Emilia R

Italy's Hidde

Best

Wishes

Phil Frampton

Phil

Published January 2000
ISBN 1 902167 01 5

MHi
Publications Ltd

Published by MH*i* Publications Ltd

P.O. Box 82 Manchester M32 8BX

Photographs: **Muriel Savrot**
and the Provincia of
Emila Romagna

Illustration: **Julia Robinson**

Book and
Cover design: **Lendon Lewis**

Researcher: **Muriel Savrot**

Editor: **Brian Crawford**

With special thanks to the
Provincial administrations of Modena and
Ferrara, Bologna Comune, Elsa Corbelli,
Emilia Romagna APT, Monica Forti,
Jane Kinninmonth, Tim Ellis, Andy Walsh,
Andrea Enisuoh, Perminder, Gail, Ellie and
Sidonie Frampton

Printed by Barton Printing Co. (Manchester) Ltd

British Library Cataloguing in Publication Data. This
publication is being catalogued and will be available at the
British Library.

Italy's Hidden Gem

CONTENTS

INTRODUCTION

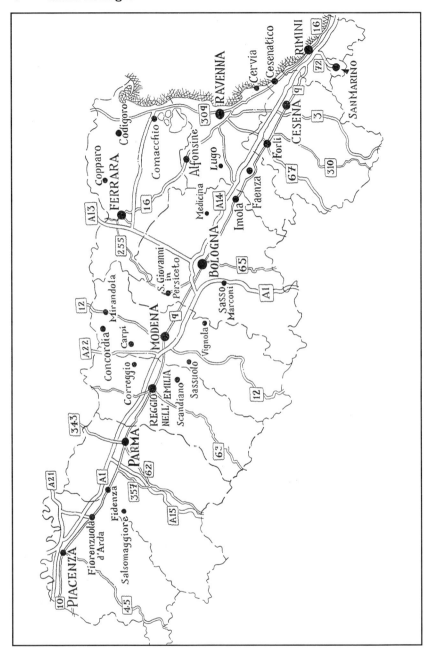

THE HIDDEN GEM **Emilia Romagna**
INTRODUCTION

As the plane flies across northern Italy and past Milan, a new and varied landscape unfolds with dramatic symmetry. Below is the ancient Roman road, the Via Emilia, which travels southeast from Piacenza to Rimini. To its north are the Po plains with its rivers meandering into the Adriatic. To the south are rolling and rugged foothills, which eventually become the towering Apennine mountain range.

In front of us is the wide sweep of the azure blue Adriatic edged by miles and miles of sandy beaches. Just before we land in Rimini, the plane flies over the legendary Rubicon which Julius Caesar's army crossed heralding the greatest days of the Roman Empire. Now it is we who have crossed the Rubicon and there is no turning back from discovering the little known region of Emilia Romagna, its beautiful countryside and towns, its sun drenched beaches and superb cuisine.

Welcome to Emilia Romagna, which has everything a visitor would want – in style. This is the land of Guiseppe Verdi, Pavarotti, Toscanini, Umberto Eco and Giorgio Armani not to mention Enzo Ferrari and the San Marino Grand Prix. Its countryside puts Parma ham, Balsamic vinegar, Parmesan cheese, and truffles onto plates around the world. Monte Cimone, peaking at 6,000 feet above sea level, is the highest mountain in the Apennine range which sweeps down Italy's spine. From the top of Monte Cimone on a clear day one can swivel round and catch sight of the country's three great protectors, the Adriatic, the Mediterranean and the Alps. Cimone's slopes provide for winter skiing, and its foothills hold centuries old castles and churches dominating tiny towns and villages.

The eastern part of the region is called Romagna but it was once known as 'the land of the castles' and, sure enough every hill and hillock seems to be graced by a castle or monastery. Here history has been excellently preserved with Romanesque, Gothic and Renaissance churches, sumptuous palaces and elegantly designed town squares at the centre of narrow mediaeval streets.

Apart from Ravenna and Ferrara all the main towns are linked by the Via Emilia. In the west, Emilia can boast the same plethora of castles and the ancient principalities of Parma, Piacenza, Bologna and Modena. None of the towns of Emilia Romagna is without its central piazza (square) dominated by a historic palace, church, or cathedral. Behind their doors one is certain to find exquisite frescoes, murals, paintings and sculptures created by the Italian masters of the time. Neither did we have to worry about missing out on the Leaning Tower of Pisa. It was hard to find a tower that didn't lean.

Perhaps the greatest attraction of these centres is that they are devoid of the crowds and the attendant hassle that stifle Florence, Venice and Rome. In the smaller towns and villages such as Guastalla, Gualtieri, Montebello and Cortemaggiore it's almost as if time has stood still. Allowed to view history's treasures in peace, we could drift back through time into the lives and works of the nobles, artisans and townspeople. These are town centres of narrow, often cobbled streets, cathedrals, palaces and theatres built to impress.

All over the region restaurants serve up a marvellous cuisine. Not much spaghetti round here but local specialities such as the big tortelloni and little tortellini, mortadella, culatello, and Parma hams, parmesan served with the nectar-like balsamic vinegar, truffles and fruits from the landscape's abundant orchards, groves and vineyards. Only when we'd been through three pasta dishes could we fully appreciate the value of the region's light sparkling red Lambrusco wines.

But what we enjoyed as much were the prices. Italy has the reputation for being expensive. Emilia Romagna is not. Travelling is cheap, food is certainly cheaper than in Britain and accommodation prices are similar. Add Italian style and we had to say it was value for money.

Finally those who want to do more than eat, rest and sight see have plenty of opportunities to play sports, get healthy at the many spas or dance the night away in the clubs. Italians love their sport and the weather provides for both winter and summer sports. The pleasure beaches are packed with people leaping around playing volleyball and basketball, the harbours with yachts and the playing fields with footballers.

We found that Emilia Romagna was a region worth discovering – a hidden gem.

GEOGRAPHY

Emilia Romagna lies in north Italy around 44 degrees and 45 degrees from the Equator. It covers most of the territory between Florence, Milan and Venice on the south side of the Po Plain. The regional centre is Bologna which is situated midway between the Adriatic and Mediterranean seas.

People often associate the cities of Emilia Romagna with the Po Plain, once under sea. The region's fate has long been linked to the ocean and geological evidence illustrates that millions of years ago, even the Apennine mountain range, which lies on the southern flanks of the region, was part of an ocean bed. Huge movements of the tectonic plates beneath the earth's surface pushed up rock to create the Apennines. Today these mountains cover almost a third of Emilia Romagna.

The rising ground and deposits of silt from the Po and the many rivers which flow into it, later created the Po plain. The plain which covers half the region is still rising, ever so slowly but without the extensive flood prevention measures, cities as far inland as Modena would still be threatened with immersion. Another consequence of the subterranean tectonic activity has been the occasional earthquake, which in the past would have devastating effects on the mountain and plains communities. Even today the region is subject to occasional tremors.

Virtually every river flowing through the territory travels north, to the eastward-flowing Po which, now trained by canalisation, spans out into its famous delta marshes. The soil left behind is rich in clays, providing the basic building bricks, pots, and decorations of the region's civilisations.

The mountains are composed of a rich geology of sedimentary rocks such as limestone and chalk, metamorphic rocks such as granite and slates and some volcanic rocks. Weathered by time the morphology of the mountains and hills has become a wonderful variety of rugged scarps, peaks, crags, near vertical rock faces, waterfalls, knolls, plateaux, and caves.

CLIMATE

On the plain, winters are cold and summers are hot. January average temperatures fall to 0°C and August temperatures rise to 30°C plus. Bologna has a May average temperature of 18°C which remains above that level till early October. Temperatures on the Adriatic coastline are mitigated by the sea and coastal breezes, making January in Rimini on average 6°C. Sea temperatures on the Rimini coast are the warmest in Italy, averaging between 25°C and 30°C between June and October.

The rainy seasons are autumn and spring, leaving dry winters with long hot summers. In the Apennine peaks, winters are colder and summers are 5°C to 6°C cooler, making the hills a popular summer retreat for Emilians and the Romagnola.

Average Monthly Temperatures in Degrees Centigrade

	Jan	Feb	Mar	Apr	May	Jun	Jul	Aug	Sep	Oct	Nov	Dec
Bologna	2.5	3.4	8.6	13.8	18.1	23.3	25.0	25.4	21.3	15.2	9.7	3.9
Rimini	6.7	9.1	10.3	13.5	17.7	21.8	24.3	23.4	20.0	10.5	9.8	5.7

Average Monthly Rainfall in Millimetres

	Jan	Feb	Mar	Apr	May	Jun	Jul	Aug	Sep	Oct	Nov	Dec
Bologna	44	52	48	57	40	35	18	22	61	47	67	61
Rimini	11	43	35	32	62	66	95	69	43	132	54	12

HISTORY

The undoubted richness of Emilia Romagna and Italy as a whole is the pre-eminence in the landscapes and cityscapes of its history. Structures hundreds and thousands of years old have survived in great numbers, despite earthquakes, floods, hurricanes, wars, and zealous redevelopers. Hardly a village, save those totally flattened during fighting in the last war, is without some church or palace more than 400 years old.

Village and town central squares date back 2,000 years. From Roman times, they were the hearts of government, combining castle, town hall, church or temple and market square. Many retain their mediaeval character.

Little of the pre-history to the Romans has survived in the region. Remains from the Palaeolithic (around 20,000 B.C) and Neolithic periods (around 6,000 B.C) have been unearthed, and are on show in the main museums. The Villanovans and Etruscans were a developing Copper and Bronze Age (2,500 B.C – 1,200 B.C) community. In 509 B.C, the Romans overthrew their Etruscan rulers and established a republic.

Etruscan civilisation in northern Italy developed into twelve city states commanding farming, fishing, industrial and trading communities. The region has several sites of Etruscan settlements and burial grounds. In **Spina** near Comacchio on the Adriatic coast, archaeologists have uncovered evidence of a great sea faring community who took goods from inland cities such as **Felsina** (Bologna) and traded with Greeks.

Digs in Bologna have found 500 huts and 4,000 graves with intricate sculptures, coins, a developed alphabet, and exquisite vases. They indicate that by 500 B.C Felsina was a semi-industrial city trading with Greece and cities in the Alps. The 5th century B.C saw the creation of the town of **Marzabotto**. South of

Tiberius Bridge

Bologna in the Reno valley, it is remarkable for its strict rectilinear street planning. Evidence of other settlements has been found at **Verucchio** and in all the major cities.

The Etruscans were challenged by migrant groups of Gauls and Celts from northern Europe. Nevertheless evidence shows that the different tribes generally co-existed. Celtic stone houses can still be seen in the wilds of the Modena Apennines. The Alps were mainly populated by the Ligurians when the conquering Romans arrived having defeated the Gauls in 191 B.C. The hill peoples were the most difficult for the Romans to subdue. Emilia Romagna was the northern frontier for Roman settlement at this time.

To consolidate the territory, Aemilius had a road built in 187 B.C from Rimini on the Adriatic to Piacenza close to the northern Mediterranean coast. This incredibly straight road, Via Emilia, travelled the southern edge of the Po plain, allowing movements of troops and merchandise. At intervals the road was defended by a fortified settlement known as a *castrum*.

The **castrum** was built to Roman precision, with a central axis where the square and forum would be. From here the *decumanus maximum* would divide the road from north to south and the *cardo maximum* from east to west. Other roads would be built parallel to these. The sites where the forum stood are still in many instances, the sites of the main piazza or town centre, as can be seen in Piacenza. The decumanus and cardo roads are often still the main town roads.

Close to Rimini is the river **Rubicone**, said to be the site where Julius Caesar launched his legendary seizure of power, leading to the great era of the Roman Empire. As Roman rule flourished great monuments, temples, bridges and amphitheatres were built. Ravenna became home to the 250 ships of Emperor Augustus's praetorian fleet.

The best of the early Roman structures left are in Rimini with its **Tiberius Bridge**, **Augustus Arch,** and Roman wall. Bologna, besieged by Mark Anthony, still has a Roman aqueduct in working order and the **Coin Department Store** in the city contains the walls of the Roman theatre. The Romans had separate administration centres for the warlike Ligurians in the Apennines. **Veleia Romea** in Piacenza is known as the region's 'Little Pompeii', excavated by the Farnese duke, whose brother excavated Pompeii.

The Roman Empire became unmanageable, and was divided into East and West empires by Emperor Diocletian. Constantinople became the eastern capital and Milan the western.

From wholesale persecution under Diocletian, **Christianity** became established as an important religion in the reign of the Christian emperor, Constantine (306-337 B.C). As Christianity became established the church, with the Pope at its head, became a powerful part of the state. In the 5th century Emperor Honorius was forced to switch the capital of the western empire to Ravenna. Architectural works flourished in the sea port city. Great temples, churches, palaces and mausoleum were built. Today Ravenna contains the best examples of **Byzantine art** and **architecture** in Italy.

Byzantine art was characterised by the combination of western and oriental styles. Figures in paintings were particularly two dimensional and static. In architecture, eastern domes proliferated, and the greatest survivors were the beautiful marble mosaics, which decorated the floors of the buildings of the period.

Under the weight of controlling its vast empire, opposition to taxes, and war, Roman rule began to decline. The population of Italy fell from around 8 million in the 2nd century to 3 million in the 7th century. The economy deteriorated. Northern peoples invaded the territory. Germanic troops under **Oadacer** seized Ravenna, making him the first Germanic king of Italy. The Ostrogoths under **Theodoric** then took Ravenna and the western empire in 493 A.D. The Visigoths, Lombards and Franks raided with ease.

By the sixth century the Germanic **Lombards** had established control of northern Italy. But by the eighth century the **Franks,** under their Carolingan leaders, were proving a superior military force. Eventually the Pope in Rome was forced to lean on the Germanic troops of the Franks to defeat the Lombards, and control the empire. The Pope conceded secular leadership of the empire to the Carolingans, making the Frankish Holy Roman Emperors the *de facto* rulers of Italy.

The rule of the Franks issued in a new stability, which saw the redevelopment of the region's cities. Papal rule at the time was through powerful regional bishops who would live in fortified palaces and control vast parts of the provinces. As papal authority had declined, so too had that of the bishops. Debauchery and corruption reached their heights amongst the bishopric and their noble flock.

North Italy's decline had stemmed, the economy began to grow, and the population grew rapidly to 10 million by the 1300s. The Popes tried to re-establish themselves as the secular power over the emperors. In order to establish a stable Papal authority, they neded to rope in the unruly bishops, gain support amongst the masses, and rebuild church funds. **Pope Gregory** fought for a redesigning of the Catholic church as sober and penitent. Elected in 1073, he introduced what are known as the **Gregorian Reforms**.

INTRODUCTION

Italian Art & Culture

For most of the last 2,000 years, the church played a key part in government, at local and national level. Religion was the ideological glue cementing the peasant mass to the rulers. The leaders of the church therefore had an interest in making places of worship attractive to peasant, merchant and landowner. The church acquired great wealth, with which rich noble landowners could command the services of the greatest artists of the day. The monasteries took over vast tracts of land. On the Po plain they played a key part in the early reclamations, draining and cultivating of the marshes.

Religious buildings and palaces became the repository of the country's greatest art works. With no great religious civil wars such as those involving the English, Henry VIII and Oliver Cromwell, many of the churches and palaces have survived and retain the best of the country's past art forms.

A point of note is that river stone and brick were commonly used to build even the palaces of the city. The region had no resources of marble and only those with great wealth could afford to import it. Those with great intentions often began building facades in marble, only to run out of cash and complete the higher facade in sandstone.

Often, Romanesque builders simply raided old Roman temples and villas, and recycled marble and other building materials as reminders of the glorious past. Roman capitals, columns, telamons and bricks often feature. This practice continued for over 500 years. Indeed, the fascination of many of the region's structures *is* the juxtaposition of styles from various centuries, as each new generation altered the buildings handed down to them rather than rebuild anew.

Pope Gregory's ally in the north was a certain **Matilda di Canossa**, a female warlord sometimes known as **Matilda of Tuscany**. She is said to have built 100 churches in Emilia Romagna to re-emphasise the central role of Catholicism. Many are classics of the Romanesque style, being the work of **Wiligelmo** and his school of sculptors from Modena, and the architect **Lanfranco**. **Modena Cathedral** is seen as the best example of Romanesque art in northern Italy. Other fine examples are the **Parma Cathedral** and **Baptistery**, **Piacenza Cathedral** and **Pomposa Abbey** in Ferrara province.

Amid the new enlightenment, in 1088 Bologna became home to the **world's oldest university**. A European centre of learning, its initial purpose was to interpret the Roman law of the Codes of Justinian brought from Ravenna. The university attracted popes, kings and the likes of **Thomas A Becket, Dante, Copernicus** and **Boccaccio**.

Romanesque Art

One of the delights of Emilia Romagna is the plethora of ancient Romanesque religious buildings. They date from the period of new found wealth in the 11th century when the merchant and artisan class began to grow in influence. The church had begun to promote a new concept of work. Toil was no longer to be seen as mankind's punishment for its sins, but a means to salvation.

Catholicism was emerging from a period of darkness, and the new emphasis on work, and on a return to early Christian mores, inspired the artists, commissioned to create new places of worship employing new methods and ideas. Worth was given to human creations as above that of use of expensive materials. Further impetus was given to the trend by the arrival of Benedictine friars with their motto of ora et labore - work and labour.

The use of the region's plentiful and cheap natural resources of sandstone and clay became apparent. Now, expensive marble used in walls, sculptures and mosaics could be dispensed with. Mosaics could be replaced by frescoes.

Artists such as Wiligelmo and Lanfranco drew their inspiration from the Roman art forms and the early Christians. In that sense the movement involved a conscious revival of Roman and early Christian traditions, while taking advantage of the new ecclesiastical direction allowing innovative techniques. They portrayed life as both a struggle and a journey towards salvation, the prospect of which was threatened by evil and sin.

Romanesque churches were characterised by facades covered with religious allegories in bas-relief, or sculptured to convey the churches' views to the illiterate masses. The interior would be decorated with frescoes emphasising, in particular, God's role at the centre of time, the link between the seasons and the Apostles and the church's role at the centre of society.

The master of design in northern Italy was Lanfranco, whose architecture involved the use of three naves and three apses, a raised presbytery above a crypt and splayed windows below vaulted ceilings. Vertical strips, and arches along with a loggia would surround the exterior. These are common features in the region's cathedrals though the churches are simpler.

For centuries, Emilia Romagna was a destination on pilgrim routes from all over Europe to the holy shrines in Rome and Jerusalem. The route to the west was known as the Via Francigena while the eastern route, Via Romei, offered a route to Rome, or down to Brindisi, where pilgrims could board boats bound for the Holy Lands.

The routes varied as to the changing political and geographical conditions in the region. Important towns en route included Piacenza, Fidenza, Parma, Bologna, Forli and Ravenna. The pilgrims brought increased income to the area, prompting the building of monasteries, shrines, castles and inns. They also brought new cultural influences from the north. Their influence is evident in the changing architecture and art forms. By this route did people such as Thomas A Becket and King Arthur find their way into the region.

Papal reforms could not stem the decline of papal authority, and ironically, the very building activity stimulated by Matilda di Canossa helped to strengthen the growing city merchant class. Opposition to the church and papal taxes increased and the **Ghibelline**, anti-papist revolt began. Supporters of the popes were known as **Guelphs,** who fought many battles against the **Ghibellines**. The region became largely an area of free city states, known as **communes,** ruled by elected leaders of the city merchant class.

The period of the communes lasted for two centuries, until the more powerful noble families began to assert themselves, often allying with the Pope or other warlords to create a large dynasty. This was the age of the emergence of the great dynasties of Emilia in the east and Romagna in the west. In Romagna, the **Estense** and **Malatesta's** emerged, threatened by the notorious **Borgias** to the north. In Emilia, the **Gonzaga** began by taking Reggio. The **Sforza** gained prominence as did the **Bentivogilio**, the **Pallavicino** and **Landi**.

Curiously, no great dynasty emerged in Emilia's biggest city, Bologna, which is reflected in its relatively modest palaces. In contrast, the Ghibelline merchants erected the **Gothic** church of **San Petronio** to rival The Vatican. The merchants of the city also began the building of **arcades** or *porticoes*, with Bologna boasting the biggest system of arcades in the world. In Piacenza, the Gothic **Palazzo Comunale** and **San Francesco church** were erected.

The city's profusion of noble families also resulted in a profusion of **towers,** which were used as a means of defence when a family was under attack from rivals. Ancient towers are commonly sighted in Emilia Romagna. **Tower-houses** are common in the Apennines. Again they were built for defence. Later, many became dove towers. Churches also built towers for defensive purposes, and bells were added to summon the mass to prayer. That almost all are leaning is due to them being built on soft subterranean clays, and further undermined by earthquakes.

With the rival nobles often leaning on the powerful Vatican troops for aid, Bologna and the other states could not hold out against papal rule for ever, which was eventually established over most of the region's city states. The legacy of this mediaeval period is the profusion of many fine **castles** and **Gothic** churches.

The economy grew and art developed. One of the great artists of this period was **Dante** Alighieri, best known for his *Divine Comedy*, which includes many references to Romagna. This Florentine's magnificently poetic writings are accredited with laying the basis for turning the Tuscan language into the foundation of modern Italian, uniting the disparate dialects and languages into a comprehensible whole. Exiled from Tuscany, he spent his last days in Ravenna where his tomb lies.

Dante is also seen as having laid the basis for Italy's finest period of art and architecture, the post 15th century **Renaissance**. Palaces and churches would be built with an emphasis on harmony of forms. The circle, rectangle, triangle and use of lines predominated. Sassuolo **Ducal Palace**, Ferrara's **Diamond Palace** and Rimini's **Malatesta Temple** illustrate the rich variety of forms from this period.

Mediaeval town planning based on narrow radiating streets was replaced with wider rectangular patterns with the piazza at the centre. As sources of pestilence, many canals were drained and replaced by streets. **Cortemaggiore, Gualtieri, Carpi** and most of all, Ferrara's **Ercole District** are classic and beautiful examples of Renaissance town planning. Commissioned by Cesare Borgia, **Leonardo da Vinci** redesigned the fort and town of **Faenza**. Sculptures adorned the squares such as **Giambologna**'s Neptune Fountain in Bologna.

Papal domination brought relative peace, and many castles were converted into summer palaces or *delizia*. A new generation of great artists emerged, adorning palaces and churches with magnificent frescoes. In Romagna, the Rimini School, led by **Pietro de Rimini,** was most influential. In Emilia the greatest artists were **Correggio**, **Parmigianino**, **Guercino**, **Guido Reni** and Ludovico and Annibale **Carracci**. Correggio was perhaps the most influential of these and is now seen as an inspirer of early Baroque. His frescoes on the domes or *cupolas* of Parma cathedral are exceptional.

Following Michelangelo and Raphael, **Mannerism** was born entwining the richness of the two greats, and inspiring many of the region's artists. Dotted around the region are frescoes using the Grotesque style popularised by Michelangelo.

The Grotesque style originates from paintings of fantasy creatures found in Nero's tomb in the 16th century, and replicated by Renaissance artists such as Michelangelo. In Italian the word Grotesque carries a meaning of a sense of fantastic absurdity – a slight difference to the modern use of the word in English.

Papal rule also brought the suppression of a thriving Jewish community. They were driven out of their homes into walled compounds, known as **ghettos** and suffered the most terrible humiliations. Ferrara ghetto has maintained many of its old features including the synagogue.

The country continued to prosper and maintain a parasitic and weak nobility. Renaissance architecture gave way to the sumptuously decorative **Baroque** style and many church and palace facades were altered. Classic examples include Modena's **Ducal Palace**, the facade of **Carpi Cathedral** and Bologna's **Teatro Comunale**.

In the 16th century the **Farnese** family secured the position of Pope and used it to aid their dynastic rule in Parma and Piacenza. The Farnese crushed the local nobility and established a powerful position in European politics. Their influence on the artistic works of Emilia is seen particularly in Piacenza with the great **Farnese Palace** and in Parma's **Farnese Theatre** and **Pilotta Palace**. When the Farnese ran out of heirs the **Bourbons** took over.

Partly inspired by the discovery of the ruins of Pompeii and Veleia in the 18th century, **Neoclassical** architecture based on imitating the old Roman Imperial styles came into vogue. Again, facades were changed to suit. Parma's ruler was **the Bourbon, Duke Ferdinand I,** who also listed the title of King of Two Sicilys. The devout duke commissioned many Neoclassical buildings including Parma's **Biblioteca Palatina**.

The French revolution, with its message of 'Liberty, equality and fraternity', shook Europe. The feudal states were too weak and divided to withstand Napoleon's revolutionary invasion in 1797. The people welcomed the troops with their more democratic ways, bringing in the **Napoleonic Code,** and an end to many feudal practices and persecution of the Jews. The tricolour became the flag of the Republicans who rose up, creating the short lived republics of **Cispadane** and **Cisalpine**. Emilia was at the heart of the rebellion and the tricolour, which would become the flag of all Italy in 1848, was first raised in **Reggio** city.

Napoleon was not so impressed by the churches artistic heritage, and many churches and chapels were turned into warehouses. Some like Rimini Cathedral were destroyed. The great leader and his generals also carried many artworks off to France.

Napoleon left little of material significance behind, though he did begin the building of the SS62 through the Modena Apennines. Known as the Napoleonic Road, it was completed by his second wife, the Hapsburg Marie-Louise who had been installed to replace the Bourbons as Duchess of Parma.

Post Napoleonic Italy saw the country under the domination of the **Austrian Hapsburgs,** who oversaw the return to power of the nobles. But they could not quench the new mood amongst the people for democracy and nationhood. Only in

Parma and Piacenza did the nobility under Duchess Marie-Louise take progressive measures to improve the lot of the people. Her great works introduced not only new palaces into the duchy but boulevards, streetlights and spa centres. The magnificent **Colorno Palace** became her summer home. The **Tabiano Spa** became her health retreat.

The French revolution of 1830 inspired new uprisings against the Austrians in Parma and Modena. Bologna, Forli, Ferrara, Rimini and Ravenna set up a government of the United Provinces, only to see it crushed within three weeks by Austrian troops. **Mazzini** and **Garibaldi** took up the cause for the **Risorgimento,** demanding the unification, liberation and democratisation of Italy.

Theatre became particularly popular and many of the new theatres were built in Neoclassical style, including **Regio Theatre** in Parma, seen as the *Little Scala*, imitating that of Milan. With a highly appreciative and critical audience, the Regio remains one of Italy's most important operatic houses. Also Neoclassical is Reggio City's fine Municipal Theatre.

By 1848, the movement for Italian nationhood and democracy reached a crescendo. Among the supporters was the great **Busseto** composer **Guiseppe Verdi**. His role is celebrated around the region with streets and theatres in his name, museums in Busseto and his home in Sant'Agata.

Garibaldi's call to insurrection in 1848 ignited new uprisings in Parma and Modena. The rebellion was defeated and Garibaldi fled through the region, escaping by sea near Comacchio. The victory of the Risorgimento was finally secured in 1859, with Emilia and Romagna voting to join Victor Emmanuel's kingdom of Piedmont. In 1860, Italian unification was finally achieved.

United under a kingdom Italy prospered. New lands were drained in the Po delta and railways were built connecting the cities. By 1900 styles began to change again and the modern embraced in the brash new style of **Art Nouveau**. The new leisure acquired by the middle classes saw the building of many spas. Their designers embraced Art Nouveau, known in Italy as the **Liberty style** of which **Salsomaggiore Thermae** is a classic example.

Art moved on in Europe through **Cubism** and **Constructivism**. Italian artists developed the **Futurist School**. **Giorgio de'Chirico** (1888-1978) reacted against this trend by setting up his **Surrealist Pittura Metafisica school** in **Ferrara**. In keeping he described Ferrara as a "truly metaphysical city...full of surprises." One of his followers was local artist **Filippo de Pisis** (1896-1956) and another, **Giorgio Morandi** (1890-1964), internationally renowned for his still lifes and monochromes. His works are on view in Bologna Town Hall's Morandi Museum.

Italy entered the First World War in 1915. Their involvement, and revolution in Russia, was to bring the country to the brink of revolution. One of the left's socialist leaders was **Mussolini**, a native of Forli. However, Mussolini turned from revolution to embrace National Socialism or Nazism. One of his right hand men was Cesare **Balbo** from Ferrara. But neither could defeat socialist Emilia without a struggle, and in 1922 a great battle took place in Parma in which Alto Balbo's stormtroopers were forced to withdraw from the city. Backed by the Italian employers, the fascist brownshirts finally came to power in Italy in 1925 crushing the trade unions and revolutionary parties.

Mussolini joined the Axis forces with Hitler during the Second World War. In 1938, he had introduced race laws aimed at the Jewish population. During the war they suffered terribly, being sent to **Fossoli** camp near Carpi, before being sent to the gas chambers in Germany and Austria. Those who opposed fascism were also interned, and many were shot. In Emilia Romagna, strong socialist and communist traditions inspired a strong opposition in the **Partisan Movement**.

When southern Italy was lost to the Allied forces, the front line of the Fascist Republic of Marshal Badoglio was in the Apennines. Many battles were fought in the region's mountains. In **Marzabotto**, German troops slaughtered 1,800 men, women and children. Every town square has a monument to those who died, and in **Carpi** is located the emotionally moving, **Deportees Museum**.

Architecturally, the period was a barren lifeless one. Indeed the net result of Mussolini's rule was the flattening of many villages in the fighting, and the destruction of scores of historic palaces and churches.

Italy's King Victor Emanuel III had sided with the fascists, and in 1946, Italy voted to become a republic. The process of post-war growth began. The rich agricultural plains of the Po furnished new food processing industries and manufacturing took off in the cities. **Ferrari** in Maranello and **Lamborghini** became household names for engineering excellence. The plains grew rich but the Apennine districts suffered.

The economy of much of the **Apennines** had been based on the plentiful chestnut trees. The wood and chestnuts, which were used for making flour, would be taken down to the market for sale. Sheep and goats provided milk and cheeses for the impoverished mountain people. The forest had shrunk to one third of its former size. Land above an altitude of 1,000 metres was reduced to purely sheep grazing land.

Disaster had struck in the 1920s when the woodlands were smitten by disease, destroying 80 percent of the trees. The threat of starvation depopulated the highlands, and with the post war growth of industry, the population streamed down to the plains in search of work. The homeless migrants filled the old palaces such as in Gualtieri and Finale Emilia.

INTRODUCTION

Today, tourism has turned the economy around. Depopulation has allowed the chestnut trees to return, and carefully controlled tree plantations have created new work. During the nineties it has became fashionable to take a second home up in the mountains.

Artistic and Architectural Glossary

Ambo	Simple mediaeval pulpit
Apse	Semicircular recess usually at the eastern end of the church
Architrave	Lowest part of entablature
Atrium	Covered area by church entrance
Baptistery	Special building for baptisms
Campanile	Belltower
Capital	Top of a column - often decorated
Chiaroscuro	Artistic method of contrasting light and shade
Chancel	Area of church containing the altar
Cornice	Top section of the classical façade
Crypt	Burial place in the church often under the choir
Cupola	Dome
Decumanus maximus (cardo maximus)	Main north-south south road in Roman town (main east west road)
Fresco	Technique of painting on wet plaster for permanent finish
Loggia	Roofed balcony or gallery
Nave	Central area of church often flanked by two aisles
Piano nobile	Normally first and main floor of palace
Portico	Arcade or covered entrance of building
Putti/putta	Cherubs (female cherubs)
Stucco	Decorative application of plaster made from lime, sand, water and ground marble
Trompe l'oeil	Art deceiving viewer by tricks of perspective
Tryptych	Painting on three joined wooden panels

EMILIA ROMAGNA TODAY

"I don't get angry. If there's a problem, there is a solution. If there's a solution, you can find it. If there's no solution, you won't find it. So there's no need to be angry."

A Naples film director touring Modena

Emilia Romagna today combines a relaxed and industrious atmosphere. The region may have Italy's highest standard of living but its politics are dominated by the left, which has long had a majority in many of the town halls including 'Red Bologna', the traditional heartland of Italian Communism. The national government is currently a centre-left coalition.

Since the poor farmers' movements in the 19th century, co-operatives have been popular, and reach into the smaller industrial establishments. Environmental control is strong and, while the region is industrious and the Via Emilia often full of lorries, it rarely scars the view. Many hamlets still retain their ancient flavour and tranquil countryside is within easy reach of the cities.

More so than in Britain, the term 'city' can be a misnomer. Only Bologna's population of 800,000 and Parma's 400,000 take on the characteristics of anything like a city in modern terms. Most of the cities are small towns on whom city status was conferred as a privilege during the Renaissance and Mediaeval eras.

Administratively, Emilia Romagna is a region of Italy with a regional government. Each of the nine provinces has a provincial government and most towns within the province have their own municipal government. Elections take place at municipal, provincial, regional and national level. The provinces are named after their provincial administrative centre or centres, as is the case with Forli-Cesena. Provincial boundaries often approximate to the old city states, and with only 140 years since national unification, inter-provincial rivalry continues, but in a more jovial fashion.

The relaxation is evident in the evening stroll or *passeggiata,* when the townspeople take to the streets on a summer evening, and at the scores of religious, culinary, musical and sporting festivals held throughout the year.

The Festival Calendar

The many Saints' days and the bountiful harvests allow for the hundreds of festivals held annually around the region. Easter, August and the autumn harvest are the major festival seasons.

Bank holidays are public holidays and are listed below:

New Years Day	January 1st
Epiphany	Circa January 6th
Easter Sunday	April
Easter Monday	April
Liberation Day	April 25th
May Day	May 1st
Whit Monday	End May
August Bank Holiday	Mid August
All Saints day	November 1st
Immaculate Conception Day	December 8th
Christmas Day	December 25th
Boxing Day	December 26th

Ferrara is famous for its **International Buskers' Festival** which, at the end of August, brings tens of thousands of people to the city streets to watch the musicians and street performers. Bologna's Summer Festival sees scores of concerts and plays performed in the city's piazzas. In the summer, Ravenna stages an **international music festival** and a **jazz festival**. Other grand festivals are being held in the main cities to celebrate the millennium.

Gastronomic festivals in the towns and villages range from the **Vignola Spring Festival** which brings out the world's biggest cherry pie, to **truffle and mushroom festivals**. Porto Garibaldi in summer stages it's **free fish festival**, while other towns celebrate honey, pork, salami, and even tripe.

Rimini has a great festival of cinema, and elsewhere one can find horse festivals, witch festivals, historic pageants and palio horse festivals as exciting as the celebrated Sienna palio.

The highlights are listed in the sections dealing with the separate provinces.

Names of Places

For the purposes of getting around and understanding names of places and sites, readers will find the following Italian words useful.

Capella	Chapel	**Paese**	Place
Castello	Castle	**Palazzo**	Palace
Centro	Centre	**Parco**	Park
Chiesa	Church	**Passeggiata**	Customary evening stroll
Comune	Local council/town hall	**Piano**	Plain
Corso	Avenue	**Piazza**	Square
Duomo	Cathedral	**Ponte**	Bridge
Festa	Festival	**Santuario**	Sanctuary
Fiume	River	**Spiaggia**	Beach
Fumarola	Volcanic vapour	**Stazione**	Station
Galleria	Gallery	**Strada**	Street
Golfo	Golf	**Teatro**	Theatre
Lago	Lake	**Tempio**	Temple
Largo	Square	**Thermae**	Baths – often spas
Lungomare	Sea front promenade	**Torre**	Tower
Mare	Sea	**Valle**	Lake
Mercato	Market	**Via**	Road
Municipio	Town hall		

INTRODUCTION

WHAT TO WEAR

As the world knows, Italians generally dress very stylishly and, Emilia Romagna being the wealthiest of Italian regions, is no exception when it comes to style and fashion. Rimini is the most stylish of the areas. Here the regular summer evening strolls are likened to fashion shows, where even designer labels don't get a look in.

Light cottons will suffice for the summer days between May and early October, but be prepared for occasional rain showers and for cooler temperatures if you visit the Apennines. Boots are advisable for trekking and visits to the marshlands, and a sun hat is advisable in the hot summer sun. Swimming in municipal pools often requires a swim cap.

If staying in hotels, it's advisable to take some clothes that do not crease because ironing is illegal in your room, Laundry service is expensive, takes 24 hours, and often non existent at weekends.

Laundrettes are few and far between in Italy. Everyone said, "Mama does the washing". Rimini has just one on the Tiberius road. It's called 'Wash' and was Rimini's first shop to be open for 24 hours a day. Bologna has a few laundrettes for its University students. If you get stuck, there are excellent laundries.

For shaving and other **electrical gadgets**, Italy operates on 220 volts.

WHAT ABOUT HEALTH?

EC citizens should pick up E111 forms available from main post offices in EC countries before arriving in Italy. The form allows them to use the Italian health services under the same terms as Italian nationals, which often means free treatment and very cheap **prescriptions.** No **vaccinations** are required but you might want to take some anti-mosquito cream. **Pharmacists** are called **farmacia** and are generally first class. Each farmacia has a list of those open at night and on Sundays. Go there and they will put you in touch with a **medico** (doctor) if you need one. In **emergencies** phone the **ospedale** (hospital) or **ambulanza** (ambulance) on tel.113. First Aid is called **Pronto Soccorso.**

The **water** supply is of normal European standard, though many people drink mineral water. Watch out for dehydration in the hot summer sun. Drink plenty of water each day and take plenty of sun tan lotion if you're worried about the sun.

WHAT TO SAY

Speaking and understanding some basic Italian words can not only be very useful but also is polite and will ease one's way around a country where only a small proportion of people speak or understand English. Otherwise French is often used as a second language and Spanish has many similar words.

Addressing people who one does not know as you requires care. Strangers should be addressed as lei. Tu is seen as disrespectful.

Useful Words and Phrases

GOOD MORNING	**BUON GIORNO**	PASSPORT	**PASSAPORTO**
GOOD EVENING	**BUONA SERA**	AIRPORT	**AEROPORTO**
GOOD NIGHT	**BUONA NOTTE**	PLANE	**L'AEREO**
GOODBYE	**ARRIVEDERCI**	FLIGHT	**UN VOLO**
HELLO/GOODBYE	**CIAO**	TRAIN STATION	**LA STAZIONE FERROVIARIA**
PLEASE	**PER FAVORE**	TRAIN	**IL TRENO**
THANK YOU	**GRAZIE**	BUS	**AUTOBUS**
MY NAME IS	**MI CHIAME**	BUS STATION	**AUTOSTAZIONE**
HOW DO YOU DO	**PIACERE**	COACH STATION	**LA STAZIONE DEI PULLMAN**
HOW ARE YOU?	**COME STA?**	FERRY	**TRAGHETTO**
FINE, THANKYOU	**BENE, GRAZIE**	BICYCLE	**BICICLETTA**
I'M ENGLISH	**SONO INGLESE**	TAXI	**UN TAXI**
DO YOU SPEAK ENGLISH?/FRENCH?	**PARLA INGLESE?**		
	PARLA FRANCESE?	TICKET	**IL BIGLIETTO**
I DON'T UNDERSTAND	**NON HO CAPITO**	NO SMOKING	**VIETATO FUMARE**
I UNDERSTAND	**CAPISCO**	CAR	**LA MACCHINA**
		MOTORWAY	**AUTOSTRADA**
I DON'T SPEAK ITALIAN	**NON PARLO**		
	ITALIANO	NO PARKING	**DIVIETO DI SOSTA**
I SPEAK A LITTLE ITALIAN	**PARLO UN PO' DI ITALIANO**	CAN I PARK HERE?	**POSSO PARCHEGGIARE QUI?**
HOW DO YOU SAY IT IN ITALIAN?	**COMO SI DICE IN ITALIANO?**	MAP	**UNA CARTA**
SPELL IT TO ME PLEASE	**LO DICA LETTERA PER LETTERA, PER FAVORE**	TRAVEL AGENT	**L'AGENZIA VIAGGI**
CAN I SPEAK TO MR...?	**POSSO PARLARE CON IL SIGNOR....?**	MAIN POST OFFICE	**LA POSTA CENTRALE**
TOMORROW	**DOMANI**	LETTER BOX	**LA CASSETTA DELLE LETTERE**
YESTERDAY	**HIERI**	STAMPS	**FRANCOBOLI**
SEE YOU TOMORROW	**A DOMANI**	POSTCARD	**CARTOLINA**
WHERE?	**DOVE?**	HOTEL	**ALBERGO**
WHEN?	**QUANDO?**	ROOM	**CAMERA**
HOW MUCH?	**QUANTO?**	SINGLE ROOM	**CAMERA SINGOLA**
CAN I?	**POSSO?**	DOUBLE ROOM	**CAMERA MATRIMONIALE**
HOW MUCH DOES IT COST?	**QUANTO COSTA?**	WITH BATH	**CON BAGNO**
WHERE CAN I FIND....?	**DOVE TROVO......?**	WITH SHOWER	**CON DOCCIA**
CAN YOU TELL ME THE WAY TO..?	**PUO INDICAMI LA STRADA PER.....?**	ONE NIGHT	**UNA NOTTE**
AT WHAT TIME IS..?	**A CHE ORA..?**	FULL BOARD	**PENSIONE COMPLETA**
HOW LONG IS..?	**QUANTO DURA...?**	HALF BOARD	**MEZZA PENSIONE**
I WANT	**VORREI**	KEY	**LA CHIAVE**
I LIKE IT	**MI PIACE**	BILL	**IL CONTO**
YES	**SI**	WHAT IS THE DIALLING CODE FOR...?	**QUAL'E IL PREFISSO PER...?**
NO	**NON**	OPENING TIME	**ORARIA DI APERTURA**
OK, I'M READY	**PRONTO**	CLOSING TIME	**ORARIA DI CHIUSARA**
YOU READY?	**PRONTE?**	EXIT	**USCITA**
LEFT	**SINISTRA**	ENTRANCE	**ENTRATA**
RIGHT	**DESTRA**	BANK	**BANCO**
YOU'RE WELCOME	**PREGO**	SHOP	**MAGAZZINO**
EXCUSE ME	**MI SCUSI**	DEPARTMENT STORE	**GRANDE MAGAZZINO**
I'M SORRY	**MI DISPIACE**	PHARMACY	**FARMACIA**
NOW	**ADESSO**	MUSEUM	**MUSEO**
GOOD	**BUONO**	HOSPITAL	**OSPEDALI**
BAD	**CATTIVO**	DOCTOR	**DOTTORE**
BIG	**GRANDE**	GENTS	**SIGNORI**
SMALL	**PICCOLO**	LADIES	**SIGNORE**
MORE	**PIU**	WC/BATHROOM	**GABINETTO/IL BAGNO**
LESS	**MENO**	VACANT	**LIBERO**
ENOUGH	**BASTA**	ENGAGED	**OCCUPATO**
HOT	**CALDO**	OPEN	**APERTO**
COLD	**FREDDO**	CLOSED	**CHIUSO**
MR	**SIGNOR**	PULL	**TIRARE**
MRS	**SIGNORA**	PUSH	**SPINGERE**
MISS	**SIGNORINA**	HERE	**QUI**
		THERE	**LA**

Pronunciation needs some care. For example:

c before e or i	is pronounced like ch in **ch**apel
g before e or i	is pronounced like g in **g**in
gn	is pronounced like ni in opi**ni**on
gl	is pronounced like ll in mu**ll**ion
hi	is pronounced like h in **h**onour
sci or **sca**	are pronounced like sh in **sh**ower

Italian Numbers

1	UNO	20	VENTI
2	DUE	30	TRENTA
3	TRE	40	QUARANTA
4	QUATRO	50	CINQUANTA
5	CINQUE	60	SESSANTA
6	SEI	70	SETTANTA
7	SETTE	80	OTTANTA
8	OTTO	90	NOVANTA
9	NOVE	100	CENTO
10	DIECI	101	CENTUNO
11	UNDICI	110	CENTODIECI
12	DODICI	200	DUECENTO
13	TREDICI	500	CINQUECENTO
14	QUATTORDICI	1000	MILLE
15	QUINDICI	5000	CINQUEMILA
16	SEDICI	10,000	DIECIMILA
17	DICIASSETTE	50,000	CINQUANTAMILA
18	DICIOTTO	1 MILLION	MILLIONE
19	DICIANNOVE		

WHAT TO BUY

Being renown for its gastronomic products, Emilia Romagna is a great place for buying items to take back for the kitchen. Superior quality **Balsamic vinegar, Parmigiano Reggiano, Parma ham, culatello, black truffles and wines** can all be bought. Hams can be bought vacuum-packed for taking back. Brisighella is famous for its **olive oil** and Val di Taro for its **mushrooms.** Monastery shops are a good place to buy **fruit wines,** health drinks and **honey** produced from the friars' fields.

Few people would want to come away from Italy without taking advantage of the less expensive, stylish **clothes** and **leatherwear**. Italians tend to go for style rather than labels. Often the fashion conscious will buy from lesser known makes, guaranteeing as good quality and more value for money. Market prices are inexpensive, especially for those Italian **football shirts** you might want to buy as presents. Leatherwear is also relatively cheap.

Jean Paul Gautier clothes are made at the **Alberto Ferreti factory** in **San Giovanni Marignano,** just south of Riccione. The cheaper **Ferreti** labelled clothes are said to be as good as those of Gautier. The region is also home to **Diesel,** their

INTRODUCTION

belts and jeans being especially cheap. **Jewellery** also tends to be less expensive than England.

Southern Romagna (around Rimini) has pretty **hand-printed cloths,** rust-printed in a time-honoured fashion, and popular throughout the rural districts for use as curtains, tablecloths and napkins. Many bargains are available at the plentiful **antique shops** and markets and the Po Delta has excellent **wicker woven furniture**, baskets and ornaments. Italian **light cigarettes** include Diana, Linda, MS, and Club.

Opening hours in summer are very flexible, though many shops close for August to enjoy the summer break. During the rest of the year, traditional times are 9am -12.30pm and 3.30pm - 7.30pm. Apart from those located in resorts, shops are generally closed on Sundays. The mid-week day on which each area closes varies. Markets tend to open from 7am till 1pm.

WHAT ABOUT MONEY?

The strong pound has recently made Italy good value for money for British tourists. Being off the main tourist track, much of Emilia Romagna is also less expensive than Rome, Venice, and Florence. Accommodation prices fall between September and April on the coast and peak during August.

The Italian **Lira** is the national currency. Arriving in Italy it's worth having some lira in your pocket for basics. It is illegal to bring more than L400,000 (£140) of lira into the country. Some hotels will accept sterling; most will accept dollars, deutschmarks and take credit cards. Travellers' cheques can be used but we resorted to using the plentiful *bancomat,* or **cash points** around the main towns. Many shops also accept Visa and American Express.

In December 1999 the rate of the lira was around 3000.00 to the pound sterling.

Lira notes come in denominations of:	Lira coins come in denominations of:
L100,000	L500
L50,000	L200
L10,000	L100
L5,000	L50
L2,000	L20
L1,000	L10
	L5

The best exchange rates are offered by banks where you **must have your passport**. Opening hours are 8.20am-1.20pm and 3.05pm-4.05pm, Monday to Friday. Both Bologna and Rimini airport have exchange bureaux.

WHAT'S TO DO?

Emilia Romagna offers more than just a sight seeing vacation. Whether on the coast, in the cities or in the countryside, there is good access to plenty of other activities bringing fun and games.

Of the **sport**, **football** is very popular and in **Parma FC**, the region has one of Europe's current top clubs. Bologna and Piacenza are also in Serie A, Italy's premier soccer league. The season lasts from the end of August till June the following year, with entry to a match costing at least L25,000.

The region has 20 or so major **golf clubs,** the most important of which is the **Modena Golf Club** which holds international class competitions. Everywhere in the region one can see helmeted cyclists. Ferrara and Ravenna are towns where cycling is the norm to get around the centres. Competitive **cycling** is popular with the Riminese and **Pantini** was the 1998 champion of the **Tour de France.**

Above all, this is **Ferrari country** and the home to **Maserati, Lamborghini and Bugatti**. Maranello in Modena is home to Ferrari and has a Ferrari Gallery, showing some of the world's best racing and sports cars. Nearby Cogniento has another veteran car gallery which all leads on to the area's **Formula One Grand Prix** race tracks at **Imola**. Nearby you will find sites where one can take lessons in **rally driving**.

As Italy's pre-eminence in international show jumping reveals, **horse riding** is very popular in the country. Whether on the coastal flats, in the pine forests, or in the mountains one will find plenty of riding stables.with horses for hire. San Patrignano in Rimini and Modena city stage international **show jumping** competitions. There is a **racecourse** near Cesenatico, and Ferrara stages a **palio horse race** through the city, rivalling that of Sienna in Tuscany.

The Apennines offer summer **treks**, **cycling** routes, hand and **para-gliding**, surrounded by beautiful vistas, forests, lakes and waterfalls in the summer. Between January and March the mountain peaks are covered in snow which provides for many **ski slopes** and **cross country skiing** routes which are well served by ski lifts from the winter resorts.

Being a sun drenched coastline makes the Adriatic Riviera an excellent place for **sunbathing, beach volleyball, sailing, water skiing** and **wind surfing**. Many international water sports competitions are held in the resorts. The Adriatic resorts have plenty of facilities for **salt water fishing** and while **fresh water fishing** is generally based on catch and return, angling in the Apennines offers delightful tranquillity.

However, what the coast is especially famous for is its **night clubs**. Often with open air floors they are inexpensive and linked by all night bus services to surrounding towns. Music, including rock, rave, hip hop, trance, garage, soul, and

every flavour of modern dance music, is played throughout the towns and resorts. The other main cities all have night spots, mainly just outside the city. The university towns, Bologna and Modena are not well known for their club scenes except during student term time, when many clubs re-open. Ferrara has many alternative music clubs, as have Rimini and Bologna.

Located in the land of **Verdi**, **Pavarotti** and **Toscanini,** lovers of classical music are in for a treat with many of the region's Neoclassical theatres offering **opera** and **concerts**. The theatres in Parma and Reggio are renown for their operatic performances and critical audiences.

TAKING CHILDREN

For the **kids** there are plenty of **fairgrounds** and **aquafairs, beach** competitions, exciting **castles** with romantic and ghostly legends, **nature trails, boat trips, agriturismo farms, festivals** and **pageants,** and **trekking** and **cycle tracks** through the **nature reserves**. The Adriatic coast is a good place to stay if one has young children. While cultured Ravenna and Ferrara are in easy reach by train or car, the countryside, castles, fairs and beaches are just a few minutes drive, cycle or bus ride away.

HEALTH SPAS

One benefit of the region's subterranean movement of rocks is the existence of some 20 or so first rate spa towns, offering beauty and health treatments. The health centres are very popular with Italians and part of the national health system attracting 300,000 patients a year.

Many spas were built in the early 1900s, and are excellent examples of Art Nouveau and Art Deco. They are often linked to or have their own hotels, restaurants and bars and organise tours of the local districts.

The main spas can be found in Rimini, Riccione, Riolo Terme, Cervia, Punta Marina, Bagno di Romagna, Brisighella, Bertinoro, Castrocaro, Castel San Pietro, Porretta, Sassuolo, Cervarezza, Tabiano, San Andrea Bagni, Salsomaggiore, Tabiano, Bacedasco and Bobbio.

WHAT'S TO EAT – A GOURMET'S DELIGHT

Emilia Romagna is without doubt, the heartland of Italian cuisine. Home to Parma ham, Culatello, Parmigiano Reggiano, Balsamic Vinegar and the black truffle, this a region where most residents will tell you that they live to eat.

The region's cuisine varies as to the natural resources in each area. The mountains offer mushrooms, truffles and chestnut flour, while the foothills offer cherries, wine and the products of other fresh fruits. The plains bring more fruit, pastas, freshwater fish, hams and cheeses, and the coast, saltwater fish, eels and market garden produce.

Throughout Emilia Romagna one will find pastas such as tagliatelle, hams, stracotto, Parmigiano Reggiano, ricotta, and Balsamic vinegar on the menus. One intriguingly named pasta for this left wing region is the long, thin, noodled **strozzapreti,** which literally translated means 'strangle a priest'.

Common to the inland region's menus are stuffed pastas, porcini and truffles. The coastal menus also include the Romagnola fried piadina breads and fish. Inland the walnut liqueur, **nocino,** is commonly served as a digestive at the end of meals.

Baked from chestnut flour, the **tigella** or **crescenta** are common to the mountains and served as flat breads such as **crescentina**, with soft cheeses or ham inserted. The equivalent in the lowland is **Gnocco fritto**, made from wheat or maize flour and fried in pig's lard. **Polenta** is a type of maize porridge also common in the mountains.

Parmigiano Reggiano - Cogniento Parmesan Dairy

Parmesan is only made in the four provinces of Bologna, Parma, Reggio Emilia and Modena and its production strictly is controlled by laws and by the co-operatives. Most production is by three or four workers on a dairy farm but now large plants like Cogniento are being created.

The Panini family owns this spacious modern dairy with 500 cows, famous in Italy for having made their money from the production of stickers.

Sr Panini explained that Parmesan is a special cheese with no preservatives. Here the cattle feed is all organically grown and even the cow's medicine must be free of preservatives.

The dairy uses 300 of its cows for milk production, and Parmesan is produced daily. We went into a shed where the milk was kept over night then partially skimmed. Two different mixes are created then put together and placed into a large copper barrel. A starter is added to begin the fermentation, after which rennate is added and the milk cooked, producing a curd.

The curd is manually removed and stood for 30 to 40 minutes, after which it is cut, shaped and stamped.

When buying Parmesan we were advised that every piece should have evidence of the Parmesan consortium mark as the only proof that it is genuine. Who knows what cheese with what additives we eat as Parmesan in England?

The wheels of cheese, with their standard diameter of 45 centimetres, are then taken to the salting room, which we found by standing on a small platform which took us down to the basement. The wheels were sat in huge baths of salted water and would stay there for 20 to 30 days to prevent any bad fermentation processes.

After the wheels are properly shaped they are stored for at least two years. Difficulties created by the length and cost of production were overcome by the formation of co-operatives, ensuring that the farmers always had some income.

Since they were so valuable – a cheese wheel costing anything upwards of L1.5million - and could be stored for so long, banks, even to this day, sometimes accept the cheese as security from the co-ops.

Leftovers are fed to the pigs. Interestingly the fermentation starter, which is the remains of the milk after the curd has been skimmed off, is considered to have medical properties. Often people will turn up at the Parmesan plants in the mornings to request some of the liquid to help heal their broken bones. Parmesan cheese is also said to be used in the hospitals to treat babies with stomach problems.

In the huge barn used as a store for the Parmesan wheels we found the strongest smelling cheeses. Some wheels here dated back to 1995. Because the cheese has no preservatives, the wheels must be washed daily to prevent sweating and the redevelopment of fermentation.

One worker was testing the cheese, knocking on the wheels with a hammer to check whether they had any empty space inside. The consortium will do the same and if the wheel passes the test and does not contain too much air, it achieves the higher grade of Parmigiano Reggiano. Those not making the grade are daubed with a red cross and kept for another year or sold as ordinary Parmesan. There were no red crosses evident in Panini's store.

We finished our Parmesan experience with a taste of Sr Panini's Parmesan – creamy, soft and very tasty - bellissimo. Each plant has a shop and, at L25,000 a kilo, it was cheaper to buy from Panini than in the delicatessens and supermarkets.

The Piadina of Romagna

Quite peculiar to the Romagna lowlands is the **piadina** or **piada**, a flat round bread made from flour and water, and cooked on a terra cotta griddle in pig's lard. The tasty bread is ordered plain, or stuffed with cured meats or cheeses. Culinary historians trace the food back to Roman times, as a basic staple for the legions camped on Via Emilia.

The advantage of the piadina for the poor was that cooking required neither yeast nor oven. Over time, where families kept a pig, pork lard was added to improve the flavour and consistency, and each area has developed its own variations. In Rimini, where it is served from bakeries, some Riminese have taken to cooking the piadina in olive oil rather than pig's lard.

Piadina al testo takes its name from the testo terracotta grille on which it is cooked. In Ravenna, a rare sight is the piadina crescione, which was a traditional filling with water cress from the marshlands. The cress is cooked, flavoured with garlic and olive oil or bacon. Today spinach, beet greens or chicory are more commonly used for erbetta fillings.

Forli's little roadside piadina shacks may serve the bread made with milk instead of water. In Cesena and Rimini one can also find piadina sfogliata, which uses more lard and sees the bread rolled out thinly to produce a crisp, flaky dough. Bakeries often have little tables outside where one can eat. These, along with the road shacks, are recommended places to try piadina, as you can watch it being made fresh. A piadina here will set you back L2,000 to L6,000, depending on your chosen filling.

DINING OUT

Italians eat in **pizzerias, paninoteca** (sandwich bars), **trattoria** and **osteria** (often one set menu for the day and family cooking), **rosticceria** (fast food and roast chicken) and **ristorante**.

Agriturismo are countryside dining - and sometimes guest house – establishments, which are supposed to only use food and drinks prepared by the local farms. Many agriturismo are actually part of a farming enterprise offering a pleasant afternoon in the peace of the countryside.

Most menus are set but the food we tasted was some of the best in the region, being fresh and wholesome. Dining at an agriturismo offers a real adventure for gourmet tourists. Meals can not be bought a la carte which means that they can be expensive but they still offer great value for money.

Cheaper eating and greater variety can be had by sharing a set meal. Other cheap meals include the huge pizzas available for L6,000 even in restaurants or the Romagnola equivalent, the piadina often stuffed with ham or cream cheese.

They say in Italy that if you want to know the best places to eat then follow the lorry drivers.

Even the fresh food in the **supermarkets** is of a high standard, which makes for easy shopping for **picnics** in the parks and mountains or on the beach. Best to take a **coolerbag** in summer.

Breakfasts and Snacks

Breakfasts are typically continental, with brioche, croissant, and breads, served with ham or cheeses and coffee. Most hotels will serve a breakfast. Eating out for breakfast is a common pastime. You'll find many locals having a snack in a bar. Pizzerias, rosticceria and ristorante offer daytime snacks like pizzas, piadina and sandwiches.

Lunch and Dinner

Five courses are often on offer in restaurants and trattoria, namely, antipasti, primo piate, secondo piate, contorni and dolci, which may all be finished off by a liqueur for digestive purposes.

Antipasto is served as a starter and may include prosciutto or other cold meats, soup, seafood or vegetables. **Il primo piate** is often pasta such as tortelloni or tortellini. **Il secondo piate** is the main meat or fish dish. **Contorni** brings the vegetables served separately. Dessert is **dolci,** which can be fresh fruits, ice cream, or flans such as Zuppe Inglese.

Smoking is still very common in Italy so don't be surprised if you can't find a 'no smoking' area.

Provincial Gastronomic Variations

In each of the region's nine provinces one can find differences in cuisine, based on availability of fresh products and traditions. Adventurous diners will have a fascinating time trying out the regional varieties which even leave room for vegetarians.

With its name lent to ham and Parmesan, **Parma** is *the* most famous for its kitchens. Other Parmigiani specialities include **prosciutto, culatello, tortelli, bollito misto** and sugary **torte**.

The pig is the king of meats in Parma where they say, "The pig is like the music of Verdi. It's all goodness with nothing to throw away." Top of the pork products is the succulent, expensive and exclusive **culatello** produced in the special humid conditions on the banks of the Po. Not much is produced and little is exported. There follows the soft, succulent **prosciutto** sweetened by the scents of olives, pine and chestnut trees blown down from the mountains and encircling the hanging hams.

Other specialities include **spalla di San Secondo**, the shoulder eaten raw, or boiled which Verdi would send, with cooking instructions, to his friends. **Salame di Felino** is another favourite, with black pepper flavouring the finely chopped pork salami.

Ask for **le delizie di Parma** and a charcuterie mix of meats comes to the table. **Bollito misto** is a selection of boiled meats with various relishes. If you've turned up your nose at tripe and onions, don't let past experience prejudice you because this region's chefs can turn into a very tasty dish. A delicious tripe is on the Parma menus as **trippa alla Parmigiana,** served in a sauce of ham, meat, and vegetables. Turkey also arrives with a recipe dating back to the Duchy of Parma, **tacchino della duchessa**.

In pastas, the main speciality is the large square, **tortelli,** which is offered with various stuffings including pumpkin with amaretti, ricotta, and the favourite **d'erbetta** stuffing includes ricotta, eggs and beet tops. With prosciutto it is common to eat **torta fritta**, a delicate crisp, fried pasta and **anolini**, a miniature pasta with a delightful stuffing of breadcrumbs, eggs, parmesan, nutmeg and juices all served in **brodo**, a clear broth of beef and capons.

West of Parma, the people of **Piacenza** have their own specialities, which reflect the province's proximity to Lombardy and Liguria. Elizabeth Farnese and her husband Cardinal Alberoni, Minister to King Philip V of Spain, were so in love with Piacentina food that they had it shipped to Spain. Truffles, salami, ribiola, cheeses and anolini were sent for the lady who ate for two, according to the cardinal.

More specific to the province today is **pisarei e faso**, bread dumplings and beans, made with gnocchetti in a sauce made up of olive oil, butter, lard, garlic, onions, pepper and the nutritional **Borlotti** beans. **Polenta** is popular and eaten **e merluzzo** (with cod) or **e quai**, with quail.

Another delicious speciality is **faraona alla creta**, guinea fowl cooked in a terracotta dish. Winter brings out **picula ad cavall**, raw or cooked mince meat with diced vegetables and the vegetarian leek omelette, **frita cui bavaron**. Here the crescenta is replaced with the **burtlena** and the wine-dunking cake is called **buslan**.

West of Parma is **Reggio Emilia** province whose cuisine has lasagne, erbazzone, chizze and, in Guastalla town, somarina – donkey slowly boiled in vegetables.

Next door to Reggio, **Modena** puts forward its claim as the home of **Balsamic vinegar.** The province produces 25 percent of all Italy's supply, and a visit to a balsamic vinegar house is a treat. Mention of the vinegar, known to have been a favourite gift of the Estense dukes, dates back to the 11th century. The rich sauce derived from grapes is a must in every Emilian kitchen, and at every dining table. Used to flavour sauces, it is also delicious when served with Parmigiano cheese.

Malpighi's Balsamic Vinegar House in Modena

At 310, Via A.Pica, set in a beautiful villa in its rose-scented gardens close to Modena city, is the renowned **Ermes Malpighi** balsamic vinegar house.

More than a dozen institutions have visited here to study the Malpighi's century old production of the sweet sauce that adorns not only the tables of Emilia Romagna, but also those across the whole of the western world.

Modena is a great balsamic producer with 3,000 families owning their own balsamic vinegar workshops. Generation on generation of families has passed down the specialist knowledge of the techniques of production. The Malpighi's are on their fifth generation as a balsamic house, which still displays some bottles from the first balsamic vinegar the family brewed back in 1860.

Ermes and his sons often give talks to visiting tourists. They are pleased to do anything that will popularise their product, which is why the United States has become a big market for the family run business. Ermes proudly showed us his press cuttings from American newspapers such as the International Herald Tribune.

Traditional balsamic vinegar is distinguished from industrial balsamic vinegar, which fails to reach the quality standards set by the Balsamic Vinegar consortium. Inside, Ermes related how balsamic vinegar was made.

Ermes took us into a storage room full of wooden barrels graded by size, and arranged in rows. The wood is also important, with oak, chestnut, cherry, mulberry and juniper being used for the barrels. This year he will produce 6,000 bottles

The wine for the vinegar comes from either the white Trebbiano Modenese grape, or occasionally, the Lambrusco grape. The grapes are pressed to make the 'sauce' and boiled to form a must. The wine is then decanted and left to ferment over two to three years in the series of barrels. The various types of wood aromatise the vinegar, which is then stored for twelve years for **Vecchio** (old) vinegar and 25 years for **Extra Vecchio**. During the process, 100 kilos of grapes are reduced down to a kilo of balsamic vinegar. That the Extra Vecchio takes a generation to produce makes it very prestigious – a syrupy, sweet, delicious experience.

The vinegar is then transferred to a locked room in the consortium, where it is tested by sight, scent and taste and verified as a quality vinegar on a scale of one to ninety. Four people are kept totally apart to judge the vinegar. The barrels that fail the quality level are sent back for re-ripening or to be sent off as industrial balsamic vinegar. The vinegar is then bottled.

Initially, balsamic vinegar was used as a digestive after meals, before becoming a sauce for the antipasti. Today it is used for soups, stews, pasta, for cooking meat and fish, and as a salad dressing. Americans, in all their inventiveness, use the vinegar on fruit, ice cream, cream caramels, bon-bons and even Chinese food. The latest fad is to put the vinegar into chocolate.

A 100 millilitre bottle will cost around £50 and £80 for Extra Vecchio. Ermes still has a bottle, which is 60 years old – priceless. **Visiting** requires making an appointment. Ermes' son, Massimo, speaks English. **Sports car** lovers might be interested in talking to the family who also make components for Ferrari. (Tel.059 280893 fax 280361)

Other Modena specialities include **tortellini**, tiny stuffed pasta balls served in brodo broth and **zampone**, a cutlet of deep fried minced pork spiced with herbs and black pepper all stuffed in pig's trotter. When zampone was made in the past, each family would add its own ingredients. Today, each producer of salami and zampone has their own recipe which has been patented. One variant is the fatty **cotechino**, served in a pig's gut. Another is **cappella da prete** where the stuffing fills a pig's cheek, which is sown in the shape of a three-cornered hat.

Desserts bring out **bensone** or **belsone**, long loaves of cake traditionally dipped in Lambrusco or sweet white wine. **Castagnaccio** is a chestnut flour based cake, flavoured with lemon rind or cocoa, and popular in the Apennines. **Cherry** cakes are especially popular, and Vignola town festival annually produces the biggest cherry pie in the world.

Tortelloni comes from **Bologna** and as the name suggests, is larger than the Modenese tortellini. It's stuffed with ricotta and herbs. Another local pasta is **passatelli**, which is served in a broth. Bologna is also proud of its **mortadella**, a firm but creamy cheese, spiced with pepper and served diced with ham. Before Indian pepper reached the area, mortadella would be flavoured with myrtle berries. Also common are green lasagne dishes, tagliatelle a la Bolognese and veal cutlets a la Bolognese. For dessert, try the local **torta degli addobbi** cake made with rice and crushed almonds.

Located on the Po delta marshes and the Adriatic coast, **Ferrara** province has a quite distinctive cuisine. Here the typical bread is **la coppia,** which comes in long thin spirals and is excellent for dunking in coffee. The main pasta served is **cappellacci,** commonly stuffed with pumpkin **(del zucca)** and served with melted butter and sage or a ragout sauce. **Pasticcio** is a crust of sweet dough filled with macaroni, then coated with a bechamel sauce seasoned with wild mushrooms or truffles, and baked in the oven.

Special meat dishes include **salama da sugo**, a salame which is hung soaked in wine for a year before being cooked. On the coast **angulle** or eel and frogs are specialities from the local marshes. Dessert brings out the rich **pampapato** chocolate cake.

Ravenna is best known for dishes of fish freshly caught by its Adriatic fishing fleets. Of these, fried **calamaretti, squid, limpets** and **cuttlefish** are common. **Eels** are also available baked or stewed on a bed of pine kernels and raisins. Ask for **rane in umido** and you'll get braised frog.

Meat dishes include **folaga,** rice with coots and **braciole di castrato** which may sound painful but its actually braised mutton chops. **Tardura** is the local pasta flavoured with eggs and parsley then cooked in a broth. **Strigoli di pineta** are a local delicacy, an edible bladder-campion that grows in the pine groves. For dessert, try **sabadoni,** a cake stuffed with pine nuts, jam and chestnuts.

INTRODUCTION

South of Ravenna, **Forli-Cesena** province has the renowned fragrant **Dovadola truffles** and ravioli stuffed with the famous **sogliano cheese** which is left to mature in caves for six months.

Piadina, the chapati-like flat bread of the Romagnola is common to Rimini province, where foods are simple and wholesome. A characteristic dish is **brodetto,** a fish stew flavoured with pepper, vinegar and tomatoes. Another is stuffed pigeon. For dessert fried cakes available include **frittelle** and **castagnole** while the local wine-dunking cake is called **ciambella.**

DINERS' GLOSSARY

Prima colazione	Breakfast
Pranzo	Lunch
Cena	Dinner

BASICS

Aceto	Vinegar
Aglio	Garlic
Biscotti	Biscuits
Brioche	Croissant
Burro	Butter
Cacao	Cocoa
Cafelatte	Coffee (white)
Caffe con panna	Coffee with cream
Chocolate	Chocolate
Formaggio	Cheese
Frittata	Omelette
Fritte	Chips
Gelato	Ice cream
Latte	Milk
Limone	Lemon
Maionese	Mayonnaise
Marmellata	Jam
Miele	Honey
Olio	Oil
Olive	Olives
Pane	Bread
Pane (nero, bianco)	Bread (brown, white)
Panino	Sandwich
Panino Patatine	Sandwich Crisps
Pepe	Pepper
Riso	Rice
Sale	Salt
Senape	Mustard
Te	Tea
Uova	Eggs
Uova al tegame	Fried egg
Uova alla coque	Boiled egg
Uova sode	Hard boiled egg
Uova strapazzate	Scrambled egg
Zucchero	Sugar
Zuppa	Soup

SERVING

Affumicato	Smoked
Ai ferri	Grilled without oil
Al dente	Firm
Alla griglia	Grilled
Alla Milanese	Fried in egg and bread crumbs
Allo spiedo	Skewered
Amaro	Sour, bitter
Arrostito	Roast
Ben cotto	Well done
Bicchiere	Glass
Bollito/lesso	Boiled
Bottiglia	Bottle
Brasato	Cooked in wine
Coltello	Knife
Condito	Seasoned
Crudo	Raw
Cucchiaino	Teaspoon
Cucchiaio	Spoon
Dolce	Sweet
Forchetta	Fork
Freddo	Cold

Fresco	Cool	**Rape**	Turnips
Ghiaccio	Ice	**Spinaci**	Spinach
Grasso	Fat	**Zucchini**	Corgettes
Grattugiato	Grated		
In umido	Stewed	**MEAT**	
Magro	Thin	**Carne**	Meat
Piatto	Plate	**Affettato**	Sliced cold meat
Poco cotto/al sangue	Rare	**Affumicata**	Smoked
Ripieno	Stuffed	**Agnello**	Lamb
Salato	Salty	**Ai ferri**	Grilled
Stracotto	Braised/stewed	**Allo spiedo**	Skewered
surgelati	Frozen	**Anitra**	Duck
Tazza	Cup	**Arrosto**	Roast
Tenero	Tender	**Bistecca**	Steak
Tovagliolo	Napkin	**Bollito**	Boiled
		Braciola	Chop

ON THE MENU

VEGETABLES

Contorni	Vegetables	**Capretto**	Kid
Aglio	Garlic	**Capriolo**	Venison
Asparagi	Asparagus	**Carpaccio**	Thinly sliced raw beef
Broccoli	Broccoli	**Cervello**	Brain
Capperi	Capers	**Cervo**	Deer
Carciofi	Artichokes	**Cinghiale**	Wild boar
Carote	Carrot	**Coniglio**	Rabbit
Cavolfiore	Cauliflower	**Cotoletta**	Cutlet
Cavolo	Cabbage	**Fagiano**	Pheasant
Cetrioli	Cucumber	**Faraona**	Guinea fowl
Cipolla	Onion	**Fegato**	Liver
Crauli	Sauerkraut	**Filetto**	Fillet
Fagioli	Beans	**Involtini**	Rolled
Finocchio	Fennel	**Lepre**	Hare
Fritte	Potato Chips	**Lingua**	Tongue
Funghi	Mushrooms	**Maiale**	Pork
Insalata	Mixed salad	**Manzo**	Beef
Lenticchie	Lentils	**Ossoboco**	Veal shin
Melanzane	Aubergine	**Pancetta**	Bacon
Patate	Potatoes	**Pernice**	Partridge
Patate pure	Potato Mash	**Polpetta**	Burger, meatball
Peperoni	Peppers		
Piselli	Peas	**Prsciutto Crudo**	Parma ham
Pomodori	Tomatoes	**Rostbif**	Roast beef
Radicchio	Chicory	**Salsiccia**	Sausage
		Saltimbocca	Veal with ham
		Scaloppina	Escalope

Spezzatino	Stew
Tacchina	Turkey
Trippa	Tripe
Vitello	Veal

FISH

Pesce	Fish
Acciughe	Anchovies
Anguilla	Eel
Aragosta	Lobster
Baccala	Dried salted cod
Calamari	Squid
Cefalo	Mullet
Cozze	Mussels
Dentice	Sea bream
Fritto misto	Mixed fried fish
Gamberetti	Shrimps
Gamberi	Prawns
Granchio	Crab
Merluzzo	Cod
Ostriche	Oysters
Pesce spada	Swordfish
Polipo	Octopus
Rospo	Monkfish
Salmone	Salmon
Sarde	Sardines
Scampo	Scampi
Sgombro	Mackerel
Sogliola	Sole
Tonno	Tuna
Triglie	Red mullet
Trota	Trout
Vongole	Clams
Zuppa di pesce	Fish soup

FRUIT AND NUTS

Frutta, Noce	Fruit, Nuts
Albicocca	Apricot
Ananas	Pineapple
Anguria	Water melon
Arancia	Orange
Banana	Banana
Ciliegia	Cherry
Fico	Fig
Fragola	Strawberry
Frutta cotta	Stewed fruit
Frutta fresca	Fresh fruit
Frutta secca	Dried fruit
Lampone	Raspberry
Mandarino	Tangerine
Mandorle	Almond nuts
Mela	Apple
Melone	Melon
Mirtillo	Bilberry
Nocciola	Hazelnut
Noce	Walnut
Pera	Pear
Pesca	Peach
Pignoli	Pine nuts
Pistacchio	Pistacchio nuts
Pompelmo	Grapefruit
Prugna	Plum
Uva	Grapes

PASTA, SAUCES AND SOUPS

Arrabbiata	Tomato sauce - spicy
Bolognese	Meat sauce
Brodo	Broth
Cannelloni	Large tubes of stuffed pasta
Carbonara	Ham, cream and beaten egg sauce
Farfalle	Bow-shaped pasta
Fettucine	Ribbon shaped pasta
Gnocchi	Little potato and dough dumplings
Lasagne	Lasagne
Maccheroni	Spaghetti tubes
Minestrina	Light soups
Minestrone	Thick vegetable soup
Pasta a fagoli	Pasta with beans
Pasta al forno	Pasta baked with mince meat
Pastina in brodo	Pasta in broth
Penne	Grooved tubular pasta
Pesto	Garlic, pine nuts and ground basil sauce

Ragu	Tomato sauce	Gelato	Ice cream
Ravioli	Ravioli	Gelato misto	Mixed ice cream
Rigatoni	Large penne	Gorgonzola	Strong, soft blue veined cheese
Spaghetti al burro	Spaghetti with butter		
Spaghetti al pomodoro	Spaghetti with tomato sauce	Macedonia	Fruit salad
		Montata	Whipped cream
Spaghetti al sugo	Spaghetti with sauce	Mozzarella	Soft cheese made from buffalo milk
Spaghetti alle vongole	Spaghetti with clams		
Stracciatella	Broth with egg	Panna	Cream
Strozzapretti	Long thin pasta	Parmagiano	Parmesan
Tagliatelle	Pasta ribbons	Pecorino	Strong hard sheep's cheese
Tortellini	Small rings of stuffed pasta	Ricotta	Soft, white sheep's cheese
Tortelloni	Large rings of stuffed pasta	Torta	Cake
Vermicelli	Thin spaghetti	Zabaglione	Sweet made from eggs, sugar and wine
		Zuppa inglese	Trifle-like cake

SWEETS AND CHEESES

Dolci, Formaggi	Sweets, Cheeses
Amaretti	Macaroons
Budino	Pudding
Fontina	Northern Italian cooking cheese

What's to Drink

Bars are common in the region but they are not big social centres in the evenings. There are some exceptions, particularly around the central squares in Rimini, Ferrara, Bologna and Modena, where young people tend to hang out. Out in the smaller towns, social activity in the evening is confined to the dining establishments. Otherwise there are plenty of places where you can sit and have a coffee, tea or a beer during the day.

If you're lucky in the cities you'll stumble across some excellent Enoteca, wine bars which stock hundreds of varieties of wine and serve food.

The aromas from the many varieties of coffees on the menus of the bars are the most telling memory of Italian street life. Espresso, cafe latte, cappuccino are commonly available. For a watered down espresso request a cafe lungo and for iced coffee request a cafe freddo. A request for a te will bring a hot black tea with lemon. Tea with milk is te con latte.

Wines

The salty sea breezes limit wine production in the area. However, located inland, Piacenza has historically had a fine reputation for wine. The great Roman scholar, Cicero speaking in the Senate, attacked his enemy Lucius Calpernius Piso for drinking too much "of those delicious Piacenza wines." The province nowadays specialises in producing the dry white **Trebbianino** from Val Trebbia, the white **Monterosso** from Val Arda and the red **Gutturnio**. Other Piacenza wines include the full bodied, red **Barbera**, the sweeter red **Bonarda** and the sparkling **Malvasia** drunk with desserts.

Reggio produces **Scandiano White** and Bologna **Montuni del Reno**. Another excellent sparkling red is the coastal area's **Sangiovese**.

Emilia Romagna's most renown wine is **Lambrusco,** but its image as a cheap unsatisfying wine is soon dispelled when drinking the real item at source. Lambrusco is a light sparkling red, and as such, an excellent companion to the heavy pastas on the regional menus. Lambrusco comes in varied degrees of sweetness and body. Both Lambrusco and Sangiovese are best drunk within 18 months of production.

Drinks Glossary

Acqua minerale	Mineral water	**Latte**	Coffee
Acquavite	Spirits	**Limonata**	Lemonade
Amaro	Bitter	**Liquor**	Liqueur
Aperitivo	Aperitif	**Lista dei vini**	Wine list
Aranciata	Orangeade	**Litro**	Lire
Bianco	White	**Mezzo**	Half litre
Bicchiere	Glass	**Rosato**	Rose
Birra alla spina	Beer, draught	**Rosso**	Red
Birra chiara	Lager	**Rum**	Rum
Birra in bottiglia	Beer, bottled	**Salute**	Cheers
Birra scura	Beer, bitter	**Secco**	Dry
Caffe	Coffee	**Selz**	Soda water
Chin chin	Cheers	**Spumante**	Sparkling wine
Cioccolata calda	Hot chocolate	**Succo di frutta**	Fruit juice
Cognac	Cognac	**Tonica**	Tonic water
Digestivo	Digestive	**Vino**	Wine
Espresso	Coffee	**Vino da pasto**	Table wine
Ghiaccio	Ice	**Whisky**	Whisky
Gin	Gin		

"Let Them Dunk Cake"

If you see diners dunking cake into their wine glasses, don't be surprised. It's a common feature in this part of the world. One's glass may get messy but it's a pleasant way to finish off the meal.

Beer (birra) is commonly available. It is served in one-third or two-third litre bottles or **alla spina** (on draught), when one can ask for a **piccola** (small) or **media** (large).

Spirits and Liqueurs

Liqueurs are often served after a meal as digestive. Local varieties include, **sassolino**, an anise based drink from the Sassuolo area, and **nocino**, a walnut based liqueur. Spirits available throughout Europe are stocked in most bars.

WHERE TO STAY

Apart from in the Adriatic resorts, accommodation can be relatively expensive in the cities. Many of the inland city hotels make their money from business customers attending the many fairs around Bologna and Modena.

The city hotels are less geared up for tourism than one might expect, and there are things to remember. Ironing one's own clothes in a hotel is illegal and few hotels have on site **laundry** facilities. The service even in the three star hotels can therefore be expensive and slow and non operational on Sundays. Many city centre hotels have no **parking space.** Even if they do, you may have to pay for parking on a daily basis. It is common in the cities for three star and lower hotels to only offer breakfast, but they usually will be linked to a nearby restaurant.

Hotel **prices** in the resorts tend to vary seasonally, with lower prices between October and May on the coast. The star guide is only a rough guarantee of prices. For example, some two star hotels may be as expensive as four star hotels. The range of prices for double rooms in Rimini can vary by six fold for the three star hotels, depending on the additional comforts provided and the location.

Unless the hotel has a five star rating, the star system of hotel rating rarely counts for an exact guide. What is on offer at a three star hotel may vary a great deal with another. **One star** hotels generally are basic and may have only shared facilities. **Two star** hotels are more comfortable, and often rooms are en suite with a phone and television. **Three stars** can vary between two star standard and very pleasant, comfortable stays. **Four stars** mean luxury and good service, with **five stars** providing a premium service. Unless otherwise stated, all accommodation prices are for double rooms.

The following is a star guide to the minimum standards hotels are expected to achieve for a star rating. It should be borne in mind that many hoteliers offer more of a service than the minimum standards.

STAR GUIDE TO MINIMUM HOTEL SERVICE STANDARDS

Facility	★★★★★	★★★★	★★★	★★	★
Reception Service	16/24 hr reception	16/24 hr reception	12/24 hr reception	12/24 hr reception	12/24 hr reception
Night Service	Porter	Porter	On request	On request	On request
Meals	Breakfast Room or served in room	No meals	No meals	No meals	No meals
Bar	Room mini-bar or 24hr bar service	No Bar	No Bar	No Bar	No Bar
Language	Heads of staff speak at least 3 languages	Heads of staff speak at least 3 languages	Heads of staff speak at least 2 languages	Italian	Italian
Room Cleaning	Daily plus afternoon tidy up	Daily plus afternoon tidy up	Daily	Daily	Daily
Fresh linen	Daily	Daily	3 times per week	2 times per week	Weekly
Air conditioning	Adjustable A/C	No A/C	No A/C	No A/C	No A/C
Floor Access	Lift	Lift	Lift if 3 storeys or more	Lift if 3 storeys or more	Stairs only
Luggage	Hotel Porter	Hotel Porter	Hotel Porter		
Phone	In room	In room	Operator service		
Bathroom	En Suite	90% en suite	70% en suite	40% en suite	Shared Bathroom

Some classic stays include Rimini's **Grand Hotel**, Ferrara's 5* **La Ducchessa** and 3* **Hotel Europa**, Bologna's 5* **Grand Hotel Baglioni**, Reggio's 4* **Hotel Posta**, Castell'Arquato's monastery stay, **Conservatorio Villagio**, Cadeo's 4* **Hotel Le Ruote ,** Forli's mountain agriturismo**, Ca Bionda** and Parma's 4* **Hotel Verdi**.

A stay in the countryside means an opportunity to stay in an **agriturismo,** akin to a guest house. These guest houses are generally cheaper than city accommodation. Car travellers can take advantage of the countryside, while being able to drive into the towns and cities, park their cars, and wander among the sites and scenery. Few rooms have telephones but they are generally clean if basic.

The cheapest accommodation used to go under the name of **locanda**. Locanda were basic guest houses, but today one can find many locanda are more upmarket and pricier than the one star and occasionally, two star hotels.

Youth Hostels exist in the main cities. Only in the Adriatic resorts is self-catering on offer. The region has plenty of **camp sites** and **holiday coastal chalets**. Camp sites run all along the coastal belt, on the outskirts of the main cities, and in the hills.

Tourist information offices will happily arrange accommodation for visitors on request.

GETTING THERE

Flying directly into Emilia Romagna is possible, with two international airports at Bologna, and Rimini. Direct flights taking just over two hours arrive from Manchester and London Stanstead to Rimini, and from London Heathrow to Bologna.

Bologna's current schedule offers two **British Airways** (Heathrow) flights and one **Alitalia** (Gatwick) flight a day from London, and flights from Amsterdam **(KLM)** Barcelona **(Iberia** and **Meridiana),** Brussels **(Sabena),** Copenhagen **(SAS),** Dusseldorf **(Lufthansa),** Frankfurt **(Lufthansa)** and Lisbon **(TAP).**

Rimini is served by a daily **Ryanair** (UK 01279 666200, Rimini 0541 569569) 2hr 15mins flight from Stanstead near London. For those wishing to travel straight to Bologna, Ryanair lay on a coach 30 minutes after flight touch down which takes 2hrs 30mins to reach Bologna Centrale rail station in the city centre. The coach returns each day from the rail station, two and a half hours before the scheduled return flight. Return coach tickets costing L30,000 are available at the Ryanair office in Rimini.

Aeradria (0541 715910) operates weekday flights from Rimini to Vienna.

Piacenza is 45 minutes from **Milan** airport, which has frequent daily flights from Heathrow and twice weekly flights from London City airport. Scheduled flights are generally cheaper than charter flight unless booked with hotel accommodation. The cheapest way to secure a flight is generally through travel agents. Some offers are listed in teletext and on the internet as well as in newspapers and weekly magazines.

Bologna is connected by **rail** all year round to the major cities of Western Europe as is Rimini in the June to September months. Travelling to Bologna from London can take 24 hours and though not cheap, is a relaxed way to travel – especially for those worried about flying. Rail tickets are valid for two months and permit stop offs en route.

Cheap offers are available for those under 26 years old who can secure an **InterRail pass** which, at £220 for the two zones covering Britain and Italy, gives one month's unlimited travel to places in between, to Turkey, Greece and Slovenia and around Italy.

Holders of **Senior Citizen Rail Cards** can buy a **Rail Europe Senior Card** for £5 which gives 30% off ticket prices throughout Europe.

Travelling by road from Western Europe, the best way into the region is via the A1 autostrada motorway connection. From Milan, this motorway touches Piacenza, Parma, Reggio, Modena and Bologna before switching south for Florence and Rome.

Distances of the main cities from **Rimini** in the south east of the region are **London** 1684km, **Amsterdam** 1482km, **Barcelona** 1355km, **Paris** 1226km, **Berlin** 1190km, **Frankfurt** 1030km, **and Geneva** 740km.

Distances of the main cities from Piacenza in the north west of the region are **London** 1316km, **Amsterdam** 1218km, **Madrid** 1599km, Paris 954km, **Berlin** 1109km, **Dusseldorf** 1030km, and **Zurich** 373km.

Visas are not required for travellers from the EC countries, North America or Australia, but visitors from the latter countries will need one if they intend to stay for more than three months. **Visa extensions** are available from the local *questura* police stations. Non Italian nationals are required to register with the Italian police within three days of arriving in the country. However those staying in hotels will be registered by their hotelier.

Getting to Emilia Romagna from Other Parts of Italy

Bologna is within a two hours drive or train ride of **Milan** airport, and three hours from **Venice** airport, making it possible to reach the region quite quickly. Domestic flights are scheduled from Bologna and Rimini airports to most parts of Italy.

Bologna's current scheduled summer flight destinations, frequency, and flying times are listed below.

Destination	Airline	Flights/day	Flying Time
Bari, Puglia	Alitalia/Minerva	One	1hr 25mins
Lamezia, Calabria	Alitalia/Minerva	One	45mins
Milan (Linate)	Alitalia team	One	45mins
Naples, Campania	Alitalia Lufthansa	Three (weekends two) One (none Saturday)	1hr 30mins 1hr 5mins
Rome	Alitalia	Six (weekends five)	55mins
Alghero, Sardinia	Italair	One	1hr 35mins
Cagliari, Sardinia	Meridiana	Five	1hr 15mins
Olbia, Sardinia	Meridiana	Four	1hr
Tortoli, Sardinia	Air Dolomiti	Two (Saturdays only)	1hr 30mins
Palermo, Sicily	Alitalia/Meridiana	Two	1hr 20mnis
Catania, Sicily	Meridiana	Two	1hr 30mins

Aeradria (0541 715910) operates flights from **Rimini** to Napoli (daily), Rome Fiumicino (twice daily, once at weekends) and Milan Malpensa (daily).

Distances of the main cities from Rimini in the south east of the region are Milan 325km, Venice 214km, Florence 159km, Rome 343km, and Naples 499km.

Distances of the main cities from Piacenza in the north west of the region are Milan 67km, Venice 248km, Florence 257km, Rome 546km, and Naples 763km.

Fast rail links to other parts of Italy connect all the regional cities. Before purchasing a ticket it's worth noting that Italy has six different classes of rail ticket and prices may vary as to the speed and comfort of your train journey.

Locale rail services stop at every station and can be very slow. **Diretto** trains stop at most stations while **Espresso** services are restricted to major towns. **Intercity** links the major cities in the region and other cities in Italy. Tickets cost 30 percent more and must be paid for in advance. Even more expensive is the **ETR 450 Pendolino** inter city service, with reservations securing a first class seat with newspaper and meal. **Eurocity** trains link up with other major European cities.

A few services are private but most are run by **Ferrovie dello Stato, Italian State Railways**. Their Principali Treni timetables are available free from the stations.

GETTING AROUND EMILIA ROMAGNA

Driving a **car** requires an up to date **International Driving Licence**. Driving for the first time abroad requires some getting used to especially if your from the left-hand driving UK. Drivers in the region tend to signal late and sometimes not at all.

The **autostrada** are motorways (maximum speed limit 130kmph), on which one normally has to pay a toll after picking up a ticket at the entry booth. Payment is usually possible by cash or credit card. Autostrada signs are in green and National or A road signs are in blue. The speed limit in built up areas is 50kmph.

Autostrada and the Via Emilia stretch in an almost straight line for 248km from Rimini in the south east to Piacenza in the north west. Distances from Rimini of the main cities are, in Romagna, Ravenna 50km, Ferrara 126km and on Via Emilia, Bologna 113km, Modena 152km, Reggio Nell'Emilia 175km, Parma 204km and Piacenza 248km.

Car hire is available from Bologna and Rimini airports, but it's cheaper to book from England where a small hatchback will cost around £180 per week as compared to £200 in Italy. Be sure to confirm that the airport car hire company has received your booking. Both airports have **taxi** ranks. Taxis are usually metered but if not, the fare should be negotiated beforehand.

For car breakdowns, dial 116 and give the operator your location, car details and registration and **Automobile Club d'Italia** will be contacted and they'll come and fix your car. It can be expensive.

Traffic is heavy and city centre **parking** difficult in the cities of Parma, Piacenza and Bologna making it worthwhile to park on the edge of the city and take a bus. Ferrara, Modena and Ravenna have substantial areas in the centre where most cars are forbidden. It is noticeable that many city workers and residents opt for riding their bicycles to get round. As a result there are plenty of **cycle hire** and in Rimini **scooter hire** (L50,000/day) places.

Taking a **bus** in town means purchasing a ticket (around L2,000) beforehand from your hotel, a newsagent or tobacconists or any place with a biglietti sign where one can buy a carnet with 8 tickets for around L10,000. Ticket prices vary. Rimini fares are L1,500 (L3,000 if bought on the bus) for one urban area and L2,500 for all urban areas. Ravenna fares are L1,200 and Ferrara fares L1,400 all valid for 60 minutes. Fares for rural routes vary with distance.

The rules for travelling by bus mean that tickets should be stamped in the machine on the bus or at the stop where one boarded. Fines of around L60,000 operate for those caught with non-valid or unstamped tickets.

Autobuses take passengers around the region or to other parts of Italy. The faster way to get around the region is to take a train (services described above). Hitch-hiking, if necessary, should never be done alone.

i Tourist Information

Tourist Information Offices are denoted by a large eye, an italicised i or sometimes the initials **IAT.** They are equipped with local, provincial and regional maps and very helpful. The offices will arrange accommodation and can arrange tour guides for the local areas.

Tour Itineraries

As the acknowledged heartland of Italian cuisine, the region is a fine place for a culinary tour taking in the fish dishes of the Romagnola coast, the Apennine simple but appetising recipes, the meats of Emilia, and the huge varieties of pasta dishes. The Pavarotti and Verdi musical tours around Modena, Parma and Piacenza provinces are popular as is the cultural trip travelling from Byzantine Ravenna to Mediaeval Bologna and on to Renaissance Ferrara before resting in stylish Rimini.

However, given that the travelling time between the major cities is so short (maximum 3 hours) and the plethora of tiny towns and villages worth, it's best to draw up your own itinerary.

Communications – Post, Phone, Fax

It's worth remembering that Italy operates on a time band of GMT plus one hour in the winter and plus two hours from the last weekend in March till the last in October. Generally speaking, Italy is always one hour ahead of the UK.

Public telephones are plentiful and accept coins or phonecards. Call units are L200 and phonecards can be bought from post offices, bars, tobacconists and newsagents. Off peak rates are from 6.30pm to 10pm. The night rate operates between 10pm and 8am and throughout public holidays. The local dialling code must be used for local and regional calls.

The international dialling code for Italy is 0039. The Italian dialling system has changed recently so that the 0 prefix for the local code should be kept. For example, Bologna (area code 051) changes to 0039051.

Key dialling codes:

Rimini **0541** Forli **0543** Bologna **051** Ravenna **0544** Piacenza **0523** Reggio Emilia **0522** Ferrara **0532** Modena **059** Parma **0521**

To make a **reverse** or **collect call** home from Italy, it is necessary to dial 172 then the country code, which will put you through to a telephone operator in your country of choice.

Post

Posting Italy from the UK costs a minimum of 34p for letter post. Post can take up to a fortnight so post early. Posting from Italy to the UK can sometimes be quicker and cost L800.

Many hotels have facilities for receiving and sending **fax** communications but few yet use **e-mail**. Fax numbers of hotels and other facilities are given in this guide where available.

Rules, Regulations and the Police

The region is quite safe though it's always wise to take precautions with valuables and baggage. Most hotels have a deposit safe for valuables and money. If you do have problems which require the law, it's worth noting that there are different types of police dealing with different aspects of the law.

Vigili Urbani are town traffic police dealing with parking fines and directing traffic. **Polizia Stradale** are responsible for motorway traffic. Thefts should be reported to **Polizia Statale** at their questura police station. They deal with crime in general. **Carabinieri** are the machine gun toting police who look like soldiers. They also deal with crime but their remit includes higher crime, drug control and public disorder.

The **emergency service** telephone number for Police, Fire and Ambulance services is 113

For any further problems, the **British Embassy** is in Rome (tel 06 4825551) and a **British Consulate** is in Florence (055 212594).

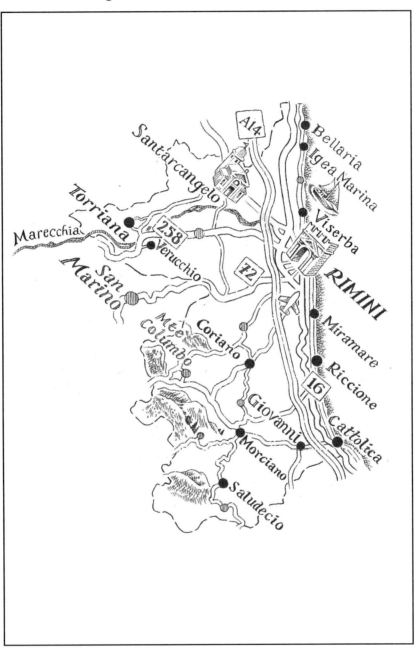

A TALE OF TWO TOWNS **Rimini**
STARTING OUT

My companion, Muriel, and I arrived in Rimini's small airport, only to be struck by the prosperity and charm of the town outside. This was not tacky Blackpool, but a charming relaxed town where the Italian penchant for cafe life and promenading through the evening is in full swing. The light coastal breeze meant that even though it was August, the heat was pleasant.

What we were to discover in and around Rimini is that the area is far from being an area of just sandy beaches, water sports and night clubs. Close by is a dramatic countryside of rugged hilltops and tranquil valleys, ancient villages, Mediaeval castles, churches and monasteries.

We found that Rimini was two towns. There are the beaches teaming with people playing sports, sunbathing or just having a laugh. But there is also the stylish town centre, with its often overlooked, Roman, Mediaeval and Renaissance buildings and squares that were delightful to walk around. We sat down at the Pescheria by Cavour Square in the middle of Rimini's Mediaeval core surrounded by beautiful buildings.

The Pescheria has huge marble slabs, said to have been used by the Romans for selling fish, but now used by market traders or by people like us looking for a place to sit with a glass of wine.

HISTORIC RIMINI

The **Pescheria** in Rimini's Cavour Square on Corso Augusto was an ideal place to get our bearings, and chart our route. If one takes the Pescheria as Roman, then the square contains all elements of Rimini's history.

In 268 B.C, the Romans chose Rimini as the starting point of the Via Emilia, which would cut across the northern edge of the Apennines and begin Rome's conquering of the Po plain. Rimini, then on the banks of the River Marecchia, was linked to Rome by Via Flaminia, and thus became a key point for trade.

Corso Augusto was the main axis or decuman for the Roman town, then known as Ariminium, the spot where Julius Caesar rallied his troops after crossing the Rubicon and marching on Rome. The stone on which he is said to have stood to address his army is in **Piazza Tre Martiri**, a short walk from the Pescheria along Corso Augusto. The Piazza was the siting of the Roman forum.

The triumphal Arco Augusto was erected in 27 B.C at the entrance of Via Flaminia and Corso Augusto. Close by, off Viale Roma on the edge of the Roman city wall, are the ruins of an amphitheatre, built by Hadrian to house 10,000 spectators.

A walk down Corso Augusto took us through the old centre, and onto the **Ponte Di Tiberio,** the Tiberius bridge with Latin inscriptions on its massive Istrian slabs. The pride of Roman architecture in the town, it was erected across what was the Marecchia river between 14 A.D and 21 A.D. In 1417, the Marecchia shifted its estuary to the north and the river was replaced with a canal.

Vital to Rimini's rise was the town's port which, on Via Flaminia and connected to Puglia in the south, was also an important pilgrim route to Rome. Its merchants grew rich and built **Palazzo dell'Arengo,** the Arengo Palace opposite the Pescheria in Cavour Square, in 1207. The name derives from it being a meeting place for the town's government.

While the palace underwent substantial restoration in 1925, its **Sallone dell'Arengo** portico and the odd bell tower still demonstrate the wealth the town had generated. The **Palazzo del Podesta** was added in 1330.

Another product of this era was the Gothic church of **San Agostino,** started by hermit monks in 1274. It underwent a reconstruction in the 18th century, but its flanks, apse and campanile (bell tower) are original. Indeed the bell tower on Via Cairoli is the highest in Rimini, rising to 180 feet.

The interior has beautiful frescoes, particularly in the apse where Giotto's influence can be seen. The campanile's chapel contains frescoes depicting the **Stories of the Virgin** by Giovanni da Rimini, master of the Rimini School of artists, while the church contains many other masterpieces from the 14th century school.

Within yards of the western side of Piazza Cavour in Piazza Malatesta, we came to the imposing **Castelo Malatesta** erected by Sigismondo Malatesta. Under restoration, its battlements recently looked inside onto the local prison. Now the castle has a Museum of Primitive Arts, devoted to ethnic artefacts from around the world.

Sigismondo's greatest legacy in Rimini town is the 15th century **Tempio Malatestiano** on Via 4th Novembre close to Tre Martyri. Its design was by one of Italy's great early Humanists, Leon Battista Alberti, who constructed it using the frame of a Gothic Franciscan church that stood on the site. He encased it in Verona marble. Alberti was inspired, like Sigismondo, by the Roman era and his classical designs and theories are said to have been the precursor of Renaissance art.

The facade contains fascinating bas reliefs, with tigers and elephants reflecting Sigismondo's imperial designs and joyous scenes with putti, nymphs and grapes – more similar to those Romanesque churches said to be linked to the occult. Sigismondo was not popular with Pope Pius II, who declared the church "a temple to devil worship", and had an effigy of the warlord burnt on the streets of Rome.

The interior was designed by Dutti and contains a 14th century crucifix by Giotto, and a fresco produced in 1451 by Pietro della Francesca, portraying Sigismondo knelt in front of the saint of the same name.

Work on the temple was never completed. After the Malatestas, Papal rule ensued and Rimini's development stagnated. Nevertheless, around Cavour Square are many pleasant Renaissance houses, and the cobbled streets and pavements of old. The square itself sports the 16th century **Pine Cone Fountain**, said to have enthralled Leonardo da Vinci, and a bronze statue of Paolo V erected in 1612. Tre Martiri contains Buonamici's 18th century clock tower, a reconstruction of an 18th century structure, and the San Antonio temple built in 1530.

Many of the artefacts and paintings telling Rimini's story, including fragments of Roman mosaics, are displayed in the civic museum, **Museo della Citta** in Piazza Ferrari, a stroll from Piazza Cavour.

Federico Fellini hailed from Rimini, as did the modern sculptor, Arnaldo Pomodoro, whose funeral monument, **La Nave Va** (the boat sails) in the civic cemetery on Via dei Cipressi, commemorates the great genius and his wife.

Rimini Town

Entry into Rimini from the north is quite verdant. Inland, one can see the rugged hills, topped with the occasional tower or castle. Rimini town is full of tree-lined boulevards.

Rimini town lives up to its reputation for offering almost everything a seaside tourist would want. The population doubles in the summer and outside of season its relative tranquillity provides a pleasant atmosphere.

Rimini's beaches have every water sport you might wish to mention, including deep sea fishing trips, sailing, windsurfing and clean waters to swim in. July brings an **international sailing race**, drawing all those seemingly thousands of boat owners from around the province. On the north end of the promenade is the **Dolphin Show Park** containing an aquarium and half a dozen performing dolphins. Shows start at 4.45pm, 6pm, 9.30pm and 10.30pm between April and October.

The town has more than a dozen **roller skating** rinks, **pond fishing** at *Lago Riviera* in Viserba and 14 parks which are good for cycling. Rimini is a **Vespa** town swarming with **scooters** and **mopeds**, but also cyclists – the best way to penetrate the centre's pedestrian areas. The town also has a **health centre** at the *Terme* (tel 751315) using Galvanina mineral water.

For those who want the more artistic side of life, there are plenty of **festivals** and **exhibitions**. July brings street musicians onto the piazzas for the town's *Buskers' Festival*. August sees the *Sagra Musicale Malatestina* **International Festival of Classical Music** and at September's end, the *Riminicinema* **International Film Festival**. One event, not necessarily just for the children, is the *Cartoon Club* which, in mid July to August, features cartoons from around the world at cinemas throughout the town.

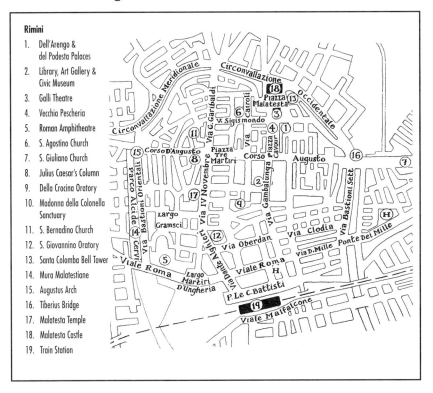

Rimini

1. Dell'Arengo & del Podesta Palaces
2. Library, Art Gallery & Civic Museum
3. Galli Theatre
4. Vecchia Pescheria
5. Roman Amphitheatre
6. S. Agostino Church
7. S. Giuliano Church
8. Julius Caesar's Column
9. Della Crocina Oratory
10. Madonna della Colonella Sanctuary
11. S. Bernadino Church
12. S. Giovannino Oratory
13. Santa Colomba Bell Tower
14. Mura Malatestiane
15. Augustus Arch
16. Tiberius Bridge
17. Malatesta Temple
18. Malatesta Castle
19. Train Station

Shopping

Saturday and Wednesday mornings are Cavour Square's **market** days. We tried both days and each time the square was packed with varied stalls jammed in side by side, selling fruit, vegetables, clothes, leatherwear, jewellery, Del Piero football shirts and other goods. The prices if anything were slightly cheaper than what we would find in Britain.

Rimini has plenty of **fashionable** shops with similar prices to the UK. One point to note is that many are shut in August. However we did find an Island shop on Piazza Ferrari selling Diesel trousers. Romagna is the home of Diesel and this pair of trousers, which would have cost £60 in England, was on sale for £20. The piazza is also a pleasant square, with gardens where in the summer one can sit around the cafe or in the tree shaded gardens. Collectors will also want to visit the big **antique market**, which takes place on Fridays during the summer in Piazza Cavour.

Shops with a regional flavour include **Le Terre** on Via Soardi selling terracotta works, **Perra Massimo**, displaying marble artistic works and **Brolli Ceramiche**

D'Arte, selling ceramics. On the lighter side there are plenty of 'sexy shops' in Rimini.

Night Life

At 9pm we decided to try the **Teatro** restaurant in Cavour Square, as it has a good reputation and was only slightly more expensive, but opted for the **Cavallieri de Rosa**, another recommended eating place in the square. The advantage of the Cavallieri is that it opens till midnight, and even later for parties.

At night we found a lively atmosphere, with young Riminese filling in the Pescheria on Cavour Square. For those who want a bit of life without throbbing music it's a good night out. Otherwise, there are plenty of restaurants, trattoria and pizzeria on the promenade – the only place in Emilia Romagna where we could see spaghetti bolognese on menus.

Clubs

For the young at heart, a trip to Rimini is a must. Dance through the night and sunbathe through the day. Clubbers praise the town's great atmosphere, with reasonable prices and a fantastic choice. The biggest clubs include **L'Altro Mondo Studios** near Miramare Beach, containing four dance floors playing commercial, trance, revival and underground for 3,000 people, and **Velvet** (Via S. Aquilina), with two floors playing dub, trance, ethno-dub, acid jazz and rock indie for up to 2,000. The lovely setting at the popular **Paradiso** on the hill in Covignano has two indoor floors and one outside playing underground, house and commercial for up to 1,500 clubbers. Some of the other larger clubs which stay open throughout the year include **Blow Up** at 209, V.le R.Elena in Bellariva, **Carnaby Club** at 20, Via Brindisi, **Embassy** at 33, Vle Vespucci, **Lo Street Club** at 7, V.le Vespucci, **Nabis** at 5, Via Schubert and **Rag** at 7, V.le Beccadelli.

Miramare Beach

Near to Rimini airport is the beach of Miramare which, while containing a couple of cafes, is clean and devoid of the customary intensive covering of deckchairs. This may be because it is known as 'the transvestite beach'. To the right of the Cafe Gustavo, gay men and transsexuals bathed or strolled on the soft sand stretching 50 metres to the sea.

Further on to the horizon, a clear day offers a view of the cliffs rising out of the sea. Beyond here are the tiny coves of the Ancona coast. One attraction is that the beach is never very busy, even on a Sunday. When we left at 5.45pm the beach was almost empty as the cafes and beach shops had closed. Nearby is **Fabialandia** a huge funfair popular with young and old.

THE RIMINI RIVIERA

Rimini is most famous for its 40km of sandy beaches, hotels, water sports and night clubs. The town itself was first established as a seaside resort in 1843, when a bathing centre was established. Now there are 700, each with an attendant hiring out deckchairs, parasols, bathing huts and sunbeds.

Fellini

For those who like a restful beach holiday, getting a sun-tan and a little light recreation, the Adriatic Riviera offers wonderfully serviced resorts. Almost every beach is equipped with snack bars, restaurants and sports equipment. The beaches are packed with bathers at the weekends, but aside from August, weekdays offer quieter times.

A typical Sunday scene sees the sands covered in rows of deckchairs, strictly regulated on the numbered beaches. The beaches are often wide enough to facilitate volleyball and basketball nets, football areas, wooden huts, and other facilities, making the beach a lively fun area. If this isn't enough there are major fairgrounds and fantasy parks close to the beaches.

On the Rimini beaches, the pink walls of the Grand Hotel are a major landmark. Fellini stayed here, and the prices make it Rimini's most expensive and oldest hotel. The Grand looks out over number nine beach which, with the least number of deckchairs, we found most attractive.

On the warm summer nights, the Riminese young and old go promenading in style around the pleasant town. Plenty of restaurants are open serving Romagnola dishes, and the popular local Sangiovese wines. After dark, the 80 or so night clubs open, bringing thousands of young visitors who flock to Europe's premier clubbing centre.

Many of the night clubs, costing L30,000 to L50,000 to enter, are serviced by the inexpensive (L4,000 for a bus pass) all night, **Blue Line** bus services sponsored by the municipalities to increase safety. They arrive and leave for places as far away as Ferrara. It's just as well because the most fashionable discos are in the hills around Rimini, in Covignano and the like. A cheaper night can be had in the summer when bars on the promenade hire DJs to set their premises rocking. The clubs will be open till 5am or so before the revellers are taken home.

Lunchtime will often find the clubbers back on the beach, taking in the sun and resting for the next night's rave.

We returned out of season, driving north along the Rimini coastline. It was October and the beaches were absent of the summer deckchairs, which swaddle the shores till the end of September. Without them the shoreline looked quite pretty. The temperature still hits 20°C plus, making it an ideal time to visit if you prefer romantic walks along the beach. Many of the hotels and cafes were shut but those that were open had knockdown prices. In Viserba just north of Rimini, we found the pleasant, if basic, Hotel Giardino (tel 0541-732336) on Via Cividale, just 50 yards from the beach and charging just L40,000 per night.

With road access restricted to residents booked in a hotel or apartment, to get to Bellaria beach one has to walk. **Bellaria Igea Marina** (15km north of Rimini) is a big complex of multi-storey tourist hotels and apartments with pleasant gardens. In summer the beaches are packed, swamping the local population of just 13,000. It's a fun place with plenty of discos, water sports, and a curious **Shell** and **Paper Money Museum** on the Torre Saracena.

Water sports include diving and snorkelling, windsurfing, sailing, shark and deep sea fishing. Being a tourist resort, the town also has plenty of night clubs, including the two dance floor, *Gallery Chez Vous* on Via Mar Jonio, playing acid jazz, soul funk and 70s and 80s music for 1100 people. The similarly sized *Lola by Rio Grande* on Via Abba aptly plays commercial and live music, while the smaller single dance floor *Manila* club on Viale Ennio plays underground and progressive music.

Beneath a hill, **Cattolica** (18km south of Rimini) is another popular and picturesque beach resort. It is an important fishing harbour and packed with sea-going vessels. Once a Roman settlement, its history also includes the 1823 visit by Napoleon's brother, Lucien who holidayed in the town with his family.

Around the end of June, the town hosts the **International Thriller and Mystery Festival** and at the end of August, a **Windsurf Day** for addicts to windsurfing. September then sees the crazy **Netturbiadi, or dustmen's Olympics.**

Market day is on Saturday in Piazza A. De Curtis and Via Petrarca. Discotheques include the *Golden Gate Disco Pub* on Via Bovio and *Esedra* on Via C. Battisti. Motonave Brigantino organises mackerel (0337-638699) fishing trips, and Circolo Nautica on Via del Porto, deep sea and underwater fishing.

Close by, **Misano Adriatico** is a smaller quieter beach resort, more suited to families. Having said that, it's not so quiet at it is located close to the world famous **Santamonica Racing Track,** where up to 70,000 spectators watch **motor racing** and **motorcycle** races. The track also runs two day sports driving, competition driving, and anti-skidding schools (tel 612540).

The town also contains *Byblos*, a 3-dance floor venue and restaurant on Via

Castello, where 1,800 ravers can dance to garage, hip hop and underground beneath a huge glass pyramid.The 3-floor, **Echoes** (Via Del Carro) has a capacity to take 1,000 people dancing to house, underground and progressive music and **Peter Pans** on Via Scacciano has two dance floors playing similar music for 1,200 people.

A quieter time is offered by the horse riding stables at **Rawhide Ranch** (tel 610088) and **Bathek Ranch** (tel 615686) and **Paolo Sylvestrini's Windsurfing School** on Portoverde beach.

With 33,000 people, **Riccione** is the province's second beach resort, a garden town with wide tree-lined boulevards. Its elegant villas and boutiques lined up on Viale Ceccarini flaunt the town's attraction for Italy's well-to-do. Located 10km south of Rimini, it offers plenty of water sports, beaches and night clubs.

However, Riccione is not just a clubber's centre. The town hosts several major festivals including, an **International Cycling Week** of competitions at the end of September, the **International Amateur Cyclists Championship** on the 24th and 25th April, the **Bit Movie Computer Art International Festival**, and from February to June, a season of concerts directed by what one brochure describes as 'notorious' directors. Several opera nights are staged in July.

Market day is Friday in Piazza Unita. Riccione is also popular for its **Terme** (tel 602201) health centre on Viale Torino, offering mud baths, massages and mineral water cures and beauty treatments.

The fun fair is on Viale Vespucci in the Spa area. Riccione has five **roller skating rinks** for enthusiasts including **Pattinodromo** on Via L. Carpi and **Giardini** on Via L. Milano. Water sports include diving and snorkelling, and trips run by **Progetto Sub Italia** (tel 0335-371423). Summer **sailing courses** for beginners and the advanced are held at **Club Nautico** (Viale D'Annunzio), with **windsurfing** available from Bathing Establishment 49 in front of Piazza L. Roma.

Aquafan on Via Pistoia must be the **largest water park complex in Europe** and a must for the kids with 2,800 square metres of water, huge sliding boards, a small children's theatre, shows, whirlpools, diving courses, restaurants, bars, picnic areas, a nursery, a gym and a disco. It's open from June to mid September from 10am to 6.30pm, with a disco from 10pm to 4pm, and can be reached on tram 11 from Rimini and tram 125 from Cattolica.

After hours there are plenty of **clubs**, the biggest of which include the nationally famous 4-dance floor **Cocorico** (Via Chieti) where 1,650 ravers are offered hard and progressive house and underground. **Walky Cup by Aquafan** contains swimming pools and contains a floor used for bubble dancing! The two indoor and one outdoor dance floors of **Prince** (Via Tre Baci) serve up commercial, garage, happy sound and global groove for 1,440, while the two dance floor **Maxie Vallechiara** accommodates 1,150 people who can dance to rock, acid jazz, RnB, funk and South American tunes.

EATING OUT

Rimini has plenty of good restaurants and during the summer, many cheap places to eat on the promenade. Places to eat of note are:

Bastian Contrario at 312, Via Marecchiese **Cavallieri della Rosa** (open till midnight), 15, Piazza Cavour and the other small restaurants around Piazza Cavour.

For those who wish to splash out more than L70,000 a head, the pricey places in town are the fish restaurants: **Aurelio** at 140, I.mare Spadazzi Bagno, **Da Oberdan Il Corsaro** in Via Destra Del Porto and **Lo Squero** at 7, I.Mare Tintori.

Cheapest places in town are the pizzeria and the Chinese restaurants which include: **Fong Shuo** at 69, Vle Dardanelli and **Li Dailing** at 108, Vle Pascoli.

ACCOMMODATION

Hotels

The Rimini Riviera has a huge number of hotels and guest houses. Prices vary dramatically within the star system, and rocket during the summer season. We have picked out some of the cheaper and more expensive stays within the star system. Prices where given are approximate for double rooms per night.

Rimini (area code 0541)

***** The only 5 star stay in Rimini is provided by the opulent **Grand Hotel** at 1, Parco F.Fellini (tel 56000, fax 56866) (£130/£200) on the promenade.

**** Top Range (£80/£150)

Imperiale, 16, V.Le Vespucci (tel 52255 fax 28806), **Ambasciatori**, 22, V.Le Vespucci (tel 55561 fax 23790).

Lower Range (£20/£60)

Ascot, 38, V.P.Di Piemonte (tel 371561 fax 372012) and **Coronado Airport**, 390, V.Flaminia (tel 373161 fax 371740) in Miramare. **Vienna Ostenda**, 11 V.R.Elena (tel 391744 fax 391032) in central Rimini.

*** Top Range (£20/£100)

Columbia, 4, V.R.Elena (tel 391104 fax 391470) and **Costanza**, 141, V.R.Elena (tel 380381 fax 380541) in central Rimini. **Guiseppe Verdi**, 8, V.Fano (tel/fax 380156) in Bellariva.

Lower Range£15/£30)

Cosmos, 23, V.Lecce (tel/fax 373175), **Ca'Vanni**, V.Mantova, 2 Ang.V.Gubbio (tel 372171) and **Santiago**, 112, V.R.Margherita (tel 375508) in Rivazzurra. **Valverde**, 16, V.Del Tulipano (tel 381431 fax 381549), **Villa Marina**, 220, V.Le Pascoli (tel 390404) and **Caesar**, 30, **V.R.Elena** (tel 381561) in central Rimini.

** Top Range (£10/£50)

Consul, 1, V.Neri (tel/fax 390466), **Naiade**, 7, V.Le Medaglie D'Oro (tel 390950 fax 392469) and **Novella**, 1, V.Le Dandolo (tel 24724 fax 786522) in central Rimini.

Lower Range (£10/£20)

Galles, 179, V.R.Elena (tel 381025 fax 389179), **Macky**, 129, V. Lagomaggio (tel 389404 fax 28682) and **Piccadilly**, 54, V.le Vespucci (tel 390962) in central Rimini.

* Cheapest stays in central Rimini (£10/£20) are at **Villa Serenella**, 23, V.le Bengasi (tel 390762), **Villa Roberta**, 7, V.P.Da Rimini (tel 381022), **Sabrina Rimini** 83, V.Pascoli (tel 381461) and **Bel Soggiorno**, 15, V.Gusti (tel 381226).

Other cheap stays can be found in Rivazzura at **Agostini**, 4, V.Brindisi (tel 373306), **Cavallino Bianco**, 24, V.Sarsina (tel 372715), **Corno D'Oro**, 4, V.Mantova (tel 372309) **Tina**, 21, V.Viareggio (tel 372023) and **Villa Luca's**, 51, V.Morgagni (tel 373542).

For the other parts of the Rimini Riviera we have included only the top of the range highlights. All the resorts have plenty of 1, 2 and 3 star accommodation, and the best way to book is via the tourist information offices which are listed below.

Riccione has the 5 star **Grand Hotel Des Bains** at 56, V.le Gramsci (tel 601650 fax 606350). Top of the range 4 star hotels include **Concord**, at 1, V.Rismondo (tel 692937 fax 691682), **Grand Hotel**, 25, V.le Gramsci (tel 694006 fax 693951) and **Mediterraneo** at 3, P.le Roma (tel 605656 fax 691262).

Cattolica's top of the range 4 star hotel is the **Victoria Palace** at 24, V.le Carducci (tel/fax 962921) while **Bellaria Igea Marina** has the **Ermitage** at 11, V.Ala (tel 347633 fax 343083). **Misano Adriatico** has one 4 star hotel, *Atlantic* at 28 V.Sardegna (tel 614161 fax 613748).

Apartments are also available to let on a daily rate. Contact tourist information for further details.

Camping

Rimini city has four main camp sites which also include bungalow facilities. Prices for adults range from £2-£3 per night out of season to £5 per night in the summer. Children have discounted rates, though some camp sites consider adults to be any one over 8 years old.

Rimini
Italia International, 112 Via Toscanelli, Viserba (tel 732882 fax 732322)
Maximum, Via Principe Di Piemonte, Miramare (tel 372602 fax 370271)
Torre Pedrosa, Via S.Salvador, Torre Pedrera (tel 720563)
Belvedere, 9, Via Grazia Verenin, Viserbella (tel 720960 fax 721723)

Riccione
Adria, 40, Via Torino (tel 601003 fax 602251)
Alberello, 80, Via Torino (tel 615402)
Fontanelle, 56, Via Torino (tel 615449 fax 610193)
Riccione, 10 Via Marsala (tel 690160 fax 690044)

Bellaria Igea Marina
Happy, 228 Via Panzini, Bellaria (tel 346102 fax 346408)
Riccardo, 310 Via Pinzon, Igea Marina (tel 331503 fax 330464)
Castellabate, 11, Via Agedabia, Igea Marina (tel/fax 331424)

Misano Adriatico
Misano Adriatico, 60, Via Litoranea Sud (tel 614330 fax 613502)
Conca D'Oro, 2, Via Litoranea Sud, Portoverde (tel 614303 fax 613304)

i Tourist Information Offices
Rimini 86, Via Dante (tel 51331 fax 27927)

Riccione 10, Piazzale Ceccarini (tel 693302 fax 605752)
Bellaria Igea Marina 10, Via L.Da Vinci (tel 344108 fax 345491)
Cattolica 1, Piazzale Nettuno (tel 963341 fax 963344)
Misano Adriatico 22, Viale Dei Platani (tel 615520 fax 613295)

Tour Organisers
Dreamtown T.O. Rimini (tel 24564 fax 51148)
Firma Tour Tour Operator Rimini (tel 355111 fax 55428)
Jordan Travel Rimini (tel/fax 376002)
Mosaic T.O. Cattolica (tel 953125 fax 954546)
Congressitalia Travel, Santarcangelo (tel 622334 fax 622451)

Rimini Tour Guides
Camas, (tel/fax 785183),
Coopservice, (tel 56029 fax 27272),
Inform Due Soc.Coop, (tel 728183 fax 773060) and
Travelcoop, (tel 677429 fax 678881)

Travelling Around
Distances from Rimini of the main cities are; Ravenna 50km, Ferrara 126km, Bologna 113km, Modena 152km, Reggio Nell'Emilia 175km, Parma 204km, Piacenza 248km, Venice 214km, Milan 325km, Florence 159km and Rome 343km.

Train Times – faster direct service

Rimini to Modena (1hr 40mins) Forli (30mins), Reggio Emilia (2hrs), Ferrara (2hrs), Parma (2hrs 20mins), Ravenna (50mins), Bologna (1hr), Piacenza (3hrs), Milan Centrale (3hrs), Brindisi (6hrs).

Trains Around Rimini and the Adriatic Coastline

Trains run frequently (journey times in brackets) from Rimini station north along the Adriatic coastline to Ravenna, stopping at Rimini Viserba, Rimini Torre Pedrera, Igea Marina (15mins), Bellaria, Gatteo e Mare, Cesenatico (30mnis), Cervia, Lido di Classe/Savio (48mins), Classe, Ravenna (1hr).

Trains run west to Santarcangelo (10mins) and south through Miramare, Riccione (15mnis), Misano Adriatico and Cattolica (25mins).

Trams patrol the coast from Cattolica in the south, to San Mauro e Mare just past Bellaria. In summer they run very frequently between 5.30-6.30am and 1.30-2.30am stopping at every town. Trams run from Rimini train station. Timetables are available free from the many shops selling bus tickets.

In summer, **Blue Line** night buses connecting all the night spots and ensuring a safe and fun journey back to your accommodation, supplement the tram service. Blue Line operates between 10pm and 5am during weekends in July and every night in August. (tickets L5,000).

Buses run inland from Rimini bus station to Santarcangelo, Poggio Berni, Torriana, and Montebello, to San Martino in XX and Coriano. Riccione buses travel inland. Coriano and Morciano and Cattolica buses go to Morciano, Saludecio, Mondaino and Monte Gridolfo. **San Marino** is served by Bonelli buses running from Rimini.

RIMINI

Rimini Airport

Rimini airport is a very smart, domestic and international airport A post box can be found to the right, as one leaves the building. Inside the building on the left is a shop selling newspapers, stamps and other goods. The airport has a bar and a hire car desk open during the day from about 8.30am till 5pm. Hire companies include Hertz and Avis. Ryanair has its own desk at the ticket office. There are no cashpoints, only a foreign currency exchange office. Getting there by car is best done by hitting the promenade and taking the road to Bellariva. It avoids the confusing signs around the complex one way system in the centre

THE RIMINI COUNTRYSIDE

We wanted to explore Rimini's rich culture, and the nearby towns, villages and countryside first. Even though Rimini is on a narrow coastal plain, ten minutes out of Rimini we found undulating green hills that roll and roll till they meet the horizon of rugged mesas, and isolated knolls deeply cut into by rivers and streams.

Hardly a hillock was without an ancient abbey or prince's fortress. No better place for understanding the phrase, "Lord of all I survey," as you gaze down on the countryside below. Here is the land of fable, the Italy of the **Malatestas**, the **Medici, Lucrezia Borgia, Garibaldi** and the **partisans.** Clay roof tops of tiny villages speckle their way up the steepest hillsides, which all but defy the motor cars which in deference, crawl up narrow roads edged by breathless precipices.

As Rimini's **Tiberius Bridge** and **Tiberius Arch** and **Malatesta temple** testify, this is a region of ancient historic settlements. The rugged cliff tops provided excellent sites for the protection of small city states, while the valleys and Adriatic coastline provided communications routes.

Evidence of pre-Roman settlements exists all over the area. By 1100 B.C the area already was occupied by quite advanced civilisations. Bronze and Iron Age artefacts have been found in **Santarcangelo, Poggio Berni, Verucchio, Torriana** and nearby **San Leo**. Indeed Verucchio's 1,000 B.C Villanovan colony is considered to be one of the first commercial settlements, whereby an Etruscan warrior caste became rich by trading along the coast.

Much of the area was later colonised by the Romans, who concentrated their settlements in the valleys to control the trade routes. The post Roman era saw the region transformed into a series of warring fiefdoms. By the 8th century it was already known as 'the land of the castles'. The nearby fortress town of San Leo has another claim to fame. Between 962 A.D and 964 A.D it was the capital of Italy under the rule of Berengarius II, and the scene of a great battle with the troops of German Emperor, **Otto I.**

But the main feature of the region is the display of the Mediaeval power of the Malatesta dynasty, which lorded over the area between the 13th and 15th centuries. Their castles and churches dominate the history of Rimini province, bringing with them tales of heroism, romance, treachery and fratricide. Battling with Popes and rival noble families, the dynasty left behind wonderful works of art. Dante also travelled through the area, recording some of its legends in the **Divine Comedy.**

The Malatestas

The region's key trade route was along the valley of the Marecchia, which descends from its source near San Leo to its mouth in Rimini town. So important was the valley that some still contest whether the Marecchia river was the Rubicon. The Malatesta took control of Pennabili and Verucchio in the 12th century, thus acquiring dominance of the middle section of the valley. From here Giovanni Malatesta launched his campaigns, defeating other rival lords. By 1355 he had established control of Rimini town. Eventually their rule stretched from Ascoli Piceno in Marche to Borgo San Sepolchro in Tuscany, and Cesena to the north.

Under Sigismondo Malatesta, the dynasty was responsible for erecting many of the area's fortresses and castles in the 15th century. They needed them to control the area as they had many rivals. Over the centuries, the Malatesta had to contest, not only with the **Borgias, Medici's, Sforzas, Gonzagas** and **Montefeltrans** but also troops of the Pope. By the end of the 15th century their power had waned. They were defeated by the **Montefeltrans**, who ruled from what is now San Leo, and the Papal troops, after which the land became a vassal of the Vatican.

Later, the area would pass to Papal rule and Renaissance architecture. During the Second World War, its hilltops and valleys would become a key battleground between the Allied forces and the Germans. Verucchio and many other castles were part of the Germans' Gothic Line of defence, which ran across the Apennines to the Mediterranean coastline. The war did some damage but the province's cultural heritage has been largely left unspoilt and, as yet, free of crowds of tourists. Virtually all its sites are within 30 minutes drive of Rimini town, which makes it an excellent place from which to reach old hamlets, the hillside and valleys.

Santarcangelo

Driving from Rimini to the small town of Santarcangelo took just ten minutes on the Via Marecchiese. What we found was a small town with a big heart – a beautiful Renaissance square of arches hiding little cafes and coffee houses.

Beneath the town lies a mystery. In Piazzetta della Monache and on Via Fabbri, leading to Via Ruggeri, one can step inside the hill, taking the entrance to a grotto. It is part of a system of a hundred or more caverns and tunnels dug into the hill on which the town stands. This particularly grotto has a long entrance and several side openings leading to a large circular cave. The origins and role of these caves remains unknown.

At night we, took a walk through the mediaeval cobbled narrow streets on the hill beneath the castle, and followed the winding road and steps up to the castle overlooking the town. On the way we passed the pretty little square, **Piazzetta delle Monache,** overlooked by the 14th century convent of **Saint Barbara and Saint Catherine,** before heading for the castle, which offers an excellent view of the town below.

The castle was first built in the 12th century and its entrance, the Campanone Vecchio, gate remains. The rest mainly dates back to 1386 when Carlo Malatesta built the square tower.

Just outside the castle walls is the **Capuchin Monastery** (1654-61). **Piazza Balacchi** has the **Collegiate Church, Chiesa Collegiata** (1744-56) with its 14th century crucifix, attributed to **Pietro da Rimini,** founder of the important Rimini school of art, and a splendid altar painting by Bonomo

Next to Via Cesare Battisti on Vicolo Denzi is **Stamperia Marchi**, a traditional fabric working shop. The town was famous for its fabric products, and inside a large treadwheel for the printing press still operates after 400 years of use.

Also along Via Cesare Battisti, we came across Sferisterio, just beneath the Mediaeval walls and two huge towers, one of which was the town prison. This area is used on Sundays for a local form of tennis known as **tamburello**. The tournaments in tamburello have their origin in an 18th century game known as bracciale, in which the rackets were spiked wooden armbands, and the ball made from pig skin or donkey hide.

One kilometre from the town, on the plain across Via Marecchiese, we visited the area's oldest church, the Romanesque pieve dedicated to **San Michele**. Built shortly after 550 A.D, it reflects the Byzantine influence of Ravenna, with fragments of floor mosaics still on view, and a low pillar of the ninth century. The church is popular for wedding services, but otherwise remains closed.

Key Events

A **European Theatre Festival** of **avant-garde** plays is staged in the open air during July. The **Balladeers'** open air music festival is held during the St Martin's Fair in early November. The **March Bonfires** are held to celebrate the eve of St Joseph's day on March 18th. **Market days** – Monday and Friday, mornings only.

Montebello

Set on a rugged outcrop of rock 23km west of Rimini, this little village, whose name derives from 'Mons Belli' (mountain of war) was the scene of a famous battle during the Second World War.

Montebello's sturdy fortress dates back to the 12th century. In 1375, the blue eyed daughter of the Marquis of Montebello mysteriously disappeared in a crevice. **The Azzurina**, as she is known, is said to be heard singing and laughing on the night of the summer solstice, and has attracted occult circles.

In 1186 it was bought by the Malatesta's and, like many castles in the area, fell under the control of the Montefeltrans and the Pope. Pope Pius II granted the castle to **Count Guido di Bagno**, whose family have held on to it ever since.

The gate tower is 13th century, the walls 15th century and the residential wing 16th century. Inside, the armoury is based on an 11th century church, which now serves as a **wine-tasting** tavern offering the best of Romagnola wines. It also contains an exhibition of 15th to 18th century jewels and furniture.

The village is tiny, with a church and a handful of small houses on narrow streets centred on a main piazza of just 20 to 30 metres. The old watchtower was originally a Romanesque mediaeval construction, with its bell ready to announce festivals and warn of danger.

A feature common to the houses is the rust-stencil print patterns, used on the curtains. This is traditional Emilia Romagna, home of such print patterns (to cover millinery) which have spread throughout Italy. Traditionally, stencil imprints are rendered in mellow rust colour or in sky-blue.

The village is peaceful, and offers splendidly dramatic views of the curiously rolling, but rugged countryside below, where the rivers have cut deep scars in the hillsides. On a clear day, we were assured, we would also see the Adriatic Sea to the west. The bountiful flora in the valley below attracts many varieties of bees, which probably explains why an annual **honey festival** is held here. The honey is excellent and available in shops throughout the village. The fair takes place on the last Sunday in August and the first in September.

We had lunch at the Trattoria Pacini in the square. The trattoria may look small from the outside but enter and after the bar, the interior opens up to seat 200 people and offer fine views from its large windows.

Saiano

The nearest hilltop to Montebello is **Saiano,** on which stands the lonesome **Saiano Monastery** with its solitary Franciscan friar, the only occupant of the whole hillside. We were going to pay the recluse a visit but it had been raining overnight making Via Palazzo, the difficult road up the hill, impassable. The presbytery of the church contains Renaissance frescoes and a sandstone cylindrical bell tower similar to those of Byzantine influence in Ravenna, and thought to be possibly 8th century in origin. Beneath Saiano, we passed the *Osteria de Malledote,* whose century old framework houses an excellent restaurant.

Torriana

In the foothills of Montebello, and opposite Verucchio, Torriana's rocky summit 1,000 feet above sea level gave us lovely views of Verucchio and the Rimini coastline. Iron and Bronze Age artefacts now in **Rimini's Civic Museum** were discovered on the hillside testifying to the settlement of the area for over 3,000 years. Until recently known as Scorticata, the town was an important fortress controlling the valley and was much fought over.

The current castle is thought to be a 15th century Malatesta construction. Sigismondo Malatesta organised a chain of towers across the area and, by means of contacting Montebello castle, the watchtower that lords the hilltop could communicate with fortresses right into Galilea. Local tradition has it that it is in Scorticata castle that the sons of Paulo Malatesta took their revenge on the Malatesta lord Giancotto. Paulo's cuckolded brother, Giancotto, infamously murdered their father and Giancotto's wife, Francesca, in Gradara castle.

Verucchio

We were now travelling alonng the ancient mountain road, up the Marecchia, which forms part of the Via Emilia. Situated 18km from Rimini, we were looking up at **Verucchio**, the fortress which dominated the lower valley. Verucchio is the town from which Giovanni Malatesta descended with his son, the 'Mastin Vecchio' to conquer Rimini town in 1295, and begin the era of Malatesta domination. Malatesta rule of the castle ended in 1462 when Frederico di Montefeltro ended a siege by sending a forged letter from another Malatesta fort. The letter promised reinforcements but the troops that arrived were Montefeltro troops in disguise.

Stood on the battlements of the 12th century **Rocca del Sasso castle** at the top of the hill, it was easy to see why this spot was favoured by Sigismondo Malatesta, and by the German army, who made the fortress a key observation point on the Gothic Line in 1943. Not only does the castle have a fantastic view of the valley, but it also dominates the town below. A single cannon remains, its barrel pointing towards the town centre. Fighting during the war, we were informed, took place in the town before the Allied troops seized control, forcing the occupants of the castle to surrender.

Sigismondo Malatesta heavily altered the castle between 1442 and 1449, adding the turrets to cope with the changing demands of warfare. The clock tower is an 18th century addition.

Below the castle is the former monastery of **Sant'Agostino,** which now has a museum housing interesting artefacts, including helmets and objects in gold and amber from Verucchio's Villanovan colony which existed in the area till the 6th century B.C. The monastery grounds also house a 14th century church, inside which are Baroque stuccoes and golden anconas.

The old part of the town, with its maze of tiny streets, alleys and steps, is a delightful experience. Here, the **Collegiata Church,** built and decorated in a bright Neoclassical style in 1874, contains a crucifix painted by the 14th century Rimini School, and one painted in 1404 by **Nicolo di Pietro.**

Down the hill, 2km away at Villa Verucchio, is the Franciscan church of **Santa Croce** part of the Friars Minor Monastery founded by **Francis of Assisi** in 1215.

Saint Francis is said to have stopped at Santa Croce hermitage, while passing through to Rimini in May of that year. At Santa Croce he is believed to have performed several miracles, including reviving a cypress plant, invoking a new water spring and ordering the sparrows to be silent while he pondered. A colossal 700 year-old cypress tree, 25 feet in circumference, still stands in the convent, and is believed to be that revived by the saint. The church has tremendous frescoes from the 14th century Rimini School.

Further down the hill, the San Martino Pieve is a Romanesque church dating back to 990 A.D.

Rimini's excellent **Golf Club** (tel/fax 0541 678122), with its 18 hole course similar to those to be found in Scotland, is in **Villa Verucchio**.

To the south of Verucchio lies the Republic of **San Marino.** Only 10km from the Adriatic coast and 24km from Rimini, this tiny state gained its popularity amongst Italian visitors because, apart from its superb location on **Monte Titano**, its duty free system offered very cheap shops. Prices have increased sharply over the years but the visitors still come in their droves.

San Marino is not a member of the European Community but we didn't need our passports to enter. Having held onto its independence since the 4th century, the state can justifiably claim to be **the world's longest standing republic**. About 25,000 people live in the country's 61 square kilometres. The shops take lira but San Marino does have its own currency, said to be very much collectors' items.

San Leo

The rock fortress town of San Leo rose almost vertically from the plains around as we drove west from Verucchio on the Via Marecchiese. The top of this incredible rocky intrusion rising almost 2,000 feet above the plain, appeared almost impossible to ascend by car. After winding up and around its cliff sides, we finally reached the car park beneath the main plaza. The night sky was lit by a full moon, and the air carried the eerie sounds of an organ beating out some tune akin to a *Hammer* horror movie soundtrack. The origin was the twelfth century cathedral, which sits a few yards above the square.

Though in Pesaro, just outside the boundaries of Rimini province, this historic town which was once the capital of Italy, is a must for visitors. That Dante visited the area is recorded in his Divine Comedy. Francis of Assisi gave a sermon in the town, being presented with Mount Verna as a gift in 1213. The town was taken over by Montefeltrano I in 1155, and for many years took his name. San Leo had a key strategic position along the M was much fought over from Byzan After 1631 it was incorporated into

The grand fortress sitting on to one side built on the edge of a hug a 15th century marvel of constructio so impregnable that in 963, a G could only take the town by means siege. Today it is a museum and pi

Inside the cathedral, Sunday service was in full swing. We wandered around the small 9th century pieve and the grey stone houses which climb up the hill, and finally into the piazza with its handful of cafes. One building on the square is given over to the Italian sculptor **Arnaldo Pomodoro**. His work was fascinating and only hunger kept us from staying longer.

Five **buses** a day take the one hour trip to San Leo from Rimini Autostazione.

Gatara

Past San Leo on the winding road to Sestino, we were in the hills of **Gatara**. Here, there are tiny rock strewn rivers abundant with fish pacing the cold waters. The area is accessible but devoid of tourists. The natural freedom of fish, fauna and flora make for a rustic paradise of greys, greens, terracotta browns and blues, gurgling rock pools, singing birds and insects humming with joy at the noon sun.

Gatara village stands almost atop of a majestic knoll supervising the hills on the opposite side of the valley. From here we could see the twins, **Simone** and the diminutive **Simoncella**, two adjacent outcrops of rock at 4,000 feet above sea level.

We were almost on the Tuscan border. The landscape is beset by the struggle between the deciduous and conifer trees for the right to climb up the steep hillslopes, once scarred by glaciers and now cut by rivers. On one such hill stands **Castillo del Bosschio**, a 40 foot solid stone watchtower from which those who threatened to make incursions into the old Italy could be spotted. Among the heather beside the tower are 5 sculptures, left by a poet who was once feted by Fellini.

ALONG THE CONCA VALLEY

The River Conca flows parallel to the Marecchia in the southern part of the province, its estuary being close to Cattolica. Flowing down from Mount Carpegna in Marche region it is flanked by gently undulating countryside of less drama than seen in the Marecchia valley. Nevertheless it is a beautiful area of rural tranquillity, villages nestling in the valleys and castles and towers occupying the hillside. The Romans extensively settled the valley and most of the towns today grew out of these settlements.

Of great significance in the Mediaeval era, many of these towns and villages have not grown apace with the rest of the north. The strategic importance of the towns in the Second World War brought devastation to many towns including Coriano, Gemmano, Montecolombo and Montescudo in particular. Rural poverty saw a major post war migration of people from the villages and farms to the cities and the shells of abandoned derelict houses can be still be seen in the fields across the valley.

Gradara

We travelled for 40 minutes from Rimini down the A14 autostrada heading towards Ancona, and made our way off at the Cattolica exit for Gradara. Almost immediately we found ourselves once more in rolling countryside. We were now in the Marche region on the border of Romagna. As suddenly, **Gradara**, the great castle of legend, came into view on our left, its massive battlements imposing over the Via Flaminia, the Conca valley and the coastline.

Neat, modern houses set in olive groves and orchards welcomed us, as we climbed the hill to the town beneath the castle. We parked outside the centuries old town walls, and climbed the cobbled streets to the castle. If the shops selling tourist bric-a-brac kept us in the 20th century, then we were transported back through time as we passed through the castle's walls, to take in its magnificent keep and battlements.

Before us was what appeared to be one of the few, still functioning, drawbridges in the region. But the ticket collectors were divided as to whether it was still in working order, the younger nodding and the older shaking his head.

Francesca and Paolo

Gradara is the home to two great legends – the story of **Lucrezia Borgia** and that of **Francesca** and **Paolo Malatesta** immortalised in **Dante's Canto Divino**.

Giovanni Malatesta da Verucchio, founder of the powerful Malatesta dynasty of Rimini took control of Gradara castle in the 13th century. The Malatesta's were thereby able to hold sway over the Marche-Romagna border till 1463.

Giovanni's eldest son Gianciotto married the beautiful Francesca but, absent from the castle for long periods, was powerless to prevent Francesca from falling in love with his brother, Paolo. It is said that when Gianciotto discovered the affair, he ordered the brutal stabbing to death of the two lovers. Torriana people believe that it was in the vaults of their castle, that the sons of Paolo then avenged themselves of his death, murdering Gianciotto. Today access to the castle battlements is denied as Francesca's ghost is said to walk them on the nights of the full moon.

Lucrezia Borgia

In the period following the murders, Gradara was known as a thriving and gay court, as it passed through the hands of the Malatestas, the Estense and the Sforzas. Then in the 1490s, the infamous Lucrezia Borgia arrived, having married its Lord, Giovanni Sforza. Her room at the castle displays much of the period furniture and Renaissance frescoes.

Alexander IV, then ruler of Rome, is said to have instructed the Borgias to use the marriage to destroy Giovanni, but the Pope dissolved the marriage in 1497. However, by 1502, Lucrezia was married off to Alfonso D'Este, Duke of Ferrara. Her brother Cesare had driven out the Sforzas, and declared himself Duke of Romagna.

A series of battles left the castle in ruins, and its grand structure was only restored in 1920. Much of it remains original, but the Francesca room is more fantasy than a strict historical replica. It's worth a visit. The views of the Rimini coastline are as thrilling, as the torture chamber is chilling.

San Giovanni in Marignano

North east of Gradara on the Morciano road, and 23km from Rimini, San Giovanni may be an industrial town, but its centre, surrounded by walls with turrets and narrow mediaeval streets in the Sant' Antonio and Scuola districts, are quite a treat for explorers. Otherwise, a special time to visit is **Witches' Night,** a festival celebrating the town's patron saint, held on June 24th. Witchcraft, sorcery, and other rites are performed in the streets to music and dancing.

Morciano

Further west up the Conca valley is another ancient town, Morciano. Documents from 1371 indicate that the old town was continually beset by flooding, became almost uninhabited and was reduced to ruins. Nevertheless its importance as a market centre continued and today, it is a busy, small commercial centre of 5,000 inhabitants.

Built in 1069, the only remains of the **San Gregorio monastery** are its external walls. They have been incorporated into a farmhouse, but the town hall is carrying out a restoration project. The legacy of the monastery is the **San Gregorio Fair,** held to celebrate the spring equinox. The fair has been held since the 12th century on the second week in March. As in San Giovanni, it is an occasion for pagan rite festivities, music, dancing and market stalls, but it also features a horse and a cattle market.

An example of work by modern sculptor, Arnaldo Pomodoro, who was born in the town, is displayed in the main square.

Further up the Conca valley, and branching into the valley of the Ventena River, lies Montefiore. On a clear day the village is noticeable from Rimini, owing to its huge fortress. Around 1350, the Malatesta Galeotto chose the village as the site for this massive fort, and **Sigismondo Pandolfo Malatesta** added significant adaptations in 1432. Today, the castle's angles and rotundity, its sheer bleak walls and clean faces, give it an Orwellian aura. Climb up to the roof terrace on a clear day and take the fabulous view from Ravenna to Croatia across the Adriatic.

In fact, the castle was more a prestigious symbol, rarely seeing battle, and was used as a palace for hunting across the valley.

The castle's cross vaulted hall and the Emperor's room contain rare 14th century frescoes by Bolognese artist Jacopo Avanzi. Its courtyard contains a decorous well from the same period. Montefiore's distinction is that it is the only private castle where Malatesta decorations survive.

Entry to the town was through Porta Curina gate, fixed in the 15th century into the fortified walls surrounding the citizens. On the main street Via XX Settembre, the Ospedale Church known as Santa Croce has 15th century frescoes, the work of the Marche School. San Paola Church on the Ghirlanda to the right of the castle has a fine Gothic portal and 14th century crucifix painted by the Rimini School.

Trekking and the Onferno Caves

Besides the Capuchin Monastery lies a path leading to the summit of Mount Auro. The surrounding area offers many interesting walks. In particular, if from the hamlet of Urbotto one follows the Ventena river upstream to the smaller tributary called Burano, the route leads you to the famous **Onferno Caves**.

The caves were originally known as Inferno, or hell, owing to the escaping winter vapours which would make the entrance seem like the devil's sanctuary. The name was changed in 1810 by a Rimini bishop, fed up of having 'hell' in his diocese. A river once flowed through the grey chalk grotto, which extends for 367 metres, and contains both an entry and an exit. The grotto has fascinating flows of red lime, the famous large chalk knolls in Sala Quarina and coral-like formations.

The anti-Papist, **Dante**, is thought to have acquired inspiration for his *Inferno* from a visit to the caves in 1305, writing in the 32nd canto:

"I heard them say, look carefully as you walk: make sure you so not squash the heads of the miserable monks there."

Be warned, the grotto is patrolled by mosquitoes, spiders, stone marten, and around 10,000 bats. Clothing for a temperature of 12° to 14°C and walking boots are recommended. A torch and helmet are supplied by the guide for the one hour walk and scramble.

The Onferno are part of a nature reserve of the same name, which covers woodland and cultivated fields, broken by the sporadic outcrop of gypsum. A hilly area, its woods house polecats, porcupine, roe deer, and foxes. Its skies are patrolled by kestrels, buzzards, Montagu's harriers, and various species of owl, making for interesting walks.

The caves, situated 30km from Rimini, are open with a guided tour in summer between 9.30am and noon and 3pm to 6pm. In April, May and October the caves are only open on Sundays and holidays between 2pm and 5pm. Information is available from the cave co-operative on tel. Gemmano 984694.

Montecolombo

Entering this old village, 21 km west of Rimini and sat in the hills between the Conca and Marano rivers west of Coriano, was like entering a ghost town, such was the stillness. We passed through the ancient fortified walls into the empty mediaeval square.

There is little else to see here but it is valuable for its serenity and the ***Ameci Mei*** (tel 984456) restaurant specialising in roast boar, and its July festivals celebrating local tripe and pasta specialities. The village is also close to the San Savino mineral springs.

Montescudo

A few kilometres west of Montecolombo in the same hills lies Montescudo, particularly known for the fine **pottery** produced from the local clay. Potters visit the nearby village of Santa Maria del Piano, reputed to have the finest pottery workshops in the province.

The village also has a fine example of a Malatesta fortress. We found the 15th century castle with its walls, watch tower and ice cellar still in evidence in the town centre. Indeed, a plaque in Latin on the walls from 1460 quotes Sigismondo Malatesta stating that he built the castle to protect Rimini town. The huge inclining walls made this castle impregnable and a key part of the defence of the Conca middle valley. Bronze coins from the Sigismondo era have been found hidden in the castle walls – apparently a favourite trick of the Malatesta's - possibly to reward future restorers of their castles.

EATING OUT

On the road into Rimini from Novafeltra is one of the town's fun eating places, *Bastian Contrario* (312, Via Marecchiese). Its food is said to be delightful and based on centuries old local recipes. The popular trattoria takes its name from the owner Bastian and his contradictory nature. He's a fun guy who will spend all day arguing with his customers, only to suddenly pull out his guitar and start up the singing.

Ro and Buni Hostaria (697, Via Mulin Bianco) in **Verucchio** is another popular trattoria with superb food. It's a big, old, farm house where the vats are still left on show and tradition is preserved. Ro and Buni gets its name from the old farmers' method of ploughing. Our friend, Elsa, explained that when a Rimini farmer wanted his plough to go to the right he would shout "Buni!" to the cow, and to go left he would shout "Ro!".

Another fine place to eat is *La Sangiovesa* osteria, (tel 620710) at 14, Piazza Simone Balacchi in **Santarcangelo** for a cultured meal in cultured surroundings. Otherwise it's worth trying some of the agriturismo eating establishments listed below in the accommodation section.

For those who wish to go **wine tasting,** there are several places around the area. These include:

In **Coriano**, *Pagnoni Adamo* at 60 Via Flaminia Conca (tel 657071), *Ronco* at 7, Via Cella, Ospedaletto (tel 656000 fax 657452) and *San Patrignano* (tel 759073) at 136 Via San Patrignano in the same area.

In **Montecolombo**, *Fattoria Del Piccione* (tel 985664) at 13 Via Roma, San Savino and *Piva Fiametta* (tel 988981) at 83, Via Abbazia.

In **Verucchio**, *Tenuta Del Monsignore* (tel 955128) at 154 Via Patarino and the *Ottoviani* establishments at 105 (tel 952608) and 203 (tel 952565) Via Panoramica.

In **Santarcangelo**, Battistino (tel 621353) at 1145 Via Emilia and *Tamburini* Luciano (tel 624030).

ACCOMMODATION

All phone numbers are prefixed with the Rimini code 0541.

Hotels

Gemmano * Centopini, 59, Via Circ. Zione (tel/fax 854064)

Montecolombo**** Villa Leri, 12, Via Canepa (tel 985262 fax 985126)

Montefiore Conca * La Loggia Dei Malatesta, 76, Via Provinciale (tel 980008)

Montegridolfo: **** Palazzo Viviani, 38, Via Roma (tel 855350 fax 855340)

Montescudo * Malatesta, 17, Via Rocca (tel 984317)

Saludecio **Locanda Porta Marinara, 1, Piazza Gioco Del Pallone (tel 981109)

Santarcangelo***Verde Mare, 1044, Via Pasquale Tosi (tel 626629)

Torriana **La Caveja, 34, Via Torrianese (tel 675412)

Agriturismo with accommodation

Montecolombo: Il Campanaccio, 5, Via Casiccio (tel 984643), Palazzo Marcosanti, 13, Via Ripa Bianca (tel 629522), Zio Monti, 3 Via Casiccio (tel 984640 fax 383074)

Monetfiore Conca: Il Vecchio Gelso, 770, Via Molino Ciotti (tel 989455)

Saludecio: Fattoria Eby, 240, Via Tassinara (tel 987847), Torre del Poggio, 145, Via Dei Poggio (tel 857190)

Camp Sites

Santarcangelo: **La Ruspante, 862, Via Balduccia** (tel 758057)

Coriano: Oasi, 33 Via Maracco (tel 658098)

RIMINI

Forli/Cesena COAST AND COUNTRYSIDE

Forli/Cesena province takes its name from the two most populous towns in the area. Once an important Roman district traversing the Via Emilia, the province went through many battles in the post Roman era, and many of the old towns were destroyed. Apart from being Mussolini's birthplace, the area is most known for Cesenatico's beaches and fish dishes.

However the flat plain and coastal towns are but a small part of a territory which reaches up into the Apennines. Its surrounding valleys lead to the Tuscan border, offering breathtaking views. The significance of these valleys for the Romei pilgrims is demonstrated by the many old churches, castles, piazzas and palaces which have lasted through the centuries. The Romei meant money, and each valley is packed with mediaeval fortresses in various states of repair. Above Forli, the Montone valley alone had seven castles by the end of the 1300s. Many still stand. But the hill region remains fairly free of tourists, making it an ideal place to explore.

FORLI

Approaching Forli, the land is very flat. **Forum Livii**, Forli's Roman name, was founded as a castrum, at the point where the Via Emilia crossed the Montone river between 100 and 200 B.C. Up Until the end of the first millennium, the city was the civic and religious capital for a territory almost as big as the province it is now the capital of. Around 1,000 A.D, it was taken over by the Ravenna archbishops, who ruled until 1315, when the **Ordelaffi** family took control for the following 165 years.

The Sforzas and Cesare Borgia had brief periods of rule, and close to Forli is Ravaldino Castle, where Caterina Sforza was besieged by 'Il Valentino', Cesare Borgia, in 1500. Thereafter, the area became a Papal state till Italy's unification in 1860.

Situated 64km east of Bologna on autostrada A14, Forli is industrialised. However, the environment is strictly controlled by the authorities. The city centre maintains its mediaeval layout. Inside are a number of interesting 16th to 18th century palaces, such as **Palazzo Manganelli**, the Romanesque-Gothic **Palazzo del Podesta** in Piazza Aurelli Saffi and the former residence of the Ordelaffi, **Palazzo Municipio.**

Forli has been a victim of the grand designs of various politicians. Napoleon's troops demolished many buildings, which were replaced with the unification of Italy. Much work was done to make the area worthy of its most notorious son, **Benito Mussolini**. Its heart, Piazza Aurelli Saffi, was redesigned in the inter war period by uninspired architects of the Fascist period.

Close by is the Benedictine friars', **San Mercuriale Abbey**, with its beautiful 240-foot high Romanesque bell tower. The abbey was built on the site of a 5th century, and later a 12th century, church at which the body of St Mercuriale, first bishop of the city, was laid to rest in the 7th century. The building was destroyed by fire and the bell tower was erected in 1180 during the reconstruction.

The Cathedral or Duomo in Piazza Ordelaffi suffered a 19th century restoration, but inside has frescoes by Carlo Cignani including his fine painting of The Assumption.

FORLI/CESENA

Travelling Around
Distances from Forli to the main cities are; in Romagna, Rimini 42km, Ravenna 27km, Ferrara 100km and on Via Emilia, Bologna 64km, Modena 103km, Reggio Nell'Emilia 126km, Parma 155km and Piacenza 200km.

Train Times
Forli to Rimini 30 mins, Bologna 34 mins, Parma 1hr, Milan Centrale 2hrs 30 mins

Trains around the Province
Trains run south eastwards from Forli to Bertinoro, Cesena (15 mins), Gambettola and Savignano sui Rubicone (25 mins).

SOUTH OF FORLI
ALONG THE MONTONE VALLEY

South from Forli, the Montone Valley rises into the Apennines, and is tracked by the SS67, which goes to Arrezo in Tuscany. The hills are topped by pine forests and provide some excellent scenery.

Terra del Sole

Terra del Sole is renowned for its well-preserved 16th century layout, a fine example of an ideal town built on the lines advocated by **Leonardo da Vinci**. The painter advised that when planning towns, "let road width be equal to building height." The Fiorentine duke, Cosimo I de Medici, ordered just that when the model town began to be built in 1564. The fortress displays perfect symmetry, and contains at its heart, the huge square, which had the town hall, church and palaces.

In the square, **Palazzo Pretorio** is one of the Renaissance masterpieces of the Tuscan architect, **Buontalenti**. Most notable are the combination of square and arched windows, and linear decoration around the three central porticoes. The fort is crossed by a road which goes south to the **Fiorentina Gate**, and north to the **Romana Gate**, which was guarded by the **Castello del Capitano di Piazza Castle**.

Castrocaro Terme

Pilgrims to Rome are thought to have begun travelling up the Montone valley to reach Tuscany from the Middle Ages. One of their stops was probably **Castrocaro Terme**, named after its spa. The town's castle is now ruins, but two rings of walls remain, along with the mediaeval quarter which contains 15th century houses. The higher wall still houses the **Muriata** clock tower, reconstructed by the Fiorentines who conquered the valley in 1403. The lower wall contains the gate of **San Nicolo,** built in 1371.

The town is best known for the healing properties of its sulphurous mud. Since 1838 it has supplied salso-bromide waters. Close to Parco della Terme is the spa.

Dovadola

Situated 20km from Forli, **Dovadola** is another town with a lovely mediaeval quarter around **Piazza Battisti**. The castle is located across the main road, and was once a stronghold of the Guidi from Modigliana, before they were forced out by the Fiorentines. About 10km upstream is **Rocca San Casciano,** named after its castle, now in ruins. Further along at **Brocconi** is the interesting 14th century bridge, **Ponte della Brusia**, with its three lancet arches.

By the time the SS67 reaches **Poggio di San Benedetto in Alp** we are 2,000ft above sea level. The village has an 11th century crypt, said to contain the relics of two Roman martyrs, Primus and Felicianus. The village is close to the scenic natural park of **Casentinesi Forest**, which contains the beautiful waterfall of **Acquacheta**, referred to in **Dante's *Inferno*** (Canto XVI).

ALONG THE RABBI VALLEY

The River Rabbi flows into the Montone, just before Forli. The road from Forli offers another route up to the Casentinesi Forest which contains the nature reserve of **Sasso Fratini**, which is closed to the general public.

Lower down the valley, 15km from Forli is **Predappio**, the birthplace and burial spot of Mussolini. A short distance out of the town on the road to Meldola is **La Rocca delle Caminate**, an 11th century castle with panoramic views. The building was rudely re-developed to serve as the summer residence of Mussolini. The modern part of the town contains the 11th century Romanesque church of San Cassiano in Pennino, which despite a poor restoration in 1934, still displays its original apse and carvings.

The top of the valley has another well-preserved old town, Premilcuore. A former stronghold of the Guidi family, it still has its castle and mediaeval quarter surrounded by the old town walls. Today the town, situated on the Tuscan border, is a peaceful holiday resort.

ALONG THE BIDENTE-RONCO VALLEY

FORLÌ/CESENA

Forlimpopoli, west of Forli on Via Emilia, was another Roman castrum. It had an unfortunate early history, having been totally destroyed by the Longobard king, Grimaoldo, in the twelfth century, only to be rebuilt and destroyed again in 1361 by papal legate, Cardinal Albornoz. Since then, the building has remained intact and the superb castle has been left to dominate the town square for 600 years. The relics of the cathedral's saint, San Rufillo, and the bishop's throne in Verona marble were not returned to the duomo until 1961. The fortress houses a museum containing pieces from the cathedral.

*A theatre was created in the castle, and was party to a famous incident in 1851 when the bandit known as **Il Passatore** took to the stage, demanding 40,000 scudos from the audience. They paid in full.*

Bussecchio contains many old villas and vineyards, olive groves beside weeping willows, illuminated by the October sun braking up the coastal haze. Hills to the right and left emerged out of the haze as we headed left on SS311, the landscape gently undulating, 2km from **Meldola**- a pleasant little town set in the hills.

Heading cast into the **Bidente Valley**, the tree covered rolling hills to our right and the pastures on the sharp escarpment to the left announce the **Apennines**.

The SS311 travels along the valley, reaching **Meldola** at its centre. The valley was another popular route for pilgrims going to Galeata. Meldola contains the arcades at its centre in Via Roma, leading into the main square containing 16th and 17th century palaces. The castle on the hill overlooking the town is a 15th century construction of Malatesta Novello.

Located 35km from Forli, the valley widens, and the road reaches the former pilgrim town of **Galeata**. Upstream from the town is the church of **San Ellero**, said to be 5th century in origin. Rebuilt in the 17th century, it still retains its 11th century doorway, and a granite tomb encasing the relics of San Ellero, a hermit turned friar. Nearby the remains of **King Theodoric**'s hunting lodge were found. A relief on the walls portrays the Ravenna-based king's supposed meeting with the saint.

Galeata also has the **Museo Civico** on Via Zanelli, which houses artefacts excavated from the site of the former Umbrian/Roman settlement of **Mevaniola**. Mevaniola is on the SS310 road upstream from Galeata, on a road off to the right before Pianetto. The settlement was Umbrian before becoming a Roman municipium, which lasted till it was abandoned in the 5th century A.D. The foundations of the forum, baths, and a small theatre can still be seen at the fenced off site.

An Agriturismo – Ca Bionde

Climbing steeply and taking care to avoid horses wandering across the road, we arrived at the top of a wall marshalling its edge. We were at **Ca Bionde**, one of the areas most well known **agriturismo** and frequented by landscape painters. At 400 metres above sea level, its beautiful views offered a vast range of routes for hill walkers. Just 30 km from Tuscany, it is also an excellent spot for combining a trip to **Florence,** while avoiding the crowds of tourists who flock to that region.

As an agriturismo, Ca Bionde contains large cattle barns, horses stables, and raise their own chicken, turkeys, guinea fowl and geese. The farm also produces bread, pasta, home made red wines, fruits, almara, rosoglio, grappa, gnoccino, mushrooms, stinging nettle shampoo, creams, and even St John's Wort body toning cream.

Ca Bionde has facilities for horse riding and archery, a fishing lake, an outdoor swimming pool, a shooting range and archery. Its restaurant offers a superb view of the valley and surrounding hills. Mountain biking is also popular here, and the restaurant contains a collection of trophies won by the local mountain bike teams.

Just above the farm is an **astronomical observatory**, seating up to 12 star gazers with a 4,900 times magnification telescope. I most enjoyed sitting on a terrace and gazing out on the hills and valleys. Rustic life ambled through the day overlooked by a stern guard of rugged, stratified escarpments made from sandstone and clay.

Full board here costs L90,000 compared to L110,000 in a similar place in Tuscany. The apartments in buildings made of local stone are very pleasantly decked out with traditional furniture. Indeed the foundations of lower apartments date back 1,200 years – old enough to be recorded in the Vatican.

CESENA

We drove the 30km west from Rimini on the A14 autostrada to **Cesena**. As we passed into Cesena we came to its residential area of houses painted yellows, golds and deep greens.

FORLI/CESENA

The old heart of the town is wonderfully pedestrianised within its 15th century walls. We parked on the outside and entered by foot through the city gates.

In the 14th century the Malatesta's took control, building the **Rocca Malatesta** on the slopes of Mount Garampo, the site of the old Roman castrum. On Viale Malatesta Novello, the fort dominates the town. The fortress is now the town hall and includes a museum exhibiting the 'Tito Balestra' art collection.

Beneath the castle and right beside Palazzo Comunale we found the town's heart, the lovely cobbled **Piazza del Populo**. At its centre is the 16th century **Masini Fountain**. From here we strolled around the narrow streets of the old centre which has plenty of shops, cafes, and restaurants. Although the town is slightly smaller than its twin provincial capital, **Forli**, it is an important agricultural and commercial centre.

Containing 200,000 books, documents and ornate historic manuscripts, Cesena's 15th century **Biblioteca Malatestiana Library,** in Piazza Bufalini, is the pride of the town. The exterior is 19th century Neoclassical but the interior retains much of the original work. Malatesta Novello ordered the work in 1452 as a library in a Franciscan monastery, and its fine reading rooms are worth a visit.

Opposite the library is the 15th century **Palazzo del Ridotto** with an 18th century facade, the work of Cosimo Morelli

The Gothic design of the Duomo on Piazza Vescovado retains its Romanesque door arch, but the facade is a Renaissance addition. The altar dates back to the 15th century. A niche in the facade has de Gaspare's Madonna and Child from the same era. Next door in the former San Biagio monastery, the **Pinacoteca Comunale** contains a large collection of paintings dating back to the 1400s.

Looking out onto the city is the Benedictine **Madonna del Monte Abbey**, where the friars still restore books and manuscripts.

Sant Agostino church on Via Riciputi was designed in the mid 1770s by Luigi Vanvitelli for the Austin friars. He had already started building the order's mother house in Rome, and as in his previous works, the transept was designed to give a sense of centrifugal motion. What is also interesting is the lack of a facade for the massive building and its huge buttresses, topped by scrolls in Istrian marble. The interior is Roman-style, plain and full of light. Much of the church's decor has been removed, but the High Baroque style 18th century pulpit and four confessionals are excellent marketry.

Depending on your taste, Cesena isn't all high culture and history. The town also has a **racecourse** for those who wish to try their hand.

Situated 10km west of Cesena, just south of Via Emilia, is **Bertinoro**, once the district's most important centre. On the slopes of Mount Maggio, the town is surrounded by vineyards. By the 11th century it was the centre for the Duchy, and by the 14th century, home to the Count of Romagna. Two ancient gates bordered the old town and cut through what remains of the walls. **Porta del Soccorso** contains the castle once used by **Barbarossa**, and now serves as the bishop's residence. Porta San Francesco leads to Polenta, and the nearby San Donato church restored in the 18th century and reputed to have been visited by **Dante**.

The town centre is in Piazza della Liberta and contains a cathedral restored in the 1500s. The 14th century Palazzo Comunale has been heavily restored. The church of Madonna del Lago has an interesting icon of the Blessed Virgin, an 8th century statue from the Byzantine period of iconoclasm.

SOUTH OF CESENA
ALONG THE SAVIO VALLEY

Cesena, being on the Savio, was another pilgrim route for the Romei. They mainly travelled up the Savio valley, where now one can use the new E7 highway, to reach Tuscany. Alternatively, one can take the slower SS71 and saunter up the valley, which is littered with the ruins of castles. About 30km from Cesena, is **Mercato Saraceno**, where this former mediaeval trading centre still has its old mills grouped around its ancient three-arched bridge.

Travelling 8km along a small road into the hills west from Mercato leads to the 8th century, late Byzantine church, **Pieve di Monte Sorbo**. The building, largely created out of the ruins of former Roman buildings, is beautifully simple inside, and contains a 15th century Umbrian painting of the *Madonna in Adoration of the Sleeping Child.*

Further along the valley is the former Roman town of **Sarsina,** where **Piazza Plauto** marks the site of the Roman Forum, and still contains traces of the marble paving. The piazza is named after Plautus, a Latin comic playwright born here in 245 B.C. Many artefacts of the Roman, and preceding Umbrian era, have been excavated, and can be found in the **Museo Archeologico Sarsinate**, near Piazza Plauto. Piazza Plauto also has the Byzantine cathedral of **San Vicinio**. The relics of the saint are kept in a chapel along the right hand aisle. These include an iron collar worn by the saint, which is still used for exorcisms.

Bagno di Romagna, 60km up the Savio from Cesena, is the linking point with Bidente valley. In the 15th century it was one of the homes of the Guidi family, and Palazzo Pretorio on the main road remains. The **Basilica di Santa Maria Assunta** is of interest in that it was designed in the Tuscan Renaissance style. Above, and east of the town, is Mount Fumaiolo, which peaks at 4,500ft above sea level. South at 3,500ft is the Mandrioli Pass over into Tuscany.

THE PLAINS AND COASTLANDS
Longiano

Just off Via Emilia, 12km south east of Cesena we came to the hill town of **Longiano**, still encircled by its mediaeval walls and overshadowed by its huge 14th century Malatesta castle. The castle has undergone several restorations, and now serves as the town hall which is open for visits between 8.30am and 12.30pm. Longiano is a pretty town, most known for its small Neoclassical 19th century theatre, **Teatro E.Petrella**, which has trained up many famous Italian actors.

Opposite, the church of Santessimo Crocefisso on Via Decio Raggi has a 13th century legendary crucifix. The crucifix used to be tied up outside the church, and in 1493, a young heifer given to the monks by the people of Gambettola is said to have knelt down to pray before it. The crucifix is also credited with saving the townspeople from the plague of 1630, and a massacre by Cesare Borgia's troops.

Now we were off to the coastal plain via the orchards of Bagniolo. Orchards could be seen everywhere. Some houses here are a very earthy burgundy colour similar to the wine. The area itself is very colourful in spring and summer because of the peach groves. On the plain we saw **cacco fruit**, a bright yellow orange fruit, very sweet with a tomato-like texture. It doesn't keep long so we had to come here to try some.

FORLÌ/CESENA

Searching for the Rubicon

We were on a quest for the **Fiume Rubicone**, or **River Rubicon**. As soon as I was aware that the river of legend was in the region, I was determined to cross it. For those unaware, the phrase, "To cross the Rubicon" means to take one past the point of no return, of not turning back.

The use of this historic phrase dates back 2,000 years to the time of **Julius Caesar**. The Rubicon was seen as the edge of the Roman Empire, which was ruled by the Senate, who elected two consuls as the executive. Julius Caesar was one of those consuls, and was returning to Rome with his troops from a victorious military campaign in land across the northern border of the territory.

While Caesar was abroad, Rome had plunged into a deep political crisis. Caesar concluded he could resolve matters by returning and seizing control. However, he required the permission of the Senate to re-enter Roman territory. Being fearful of Caesar's intentions, the Senate withheld that permission.

Caesar felt he had to get to Rome or lose this opportunity. By crossing the River Rubicon, he re-entered Roman territory and he had technically declared civil war on the Senate, a war from which there was no turning back.

Caesar went on to conquer Rome and lay the basis for the great expansion of the Roman Empire throughout Europe and the Middle East.

My first sighting of the Rubicon had been a huge disappointment. We crossed a four foot wide ditch, some 15km from the coast. Caesar's troops could have crossed here with a small hop. What a show for such a momentous act of rebellion. There must be more to this, I thought and resolved to investigate further.

We thought we had found the great river when we reached the harbour in **Cesenatico**. Yachts with scarlet sails and black striped hulls sat in the water. Fishing boats were decorated in ivory bold relief. We had found the **Museo della Mare**, with its display of more than a score of sea going boats dating back 75 years. It's worth a visit – but this river wasn't the Rubicone. It was the harbour canal.

Eventually, in **Gatteo**, close to the Via Gramsci and Via Toscanini we reached the mouth of the Rubicon. At around 10 metres wide, the river was a little more impressive than what we had seen inland. On the south bank is a small beach, some rocks, and above them, a small cafe. Just before the river reaches the sea, a few small Chinese fishing nets sit on the riverbank, beside a dozen or so small boats used by families for recreation.

Crossing the Rubicon here means swimming or crossing in a small paddle boat.

Later on in the trip more of the story of the Rubicon began to surface. As late as the 1930s, few people were certain which river was actually Caesar's Rubicone. It could have been any one of several rivers flowing from the Apennines into this part of the Rimini and Cesena coastline.

Then, the story goes, the fascist dictator, Mussolini took a hand, and gave the august name of Fiume Rubicone to the current river passing through Gatteo Mare. His decision to canonise the tiny rivulet left nine other townships disputing the case, and offering up their own rivers as the true Rubicon. Indeed much more influential rivers such as the Marecchia, which has carved a deep valley through the hillside, would seem to have a strong case. However, without being aware of all the considerations of Roman territorial borders, I, nor it seems anybody else, can put a winning case for any particularly river. What cynics would point out is that the current Rubicone flows uncomfortably close to Mussolini's birthplace in Forli.

FORLI/CESENA

FORLI/CESENA

Leonardo da Vinci

Cesenatico is a pretty coastal town of two to three storey buildings, much more in the Italian traditional style than the bulging Bellaria. Around the streets are many attractive wall paintings by local artists commissioned by the well-to-do of the town. In the Piazza Conserve we were surrounded by such paintings, mainly of the town and its features. We arrived at the main square, with its Garibaldi statue looking out over the boat-ridden **Leonardo da Vinci Canal** flowing through the heart of the town, and came to the beautiful **Teatro de Cesenatico**, described as a chocolate box. The canal was designed by Leonardo da Vinci, who was commissioned by none other than Cesare Borgia back in the 16th century.

At Cesenatico we looked round the attractive harbour. Close by, the **Museo della Mare** stood the 18th century parish church of **Santi Giacomo e Cristoforo**, notable for containing a painting by **Guido Cagnacci**, which uses trompe l'oeil making St Joseph, bathed in light, appear to walk towards the viewer. Also here is the peculiar solid square house, said to be that of the poet Marino Moretti.

However, the town's main attraction is its 7km of sandy beaches and 360 hotels. The resort is also a fishing harbour and renown for its fish gastronomy. The fishermen's area contains 70 restaurants, devoted to serving up their ocean fresh catches bought each morning from the fish market.

The town is another cyclist's paradise, with 22 **cycle routes** and the annual 200km **Brevetto Apennino dei Nove Colli** cycling display. **Yachting** is a popular sport in the town hosting for the last 20 years an **international catamaran race** to mark the start of the sailing season. **Beach volleyball** enthusiasts are also attracted to the shoreline, which hosts many national volleyball competitions. The town also has **Atlantica**, a large aquatic park with swimming pools, slides, gaming saloons, restaurants and ice cream parlours.

The town has plenty of hotels and for those wishing to budget 1,900 apartments and three camp sites.

South of Cesenatico towards Rimini are three much smaller resorts, **Gatteo a Mare, Savignano Mare** and **San Maure a Mare**. With a quiet town, beach sand sculpture competitions, fishing at the Rubicon's mouth and its July **Festa della Micizia Cat Festival**, Gatteo sounds like a fine place for a relaxing family holiday.

EATING OUT AND ACCOMMODATION

Apart from the many fish restaurants in an around Cesenatico, the best thing to do is to head for an **agriturismo**. The best of these is probably Ca' Bionda with its scenic location.

The following all have accommodation and dining facilities and are situated in or in the foothills of the Apennines:

Ca' Bionda (tel/fax 0543 989101), web site http://www.cvc.fo.it/aziende/cabionda, 42, Via S.Giovanni, Cusercoli.

Bacino (tel 0543 912023 fax 918540), 24, Loc.Vessa, San Pietro in Bagno
Casalino (tel 0547 948489), 83, Via tezzo, Tezzo, Sarsina
Casa Vallicella (tel 0546 943911) 21, Via S.Valentino, San Valentino, Tredozio
Pian Di Stantino (tel 0546 943539) Podere Pian Di Stantino, Ottignana, Tredozio
Ridiano (tel 0546 942351), 2, Podere Ridiano, Fregiolo, Tredozio
Scarzana (tel 0546 943446), 1, Via Scarzana, Scarzana, Tredozio
Poderone (tel/fax 0543 980069), 64, Via Campigna Poderone, Campigna Santa Sofia

Lowland or coastal agriturismo include:

I Portico (tel 0541 938143) with its swimming pool on Via Rubicone Dx II Tratto, Capanni, Savignano.
Ai Tamerici (tel 0547 672730), 60 Via Mesolino, Cesenatico
Due Ponti (tel 0547 87604), 106, Via Fenili, Sala Di Cesenatico
Malbrola (tel 0546 941585), 5 Via S.Martino in Monte, Modigliana
Casetta Dei Frati (tel/fax 0546 941445), 8, Via Dei Frati, Casetta Dei Frati, Modigliana

Accommodation in the coastal resorts is plentiful and very busy in the summer.

i Tourist Information Offices:

Forli tel/fax 0543 712434

Bagno Di Romagnola tel 0543 911046 fax 911026

Castrocarme Terme tel 0543 767162 fax 769326

Cesena tel 0547 356327 fax 356329

Cesenatico tel 0547 674411 fax 80129

Santa Sofia tel 0543 971297

FORLI/CESENA

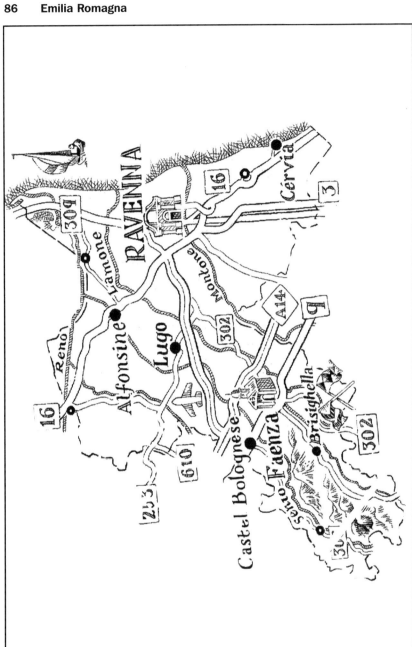

BYZANTINE **Ravenna**

We journeyed off to Ravenna, the former Byzantine city, containing the most popular cultural attractions in the region. Getting into the heart of the small city by car involved negotiating the one way system. Unprepared, we spent a frustrating 45 minutes travelling north, east, south, and every which way until we reached our hotel in the one way, Via 4th Novembre. To add to this, like the other hotels in the centre, no parking space was available so we had to drive around again to find a car park.

RAVENNA

Ravenna city is the administrative centre for the province of the same name. The city's greatest historical value is the precious heritage of some of the most important buildings from the Roman/Byzantine era. Its role as a cultural centre has been accentuated both by Dante and Lord Byron, who both spent time in the city, and the development of a fine tradition in classical music. Not surprisingly, the beautiful 1,500 year-old buildings, a clash of Byzantine and Roman styles, and the presence of two of the written word's most controversial figures, promote much debate. Ravenna is a city of contradiction and debate, contrasting styles and stories, which make a visit even more worthwhile.

On the flat coastal plain, it is close to many beaches, pine forests and several picturesque little villages in the foothills of the Apennines. Once by the sea, the settlement grew up as a port believed to be Umbrian in origin. By 82 B.C the Romans are said to have landed their fleet in the port. Ravenna was a town of inter-linked islands, protected by the delta marshes and the sea, ideal for the fleet. Houses were raised on poles, and its islands were linked by bridges.

The Roman Emperor, Augustus, stationed a Praetorian fleet of 250 ships in the port to police the Adriatic. Ravenna's port, Classe, was born. The surrounding land began to silt up, and was eventually drained. Today Ravenna is 9km from the sea.

Ravenna's historical importance dates back to 402 A.D. The Emperor Theodosius the Great had two sons and a daughter, Galla Placidia. He had given one son the Eastern Roman Empire and the other, Honorius, the west. In 402 A.D, Honorius moved the western capital from Milan to the fortified city of Ravenna, due to its apparent invulnerability, being defended by water.

The city became a thriving port and for years was the most important in the Roman Empire. Its counterpart was Constantinople, capital of the Byzantine, or Eastern Roman, Empire. When the Western Empire collapsed in 476 A.D, Ravenna was seized by the 'barbarian' troops of Odoacer, only to be captured by the Bavarian Ostrogoth king, Theodoric the Great, after a three year siege.

Ravenna again prospered. By 540 A.D, the troops of the Eastern Emperor, Justinian had captured the city from the Goths, and the Byzantine era began. Ravenna, as the Prefecture of Italy, remained an important city. Byzantine rule saw a new period of construction of fine churches and palaces. They brought fine marbles and mosaics and mixed the styles of East and West.

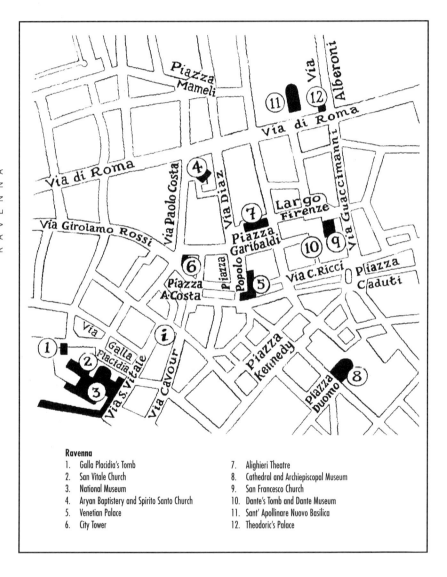

Ravenna

1. Galla Placidia's Tomb
2. San Vitale Church
3. National Museum
4. Aryan Baptistery and Spirito Santo Church
5. Venetian Palace
6. City Tower
7. Alighieri Theatre
8. Cathedral and Archiepiscopal Museum
9. San Francesco Church
10. Dante's Tomb and Dante Museum
11. Sant' Apollinare Nuovo Basilica
12. Theodoric's Palace

A WALK AROUND THE CITY

The 16th century building housing **Ca de Vin** in Via C.Ricci formerly belonged to the **Rasponi** family, one of the city's famous dynasties, before becoming a wine tasting hall. It is not a bad place to start off on a tour through the historic centre.

Being near to Venice, Ravenna often came under the influence of its powerful Venetian neighbours. Venice ruled over the city in the 15th century. The Venetians rebuilt the city centre, dismantling many churches and re-using the material.

Crossing Via Gordoni we came to Via Cairoli, a typically narrow Venetian street where one can see the sober brick buildings with balconies sporting geranium pots beneath Gothic Venetian style windows.

Via Cairoli led us to the main square, the **Piazza del Populo**. The city hall is also a Venetian building from the 15th century but it was completely rebuilt in the 1600s. The variety of capitals on the columns in the arcade is due to them having been taken from old churches destroyed by the Venetians.

The two statues on the town hall facade are of Apollinare, the city's patron saint and of the soldier, Vitale. San Apollinare arrived in the nearby port of Classe in the 2nd century A.D to spread the Christian word among the Roman fleet, and had some success before being stoned to death. Vitale is said to have been a great military leader who was persecuted in Nero's reign on account of him being a Christian.

The 18th century clock tower on the bank opposite the town hall was designed by Camillo Morigia, also the architect of **Dante's Tomb**. The buildings around the square are of late 17th and 18th century construction. We then went off by foot down Via 4th Novembre and left on to Via Cavour towards San Vitale and the **tomb of Galla Placidia** in the north west of the city. On the way, just off the Via 4th Novembre we found the city's **covered market** where meat, fish and vegetables are on sale.

We came to the 13th century church of **San Dominic**, with its attractive facade, currently undergoing restoration. The top of its tower had a covering of rugged diamond-shaped bricks and we thought it was pretty. However, we were informed that rather than being the facade it was simply the base for a decayed marble overlay, which would be replaced when the building was restored.

While in Ravenna, Lord Byron had a great romance with **Teresa Guiccoli**, who lived at the **Palazzo Guiccoli** 54, Via Cavour. Byron soon took rooms at the Palazzo and immortalised **Lady Guiccoli** in his works. In 1821 the poet left Italy and died in Greece three years later. We entered the beautiful inner courtyard of the 17th century building but were prevented from exploring further, as the building is now a police station.

R A V E N N A

Ravenna's National Museum

We entered a huge forbidding building, a former Benedictine monastery built in the 18th century. It is now a **National Museum**, principally for archaeological displays. The same premises incorporate San Vitale and the adjacent mausoleum of Galla Placidia.

The National Museum has a huge room, which was the refectory for the monastery, with 14th century frescoes and paintings from the Rimini school, in particular, **Pietro de Rimini.** His works can also be found in the Abbe Pomposa in Ferrara province. Upstairs is the archaeological museum, packed with artefacts, fragments of frescoes, sculptures, furniture, and carvings from the Roman and Byzantine periods.

Crossing an 18th century building, we entered a very large 16th century cloister, which formed part of a set of three in the monastery. Ancient wells sit around, watched over by a statue of Pope Clemence XII.

RAVENNA

San Vitale

Ravenna, built on former marshland, is sinking and San Vitale has sunk a metre below its surrounds. This explained why we had to walk downstairs to get into the rear of the church. Nevertheless some of the fine 6th century marble mosaic floor remains, particularly close to the front entrance. The surviving mosaic was renovated in the 16th century when the rest of the current floor was laid. The sinking city was often subject to flooding and no other ancient mosaics have survived in the area.

San Vitale is a brick built basilica with an octagonal plan, reaching right through to the octagonal dome. Outside, the front of the building is supported by two large flying buttresses which, as long ago as the 11th century, were erected to prop up the outward leaning walls, indicating how unstable the land beneath has been for over a millennium. This also accounts for Ravenna's many leaning towers, the most extravagant of which leans two metres. The civic tower itself has had to be re-enforced with metal to prevent collapse.

The height, size and symmetry, coupled with its magnificent decoration, makes San Vitale an imposing building. Part of its magic is due to the city being an important meeting place between Rome, Milan and Constantinople – a cultural lake into which flew the styles of east and west. Typically Syrian in influence are two small apses.

The works of the vying oriental and occidental artistic schools give the church an extra fascination.

Two different schools of mosaicists were used to decorate the church. Around the choir area, one can see a profusion of green in the naturistic landscapes, and great movement in the characters. However, the Byzantine mosaics contain gold backgrounds, with static individuals facing the viewer.

To gain some idea of how magnificent San Vitale was, one needs to take a step forward, and imagine the overall appearance by adding marble to its walls. Sadly, the marble was removed for recycling elsewhere. Nevertheless, the added piped choral music proved that the building was still awe-inspiring. San Vitale is now a parish church, and during the summer holds a series of organ concerts.

Galla Placidia's Tomb

Standing on the paved area outside the front entrance to San Vitale, the concentration of religious buildings is evident. As Ravenna became a capital city and expanded in the 5th century, the imperial court constructed many churches.

Opposite the entrance of San Vitale, **Galla Placidia's Tomb** was originally attached to the adjacent church of Santa Croce. Now it is free standing. Galla Placidia is known to have ordered the construction of Santa Croce, but whether she commissioned the tomb is disputed, there being no record.

As the daughter of Theodosius the Great and sister of Honorius, Galla Placidia is thought to have wanted her tomb to be placed in the imperial city. A marvellous example of Greco-Roman art, the tomb was built in the early 5th century and the resplendent interior, contrasting to the sober exterior, is the original work.

The interior is crucifix shaped, containing three sarcophagi. Mosaics totally cover the walls. Omnipresent is the cross, symbol of salvation. The drinking doves symbolise the dead being purified with water. There is also a beautiful gold tapestry mosaic.

Above our heads 800 gold stars glittered on a dark blue, night sky background. The dome has an eastward oriented cross, at odds with the rest of the tomb. The cross is aiming towards Jerusalem and the sunrise. The apse of the mausoleum could not face to the east, as was traditional, because it was attached to Santa Croce church. Hence the eastward facing cross inside is an artistic attempt at a correction.

The mausoleum contains three coffins, but not that of Galla Placidia. She died in Rome and was buried there. However, the right-hand sarcophagus still contains Galla Placidia's son, Valentinian III, and the left, that of her husband Constantius III. Young boys opened the front sarcophagus in 1577, resulting in damage, caused by contact with air, to the two female bodies, which had to be removed.

RAVENNA

The area around San Vitale still contains many 5th century sarcophagi. Before leaving, take a look at the Renaissance building of the Superintendent, to the rear of San Vitale, with its delightful spiralling pink columns of Verona marble.

Dante's Tomb

"Here I lie buried, Dante, exiled from my birthplace, a son of Florence, that loveless mother."

We moved on to the Via Dante Alighieri, at the end of which, close to the monastery and church of Francis of Assisi, is the **tomb of Dante**. Completed in 1782, the Neoclassical construction was designed by Coniglio Morigia. The current mausoleum replaced the Venetian built funeral chapel.

Dante was exiled for political reasons by Florence, and was taken in by the city's powerful family, the Da Polenta. He died three years later in 1321. Dante tells of the tragedy, which took place in Gradara castle, of Paulo and Francesca, in his *Divine Comedy*. The heroine Francesca da Rimini was a Da Polenta born in Ravenna. When Francesca went to Rimini, she believed she would marry Paulo, but found herself wedded to Gianciotto, his brother.

Dante's great contributions to Italy not only include his epic tales. He is ascribed with being the founder of the Italian language. The spoken language prior to Dante is known as the 'lingua vulgare', and the Divine Comedy was written in this style.

The sarcophagus contains Dante's body and dates back to 1327. The tomb's inscription bitterly attacks Florence for its ingratitude to Dante. In the spirit of Dante's wishes, the city of Ravenna jealously guarded its possession of the revered writer's corps.

For 600 years, Florence would be left regretting the loss of one of its most brilliant writers. Indeed, Michelangelo wrote to the people of Ravenna demanding the return of the body.

In 1519 the Medici Pope, Leo X, also ordered that Dante's corps be sent to Florence. However, Ravenna was opposed, and Franciscan monks hid the body, the hiding place of which was not revealed for over 300 years. Only in 1865, when a portico of a building in the Franciscan cemetery next door was being demolished, were the bones discovered in a small box which had been walled in. Another story has it that some of Dante's ashes were removed to a library in Florence in 1865 and rediscovered in 1999.

The whole area is seen as a highly sacred part of Ravenna, and Dante's tomb would attract artists and poets from around the globe. On the other hand,

Florence's counterpart to Dante's Tomb is the church of Santa Croce. The church has an empty grave, recalling how Dante was not buried there.

The cloisters of the monastery next door to the tomb house exhibitions on the *Divine Comedy*. One of the exhibitors here was the late **Henry Moore**. Upstairs is the **Museo Dante**, which has a fine library.

San Francesco is a Romanesque building, built on the foundations of the 5th century Church of the Apostles. This church was very dear to Dante, and his funeral was held here within yards of where his tomb lies.

The crypt beneath the apse has sunk. To see by how much, we put some money in the light meter, and looked down onto the 5th century mosaic floor, which is now so close to sea level that any rain takes it below the water, which has to be regularly pumped out. Note the goldfish placed there by the Franciscan monks.

The main chapel is that of the **Da Polenta**, Ravenna's ruling family. The chapel contains traces of paintings by Pietro da Rimini.

Next door to San Francesco church is the **Dante Centre**, set up in 1963 by the church's Franciscan friars to encourage the study of Dante. The centre has a library containing 10,000 books and microfilm about the man and his works, and 3,000 objects related to Dante including paintings, coins, and medals. The cloisters are used to mount exhibitions, including the **International Biennial Dante Exhibition**, which attracts sculptors from around the world.

RAVENNA

San Apollinare Nuovo

San Apollinare, the Palatine church of Theodoric the Great, is one of Ravenna's oldest and most fascinating religious monuments. San Apollinare was the first bishop of the city and remains the patron saint.

The chapel was part of the classical early 6th century 'palace' of Theodoric next door. However his main palace has been unearthed, and there is some dispute about the role of the 'palazzo'.

Inside the church, the paintings and frescoes date back to the time of Theodoric. The exceptions are the two freezes beneath the ceiling on either side of the church depicting processions. The processions, one of male saints and one of female saints, were painted in 561 A.D, the Byzantine era of the Emperor Justinian. They are proceeding from Ravenna, the earthly city of Klossus (the fleet) to the throne of god. Their Christ sits on a huge cushion as if he is floating. Another extraordinary feature is that, as in the Galla Placidia, each saint's toga carries letters. These letters are said to form an anagram believed to explain the Pentecost – the mystery of the Holy Spirit. The exact interpretation is still disputed.

As we walked towards the apse keeping an eye on the ladies we became aware that their faces and eyes appeared to be moving, watching us. This particularly trompe l'oeil is applied to great effect.

The women follow the three wise men to the throne of Mary, the Madonna, indicating that the painting is post 431 A.D. In 431 A.D. at Ephesus, the church declared that Mary was the mother of god.

The palace depicted in a painting of the city has an intriguing glitch. Open hands can be seen on the columns. The hands are completely unconnected to anything else. It is believed that the individuals to whom the hands were supposed to belong were painted out of the freeze. The personages represented in the original freeze were the Arian Ostrogoths, Theodoric's people. The Ostrogoths were Christians but not Catholics and did not believe in the Divinity of Jesus and hence the Holy Trinity.

When the Byzantines threw the Ostrogoths out of Ravenna, Justinian handed all their property to the Catholics. The church was converted into a Catholic building and the heretics painted out of the freezes – and crudely so. Curtains were painted over the personages. However, the silhouettes are still noticeable and the occasional hand and arm remains on the columns. Similarly, it is believed that the processions of male and female saints replaced the original depiction of a parade by the nobility of the city.

Very close to the ceiling on the left, one can see the miracles performed by Jesus. On the right are depictions of his last days and his death. Each is a story beginning at the apse end and moving on towards the facade. Notably there is no picture of the crucifixion of Christ, which, prior to the Byzantine era was seen to be a particularly cruel and distasteful scene.

Spirito Santo

Spirito Santo is thought to have been the first church to be constructed by Theodoric once he had conquered the city. His Arian non-Catholics needed a church of their own. The floor and columns later had to be raised but otherwise, the interior of the very luminous church, which contains a marble ambo from Theodoric's time, is original.

The octagonal **Aryan Baptistery** opposite was also built in Theodoric's time but its floor has been allowed to sink and is now six feet lower. With a very simple exterior, the baptistery has elegant decorations inside. In Piazza del Duomo, the **Cathedral Baptistery** of the Catholics is also octagonal, and was built in the early 400s by Bishop Ursus. It too has sunk, leaving the former entries to the four apses only recognisable by traces of the archways above their doors. The original floor is nine feet below the ground.

The interior is a harmonious combination of multi-coloured marble, marketry, mosaics and stucco. The dome is a beautiful mosaic with the naked Christ being baptised at the centre by St John. Around them the Apostles led by Peter and Paul are adorned in a mosaic of golden robes. Stucco decorations added in the 5th century sit alongside the windows and the whole circular impression is designed to convey the permanent wheel of life and the heavens.

The **Ursian Cathedral** is also 5th century in origin, and takes its name from its founder, Bishop Ursus. However, the cathedral was demolished and rebuilt by 1745 to the design of Giovanni Buonamici. Two sarcophagi of 5th century archbishops and a 6th century pulpit survived. Otherwise, the mosaics and marble fragments from the old cathedral, including a Bishop's ornate 6th century ivory throne, can be found in the nearby **Archiepiscopal Museum**. The museum is a treasure house of artefacts collected from the 5th to 8th centuries, and part of any tour of Roman/Byzantine Ravenna.

One can pass through the museum to a 6th century chapel, standing behind a small atrium in St Andrea's Oratory, which displays an unusual portrayal of the **Warrior Christ**.

Street Life

The main piazza is a gathering point known as **Piazza Salotta**, where between April and October inhabitants and tourists come to sit, drink and talk in the cafe bars. The summer evenings see rock and folk music festivals in the square.

Many of the cobbled streets of the central city are designated as for pedestrian and cyclists use only. With it being a Thursday afternoon, when the shops are regularly closed from 12.30pm, walking around the historic streets was quite relaxing.

Like Ferrara, flat Ravenna is a cyclist's city, with twice as many bicycles around as residents. The newest of the cobbled streets have central tracks for the bikes. If we had spent any longer in the city, it would have been advisable to hire our own bicycles.

We spent a warm October night in Ravenna. As it was out of season, we could only find one bar open in the centre. The bar is in the Piazza del Populo, and drew fewer people than the nearby McDonalds. Some restaurants were open but there are plenty of places to eat and drink during the spring and summer months.

We took an evening walk around the narrow streets of the pretty and tranquil city coming to the old city walls and the castle's keep and drawbridge at the Via Banca Leoni. The next day we went down to the river and discovered that the city still has a small port on the river, which flows down to the sea.

Festivals

In keeping with its cultural heritage, Ravenna has plenty of festivals, the most renown of which is the **Ravenna Festival of Operatic and Classical Music**. The concerts and operatic performances are held during June and July in San Vitale, San Apollinare in Classe and other fitting venues. Famous conductor, **Ricardo Mutti** now lives in Ravenna, and makes regular appearances at **La Scala** and the **Teatro Ligeri Festival** performances. **Rocca BranceLeone** stages the Jazz Festival in July and San Vitale has its **Organ Music Festival** in August. Piazza Salotta has plenty of performances from modern and classical musicians.

OUTSIDE THE CITY

Theodoric's Mausoleum

Theodoric's monumental **Mausoleum** is 2km from the city centre in Compo Coriando, a popular burial place for the Ostrogoths. Built from huge slabs of Istrian stone, the decagonal exterior encases a circular interior on two floors. A monstrous monolith of Istrian stone, 36ft in diameter and 10ft high and weighing 230 Italian tons, covers the ceiling. The interior of the dome is argued by some to have been created to resemble the type of Asiatic tent lived in by Theodoric's ancestors.

The roof contains a large crack, which in Ravenna legends is said to have been the work of lightning. The king commissioned the mausoleum, but Theodoric's death by lightning had been foretold. A storm blew up on the day his death was predicted. Though he used the tomb for shelter, a thunder bolt struck, splitting the stone and reducing the Ostrogoth leader to cinders. His empty porphyry coffin lies on the first floor.

Classe, 5km south east of Ravenna and the city's former sea port, home of the fleet, silted up by the 6th century and is now well inland. San Apollinare arrived here to convert the Roman legions and the church of **San Apollinare in Classe** was erected in the saint's honour in 549. For miles around one can see its 123ft high 10th century bell tower or campanile, with its one, two and three opening windows supported by white columns.

Inside two rows of huge marble columns with horizontal veins police the wide central aisle. The sides of the walls should be imagined as decorated in marble panels. Unmatched in Italy, the panels were taken away by 15th century warlord Sigismondo Malatesta for his heretical temple in Rimini.

The dome in the apse of the basilica is 6th century and a marvellously simple combination of colours with San Apollinare pictured beneath a medaillon containing a large jewelled disc and a cross studded with precious stones in a gold sky.

Mosaics

Inspired by their heritage, the artists of Ravenna have maintained the skill of mosaic making. Many places in the town, and resorts such as Lido Adriana, host two-week holiday courses in the basics of the art. In addition, some of the best international mosaicists have come together to produce a marvellous array of mosaics in the city's **Park of Peace**.

EATING OUT

One place for a fine meal is the historic setting of **Ca de Vin** on the Via Ricci. It serves traditional Ravenna dishes, and carries a large wine selection. Nearby, there are several restaurants in and around the main square. Outside the city there are several **agriturismo**. Some are listed in the accommodation section. Those without accommodation include **Il Lupo** at 356, Via Sant'Alberto in San Romualdo, **La Valetta** at 21, Via Forello in Sant'Alberto and **Staggi** at 199, Via Staggi in Porto Fuori.

ACCOMMODATION

area code 0544

Hotels

Ravenna city has plenty of accommodation, mainly in the medium range. We stayed in the **Hotel Centrale Byron***** (tel 212225 fax 34114) at 14, Via IV Novembre in the centre of the city. It is a pleasant stay and costs £40/£50 per night. The only disadvantage is that it is in the pedestrian area, which made parking difficult – though there is a facility for loading and unloading luggage and passengers.

It is also possible to stay close to the city in one of the coastal resorts, or in an **agriturismo**. Ravenna's **youth hostel** or **Ostelli della Gioventu "Dante"** (tel 421164) is at 12 Via Nicolodi and costs around £5/£7 per night. **Camp sites** are plentiful on the coast.

***** The city's two 4 star hotels are the **Bisanzio**, (tel 217111 fax 32539) at 30 Via Salaria and the **Jolly Hotel Mameli** (tel 35762 fax 216055) at 1, Piazza Mameli.

*****The cheapest of the three stars are the **Minerva** (tel/fax 213711) at 1/A, Via Maroncelli and the **Roma** (tel 421515 fax 421191) at 26, Via Candiano. Others include the **Astoria** (tel 453960 fax 455419), 26 Circ. Rotonda and **Italia** (tel 212363 fax 217004).

****The most expensive two star hotel, at £50/60 a night is the **Casa Amica** (tel 421566) at 11 Via Trieste, while the **Mocadoro** (tel 450272 fax 451172) at 18 Via Baiona is half the price. **Piccolo Hotel** (tel 450792 fax 451540) is on the same street as the latter, as are lodgings at **Mengozzi Lina** (tel 451339)

***Cheapest of the one star hotels, at £25/night is **Al Giaciglio** (tel 39403) at 42 Via R. Brancaleone.

Agriturismo with accommodation close to the city include **Agriturismo 2000** (tel 417303) at 293 Via Santerno Ammonite, Santerno, **La Manera** (tel 433247) at 166, Via Staggi, Porto Fuori, **L'Azdora** (tel 497669) at 14 Via Vangaticcio in Madonna dell'Albero and **Martelli** (tel 401744) at 429, Borgo Montone in Borgo Montone.

RAVENNA

i Tourist Information Offices

Ravenna: 12, Via Salaria (tel 35755 fax 482670)

Travelling Around

Distances from Ravenna of the main cities are: in Romagna, Rimini 50km, Ferrara 75km and on Via Emilia, Bologna 66km, Modena 105km, Reggio Nell'Emilia 128km, Parma 147km and Piacenza 189km.

Train Times (faster direct services)

Ravenna to Ferrara 1hr 15mins, Rimini 50mins, Bologna 1hr,

Trains Around Ravenna and the Adriatic Coastline

Trains run frequently (journey times in brackets) from Ravenna station south along the Adriatic coastline to Rimini, stopping at Classe, Lido di Classe/Savio (15mins), Cervia, Cesenatico (30mnis), Gatteo e Mare, Bellaria, Igea Marina (45mins), Rimini Torre Pedrera, Rimini Viserba, Rimini (1hr).

Trains run westwards from Ravenna to Russi, Bagnacavallo, Lugo (20mins) and Granarolo, and to Faenza (30/40mins) and Riolo Terme (50mins).

Trains run southwest from Faenza to Brisighella (10mins), Strada casale and S.Cassiano (25mins).

Trains run northwest from Lugo to Alfonsine (18mins) and Lavezzola (25mins).

THE RAVENNA ADRIATIC

Being so close to the Adriatic beaches, a visit to Ravenna can be much more than a tour around its cultural splendours. The beaches are sandy and well equipped, with restaurants, bars, hotels, camp sites, deckchairs and fun fairs. Closest to the city are the **Lido di Dante**, **Lido Adriano**, **Punta Marina Terme** and **Marina di Ravenna**.

Between the city and **Lido di Dante** lie 10 acres of the pine woods, so loved by Dante. Close to the beach, you'll find camp sites, flats and villas, but no large complexes. **Lido Adriana** has the **Auai Auai Aquapark**, and is more fun oriented. **Punta Marina Terme** and **Marina di Ravenna** are further north and also backed by pine forests. About 13km from Ravenna, **Marina di Ravenna** is the city's eldest resort, with a large tourist harbour capable of berthing 800 boats. It boasts a show ground for **show jumping**. At these resorts you'll find discos, bars, swimming pools, skating rinks, tennis courts and riding stables. Punta Marina Terme doubles as a **spa centre**, offering seaside cures.

Marina Romea is on the north side of Porto Corsini, at the outlet of the River Lamone. It is an old resort and the **Capanno Garibaldi**, almost submerged in water, is a reminder of Garibaldi being saved from the Austrian troops by the people of Ravenna who hid him in 1849. For riding enthusiasts, it is home to Italy's second most important **horse riding centre**.

South of Ravenna

South of Ravenna, past Classe, the Apennines came much more into view. To the west of the main road are a scattering of small lakes in the flat salt marshes, where salt is naturally produced. To the east can be found miles of pine forests, first planted by the Romans to supply the fleet at Classe.

Just off the Rimini-Ravenna road, we arrived at the **Lido di Savio**, with its **naturist beach** at the north end. It being October the beach was deserted, allowing us to stroll in 23°C fully clothed, without embarrassment, along a sandy shoreline edged by maritime pine woodland as far as the eye could see, and on to Ravenna.

Two restaurants sit on the beach, and 200 metres further south are scores of hotels. To the north, the woodlands contain several **camp sites** and **horse riding facilities**. Apartments are also available to let. One thing to note is that even in the summer, you won't find the ubiquitous deckchair here. It is a truly natural beach, and for 10km to the north, one can find no other facilities. Dotted with shells, the shore is ideal for children. Our friend insisted that apart from in the busy month of August, nudists or not, she would feel happy taking her children to Savio.

After Savio, on a clear day San Marino comes into view sat on a mountain. Situated 11km south of Ravenna on the Rimini road, we arrived at the fun park of **Mirabilandia**, the biggest fun fair on the Adriatic Riviera. The fair has a special area for toddlers called **Bimbopoli** with six fun attractions. The big dipper is called **Sierra Tonante**, and reaches 100km an hour. There are also water slides, raft rides, brass bands and restaurants.

Further south we came to **Milano Marittima**, which has an attractive natural park with several camp sites and accommodation close to the town. Together with **Cervia** it forms a large seaside tourist resort.

We ventured inland on the road to Castaglione. This is a land of fruit orchards, fields of cabbages, spinach, beans, strawberries and farms. Beside the road were small shacks selling **piadina** and **cascione**, a pizza-like sandwich snack costing usually L1,000 or up to L3,500/5,000 with fillings such as prosciutto.

The marshes to the west of the Ravenna-Rimini road offer a peaceful place for **bird watching** and **walking.** Plovers, sandpipers, little egrets, spoonbills and widgeons flit around the waters. **Magazzini del Sale** was once a great salt warehouse and gives a picture of what life was like for the salt sifters. Mud similar to the 'liman' of the Black Sea is taken from the salt flats and used in Cervia's spa centre.

The town is former Italian soccer manager, Arrigo Sacchi's, favourite spot for his summer holidays, and has plenty of sports facilities and sporting events. **Golf courses**, **riding stables**, 130 **tennis courts**, **Le Siepe** showground staging top class **show jumping competitions** and **beach volley competitions** offer plenty to do. Via Jelenia is the home of the **Adriatic Golf Club** (tel 0544 922786 fax

993410) with its 18 hole, par 72 course. In addition the coastline has a harbour, mooring 350 tourist boats and boats for **deep sea fishing, wind surfing** and

water skiing not to mention the sandy beaches full of sunbathers.

Interesting international festivals in Cervia include 'Arrivano dal mare', the **puppet fete** and 'Cervia Volante', the **kite fliers' festival**. There's also the Ascension Day '**Marriage of the Sea Festival'** celebrated since 1445, and accompanied by a costumed procession, a **sailor's fair** and **climbing the greasy pole** - over the water. June brings 1,500 dancers for an **international dance festival** and July/August, **open air theatre and ballet** organised by Cervia's Summer Theatre. August 10th is the day of the **San Lorenzo Fireworks Festival**.

Special shopping opportunities include the **antique and crafts street market** in the old town and the Piazza Andrea open market every Thursday. Best meal to try is the grilled blue fish, a speciality of the Ravenna Riviera.

RAVENNA

ACCOMMODATION
(area code 0544)

Cervia
**** Cervia itself has the **Grand Hotel Cervia** (tel 970500 fax 972086), 9, LM.G.Delcdda and **Nettuno** (tel 971156 fax 972082), 34, Lm.D'Annunzio. **Garden** (tel 987144 fax 980006) is at 250 VI Italia in Pinarella and **Capriccio** (tel 980308 fax 980316) at 12 Via Montefeltro in Tagliata.

***The resort has at least 50 three star hotels, the cheapest of which are the **Sedonia** (tel/fax 971258) 82, Lm Deledda and **Riz** (tel/fax 71340) at around £25 a night. Visitors can expect to pay twice as much at the **Summer Dream** (tel 715190) at 90, Lm Deledda

and **Villa Mare** (tel 971200 fax 970054) at 84, Lm Deledda.

Most two star hotels are around £25 a night, and include, also on Lm Deledda, the **Alda (tel 971240) at 20, **Lusa** (tel 71776) at 66, **Marina** (tel 9712470 at 50, with the **Moderno** (tel 71936) and, at 64, **Wally** (tel 72354).

*Cheapest of the one star hotels are the £15 a night **Saretina** (tel 71754) at 122 Lm Deledda and £20 a night **Aurora** (tel/fax 971110) at 77, VI Colombo.

Milano Marittima
****Milano Marittima has 21 four star hotels, the priciest of which are the **Marie E Pineta** (tel 992262 fax 992739) at 40 VI Dante and

Miami (tel 991628 fax 992033) at 31, Il Traversa, both costing around £120 a night in season.

***The resort has at least 100 three star hotels. The cheapest at £15/20 a night is *Oasi* (tel 994222) at 8, XIV Traversa. Otherwise expect to pay £25/£40 a night. Similarly with **star and * star accommodation.

Camp Sites

There are 20 camp sites spread across the Ravenna Riviera, with the biggest in Punta Marina having a capacity to take over 2,600 campers. Sites close to Ravenna include: in Casalborsetti – *Adria*, (tel 445217), *Pineta* (tel 445298), *Reno* (tel 445020) and *Romea* (tel 446311) all on the Via Spallazzi. In Lido di Classe, *Bisanzio* (tel 939532) at 48 ia Marignolli. In Lido di Dante, *Classe* (tel 492005) on Via Catone and *Ramazzotti* (tel 492250)

on Via Paolo e Francesca.

In Marina do Ravenna, *Piomboni* (tel 530230) at 421 Viale della Pace and *Rivaverde* (tel 530491) at 301, Viale delle Nazioni. In Marina Romea, *Villaggio del Sole* (tel 446037) on Viale Italia. In Punta Marina Terme, *Adriano*, (tel 437230) and *Coop 3* (tel 437353) on Via Campeggi and *Villagio dei Pini* (tel 437115) on Via della Fontana.

Cervia has three camp sites at Pinarella: *Adriatico* (tel 71537) 33, Via Pinarella, *Pinarella* (tel 987408) at 52 Via Abruzzi and *Safari* (tel 987356) at 130 Viale Titano.

i Tourist Information Offices

Milano Marittima: 107, Viale Romagna (tel 993435 fax 992515)

RAVENNA

ON THE ROAD TO BOLOGNA - THE PLAINS

We were travelling from Ferrara on the Ravenna road across the plains. To the west we could see the Apennine foothills rising through the haze. The landscape was dotted with the clay-tiled roofs of farm houses and the occasional church. Vineyards, trees and shrubbery increased as we neared the coast.

We passed through Alfonsini, a pretty little town of two storey buildings surrounded by plenty of trees and orchards almost like an oasis in the parched surrounds.

Bagnacavallo

We turned south to cross the plain towards the Ravenna Apennines. Situated 19km away from Ravenna, on the road to Bologna, is the town of **Bagnacavallo**, most noted for its 7th century church, **San Pietro in Sylvis** on Via Garibaldi. Said to be one of the best preserved old churches in the region, it was built when the Exarchs were controlling Ravenna. The style reflects the transition from the Byzantine style to the Romanesque. Much of the mediaeval town has disappeared, but the main square, **Piazza Liberta**, contains a 13th century Civic Clock Tower. The bandit, Stefano Pelloni, known as 'Il Passatore' was imprisoned in the tower in 1849. Also original is the layout of the town, which radiates out from Via Mazzini. The winding streets were probably forced on the planners by the sharp bend in the Santerno river.

Via Mazzini contains some fine Baroque palaces and the 15th century church of San Michel Angelo, which was reworked following an earthquake in 1688. Away from the centre, at the end of Via C.Battisti, is Piazza Nuova, a cobbled elliptical-shaped square. Surrounded by 18th century arcades, it holds a busy market day. Visitors on the trail of **Lord Byron** might also wish to visit the enclosed convent at the Church of San Giovanni where his daughter Allegra lived and studied till her death.

Lugo di Romagna

RAVENNA

Lugo (32,000) is a small but important market town a few kilometres from Bagnacavallo, close to the A14 autostrada from Ravenna. Digs in the area have revealed traces of a Fiorano tribe, said to have settled here in 5,000 B.C. Being at the crossroads of the routes from Ferrara to the south, and from Bologna to Ravenna, it took on additional importance in the Middle Ages.

Historic relics include the Latin cross-shaped **College of San Francesco**, which still has its 13th century portal and fragments of Romanesque frescoes on the walls. The town's castle was built in 1298, and its crenellated, cylindrical ramparts and 14th century fortifications are well preserved. Inside, through the internal gardens, the grounds contain attractive hanging gardens.

In 1337, soon after the castle was built, the town came under the control of the Estense based in Ferrara. Like Ferrara, the town was ceded to the Vatican in 1598.

The town centre is mainly 18th century in origin. Opposite the castle around Piazza Mazzini is the **Pavaglione**, a grand quadruple arcade covering an area of 132metres by 84metres, which was erected in 1783 as a market for silk cocoons, and is still used today as a major market.

Gioachino Rossini may have been born in Pesaro but in his formative musical years after 1802, he lived in Lugo. The 18th century **Teatro Rossini**, partly designed by the Bibienas is dedicated to the composer. The **Callido** and **Gatti** organs on which the young Rossini practised are in the **Chiesa del Carmine**, and the house where he lived is still standing, part of opera lovers' itineraries.

ALONG THE LAMONE VALLEY
Faenza

We left the A14 autostrada, arriving at the pleasant town of Faenza on Via Emilia, and immediately became entangled in its one way system, which forced us to return to square one in our attempts to reach our destination.

Faenza, in the clay belt, is noted for ceramics, and in particular for the fine artistry of its majolica. The **International Ceramics Museum** on Via Baccarini houses one of the world's largest collections of historic and modern ceramics, including the works of Picasso and Chagall and 13th century local creations. The town has had a traditional link with Tuscany and Florence, which enriched their artists during the Renaissance period. The museum has a large collection of Faenza pottery from the same period. Opening hours are 9.30am to 1pm and 3.30pm to 6.30pm but the museum is closed on Mondays.

Potters come from all over the world during September and October for the town's **ceramic festivals**. Outside the town, another potter's haunt is the Villa Case Grandi dei Ferniani with a display of Faenza pottery between 1700 and 1900.

Another legacy of the Renaissance period and Tuscan influence is the fine cathedral in the central Piazza della Liberta. Built between 1474 and 1511 to Fiorentine Giuliano da Maiano's design, it is a splendid three tier symmetrical duomo in brick. Its unfinished marble facade is a rich combination of circles, rectangles, arches and linear decorations. The interior contains a large collection of period sculptures and frescoes, and the 15th century tombs of St Emilian, St Terence, and the beautiful St Savino tomb, carved in marble by Benedetto da Maiano in 1475.

Piazza della Liberta contains the site of the Roman forum, situated where the cardo and decuman principal Roman axis roads met. The decuman gate of the Roman town Faventa, is in the square. The square has a large fountain with bronze sculptures dating back to the 17th century, and the Goldsmiths' Portico of open arcades opposite the Cathedral. Treats for those who prefer Neoclassical buildings are the luxurious Palazzo Milzetti on Via Tonducci and the **Teatro Masini** theatre completed in 1787. Palazzo Milzetti now houses a museum of Neoclassical art, and is open on weekdays between 8.30am and 1.30pm.

Outside the town, the lower valley is littered with larger villas. Above are the soft selenite/chalk hills, which provide beautiful treks with fascinating green landscapes of woodlands, cut into by swallow holes, ravines, and gorges, and dotted with the ruins of old castles. Tuscany, eat your heart out! **Grotto Tanaccia Karstic Park** and **Carne Natural Park** have visitors centres, with refreshments for base camp. Golfers can take some time out at **Golf Club La Cicogne** (tel/fax 0546 622410) with its four hole practice circuit on Via Saint'Orsola.

RAVENNA

Brisighella

Burgundy, lemon, lilac, scarlet and green vied for the autumnal landscape as we passed Faenza going south on the SS302. We were soon in a wide valley topped by a mix of conifer and deciduous greens beneath the vineyards and orchards on the lowland. We passed the Ristorante Cardinale as we began a gentle climb back into the junior Apennines. Crossing the River Lamone we were in Brisighella, 15km from Faenza. Once again, the one way system took us on an impromptu tour, until we found ourselves in the centre of the mediaeval village.

The rotund twin towers of a castle appeared up on a knoll above the town. It was the 14th century rocca of the ruling Manfredi's, later restored in the 1500s. Then a shock; almost by its side but perched on its own rock outcrop, appeared not another rocca but a tiny 13th century tower dominated by its huge clockface. The castle houses a small museum of life in Brisighella.

We climbed up the hill through the pine trees above the village, and saw how the castle and clocktower lord over the beautiful villas below. We soon reached the third hilltop on the side, and the chateau-like shrine of **Cava del Monticino**, built in 1758 to house an ancient terracotta statue of the Virgin Mary.

Above the chateau, the splendid view of the mountains, patchwork fields and woodland, the rocca and the rustic life below was set in a water colour haze and reminiscent of a Turner landscape. Majestic and eye watering, this was a sight not to be missed. But we were in Brisighella to explore its famous mediaeval streets and traditions, and so descended back into the village where we were soon lost again in the one way system.

We alighted in the little Piazza Reduci, which has a small duomo completed in 1697 by Sylvani. We sat in the Cafe Masini across the square drinking espresso and tasting the salami. The town is known for its excellent extra-virgin olive oil, its cheeses, charcuterie and salami. Close by was the hotel and restaurant, Gigiole, worth remembering for a stay over during the town's **Mediaeval Festival** and the November festival '**To his majesty the truffle**.'

We walked up the mediaeval Via Naldi to the main piazza, **Piazza G. Marconi**, which is hardly a square now but a widened street, with buildings looking worn by the centuries. The **Maghinardo Palace**, now the town hall, is here, alongside a small ceramics shop, wine shop, and restaurant. Little alleyways lead off and we imagined the horse drawn carriages rattling across the cobbled stones and through the small entries. Via Metelli is a similar part of this maze of tiny streets such as the Via Fensoni, completed in 1639, with buildings declaring their 16th and 17th century origin. Via Lapescoli contains a small park.

Out of the town and up the valley we reached **Pieve del Tho**, a Romanesque church built in 909, and now called San Giovanni in Ottavo. This simple church with its atmospheric crypt was probably rebuilt in 1100, as one of the pillars has the date carved on it.

One classic Romanesque feature is the abundance of borrowed materials used in construction. The oriental granite pillars in the two aisles were taken from a Roman military memorial site. A Corinthian capital is used as a holy water stoup, and other pillars have capitals from Roman buildings.

Brisighella Spa (tel 0546 81068 fax 81365) is on Vialle delle Terme and offers health and **beauty treatments**, **macro-shiatsu** and **reflexology**. The village is best known for its **Mediaeval Festival** in July, when the locals dress up in mediaeval costumes and re-enact the dances, customs and rites of yore.

ALONG THE SENIO VALLEY

The Senio river flows from the Apennines, close to the frontier with Bologna, and down into Lake Comacchio. We took the SS306 south from Castel Bolognese to visit its upper reaches. By the time the SS306 reaches **Riolo Terme,** 50km from Ravenna, and the same distance from Bologna, the hills are gently rolling. Above the town to the south on Mount Mauro lie the ruins of a mediaeval castle, and to its south the beautiful gushing ravines of the Rio Basino. It is a marvellously tranquil setting for this 19th century spa town.

It is hard to imagine the tumult, which must have existed here when Cesare Borgia (Il Valentino) and his troops stormed the town castle's bastions in 1500, defeating the 300 soldiers on guard. **The Rocca**, built in 1388 by the Bolognesi family, is still intact, and nowadays used for art exhibitions and concerts. The walls of the old borg are also still evident. Beside them is the **Parco Sotto le Mura**, containing bronze sculptures by Giovanni Bertozzi and, on Via Limisano, the 18 hole very technical par 72 golf course of **La Torre Riolo Golf Club** (tel/fax 0546 74035).

The Art Nouveau buildings of **Riolo Bagni Spa** (tel 0546 71045 fax 71605), a spa once visited by Lord Byron's mistress, offer traditional cures for respiratory problems and up to date treatments including **hydro-massage**, **saline bromidic treatments**, a **gym** and a **beauty centre** with **mud treatments**. The spa also has a **Terme Bimbo** for the children. Beside the spa is an old park containing centuries old redwood trees. To the west on Via Rio Vecchio is **Acqualand**, a 70,000 square metre inland water park resort with slides, hydro-massage, solariums and water games.

Along SS306, as its name suggests, **Casola Valsenio** is in the valley of the Senio River. Apart from having been founded 1,000 years ago by the Benedictine monks, it is known for its wonderful flora. The **Medicinal Garden** is the most renown in Italy, combining medicinal, aromatic and cosmetic herbs on show to visitors. The town also has the 'Lavender Road', flanking travellers on the road out to Brisighella, and the 'road of plants of long ago', with its ancient and rare species planted along the road to the Santerno valley.

The Benedictines' Abbazia di Valsenio still stands between the SS306 and the Senio on the Faenza side. Two historic towers overlook the town. The 14th century civic tower, with its clock installed in 1560 to put an end to the citizens being, "dependent on nature" and the 16th century Ceruno Tower of the feudal Ceronesi lords who controlled the Senio.

Down river in these Cotswold-like hills, is a protected area known as the **Chalk Vein**, or **Vena del Gesso**. This area is interesting for botanists, geologists, and other travellers, due to its grottoes and swallow holes, one of which, the **King Tiberius' Grotto**, is 1,000ft deep, and offered up pre-historic artefacts of a past people. The hill overlooking the town from the west is the pine covered Monte del Pini, south of which stands a restored 12th century fortress, which was also the site of a battle during the 2nd World War.

ACCOMMODATION
(area code 0546)

Hotels

Smack in the centre of **Faenza** is the attractive four star **Hotel Vittoria** (tel 21508 fax 634440) at 23 Corso Garibaldi. The other four star hotel is the **Cavallino** (tel 634411 fax 634440) at 185, Via Forlivese. The **Class Hotel** (tel 46662 fax 46676) at 171 Via San Silvestro is three star.

The plushest hotel in **Riolo Terme** is the four star **Grande Albergo delle Terme** (tel 71041 fax 71215) at 15 Via Firenze. The spa resort has six three star hotels at around £40 a night. They include the **Cristallo** (tel 71160 fax 71879), **Senio** (tel 71154 fax 74319) and **Villa Italia** (tel 71086 fax 71943) all on Via Firenze. Two star hotels on this street include the **Alma** (tel 71097 fax 71935), **Franca** (tel 71236 fax 71873), **Lea** (tel 71019) and **Villetta del Sole** (tel 74364).

Brisighella has the four star **Gigiole** (tel 81209 fax 81275) at 5 Piazza Carducci. The more expensive three star hotels, **La Meridiana** (tel/fax 81590) and **Terme** (tel/fax 81144) are on VI. Terme, while **Tre Colli** (tel 81147 fax 81203) at 9, Via Gramsci and **Valverde** (tel/fax 81388) at 14, Via Lamone are cheaper.

Agriturismo

Near to Faenza there are several **agriturismo** with accommodation. They include **Il Laghetto del Sole** (tel 642196) at 37, Via Pittora which also has camping facilities and **La Germana** (tel 43359) at 6 Via Germana.

There are several **agriturismo** with accommodation close to **Brisighella**. They include: **Il Palazzo** (tel 80338) in Baccagnano, **La Rocca** (tel 40250) at 16, Via Gabellotta in Pietramora, **Relais Torre Pratesi** (tel 84545 fax 84558) in Cavina, **Villa Corte** (tel 85798 fax 88087) at 9 Via Corte in Castellina, **Valpiana** (tel/fax 88050) at 7, Via Tura in Casala and **Torre del Marino** (tel 89190 fax 651040) at 45, Via Torre del Marino in Villa Vezzano.

There are also other agriturismo which only serve food. They include: **Villa Severola** at 196 **Via San Silvestro**, near Faenza,

_i_ Tourist Information Offices

Faenza: 1, Piazza del Populo (tel/fax 25231)

Riolo Terme: 2, Via Aldo Moro (tel 71044 fax 71932)

Brisighella: Piazzale Stazione (tel 81166)

R
A
V
E
N
N
A

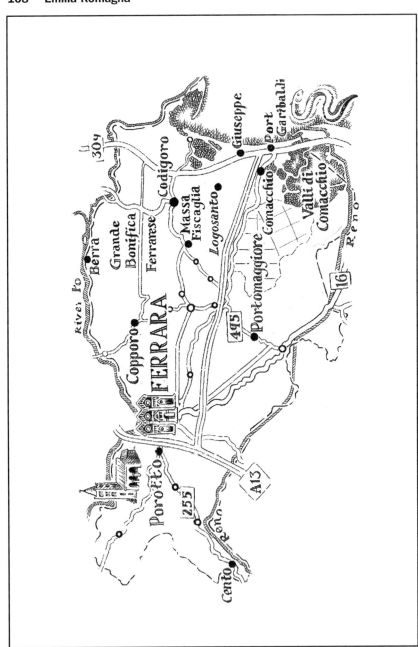

Ferrara's SHROUDED SPLENDOUR
FERRARA

We were on the A1 travelling up north to Ferrara. It is a fast road in the Reno valley flankcd by the forested slopes of the Apennine mountain range. Reaching the outskirts of Bologna the mountains become gentle hills and north of Bologna we were back on the flat Po plain with clay-tiled houses amid neatly divided fields.

"Ferrara is a truly metaphysical city...full of surprises. In some parts of town, besides offering splendid apparitions of subtle, spectral beauty which are simply awe-inspiring to even the cleverest of passers by educated in the mysteries of intelligence, this city also offers the advantage of preserving, in a unique way, remnants of a great mediaeval past that lives on, somehow, mysteriously, indefinitely, and inexplicably animating the city...especially in certain areas, these remnants of the past are mysteriously suspended between heaven and earth like embalmed nocturnal animals hanging from the ceiling of an alchemist's laboratory."

Giorgio de Chirico, 1918 founder of the Metaphysical school of painting

Ferrara City

Ferrara is my favourite Italian city. Our first trip to the ancient town was in 1997. I had just read, Stendhal's *Charterhouse of Parma* as part of my introduction to north Italy. What was interesting was that while Stendhal's hero stayed in Ferrara when fleeing from the Milan police, the town itself is not considered worth a mention. Add to this Goethe's description of Ferrara in his diary of his Italian travels as a sad and sorry city and I expected a drab industrial town.

Indeed, as we crossed the plain approaching the city there was not a feature in sight to give the landscape some relief from the relentlessly flat horizon. When, on the edge of the city, we passed through 1950s style Communist-built squat dull apartment blocks, my low expectations seemed to be realised. But suddenly the blocks disappeared and we were in the centre delighted to be surrounded by a deluge of grandiose period architecture.

Ferrara has an intriguing feature almost unique to Italy. Walking around is like journeying back through the ages, leaving the current crop of modern, brightly painted bungalows, and briefly stopping off in the fifties, surrounded by platoons of dull municipal apartment blocks, before travelling back to the Renaissance period, and finally coming to a halt in mediaeval times. The overall effect of a stroll through this beautiful city for explorers is a journey through 1,000 years of history.

Perhaps Stendhal and Goethe were responsible for keeping the tourists away from this city; its relative absence of visitors is inexplicable. Nevertheless, the reward awaits those who wish to take advantage of its relaxing, narrow streets, beautiful palaces, and tranquil parks. In fact, Ferrara's historic architecture, university, and traditions, make it a very cultured city. **Giorgio Bassani's** masterpiece, *The Garden of Fitzi-Contini* was filmed here, and here **Giorgio de Chirico,** founder of the Metaphysical avant garde art school, gained inspiration.

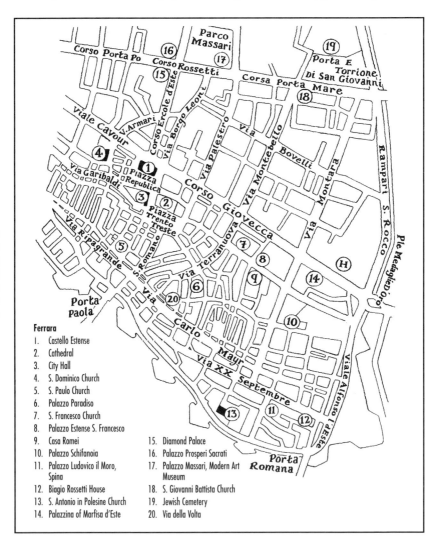

Ferrara

1. Castello Estense
2. Cathedral
3. City Hall
4. S. Dominico Church
5. S. Paulo Church
6. Palazzo Paradiso
7. S. Francesco Church
8. Palazzo Estense S. Francesco
9. Casa Romei
10. Palazzo Schifanoia
11. Palazzo Ludovico il Moro, Spina
12. Biagio Rossetti House
13. S. Antonio in Polesine Church
14. Palazzina of Marfisa d'Este
15. Diamond Palace
16. Palazzo Prosperi Sacrati
17. Palazzo Massari, Modern Art Museum
18. S. Giovanni Battista Church
19. Jewish Cemetery
20. Via della Volta

FERRARA

A plague, leading to the demise of Ferrara, as described by Goethe, and the 1598 departure of the Estense and their retinue, for a period, left Ferrara a deserted, almost empty city. Add to this, the city's famous winter shroud of fog, and one can imagine why Goethe described the place as an unnatural and 'dead' city.

Much of Ferrara centre is pedestrianised, its 150,000 residents being reputed to possess three bicycles each. Locally they say one is for everyday use, one is elegant for rendezvous and Sunday best, while the third is for sporting recreation. We watched as people drove to the edge of the city, parked their cars, and hauled their fold away cycles out of the boot. The tinkle of bicycle bells is more reminiscent of Ferrara than the toot of a car horn. And, as in Ravenna, bikes are available for hire; simply the best way to see this romantic, and relaxed city.

The Making of Ferrara

Records of human inhabitation in this area go back to the Bronze Age at nearby Bondeno. The modern city is believed to have been founded in the 8th century on the banks of the River Po, where the Via Ripagrande now runs and the mediaeval buildings still stand. The other two roads which ran parallel to the river were the 2km long Via della Volte (street of arches) and the oldest, the Ragno. The Po's route shifted due to flooding in the 12th century, and moved to pass 6km north of the city.

The church and the Longobards controlled the city in 986, when Pope John XV gave it Theobald of Canossa. But in the age when church rule began to weaken, the noble families increased their power, and the **Estense** emerged at the head of the anti-Papist faction. Obizzo D'Este took control of the city in the 13th century.

The Estense were cruel and oppressive rulers, and in 1385 sparked a people's revolt against new taxes. The tax adviser to the Marchese Nicolo II was murdered, and the castle was ordered to be constructed forthwith. The Este built fine palaces and churches, and when they ran out of male heirs in 1598, forfeiting the province back to the Pope, they left behind the beautiful legacy of the **Renaissance District**.

Papal rule was equally oppressive for the people who destroyed the Papal fortress in 1859. The people had welcomed Napoleon's troops in 1797, and took part in the Cisalpine and Cispadane Republics, which fought against papal rule. The only blot on the area's history was that Cesare Balbo developed a strong fascist following in the city.

F E R R A R A

The old, high, mediaeval walls were destroyed as the city expanded. Today the city still retains 9km of its 15th to 19th century boundary walls, and it is possible to cycle around them. The walls are quite low as was the Renaissance style, accommodating to the introduction of gunpowder and cannon. The thick low walls defending the city allowed the cannon to fire at their targets on the ground.

The walls were surrounded by a 33 metre wide, deep moat, and the green moss on the walls indicates the old water line. In this mini canal, the Este family organised boat fights, using soldiers, for their pleasure. The moat was drained in the last century because, in the humid conditions, the abundance of water allowed mosquitoes and malaria to fester.

The University of Ferrara

The city's university was established in the 14th century. The seat of the University is the Estense-built 15th century Palazzo San Francesco (or Palazzo Renata di Francia).

Palazzo Estense has a special story. In the 16th century, Renata, wife of the then Duke of Ferrara, Ercoli II, was imprisoned here. She was sister to the French King Louis XII and a Calvinist. As duchess, she invited Calvin to Ferrara, enraging the Papacy. Fearful of the consequences, the duke imprisoned her for two years, preventing her from seeing anybody, including her children.

The **Palazzo Marquisa D'Este** was a delizia for the Estense. Delizie were palaces built as 'delights' for the dynasty. Used for the enjoyment of the family rather than military or administrative purposes, they were often built on the edges of the cities where they would be attached to vast parks or hunting grounds. Built in 1559, it was a small summer palace.

After the last Estense duke died without an heir, the Estense were forced to leave Ferrara in 1598. However, the Duchess stayed on in the city, remaining a wealthy and important personage. She left behind a legend for the Ferrarese.

It is said that should one stand in front of the palace at midnight, one will see the door open, and the libertine Duchess make her exit, seated on a chariot drawn by four horses and followed by all her former lovers. Some say the legend was only created because the Duchess refused to submit to the 16th century ruling that women must wear hats and cover their head.

Inside there is a small museum with period furniture brought from around Italy, excellently recreating the atmosphere of a typical 16th century palace. Frescoes painted by the Ferrara school of Cosimatura cover the ceilings with the fantasy creatures of the Grotesque style, so common in the late 16th century.

The artist, Felipe Bastiano, influenced by his study of Michelangelo's work in the Sistine Chapel in Rome, introduced the Grotesque style used in the palace, the castle and in many of the other palaces.

MEDIAEVAL FERRARA

We entered Ferrara from the south side. The old city walls had been converted into a cycling track. Once inside the old boundary, the streets, overlooked by old clay brick Renaissance and Gothic buildings with shuttered windows, become narrow, cobbled and replete with history.

We passed the beautiful Renaissance palace on Via XX Settembre, the Palazzo Costabili designed by Rossetti, and now the city's **National Archaeological Museum**, housing the richest collection of antique Attican (Greek) vases in the world.

The basis of the collection originates in the unearthing of the ancient town of Spina, which dates back to the 6th century B.C and lasted till the 3rd century B.C. Two of the town's necropoli were discovered, in which attic vases had been placed alongside the corps of the dead.

On Via Gamboni, we arrived at **San Antonio in Polesine**, the convent of the silent nuns of St. Beatrice. The convent dates back to at least the 12th century. The father of Beatrice was an Este, and made a present of this former Augustinian monastery to Beatrice. Beatrice turned the monastery into a convent where she lived reputedly performing miracles of healing. She was canonised in 1272.

We knocked on the convent door and requested permission to enter. The convent is only open to the public between 9am and 11.30am and 3pm and 5pm. On Saturdays prayers require closing at 4pm.

We were in the inside church, which dates back to the 12th century, and is the oldest part of the chapel. Frescoes carried tales from the New Testament from the Slaughter of the Innocents to the Crucifixion. The middle section contains 14th century walls and a Felipe painted 16th century ceiling, typically covered with Grotesque figures.

We whispered our way through the chapel to the outside church, with its beautifully carved 15th century stalls, where the friendly nuns were gathering to pray. One especially interesting feature was the fresco of Jesus climbing the cross for his crucifixion, an unusual representation of Christ's willingness to play his part.

The tomb of Beatrice is outside between the chapel and the dormitory by the beautiful gardens. She died in 1262 at the age of 36, having founded the convent in 1254. Her corps was taken away intact in the 16th century. Since then the tomb had dripped water, said to be Beatrice's tears. The tears are collected and given to the sick for healing purposes.

There is a small parking area just by the convent's serene cherry tree garden. We sat in the August warmth beneath a large cherry tree in its wistfully tranquil gardens just outside its walls. The tree is so popular that when it comes into full bloom, forming a huge pink umbrella traditionally on April 23rd, visitors arrive from miles around to see it.

We walked on through an area of cobbled streets, and buildings with most elaborately carved and decorated gables, and pots of geraniums hanging from the upper windows. We had parked our cars wherever we could, as parking was very difficult. Here, we came to the 11th century church and bell tower of San Gregorio.

The 14th century Carmellino house close by has one of the few examples in the city of a house extended and jutting out on the first floor to increase space, a building method more common to Bologna.

Many of the ancient houses here are still occupied. The owner of 2 Vicolo Granchio seems to have had a private theatre built into his house for rehearsing his plays, which explains why the house suddenly juts out into the narrow street by the side of what is believed to have been a canal.

We turned right into the Via Giuoco del Pallone. Number 29 used to be a palace belonging to the family of Ariosto, the poet. Number 31 was a house for storing salt and offloading it into boats on the canal.

At the end of the street is the former **Palazzo Paradiso**, now the public library. From Via Pallone we could see into the great house with its old frescoes and herbal gardens. Alberto V of the Estense built the house as the Estense's first delizia in the 14th century. The Duke went to Rome and obtained papal permission to build Ferrara's first university. The building situated on the corner of the Via Scienze is also known as Ariosto's Library. **Ariosto's tomb** lies inside.

In 1567 the palace became the seat of Ferrara University, and remained so until the 1960s, when the seat was moved to another palace. Besides the frescoes and Ariosto's tomb, the building is also worth visiting for its **anatomic theatre**, which dates back to 1771. The high chair in the theatre is said to have been for the local authorities to watch over the dissection of the corpses.

The courtyard contains a small café, and a delightful glass pain intrudes into the cobbled pavement, and shows off the old water collection and storage system below.

Now we came to Sant' Aniese and Sant'Aniesina, which belonged to the science faculties at the University. We were in the Via Carboni, where the residents, including those in the beautiful house close by still owned by relatives of Ariosto, must somehow get used to the strange, loud and long musical chimes of Sant'Aniese's bells.

Taking us to some more churches, our guide informed us that while mediaeval Ferrara has a plethora of churches, the city nowadays does not really know what to do with them. We visited the old church of St Peter, now converted into the Cinema Minion and used for showing erotic films. The cinema, whose facade is still that of the old church, has, perhaps understandably, been burned down more than once. One of Emilia Romagna's biggest enigmas is, after all, the co-existence of heavy devotion and disrespect for the church.

We turned from Via Ripa Grande onto the parallel, quite charming, street of Via della Volte. The 800 year-old narrow, cobbled street is crossed by a series of a dozen or so arches. This was just a small section of the street, which was once as long as the town itself.

Over time, the arches have been subject to all the pressures of Ferrara's shifting sub soil, causing movement of the linked buildings, almost all of which have been twisted into irregular shapes. Once, the arches allowed the merchants to cross over a canal, now the Via Volta, into the town. Today they are mainly out of use. The street was once the centre of the red light district, now long gone, leaving a very quiet and mysterious aura on a foggy autumn night.

Close by is the church of San Paulo, built in the 900s, but so damaged by an earthquake in 1570, that it had to be completely rebuilt. The interior is notable for its display of 16th century Ferrara paintings particularly the Resurrection, the Annunciation and the Circumcision by Bastianino, where he combines the styles of Michelangelo and Titian.

Many of the city's streets were formally canals, as their names sometimes indicate. Until the 12th century Ferrara had an important port. However the Po, which serviced the area, shifted further north leaving the city isolated. Modern transport and hygiene requirements made the canals redundant, and today none pass through the city. Only the Po di Volano passes near, just outside the southern walls of the old city by the Via Volano.

Via San Romano is the city's second oldest street. It linked the port with the market square by the Cathedral, and now leads to Bologna. As the Pope also owned Bologna, he built a wonderful gate on the city's edge. Though extremely narrow, it is still a very busy street, with plenty of shops catering for people as they pass from the suburbs through the gate into the city.

Here we found a **pasticceria**, where the typical Ferrarese bread was being hand made in twisting round spirals. Group tours are available for those who wish to see traditional bakeries.

The Via Mazzini was busy and while shopping, we had to watch out for the cyclists in this most cycling of cities. It brought us out at the Cathedral close to the castle.

FERRARA

THE CASTLE AREA

Around the castle are many cobbled streets. As we walked along it was as if one could here the horses cantering along and heading beneath the porticoes leading into one square or other.

It was Sunday morning and we were outside the cathedral, around which the area is closed off to motor vehicles. There was a quiet pedestrian hum about the square. No roaring engines, no horns, no church bells yet. Just the rattle of bicycle wheels on the cobble stones and scores of old men stood around in the square, with their pipes and bicycles, relating and debating their news. The younger men and women preferred to fill the chairs of the cafes, whose clientele spilled out into the square. A perfect sunny Sunday.

Ferrara's Duomo

Constructed in 1135, The Duomo or Cathedral lords over the piazza. Its facade tells a story. No particular artists have been accredited to the original construction but the main portal on the arch is a sculpture inscribed by Nicholaus, the Romanesque artist. Nicholaus was a pupil of Wiligelmo, whose school decorated many of the mediaeval churches of the region. Nicholaus' sculpture is of St George, the city's co-patron, slaying the dragon, and the cathedral replaced the church of St George as the most important ecclesiastical building in the city. That church can still be found near the city walls.

The cathedral's Porta dei Mesi was destroyed in 1717, and walking down the cathedral's south side, one can see the gap which was left. The Porta della Staio was also taken down because both had to be removed to accommodate the increasingly powerful merchants, who wanted their long arcade, or loggia, originally built in the 15th century, to be extended.

Inside the cathedral we were overwhelmed by the array of brilliant frescoes. Outstanding were the Il Guercino altar piece, portraying St Lawrence and Bonacassi's 15th century Madonna della Grazie in the right hand aisle. The third altar also has a fresco by Bastianino with the Madonna among the clouds.

Up above, surrounded by stucco work of the same era, the apse had a wonderful fresco of the Last Judgement completed by Il Bastianino in 1580. It is thought to have been inspired by Michelangelo work in the Vatican's Sistine chapel.

Leaving the Duomo, we turned left to look at the side of the cathedral facing Piazza Trento e Trieste. Along the side runs the lovely ramshackle arcade, known as the Merchants' Gallery or Loggia dei Mercia. To the left is the 10th century church of San Romano, with its clear Gothic additions to the facade. Inside San Romano has pre-Romanesque terracotta decor in the apse, and behind the church, a beautiful cloister.

The Castle

Castello Estense, the superbly solid and imposing castle, was built in the 14th century. Replete with all its intricate battlements, moat and drawbridge, it remains one of the best to visit in the region.

Giulio D'Este was 25 years old when he was imprisoned in its dungeons and only released at the age of 81. Some 40 years previously, his lover, former Duchess of Ferrara, Lucrezia Borgia, had passed away and her body encased in the Corpus Domini Monastery of the Clarisse nuns. The dungeons also housed Parisina, the subject of a poem by Lord Byron. The young wife of Nicolo III was caught in the act with the prince's son Ugo and the hedonists were both imprisoned before being beheaded.

We were at the Porto degli Angeli on the Corso Ercoli I D'Este, famous for the passage through of the departing Este family. The gate was then permanently closed to prevent their return. The Estense may have left behind a legacy of fine architecture and artistic works, but their brutal rule was not appreciated by their over-taxed, long suffering subjects.

The people welcomed the arrival of the cardinals of the Pope in 1598 but Ferrara, being a rich city surrounded by a fertile plain, was squeezed to supply Rome. In addition, the financially important 2,500 strong Jewish community virtually upped and left, depriving the city of much commerce.

FERRARA

CASTELLO ESTENSE

The Jewish Quarter

Off to the side of Via San Romano is Via Ragnio, a very old street where a 12th century house was discovered. More significantly, it marks the edge of the old Jewish ghetto. Between Via Ragnio and Via Della Vittoria on San Romano is a house with bricked up windows, having been Jewish owned, with its windows facing onto a Catholic Street. The narrow street of Via Della Vittoria was one of the ghetto's two most important streets. The cobbled street of river pebbles gently inclines from the river bank, and we could hear the rattle of a bicycle freewheeling down towards the city centre.

Number 41 was destroyed by the fascists during the Second World War, and number 39 was a house for the Jewish destitute. Via Vignia Latta, another ghetto street, contains at number 69, one of the ghetto's most ancient and interesting houses. In fact, owned by the Jewish community, it is now a set of apartments surrounding a courtyard protected from the street by huge wooden gates.

The wooden balustrades and balconies are all original 14th century, and old Jewish ghetto families are in residence as tenants. The residents were welcoming but visits are only possible with an introduction from a tour guide.

Ferrara's Jewish community was once the most influential in Emilia Romagna. Jewish presence in the region was recorded as early as 1200 A.D and reached its height in the 15th and 16th centuries when Jewish communities existed in many towns.

The statutes of Lugo in Ravenna province drawn up by a 13th century Archbishop of Ravenna declare a "penalty for a Jew who leaves his house in Holy Week: fine of 10 lire."

The period when the community reached its most influential coincided with the rule of the Estense dynasty over the area of Emilia. The Estense's coveted the Jewish community which, like the Estense, was threatened by the Popes. While the Popes attacked the Jewish people, the Estense welcomed Jewish exiles from around the world. Many of the exiles able to get to Emilia brought their wealth and talents to the region. Ferrara's community was able to support at least ten synagogues, catering for the different needs of the Ashkenazi, Sephardim and Italian Jews.

Around Emilia one can find examples of Jewish ghettos created at the behest of the Estense, and situated almost adjacent to the Estense castles.

FERRARA

In contrast, where the cardinals took control in the region, Papal dictats drove many Jews out of their homes and cities, or corralled them into walled ghettos. The Jews who were in these ghettos were subject to substantial humiliation and repression. Houses were forbidden from having windows looking out into the rest of the city.

In 1598 when the Estense family left Ferrara, many of the city's Jewish families, fearing Papal reprisals, fled their homes and synagogues. They moved with the Estense into the remaining territory of Emilia, forming new ghettos in towns such as Finale Emilia.

Save for two brief periods, during Napoleon's reign and the 1848 revolution, the Jews who stayed in Ferrara were interned here from 1627 until 1859. The Ducal Chapel in the Palazzo Comunale was a symbol of their repression. Each Sunday, all those in the ghetto were rounded, up and herded to the chapel for indoctrination in the Christian faith. As they walked through the main square they were subjected to the abuse of the crowds

During Mussolini's reign, many Jews were persecuted under the barbaric racial laws, most notably during the war when they were rounded up and sent to the concentration camps.

It is a story eloquently told in the writings of ghetto teacher Gorgio Bassani, the author of The Garden of Fitzi-Contini and The Long Night of '43, both of which were made into celebrated films. Today the city still has a small Jewish community, some of who still live in the old ghetto beside the Via San Romano. The remaining synagogue at 95, Via Mazzini is one of the oldest in Italy.

Tour groups in Ferrara can arrange itineraries for those who wish to delve further into this community's fascinating history.

THE RENAISSANCE DISTRICT
Addizione Ercoli.

Viale Cavour, which becomes the Corso Giovecca, cuts across the north side of the city, and is the boundary between the Renaissance district to the north and the mediaeval area situated to the south. The Estense Castle on the Corso Giovecca denotes the limit to the old mediaeval city. The Renaissance district began to be constructed at the end of the 15th century.

The Estense Duke, Ercoli I, ordered the creation of the northern area. For the prestige of the family, he wished to create a new aspect to the city, which, in its mediaeval area, was quite dark and dingy with very narrow streets. The Estense's rule was also threatened by the Venetians to the north, who coveted the family's control of the salt trade. The city needed additional protection. So rather than construct in the old quarters, he ordered the creation of a new district, the Addizione Ercoli. At that time it was believed to have turned Ferrara into Europe's most modern city, and heralded a new phase of town planning.

The Addizione Ercoli was begun in 1493 and based on two axes, the Corso Ercoli I, after the Duke who ordered the construction, and the Corso Rossetti, after the architect responsible for its design. All the most important buildings of the period lie along the Corso Ercoli I, along which were planted black poplars (black being a reference to the bark of a type of poplar common to Ferrara). Here the Estense and their courtiers were housed.

On the right hand side by the Viale Certoso we found two classic Renaissance buildings, now part of the university. Typical of the buildings of the period are the decorative columns on each corner with putti and capitals.

On the left between Via Guarini and Corso Porta Mare is the Parco Massari a large park laid out in the 18th century. The park featured in the film of *The Garden of Fitzi-Contini*, as did the Diamond Palace, the Corso Ercole I, and the small red brick building in Greek classical style, known as the Coffee House which is the only one left of seven gates into the park.

The pretty park, which is open to the public, has trees planted in the 1700s, and exotic plants. However, fans of the film will not find the Palace of Fitzi-Contini in the park. The palace portrayed in the film as being in the gardens is actually situated close to Milan.

We strolled on to the centre of the district at the junction between the two axes, Corso Ercole I and Corso Rossetti. Here we could see how Rossetti's plans combined the use of designs based on the traditional Ferrara buildings with new Renaissance styles.

The Diamond Palace

Studded with diamond shaped stones, Palazzo dei Diamanti on the corner of Corso Rossetti and Corso Ercole I is one of Ferrara's finest buildings. The large palace, with its exquisite decorations, was designed in 1493 by Rossetti for Sigismondo, brother to the Este duke, Ercole I.

The diamond shaped stones are more typical of Florence. The remarkable design has the facade built with three levels. The highest tier of stones has their points directed upwards. The central tiers of stones point horizontally and the lowest tier point towards the earth. The effect created is an optical illusion, making the palace look taller than it is.

One morning we arrived to find the building's reflection of the sun's rays playing such tricks, that it was as if the diamond studs had been flattened. On close inspection, we noticed that the point of one of the lower stones was damaged. This is believed to have been caused by someone investigating the legend that one of the stones has a real diamond hidden in it.

The building houses a **National Museum**, which holds exhibitions and has a permanent collection of paintings dating back to the 13th century. Its courtyard has all the classic Renaissance style portraying harmony, balance, and nature in its design. Similar to a monastery cloister it was a place for the muse and the scholar.

The Palazzo Massari has a collection of modern and 19th century paintings including, De Pisis and Giovanni Baldini from Ferrara and the Futurists.

The Palio

The Palio is the famous annual horse race. Not so well known as that of Sienna in Tuscany, it dates back to the 13th century, and is the oldest Palio in Italy if not in Europe. Dedicated to Ferrara's patron saint, St. George, it takes place on the last Sunday in May.

The Palio involves four races, the Pucci, the Pute, the She Ass, and the Horse race.

The three weeks proceeding the Palio involve celebrations and preparations. Flag-waving games and competitions take place the day before the Palio, the trial for the horses taking place in the afternoon. Each quarter of the city has a team, sending one representative in each race. Due to its dangerous nature, the horse race is normally run by professional riders.

On the day of the Palio, a procession takes place from the castle, in which the nobility at the court is represented as appearing on the streets. The court and the representatives of the city districts appear in costumes based on mediaeval styles, carrying their banners and symbols. They proceed along the Corso Ercoli Primo from the castle to the Diamond Palace, before turning right towards Ariosto Square where the games are officially opened.

FERRARA

EATING OUT

A good restaurant is *Fantastic Thursdays*. The *Il Cupo*, serves traditional food costing L25,000 a full meal, or single menu items. The best way is the Italian way - share the meal between two or three and the price comes down to about L20,000 including wine. The *Three Steps* is another good restaurant, on the south side just over the canal.

Cheapest are the pizza places such as *Orsucci* (closed Wed) at 76 Via Garibaldi, *Guiseppe* (closed Tues) at 71 Via Carlo Mayr and the paninoteca, *Al Pastiglione* (closed Sun) at 4,Vicolo del Teatro, which sells a variety of sandwiches and beers.

In the middle range are *Trattoria da Noemi* (closed Tues) at 31, Via Ragno and *Osteria degli Angeli* (closed Mon) at 4, Via delle Volte. For a splurge *Provvidenza* at 92 Corso D'Este is a safe bet in comfortable surroundings.

Local Specialities

Cappellacci della Zucca – like a big sweet and salty tortelloni filled with parmesan and pumpkins, served with a tomato (a la pomodoro) or meat tomato (a ragu) or with butter (buro e salvia).

Salamina de Sugo – a 14th century large pork sausage produced with 8 kilos of tongue and offal, minced with salt, spices, and a red wine, Bosco Ericheo. After two hours the meat is stuffed into the skin of the pig's penis, before being hung for up to a year. After being soaked for a night and washed in water, it is placed in an oven for five hours. It is then removed, placed in a bag, and boiled in water, during which time the salamina must not touch the edge of the casserole or it will explode. Cooked again, it is then ready to be served with a puree of potatoes.

Nights Out

Ferrara has a *theatre of music,* with excellent concerts including performances twice a year under the guidance of the director of the Chamber Orchestra of Europe and the Berlin Philharmonic, Claudio Abbado

Ferrara *night clubs* are on the outskirts of the city. *Arrenche* is a pub with live jazz music in the centre. The *Pelodoccha* is a fun bar, with music, and dancing, and the occasional film or live performance. Located a kilometer from the centre is the *Quo Vadis* disco, with *Sinatra* 10km away and *Adelaide* 12km away. The *Giardini Sonore* is a special place, with music evenings and small festivals, exhibitions and bar.

The Brindisi is an *enoteca* where one can drink wine. It is the oldest enoteca in Ferrara, and one can taste various wines and eat prosciutto. It is frequented by artists and students, as are the pavement cafes in the square by the cathedral. They close at 11pm and the square is a very pleasant, relaxed spot for an evening's drinking.

Discos open at 10pm, but locals often don't arrive till 1am, with closing time at 3pm. For later night dancing one has to go to Rimini. Special cheap buses are available to take clubbers to and from the local discos and even to Rimini.

ACCOMMODATION
(area code 0532)

Hotels
*****The plush, elegant, **Duchessa Isabella** (tel 202121 fax 202638) on Via Palestro and close to the centre is a must for those who wish to be pampered in luxurious surroundings. This 16th century mansion still has many original doors and frescoes. Nothing is spared for service and luxury so much so that the owners have a horse-drawn landau available to take gusts around the city. Stays cost £120/180 per night.

**** Four star hotels include the **Annunziata** (tel 201111 fax 203233) at 5 Piazza Republica, **Astra** (tel 206088 fax 247002) at 55, Viale Cavour, **Jolly H. de la Ville** (tel 772635 fax 772645) at 11 P. le Stazione and **Ripagrande** (tel 765250 fax 764377) at 21 Via Ripagrande.

***Of the three star hotels, **Hotel Europa** (tel 205456 fax 212120) on Corso Giovecca is a special stay. The second owner of the hotel, Count Bottoni, helped finance Napoleon's invasion of Italy. As a mark of thanks for the Count's assistance, the Emperor sent Bottoni a painting of himself and his wife, Josephine. The picture still adorns the special suite, which also contains fine period furniture and stucco decorations. For £50/80 a night it is not a bad luxury stay.

Also of note is **Locanda della Duchessa** (tel 206981 fax 202638) in Vicolo del Voltino, which is almost as luxurious as its parent hotel, the Duchessa Isabella.

Others in this range include the **Carlton** (tel 211130 fax 205766) at 93, Via Garibaldi and **Nettuno** (tel 977155 fax 977154) in Via Pigna, Nord Ovest (tel 52083 fax 773145) at 52 Viale Po and Touring (tel 206200 fax 212000) at 11 Viale Cavour.

Hotels in the two star range costing around £35 a night include the **Impero (tel/fax 63717) at 117, Via Ravenna, **Nazionale** (tel/fax 209604) at 33, Carso Porta Reno, **San Paulo** (tel/fax 762040) at 9, Via Baluardi and **Santo Stefano** (tel 206924 fax 210261) at 21 Via Santo Stefano).

*Cheapest of the hotels in this range is the £15 a night **Tre Stelle** (tel 209748) at 15 Via Vegni, followed by the £25 a night **Casa degli Artisti** (tel 761038) at 66 Via Vittoria.

For budget travellers there's also **Ca' Spinazzino** (tel 725035 fax 722171) outside the city in Spinazzino, which is a £15 a night **agriturismo** with accommodation The closest **camp site** to Ferrara is the **Campeggio Estensi** (tel 752396) on Via Gramicia costing £2/3 per night per adult with children under eight free.

Sports
Golf, **cycling** and **swimming** pool facilities are available just outside the northern city walls in the Addizione Verde, a designated green recreational area. **Fishing** is common in the canals to the north. **Cus Ferrara Golf Club** (0532 750396) is just outside the city walls at 41, Via Gramsci. The nine hole par 33 course is narrow and bunkered.

i Ferrara's Tourist Information Office is in the Castello Estense (tel 209370 fax 212266).

Shops close in Ferrara at 7.30pm in winter and 8.00am in summer.

FERRARA

THE PO DELTA PARK

The Delta Park was established as a protected area in 1988. It has six centres, including Comacchio, the salt lake area of Cervia, Mesola and Goro with a forest dating back to the Mediaeval era, and a unique species of tiny deer. Stretching from the Venetian boundary to Cervia south of Ravenna and inland to Argenta, it is an area of beautiful marshland, lakes, salt flats, woodland, sand dunes, and beaches, almost unequalled in Italy. Whether in the summer haze or the autumn mist it is a perfect compliment to a visit to Ferrara city, and a must for lovers of simple nature.

ON THE ROAD TO COMACCHIO

F E R R A R A

En route to Comacchio we travelled straight down the Via Rossonia. It was built under the fascists to get to their town of Tresigallo. Flanked by Poplar trees it nevertheless offers a wind break, a pleasant shade from the sun, and an equally pleasant insertion into the flattened landscape of orchards and corn fields. Tresigallo was built under fascist instruction in the thirties with houses quite similar, observed Muriel, to those built for German troops in Calais.

The fields along the road are planted with every manner of fruit, including apples (for which Ferrara was said to be the capital), peaches, nectarines, apricots, pears, and melons. In addition, soya, pumpkin (for the local speciality of capallachi della zucca), carrots, asparagus, flowers, and a smattering of small copses give character to the plain.

Just beyond Tresigallo, north of the Ferrara-Comacchio A13 autostrada, are the towns of Migliarino, Migliaro, Massa Fasciglia, Codigoro and, further south, Ostellato. Turning northeast along the banks of the Po di Volano, the first town is

Migliarino, once a part of Migliaro. It grew in importance to the point where the local worthies moved the administration of the district to Migliarino. The area is most noted for its fine 19th century villas and the 17th century Villa Forti, near to which is its seven storeyed Torre Pavanelli.

Further downriver is **Migliaro**, a much fought over town in the 13th century. Believed to have been set up by a revolt of 1,000 soldier-farmers from Massa Fiscaglia, its citizens were notorious for their rebellions against the Estense. The site called *catena* on Via Estense is said to be where the Estense had their delizia. The catena or chain was used to block off the street. The villa's cellars are said to have contained the infamous *pozzo rasoi* wells, crossed with sharp blades, into which the Estense would toss their enemies.

The oldest building in the town is the 16th century Renaissance Palazzo Rosso on Via Ariosto, which was once the magistrate's court. Also of note is the church with a canvas by Guercino and its stumpy bell tower, which, before its spire was added, was once a lighthouse for guiding fisherman through the Po fog.

Past Massa Fiscaglia one reaches **Codigoro**, also on the Po di Volano, and once part of the domain of the Pomposa abbots. From the 11th century the abbots ruled the town. Their headquarters was the Palazzo del Vescovo in the centre. Known as the Domus Dominicata, it has lost its original form but the 17th century restoration is a fine example of the Venetian-Chioggia style.

In 1981, a nesting site for heron was discovered nearby in the reserve now known as **Garzaia**. Today over 700 nests for night heron, squacco heron, red and blue heron, as well as little and large egrets, have been spotted on site. Codigoro alternates with Comacchio in staging the annual **Ballo e Bello Ballet Festival**. It also has rich cuisine based on the local wildlife of eels, frogs, pheasant and coot.

About 30km from Comacchio we passed **Flanagan's Irish Pub** which I noted down in case I ever wanted a pint. We were late to pick up the boat which would take us around the lake and its marshland.

Comacchio was a collection of 13 islands. The town has only been connected to the inland since the 19th century. In the late 1900s, vast amounts of the surrounding marshland was drained and reclaimed. Today, two thirds of Ferrara province is below sea level, and many of the roads are notably raised above the level of the surrounding fields.

As we approached Comacchio lake there were plenty of the Chinese fishing nets known as *bilancioni* on the river. Mullets and shrimps are the common catch.

Around 70 years ago, archaeologists discovered the ancient Etruscan and Greek settlement of **Spina** 4km from Comacchio town. A city and its harbour were found under the water. Two necropolises were initially discovered in Valle Trebba and Valle Pegga.

FERRARA

Around 4,000 tombs were found inside, containing a large collection of ceramic objects. Many of the tiles were Greek or Attican in origin, and scientists initially concluded that the city was Greek. But Etruscan objects later found indicated that Spina was probably an outpost trading station and port for Bologna. It appears that Spina became an important trading centre for northeast Italy, and attracted many Greek merchants and sailors.

In the 4th century Greek symposium, the Greeks would have festivals of eating and drinking while lying on divans. There is evidence that the Etruscans feasted in this way and took up many other Greek customs. Work is still going on so visits are not possible but some of the find can be seen in Ferrara's archaeological museum, San Ludovico il Moro.

We arrived by the lakeside at **Bettolino di Foce** (tel 0337 592051), a wonderful restaurant specialising in local eel and fish dishes. Eel comes in every form - eel risotto, eel marinated in salt and vinegar, smoked and grilled eel and eel stuffed in a cabbage, a local end of year favourite that has to be ordered in advance.

COMACCHIO BASIN

In the past Comacchio, was divided into four quarters, and each had a main fishing station, as well as many smaller stations. Watchtowers would be used to control the region particularly during the night when poachers would arrive.

As we sat on a tour boat passing across the lagoon, a common heron flew by with its grey wings. We also saw the small white egrets, spoonbills, and other types of heron. Throughout the year, up to 400 species are known to nest in the park. Our guide said that protection has attracted birds which never previously visited the area, such as the slender headed gull, which used to nest in the Camargue in France.

Eels born at sea arrive in the lagoons as small fish, and develop in a protected environment of warm and salty water. After five years the eels return to the sea

Comacchio
1. Bosco della Fasanara
2. Bosco della Mesola
3. Casone Cannevie
4. Valle Bertuzzi
5. Lido della Nazioni

to reproduce, leaving the lagoon and heading for the Sargasso Sea. The eels are drawn through several triangles (lavoriero) which through an ingenious method, trap the smallest eels first and finally the largest. Other fish such as bass and silverside are also caught.

The lavoriero are based at the fishing stations around the Comacchio Basin. Occasionally one of the seven watchtowers comes into view. This is eel country and 100 fishing stations existed here at the height of eel fishing in the last century. Now only seven stations survive, the old stations having been turned into museums.

Comacchio is now an official conservation area, but the reliance of the people on the fishing industry has long required them to secure a balance with natural rhythms, allowing fish stocks to replenish. The well-organised, municipally controlled system allowed for this level of planning.

Traditionally the eel season runs from March to the beginning of May, and continues from September through to December. The atmosphere was very damp and the fishermen would only spend two to six weeks on station. At the station we could see their tiny beds made of reeds. Rats were a big problem so the ingenious fishermen hung their baskets of food from upturned bottles attached to the ceiling. Whenever the rats tried to reach the food by climbing down the bottles they would slip to the floor.

A common local dish is *a becco d'asino*, which literally translated, means a donkey's snout. However, this is a local expression meaning to make do with whatever is available, which usually means eel soup, which is made by cooking an eel with browned onions, salt, pepper, a little vinegar, lemon rind and some tomatoes.

FERRARA

Boats are available to pass though the marshes, which, with large stocks of fish, are a birdwatcher's paradise. Nesters include avocets, pratincoles, black winged stilts, and shovelers, gadwalls, great scaup ducks, coots, pochards and the sheldrake. Other birds which find there way to the marshes include ibis, spoonbills, marsh harriers and small grebe.

The best times to watch the birds are during the nesting times in April and September. In September we found the sight quite charming, as the sun set on the waters and the birds took to the air for their evening meal.

Arriving in **Comacchio town** was easy but finding a parking place near the centre was less so. The guide assured us that to see the town properly required a lot of walking. Some of this could be avoided by hiring a cart or a small boat.

Comacchio town has a former cathedral, which appears to date back to the 8th century, though local archives record the town as having existed since the 6th century. In 1981 a 1st century B.C Roman vessel loaded with cargo was discovered in the area, and a 5th century burial ground was found, indicating that Comacchio was probably a village prior to the 6th century.

Originally the town was based on 13 islands criss-crossed by canals and bridges. Contact with the rest of the world was only possible by boat. Many of the reputed 40km of canals have now been turned into roads, but there are enough left for the town to be known as "Little Venice".

Many of the pretty white washed buildings in the town date back to the 17th century when the Papal cardinals tried to display their renewed authority by demolishing many houses and rebuilding the town. The town has many monasteries. Our guide took us to the 17th century Capuchin sanctuary of Santa Maria.

We wandered through the cobbled streets and found some 'androne' small archways that lead into a walled courtyard of houses – villages within the village. The centuries-old complexes, each with a name, are quite unique, with their long corridors leading through the house to a patio, a vegetable garden and a small boathouse.

And what a place to shop the busy little town is. **Market day** is Wednesday and the stalls were full of fresh fish, lobster, mussels and calamari, all furnished by the coastal waters and swampland.

The canals are connected through to Porto Garibaldi to the east. A new canal was built in the 17th century to the port, allowing more sea water to enter the town's canals and increasing the level of hygiene.

FERRARA

We stood on the 17th century **Trepponti,** a bridge, or three bridges, where three canals meet. The bridge was a gate into the town, and two watch towers, added later in the century, still stand. Below, special flat boats called *batanna*, also known as *Comacchina*, were moored. Free excursions are available from in front of the fish market, which can be seen from the top of Trepponti. The fish market is as old as the bridge. Each morning locals arrive to buy freshly caught fish. A photographic exhibition in one of the shops gives an excellent indication of what life was like in the town.

And just further on is **Ponte degli Sbirri,** Policeman's Bridge, built in 1631 and designed by Luca Danesi, who was also responsible for building Trepponti. It leads, not surprisingly to the prison, which was the accommodation mainly used to incarcerate poachers. When we were there it was being converted into a museum to house a Roman boat dating back to Augustus Caesar's rule.

Suddenly, we were interrupted by a cheerful train of well wishers and a photographer following a couple in their wedding apparel. As is tradition, they were displaying the beauty of the future bride's dress to the townsfolk, before getting married the following day.

Next to the old prison is the 19th century **Palazzo Bellini**, whose facade displays some fantastic masks. Now the library, it also houses an art exhibition, and possesses grounds at the rear which are used for a **jazz festival** (July 11th to 16th), exhibitions and concerts.

Back in the centre of the town the **Felice Cavolotte** civic tower, built in 1826, was built after the 14th century tower was blown down in a gale. The tower was built for the municipality. To the left on Via Mazzini is the **Loggia Del Grano**, which from the early 17th century was used as a grain warehouse.

Further on is the main church, which dates back to the 17th century. The **San Cassiano** was a cathedral till the bishopric was united with Ferrara. Its grandiosity compared to the rest of the town was intended by the cardinals to symbolise the power of the Papacy. The tower is a later edition as the original larger 48 metre high tower also fell down.

An interesting feature is the monumental altar, carved out of a huge marble block discovered by the clerics. San Cassiano was a bishop who was murdered by his students. The bulbous basis of the church tower is said to be caused by the necessity of placing San Cassiano's relics inside it. August 11th/13th sees the **Feast of San Cassiano**, celebrated with traditional races of the batanna boats.

Pomposa

We took the Venice road north to the Abbe Pomposa and into Ferrara province, clinging to the coastal flats. Initially, the tree-lined road passed through a very pretty area of woodland, streams and rivers. We passed by a restaurant called the Ca Del Pino which, set in the woods, looked like a pleasant place to stop off on a long trip. The Abbey is just off the main SS309 road, sometimes called the Romea Road. We watched out for a small signpost but the tall tower of the Abbey was easily visible from the road.

Pomposa was once an island between two branches of the River Po, the Po di Goro and the Po di Volano. An abbey was situated on the island as early as the 7th century. But the current abbey was built in the 11th century. This was the golden age of the abbey, when a famous abbot called San Guido was based here. A hundred Benedictine monks lived in the abbey, and with the abbot being both the religious and civil power on the island, the abbey became an important economic and social centre. Justice was administered from the Palazzo della Ragione which stands to the side of the building.

With their motto, 'to work and pray all the day', the Benedictines were very hard workers. They drained, reclaimed and cultivated the surrounding marshland, building canals and sluice gates. The monks also spent much time copying out by hand the most important books of the time. Unfortunately, most of what became a very famous and significant library has now been lost.

The atrium, and the tall, typically leaning, bell tower of the abbey are 11th century. The tower, built 50 years after the atrium in 1063, was clearly constructed using a great deal of material recycled from other buildings. The atrium had a particular use. At the time it was built people who had not been baptised could not enter a Catholic church and listen to the mass. The atrium, the type of which there are few left in Italy, was effectively a covered lodge from where the unbaptised could hear the services.

The Romanesque style is shown by the many symbols on the wall such as the peacock for infinity, the eagle and the lion. The overall effect was to create a highly decorated, fascinating facade such as one rarely finds in the rest of the region.

The interior was refurbished in the 14th century when much of the island was reclaimed by water and the abbey went into decline. Enter the church and turn left to face the front and you will see fascinating frescoes on the wall with terrifying scenes of life in hell.

The first church had seven bays and two more were added before the atrium was built. The church has a high ceiling and heavy decoration on the walls but nevertheless is quite simple in appearance. The central floor is covered with mosaics, the oldest being that nearest the altar dating back to the 6th century. It was probably taken from a church in Ravenna.

To the right of the church are the serene remains of a cloister, overlooking which is the monks' 14th century dormitory. The chapter has some beautiful early 14th century monochrome frescoes and a Giotto inspired fresco of the crucifixion. The mullion windows are painted in pink and blue. The chapter was so-called because its function was to allow the monks to read a chapter of a particular book. Later on this chapter became a counsel room, making the most important decisions regarding the monastery including choosing the next abbot.

Besides the abbey is a restaurant, a pizzeria and bar, and just further along the road north we later stopped by the roadside at fruit stalls sporting all manner of exotica; huge pumpkins, gourds and melons. Indeed, the area has its own annual **Festival of the Melon** on July 21st. Another local speciality is the white wine, **Uva d'Oro** from the grape of the same name. The grape was introduced from France by Renata di Franca, sister of the French Louis XII and wife of Estense Duke Ercole II.

Close to the abbey in the sand dunes and pinewoods are the villas and chalets of the seaside resort, **Lido di Pomposa**.

The Ferrara Riviera

From Goro on the Venetian frontier to Spina, a string of resorts bordered by the SS309 Via Romea, spread out along 25km of coastland. They offer relatively cheap accommodation for taking in the beaches, the marshlands and the historic town centres.

Lido delle Nazione has a large artificial lake, which attracts plenty of migrant birds including blue heron, tufted duck, merganser and great crested grebe. Other visitors are holidaymakers enjoying the canoeing, sailing, rowing, and the nearby beach and discos. It is known for the free range breeding of black bulls and splendid white Camargue Delta horses in the wilds of Spiaggia Rome. Plenty of stables offer **horse riding** trips.

To the south, **Porto Garibaldi** is a fishing harbour, and has boats available for hire to go night fishing at sea, deep sea mackerel fishing, or a trip through the marshes. In the morning, rise early for the **Mercato del Pesce**, fish market to collect your tuna, or take a boat at the Marina degli Estensi, a modern harbour with moorings for 300 boats.

Otherwise a good day to visit the pier is August 14th when tables and chairs are laid out and fried fish, bread, fruit, and bosco wine are handed out to visitors during the town's **Hospitality Fest**. Bands play along the entire waterfront and the night culminates in a spectacular firework display.

With broad shallow beaches, **Lido degli Estensi** and **Lido di Spina** are upmarket resorts, with attractive villas in the pine woods. The former has the fashionable shopping street, Carducci Avenue and the latter, the splendid **Remo Brindisi Contemporary Art Museum.** Built in 1973, the museum, which is open between May and September, was designed by Nanda Vigo and inspired by the Bauhaus movement. Inside are works of Picasso, Modigliani, Fontana, Dali, Chagall, De Chirico, Morandi, Guttuso and Brindisi.

Mesola and the Towns on the Venetian Border

From Pomposa we headed north on the SS309, Via Romea to the nearby town of **Mesola,** with its classic castle housing a library and an aquarium. The castle, on the right bank of the Po di Goro, was built in 1579 as a delizia for the Estense, and an advanced defensive position against the Venetians to the north. The central building has a large tower with battlements at each corner. It has been heavily renovated but what remains fascinating is the ancient circle of arcades, stables and courtiers' houses around the fortress, which now contain shops and market stalls.

The dukes used the vast tracks of land of the Bosso di Mesola behind the castle as their hunting ground. We wandered around the beautiful woodland and marsh area with its fishing lakes, oak, elm and ash trees, water rushes, weeping willow and roaming deer, skunks and weasels. South of Mesola we came across Torre dell'Abate. This tall watchtower over the marshes is also a splendidly intact 17th hydraulic plant, containing a cafeteria.

The wide **Volano** beach and its resort are in a picturesque part of the coast bordered by a large pine forest and marshland. We visited the superbly tranquil marshland nature reserve of Valle Bertuzzi on the Po di Volano seeing all manner of birds including a gold-red pheasant with its white neck. Here, grey mullet and eels hide in the shallow waters as heron stalk, and reed warblers and bittern flit through the air.

We dined at **Cannevie** (tel 719103 fax 719108), the old fishing station and 16th century Porticino fishing house near Volano, an excellent simple fish restaurant on the marsh. Here eel starters were available for L14,000. Meals would cost L70,000 with anti-pasta, pastas, fish, eel cooked inside a cabbage, and a sweet, followed by ciambella, the cake which is dipped in one's wine glass, and more spirits to settle the stomach.

Further west and upriver of the Po, di Goro are the towns of Berra, Copparo, Bondeno and Stellata. Close to the Po, these towns were historically subject to devastating floods and brutal wars between the Ferrarese and the Venetians fighting for control of the river.

Typically the area around **Berra** changed hands between the Venetians and Ferrarese. Most of the area was only reclaimed after Italy's unification, much remaining as marshland, ponds and woodland. Between the Polesalla and Ariano-Corbala bridges is the remaining **ferry station**, still taking people across the Po to Villanova Marchesana in Venezia.

Around Cologna there are the remains of some of the ancient *golenanti* river dwellers' houses, which would often be immersed in the floods. East of Berra by the Po, **La Porta della Delta** is an old golenanti settlement, which has been restored and converted into a resort, with restaurants, campsites, sports facilities, and boating.

FERRARA

EATING OUT

En route to Comacchio there are a few **agriturismo** around **Ostellato**. These include the **Novara** (which has accommodation, bookings tel 651097) at 61 Via Ferrara in Dogato and, in Ostellato, *Tassone* at 24a Via Mezzano, **Valli di Ostellato** at 1 Via Argine Mezzano and **Belfiore** (for accommodation tel 681164 fax 681172) at 27 Via Pioppa.

The coastal area has some excellent places serving fish and eel dishes, including *Bettolino il Foce* and **Cannavie**. **Comacchio** itself has plenty of trattoria serving traditional fish and meat dishes.

ACCOMMODATION
(area code 0533)

The only hotels in **Comacchio** itself are the one star *La Pace* (tel 81285) at 21 Via Fogli and *Trepponti* (tel 312766) at 3,Via Marconi both costing £20/25 a night.

****Those who wish for four star stays nearby can go to the £35 a night **Alfieri** (tel 380162 fax 380165) at **Lido del Scacchi** or the £50 a night **Delle Nazione** (tel 379276 fax 399195) in Lido delle Nazione.

The beach resorts have plenty of two and three star hotels at £25/50 per night. For the cheapest hotels there are a few in the 1 star category at £15/20 per night including **Ariston** (tel 327483 fax 327241) and *Canoa* (tel 327876) in Lido di Porto Garibaldi.

Cheaper accommodation is available in an **agriturismo** with accommodation for £13/15 per night at *Quieto Vivere* (tel 33359), 96, Viale Raffaello in **Lido di Spina** and *Ca' Laura* (tel 794372) at 70, Via Cristina in **Bosco Mesola.**

Camp sites include:
Lido di Spina: *Camping Spina*, 99, Via del Campeggio (tel 330179 fax 333566) and

International Camping Mare e Pineta, 67 Via Acacie (tel 330194 fax 330052)

Lido degli Scacchi: *Campeggio Ancora* 25, Via Republiche Marinare (tel 381276 fax 381445) and *Camping*

Florenz, 199, Via Alpi Centrali (tel 511448 fax 380428)

Lido di Pomposa: *Campeggio Vigna Sul Mar*, 20 Via Capanno Garibaldi (tel 380216 fax 325620)

i **ComacchioTourist Information Office** (tel 310147 fax 310148) is at 12 Via Buonafede (e-mail: **informazioni@comune.comacchio.fe.it**).

Guided tours of Comacchio Lagoon are offered by CASVDC (tel 81159 fax 313053) at 200 Via Mazzini, Comacchio.

SOUTH OF FERRARA

Just between the autostrada and SS16 are the small towns of **Voghiera** and its satellite, **Voghenza**, which lie 5km south of the Gualdo exit from A13. Prior to the 9th century, **Voghiera** on the Sandalo river was an administrative centre for the whole of the province. Both the Etruscans and Romans used the town as a capital. A necropolis, with 67 sepulchres containing perfume bottles, glass bottles, ceramics and other artefacts in gold, onyx, amber and bone, were found two kilometres away in **Voghenza**. Many of the items are on display in the Belriguardo Antiquarium.

Sacked by the Lombards, Voghiera only returned to prominence in the 1400s for the amusement of the Estense. Just outside the town is the beautiful, and first of the Estense delizia. Duke Nicolo III built Castello di Belriguardo in 1435. A canal was dug in the long dry Sandalo river bed, and entered the castle's mile long moat so the duke could arrive by boat.

The sumptuous battlemented castle with crenellated walls, painted towers, two loggias, stables and servants' premises, had 50 frescoed rooms. It is open by appointment. Its park hosts the July/August **Estate e Belriguardo Festival of Theatre** and concerts.

The town's 12th century church of Nativita di Maria Vergine has an interesting fresco over the vault of the apse. The Virgin Mary looks down from the centre and beneath her feet, in Latin, is inscribed, *"ipsa conteret caput tuum."* – she will trample your head. Nice.

South on SS495 we were back on SS16, and passed through **Argenta**, an industrial town 30km from Ferrara, whose architectural history was largely obliterated by wartime bombing. At the south end of the town is a classic red clay church, San Giorgio. Built in 569 A.D, it has a splendid marble portal by Modigliana, with the cycle of the seasons and inside a Byzantine altar and a mosaic floor.

Across the river Reno, set in the marshlands of the Delta Park, is **Campotto Oasis,** which houses the park's Natural History Information Centre at Campotto Casino. Water lilies, reeds, cattail and flowering rushes in the Oasis marshlands offer a special attraction to certain birds including purple and blue heron, osprey, sparrow hawk, buzzards, harriers, coots, cormorants and several varieties of duck.

Cento

Along the SS255 west from Ferrara, on the left bank of the Reno river bordering Bologna and Modena is **Cento**. Cento is an important market town, with a lovely historic centre named after its famous son, the 17th century artist Francesco Barbieri - Guercino. Its elegant 16th and 17th century palaces include the town hall and the crenellated Palazzo del Governatore, built with its clock tower in 1502, bordering Piazza Guercino. The latter now contains **A. Bonzagni**, a gallery of contemporary art (open 8am –2pm, closed on Sundays).

Not surprisingly, several of Guercino's works are on display in the Pinacoteca Art Gallery in Via Matteoti (open weekdays 9.30am – 12pm). Four of his pieces can also be found in the second chapel on the left of Il Rosario church. More of his work is on show in the attractive Baroque church of San Biaggio, along with wooden choir stalls carved by Vincenzo Rossi in 1743.

The artist cannot avoid being part of a visitor's itinerary, and the Corso Guercino is where you'll find the mediaeval streets and well preserved wooden props which hold up the arcades of Casa Pannini and other buildings.

Cento Golf Club (051 6830504) is at 4 Via dei Tigli with a nine hole all par 3, course with double starts allowing for an 18 hole round.

FERRARA

ACCOMMODATION
(area code 0532)
Argenta

****Villa Reale** (tel 852334 fax 852353) 16a Viale Roiti

***Centrale** (tel 852694 fax 852235) 1d Via G Bianchi

Cento

****Al Castello** (tel 6836053 fax 6835990) 57, Via Giovannina

*** Al Castello Dip** (tel 6836066 fax 6835990) 57, Via Giovannina

***Europa** (tel 903319 fax 902213) 16 Via IV Novembre

* Sole** (tel 904546) 28 Via Donati

Ferrara
terra e acqua

Ferrara is a city of culture, noted for its gastronomy and its surroundings that include the Po Delta and the wide beaches of the Commachio area.

Ferrara is a welcoming place, all year round. This spring, Ferrara's cultural season begins at the Diamond Palace with an exclusive world exhibition of the art and ceramics of Picasso, featuring pieces especially loaned to the exhibition by the artist's grandson. (The exhibition takes place from 20th February to 21st May (for information, telephone Ferrara tourist office on 0039 0532 299303). As well as the masterpieces of Picasso, one can admire the colours of the herons, shelduck, kingfishers and deer that live among the tamarisks, reeds, pines and sand dunes of the Po Delta Park. The Po Delta is the largest area of wetlands in Italy. In this area tourism, nature protection, agricultural activity and education and respect for flora and fauna exist in harmony with each other.

One can also admire the colour of the gastronomy and produce of Ferrara. These include the salama da sugo (a typical local salami), various types of fish (amongst them, the Valle eel), topini (a dessert from Comacchio), sweet truffles, clams and vino di sabbia (a local wine).

There are also the colours of the province's monuments and buildings.

A suggested itinerary for the first time visitor is to take a walking tour within the recently restored city walls, exploring the Romanesque cathedral, the renaissance Estense castle and the medieval part of the city with its Jewish quarter. In the province of Ferrara, one can find the delightful Pomposa Abbey, a Romanesque construction which is one of the "must see" places on the Via dei Romei pilgrim route. One is also recommended to visit Comacchio; a city located on 13 islands, which is well known for its sixteenth century bridge "Trepponti". A Roman Ship Museum will open up in September.

One should also not miss the Estense attractions such as the Mesola castle, the Verginese and the city of Cento, which houses the world's largest collection of paintings by Guercino.

Ferrara, Renaissance city, and the Po Delta are recognised as *World Heritage sites* by UNESCO.

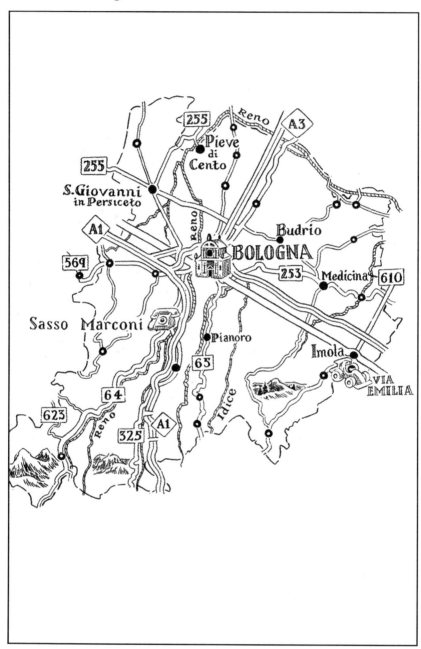

Bologna THE BEAUTIFUL

We picked up our rented car at Bologna airport. When we arrived at the town hall we were told that we were lucky the police had not stopped us. We had been driving around in a prohibited area for ten minutes. We had to get to know our road signs.

We were at the centre of a historic and beautiful city. It is one of Italy's finest and best preserved ancient city centres. Driving around in the busy traffic is tiresome and parking difficult but everywhere seems to be history – a network of old palaces, castles, churches, porticoes and arcades. During the 13th century, the town got the nickname, 'la Dotta, la Grassa, la Rossa' – the learned, the fat and the red – due to its notable university, cuisine and use of terracotta.

Nowadays the main antagonism is between the motor car and the historic centre but the story of Bologna is in its buildings – continuous development through the clash of antagonistic factions; the Bolognese and the Ravenna Byzantines, the Guelphs and the papal Ghibellines, Bologna and Rome, church and nobility, Bologna and Modena, communism and fascism.

The Shaping of Bologna

The city's origins date back to the Etruscans in the 6th century B.C when the town was known as Felsina. Firms in the city and the inhabitants are still today called Felsinians.

In the 3rd century B.C, the town was occupied by the Celts, sometimes known as Gauls. The Celts lived in Boii, as they renamed the town, alongside the Etruscans and absorbed much of their culture. Indeed, the particular accent of the Bolognese is on occasion attributed to their Gallic origin. The Celts are also believed to have introduced pig farming to the region now famous for its pork products.

The present name of Bologna originates from when the Romans renamed the city around 189 B.C after conquering the Celts and renaming the colony as Bononia. Their streets lie beneath the area around Ugo Bassi, Via Rizzoli and Via 4th Novembre. The walls of the ancient theatre can be found elegantly displayed in the Coin Shop where it was discovered.

Bologna centre's grid street layout and radial roads to the outskirts have their origin in the Roman era. Most notable of all is Via Emilia the Roman road which still links Rimini to Bologna and Piacenza. At the city's heart it is now Via Ugo Bassi, which formed part of the decumanus maximum. The Romans left behind the remarkable Setta aqueduct, which is still used to this

BOLOGNA

day. They also drained the surrounding area reclaiming it from the Adriatic swamp land and bringing great wealth to the city.

From between 200 A.D and 300 A.D Rome faced invasions from the north and for the first time in the 6th century, defensive circular walls were built in Bologna and can still be detected in aerial photos of the city.

Longobard rule came between the 8th and 11th centuries using Bologna as a frontier town in their wars with Ravenna's Byzantine rulers. The eleven watchtowers that adorn the centre's skyline were built by the noble families in the last decades of Longobard rule. The **towers** were symbols of the wealth and power of the families and 100 were erected between the 11th and 12th centuries.

The towers heralded the Middle Ages, Bologna's most important period. In 1088 Bologna established what is now Europe's oldest university based on the study of Roman law. Bologna became famous for its silk and pork production.

In 1249 the troops of the three Guelph comunes of Bologna defeated Emperor Frederick II at Fossalta near Modena. The Emperor's illegitimate son, **King Enzo** of Sardinia who lorded over the city, was captured. He was imprisoned in Bologna till his death 23 years later which was greeted with great festivity and celebrated by an annual festival for the next 500 years. Bologna's power so increased that it became one of Europe's ten most important cities and by 1274 the Emperor's camp had ceded their claim on Bologna to the Vatican.

During this time war and expansion of the city meant the creation of a 9km long second city wall which itself had to be replaced 80 years later when the town's 50,000 people had spilled out over the boundary. The main gates of the second wall can still be seen while a third wall can be followed.

Throughout the Middle Ages Bologna, shunning oligarchy, had a form of democratic rule, first of the craftsmen's guilds and then of the noble families. Amongst the noble families, the art-loving **Bentivoglio** family was *primus inter pares*. Nevertheless the nobility elected their leaders. This domination of relatively insignificant nobles devoid of vast wealth is reflected in the city, which rather than having one or two great palaces or monuments dotted about has an abundance of beautiful but comparatively modest buildings.

In 1506 rivals to the Bentivoglio came with Papal troops to Bologna ousting the Bentivoglio from the town and beginning Papal rule which lasted till the Risorgimento in 1859. From the Santo Stefano church complex outward, the church created 100 monasteries and another 100 ecclesiastical buildings to surround and control the city.

However the Pope's Pontifical Delegate ruled in tandem with the representative of the other 40 noble families thus maintaining stability and the municipal power of the nobility. The absence from the buildings of the Baroque style, which originated in Rome illustrates that despite Vatican concessions, the nobility remained antagonistic to their Papal rulers.

Bologna also retained an ambassador at Rome. Ironically he was called the Mortadella Ambassador after the locally produced salami.

After the French Revolution, Napoleon's troops arrived in triumph marching from Modena along the Via Emilia. Many churches suffered in the occupation being used as barracks or ransacked. But the people welcomed the troops, bringing the principles of liberty, equality and freedom to the city. Napoleon's rule turned the Bolognese to believing themselves as firmly anti-Papist Italians and laid the basis for future revolts against both the Pope and the Austrian Emperor.

The Bolognese then fought in three national wars of independence until in 1859, when they joined free Italy after a referendum. Papal rule was over. The city was last occupied by Hitler's armies which began in 1943 and ended on 21st May, 1944 with the entry of the partisans and the Allied troops. German troops may have damaged the people but most of the city's rich buildings remained intact. It was actually Allied planes which inflicted most damage with bombing raids doing severe damage to the Archiginnasio, the Anatomical Theatre and the area around the railway station.

Since then the city has prospered and grown to a population of 800,000. It is the region's most important city and also known as '**Red Bologna**' for its long standing tradition of electing communist local governments.

Communist rule has not prevented Bologna from being an important engineering and commercial centre. Perennially, hundreds of industrial exhibitions and 'fairs' take place on the edge of the city attracting people from around the globe. One consequence for holidaymakers is that hotel prices in the city are quite high and visitors would be advised to stay on the outskirts. On the other hand, being close to both Florence and Venice, the city's attractions are often overlooked making more pleasurable conditions for those who do go sightseeing. By the way, don't bother asking for spaghetti bolognese. As far as the Bolognese are concerned, there's no such thing.

Bologna

1. Tourist Information bureau (*i*)
2. City Theatre
3. National Art Gallery
4. Town Hall
5. Civil Archaeological Museum
6. Academy of Fine Art Collection
7. St Petronius Basilica

8. Botanical Gardens
9. Palace of the Podesta
10. Neptune Fountain
11. Hall of the Notaries
12. Archiginnasio
13. Guglielmo Marconi's Birthplace
14. Tombs of the Glossatori

15. Altabella Tower
16. Garisenda & Asinelli Towers
17. Isolani House
18. Santo Stefano Basilica
19. Torresotto Tower

The Town Hall

On another occasion in Bologna we took a bus along the Via Indipendenza. We had discovered that it was not advisable to take a car into the city centre because of parking problems. Built in the late nineteenth century, the Via is the only straight road you'll find in Bologna, having been built to carry people from the centre direct to the railway station. The buildings overlooking the street are characterised by huge great porticoes around 7 metres high.

The bus took us close to Piazza Maggiore to Bologna's imposing town hall. The Palazzo Comunale is one of the city's splendours. Built between the 13th and 15th century. It was a fortress for a century and thereafter a palace. Entering via the horses' staircase of small sloping steps was quite a treat.

Whether there are 61 or 62 steps to the first floor, we couldn't agree, even though we counted them twice stride by stride. Have the argument yourselves. When leaving skip down the elegant staircase and one can imagine the clatter of the horses as they rode out into the town.

The Pope's representatives occupied the palace from the 16th century till the mid-1800s while Bologna was under the Papal rule of the kingdom of Rome. As the Pontifical Delegate lived on the second floor, the horse steps were required to reach his home.

The Council Chamber

We entered the splendid council chamber where all major decisions for the town have been taken since the 15th century. Here the Bentivoglio had the council of the nobility. Later this would be the meeting place for the Papal delegate and representatives of the nobility. Today the city council meets every Monday and the mayor sits in the middle surrounded by his council department heads and city councillors. Here the left wing parties sit on the right as the majority and the right take their seats on the left.

The walls and ceiling are decorated with marvellous 15th century frescoes of Dentoni, known for his combination of architecture and figures. In a trompe l'oeil the pillars on his paintings follow the moving onlooker.

Up the second flight of horse steps to the Pontifical Delegate's residence and we entered the Museo Giorgio Morandi (1890-1964). Named after the impressionist painter it contains the late artist's works and a recreation of his studio. (Opening times 10am to 6pm, closed on Mondays, entrance costs L8,000).

Our main delight was the large Waiting Room for those wishing for an audience with the Pope's representative. The Pontifical Delegate lived in the rooms now used for the municipal art exhibition. Frescoes from the 16th and 17th century adorn the walls, representing the most important events of the town's history.

The large Farnese chapel, one of 12 chapels in the town hall, is being painstakingly restored. When Napoleon's atheistic troops arrived they covered the frescoes with clay and turned the chapel into a store. Now one can once again see the magnificent frescoes of the Holy Virgin by Prospero Fontana, a follower of Raphael and Michelangelo.

BOLOGNA

The town hall was built over three different periods. The oldest part includes the arcades and the clock tower from the 13th century. Known as **Accursio's tower**, the clock was added centuries later. Originally the tower was a watchtower owned by Accursio a law teacher at the university. He sold the tower and his house to the town and they became the nucleus of the town hall.

From the main door to the left below the Red Room is 15th century and to the right was completed in the late 16th century.

Devoid of access to cheap marble, the architects exploited the malleability of readily available baked clay for decorative purposes. We were told this was the real reason why the city was called Red Bologna and not its radical political traditions.

To emphasise the point our guide showed us a beautiful 16th century terracotta statue of the Madonna created as a tribute to the Bologna-born Pope Gregorio XIII. The Bolognese Pope reformed the calendar ending Caesar's shorter years, introducing 365 days to our calendar now known as the Gregorian calendar.

Back out in **Piazza Maggiore**, the buildings opposite the town hall were being restored with funds from Benetton and were covered with hordings carrying the faces of Benetton's smiling faces.

Opposite our cafeteria was the Basilica San Petronio and behind us the **Asinelli tower**, leaning like the Bolognese to the left.

Piazza Maggiore is the heart of the town. Once the thriving market square, it is where all the most important political, municipal, festive and cultural events such as the New Year's Eve celebrations and concerts are held. One part of the square is even known as Bologna's Hyde Park Corner where old people in particular carry on an age old Sunday tradition of meeting to discuss the world and its uncle.

To create the Piazza the 12th century municipal government destroyed eight small churches and, in the following 300 years the area around the square was built to something like what is on view now.

BOLOGNA

Palazzo dei Notai

To the left as one looks at the Town Hall is the **Palazzo dei Notai** which was the seat for the corporation of notaries. The line cutting across the building emphasises that the building was created in two different periods. To the left the building was erected in the 14th century – now it has a bar. To the right, the building is of 15th century origin.

Looking to the left of the Town hall is **Neptune's Place**, which takes its name from the beautiful fountain with Neptune portrayed in his glory surrounded by maidens. The Medici Pope Pius III was the first in the city and created the statue of Neptune, god of the ocean, to illustrate his power. Neptune's left hand reaches out to the old town calming the waves – the people of Bologna. Late 16th century once again, the style, used here by Flemish sculptor Giambologna, is heavily influenced by the works of Michelangelo.

Pictures of martyred partisans who fought in the 1939 to 1945 war and were shot in the square adorn the town hall wall just behind Neptune. The Bolognese do not intend to forget their victorious fight in the nearby hills against fascist tyranny.

Opposite the town hall on Neptune's Place is The Golden Prison, **King Enzo's Palace**, in which the victorious Bolognese comunes imprisoned Enzo after the 1249 Battle of Fossalta.

Arengo's Tower

When we came to the 12th century **Arengo's Tower** opposite the town hall in Neptune's Place we could notice its unique structure. It has no base on the ground but a base in the two adjacent buildings, its mass resting on the central vault of the cross-shaped portico. The statues in the four corners represent the four saints of Bologna, San Franciscus, San Domenicus, the city patron Petronius portrayed with the city in his hands and the soldier Propolus.

We walked under the base of the tower and discovered a fascinating phenomenon. Muriel walked over to one corner of the base beneath San Domenicus and I to Petronius's corner diagonally opposite. When she placed her face very close to the corner I was able to hear her as she whispered by listening in the opposite corner. How it works nobody seems to know but it must have been a handy spot for intrigue and fun and games. The phenomenon was rediscovered by two children at play, then historians joined in.

The San Petronius Basilica.

Bologna is unusual in that its main square has no cathedral. Instead the cathedral, dedicated to St Peter, is relegated to a spot at the beginning of Via Independenzia while the basilica of St Petronius dominates the piazza. Behind this story is the age long rivalry and enmity of the local nobility and the Vatican.

The cathedral as the seat of the archbishop was linked to Rome. But the nobility decided to build its own church in the square. They aimed to build a church to their patron saint, Petronius that would be bigger than the Vatican. Not one lira of Rome's money would ever be requested to finance its construction. It would be paid for by the people of the city and become a symbol of freedom from Rome.

Symbolic of the basilica's anti-Papism is the tomb containing the relics of Eloisa Bonaparte, Napoleon's sister.

The Bolognese aimed to have a beautiful church with a facade of marble. The first stone was placed in 1390 starting with the facade. The church was unusually built backwards. The chapels followed and after 300 years with the main altar in place, the basic format of the church was complete. As they ran out of money the facade remains incomplete.

The basilica is 60 metre wide, 132 metres long, 51 metres high at the facade and 45 metres high inside. These monstrous Gothic proportions were meant to be extended until the church was 224 metres by 150 metres but eventually expansion was blocked by the wiles of the Pope and by finance. Nevertheless the town managed to create, what is said to be, the fifth biggest church in Christendom. Once the town was in the hands of the Popes, they used it. For example Pope Clement VII crowned Emperor Charles V here in 1530 and 100 years later it would be the venue for two sessions of the famous Council of Trent.

Entering, a sign warned, 'No eating ice cream' and 'No walking arm-in-arm'. We were enthralled by the dramatic Gothic height of the interior and its overwhelming simplicity. The use of red and white on the pillars cleverly enhances its luminosity. A peculiarity of the church is that it lies south – north and not east – west. The reason given by the creators was lack of space to build but many believe that it was another expression of defiance against the Pope. The overall effect was to increase the light entering first from the east and then from the west.

Inside our guide, pointed to a half window, evidence of how the planned expansion of the width of the church was halted. The magnificent architecture by Giacopo della Quercha, a Sienna sculptor is said to have inspired Michelangelo who stayed in the city for some months.

Suddenly Roberta stopped us and pointed to the floor where we were standing on a 17th century sun dial painted into the floor by Cassini. A sunbeam was pointing to the chart at exactly the correct time, day, month plus, for those interested, the horoscope (horoscopes were important for sanctioning various activities). Said to be one of the most perfect in existence, the length of its line is one six hundred thousandth of the earth's meridian.

Arriving almost midway down the church to where the builders had reached by the late 16th century, the main altar stands in the middle of the church. The frescoes behind once again employ perspective to create an image of rounded pillars and 3D.

Back outside to the rear of the basilica we had a perfect view of the buildings sudden halt. Not only half windows but doors appear and bricks jut out from the edge of the wall waiting for cement or a marble overlay. The rupture marks the time when, during the late 16th century, the altar had been built and work was being prepared to extend the wings making the church bigger than St Peters in the Vatican.

By then the Papacy were in control of the town and, to block the extension, the wily Pope Pius IV quickly ordered, right next door to the basilica, the building of the Archiginnasio. From Piazza Galvani we could see the jutting brickwork still waiting after 400 years for the next mason.

The Archiginnasio designed by Morandi, known as 'Il Terriblia' was completed in two years and became the first seat for the university. Nevertheless the university welcomed the construction as previously the faculties were spread all over the town with no centre. Morandi added del Pavaglione, the portico which links Piazza Maggiore to Piazza Galvani, and which helped pull the university schools into a single whole.

The Towers and Arcades

Just behind the basilica in Galvani Square we stopped to look at the mediaeval courtyard structure. It is the only place in the city which maintains the old structure. The arcades link around the tower, Torre Galuzzi, which would be the only building made in brick. The whole family and their relatives would live around the tower. When families were attacked by their rivals, they would fight first on the ground floor, move up to the first for further defence and as a last resort go to the top of the tower.

By the 13th century 100 towers pierced the skyline. The higher the tower the more wealthy, and better defended, the family. The Asinelli tower in the centre rose to 97 metres, its base being created into a small fortress and a dungeon. It is at the end of Via Rizzoli. Climb its 500 steps and you'll discover panoramic views of the city. Don't worry that it leans 4ft or so. Next door is its diminutive, the Garisenda tower leaning 11ft.

Torre Galuzzi is 36 metres high but the norm was 60 metres. Now a restaurant sits under the tower and takes the same name, the Torre Galuzzi in the Corta Galuzzi. The restaurant is excellent, but meals cost at least L80,000.

Bologna boasts over 40km of arcades or porticoes – the biggest collection in the world. In the city centre almost every building seems to have its porticoes providing sunshade, rain shelters, walkways and shopping malls.

The arcades came out of the University city's pressure for space, as the number of students expanded during the Mediaeval period.

BOLOGNA

On Via Dettosci, Strada Maggiore, Via Clavature, Via Caduti and streets just off the Via Castiglione are old mediaeval buildings whose structure demonstrate how the Bologna's arcades began. They are said to have started because of the need to accommodate the expanding numbers of university students. Building another floor on the two storey buildings was too expensive.

Pushed for space and money, the families began to expand their houses by extending the first floor into the street. Wooden poles or planks wood then hold up the structure on the ground creating a portico. As more and more families followed suit, arcades were created linking houses and streets. Later the areas beneath the poles would also be walled off occupying the public earth. The Roman-Gothic Casa Isolani in Strada Maggiore is one of the best examples.

In 1116 the municipal government took up the arcade principal ordering them to be built everywhere. At the same time, a minimum height of 7 Bolognese feet (2.66m) was stipulated for the arcades allowing a man on horseback to ride beneath and thus protecting the public highway.

In some areas we even saw the old wooden beams still in place – though they are probably more recent restorations.

The Coin Shop

On Via de' Carbonesi we entered the Coin shop, not for shopping but to see the well preserved remains of a 1st century B.C Roman theatre, enlarged in the 1st century A.D. (open 9.30am - 1pm, 3.30pm - 7.30pm).

The site of the shop had been cleared. When the area was being prepared for construction, the theatre was discovered. The shopping chain, Coin was able to continue building providing they kept the remains on view. What they achieved is a very stylish presentation set in the basement amid displays of their clothes.

The floor of the site is full of coins. An old Roman tale has it that if one turns one's back and makes a wish while throwing a coin over one's shoulder, a return to that place is guaranteed. I followed suit, my coin landing in the theatre and I was back within the month.

On Via Dotes we had a perfect view down the street with its mediaeval buildings. Then we came to Santa Maria de la Vita on Via Clavature opposite the town hall, which inside on the right has a beautiful complex of statues representing the transition of Christ's body to the tomb.

Europe's Oldest University and the Anatomical Theatre

Now we were on the way to the Anatomical Theatre, which is adjacent to the city's basilica on Via dell' Archiginnasio. This is in the old university created to stop the basilica's expansion.

Founded in 1088 and dedicated to studying Roman law, Bologna University is the oldest in Europe. The university had no seat until 1663. The various faculties were spread about buildings in the city, lessons being held in offices, the churches and even the open air. So the Pope's order to create the central seat of the university which houses the anatomical theatre benefited the town.

The entrance to the university opens into a beautiful hall decorated by more than 7,000 coats of arms. Our guide, told us how in the Middle Ages, the students chose and paid their professor, grouping into corporations on the basis of their home towns, religion, and so on, to do so. The coats of arms represent the different corporations illustrating how the students attended from all over Italy and Europe. The university seat was based here till 1803 when the invading Napoleon ordered it to be moved to 33, Via Zamboni where it remains to this day. Consequently the building housing the theatre is now a public library. We had to rush because, as a public building, access is denied after 1pm.

Two staircases ascended from the entrance hall. The staircase to the right led to the facilities for the students of law and that to the left was for the artists and the other disciplines including astronomy, maths, oratory and medicine. We climbed the steps to the left. Every aspect of the walls and ceilings are finely decorated with coats of arms or elaborate carvings and this sight made our visit worthwhile for this alone.

At the centre of the seventeenth century **anatomical theatre** is a table on which corpses were laid. A lecturer would sit high up on a chair some distance away, while an assistant stationed beneath him would point to the relevant parts of the corps using a long pole. A cutter would stand by the body to carve it open as directed by the pole. Another assistant would display the various joins and innards to students. It was *truly* a theatre.

The theatre is totally made from the wood. Twelve statues representing the most important physicians of the age adorn the walls. Two very detailed statues known as, 'the unpeeled ones' on display need no further explanation. Above these are astronomical signs and our guide explained that in the middle ages no operation could be carried out if the arrangement of the stars were not auspicious.

Wooden shutters mark a window high on the wall opposite where the lecturers stood. This window was placed there on the orders of the clergy. Abhorring but unable to ban anatomy, the clerics, known as 'the contradictors' would regularly push open the shutters and stand barking questions at and arguing with the lecturers with the aim of catching them out in order to discredit both them and their chosen profession.

In this continuing struggle between science and religion, the church only permitted these experiments from the eighteenth century. The experiments were held in January or February when the cold winter weather delayed the rotting of the corps. Close by, the university has a wax museum with reproductions of the bodies. The theatre was damaged in the war by allied bombs but the restoration work has returned the chamber its magnificence.

Just outside on the parade beneath the basilica are some of Bologna's most exclusive shops such as Ganarini's, the city's most exclusive coffee shop sporting exquisite cakes and sweets.

San Domenico

On Via Garibaldi in the attractive Piazza San Domenico is the church of the same name, housing invaluable works of art. The church was built on the death of San Domenico in 1221, and contains his relics in a splendid marble tomb decorated by Pisano.

In the 18th century Dotti redesigned the church. From the exterior one can see how two Romanesque churches were brought together to make a single luminous whole.

The church is noted for its statues of Saints Petronius and Proculus and of an angel, all by Michelangelo and the wooden choir stalls by de Bergamo. The latter are masterpieces of Renaissance inlaid work and, at the time, were described as the 8th wonder of the world. The church also contains beautiful frescoes and paintings by Reni, Carracci, Lippi and Il Guercino

BOLOGNA

The Seven Churches of Santo Stefano

We walked over to the piazza of Santo Stefano beside which are the Seven Churches - reduced to five 5 this century. Known as 'The Holy Jerusalem of Bologna', this Romanesque complex is the most important religious complex in the city. Inside there is a symbolic path representing the Passion of Jesus Christ.

Bishop Petronius, establishing his popularity in the city, began the atmospheric complex, including 'The Crucifix Church', 'The Crypt', 'The Church of the Holy Sepulchre' which includes a perfect replica of the Holy Sepulchre and San Petronius' tomb, 'The Church of Vitale and Agricola', who in the fourth century became Bologna's two first martyrs and 'The Church of the Martyrium'. The site contains the relics of Santo Stefano and an interesting cloister. The complex opens at 9am then closes at noon to re-open from 3.30pm until 6.00pm.

The **Santo Stefano Piazza** is unusual in that it is a triangular shaped 'square'. The streets leading to the square sport elegant, but modest, Renaissance buildings, the most attractive of which are in the piazza itself. Nearby on Via San Stefano is the beautiful Gothic Palazzo della Mercanzia built in 1384.

That Bologna is devoid of many grand buildings, but sports many attractive less dramatic homes, towers, churches and palaces, is a product of its particularly feudal past where the city state was governed not by one ruler but by many noble families. Some of these such as the Bolognini and Lupari still live in the city.

The noblest families would live around San Stefano. Every two months the city's nobility would elect new leaders. The elections would be accompanied by a fortnight long feast hosted in the homes of the lords and ladies. Consequently these homes would have to be like theatres with beautiful facades, fresco-covered ballrooms and grand staircases.

Corte Isolana belonged to such a family, the Bolognini and is still quite superb. Outside its steps appeared a popular place for a lunchtime break, with young people sitting in the sunshine reading college books and novels. We continued to explore the lovely narrow pedestrianised streets emanating from the square.

OTHER CHURCHES

Also on Via Farini is the 13th century church of San Giovanni in Monte with its 14th century interior frescoed by Il Guercino and Prugino.

San Francesco Basilica

The basilica of **San Francesco** in the Piazza of the same name was built in the 1200s and is one of the oldest Romanesque-Gothic style churches in Italy. An apse flanked by two elegant bell towers, one dating to 1260 and the larger to the 1400s, backs its imposing facade. The lofty interior with its great marble altar piece is quite magnificent and the tomb on the side wall of Pope Alexander V emphasises the importance of the San Franciscan church

Annexed to the church are the tombs of the **Glossatori**, among them Accursio (of Accursio's tower) who re-interpreted Roman Law and whose work laid the basis for the university.

San Giacomo Maggiore, just off Via Zamboni in Piazza Rossini is 13th century in origin, the product of Augustinian hermit monks. It was redesigned in the 1400s and 1700s and, with its imposing facade (a portico supported by slender fluted sandstone columns and beautiful friezes and frescoes) is said to be one of the finest examples of Renaissance Bologna.

The Cathedral of San Pietro

7 Via Indipendenza is the site of the cathedral of San Pietro where a church has stood since the time when Christianity became established in Italy. Some of the remains date to the 10th century. The 12th century bell-tower retains its Romanesque features. The rest of the building collapsed in 1599 and was rebuilt from 1605 and lengthened in the 1700s on the orders of Bologna-born Pope Benedict XIV. Inside, in the lunette above the high altar is a fine work by Carracci (1619) portraying the Annunciation.

Madonna di San Luca Sanctuary and the longest arcade in the world

West of the city on Monte della Guardia hill, the Madonna di San Luca sanctuary boasts a wonderful treat as it can be reached from Porta Saragozza via a 40 minute walk along a colonnaded portico with 600 arches. The longest arcade in the world, it was built between 1674 and 1739.

The sanctuary was built by a group of devotional women in the late 1100s around an icon of the Blessed Virgin with Jesus Christ. In 1723 architect Carlo Francesco Dotti designed its complete rebuilding on a centralised plan harmonising with the hilltop. Inside are paintings by Guido Reni and Donato Creti amongst others. Outside is a marvellous view of Bologna city. To complete the trip, close by is the **Pizzeria Coffee Shop Vito** in Via Monte Albano with 30 different pizzas on the menu. Porta Saragozza is near Bologna's football stadium and can be reached by taking the 20 bus from the city centre

Teatro Comunale

On Piazza Verdi in the student quarter, the Teatro Comunale, Bologna's magnificent opera house is said to rival Milan's La Scala. It was opened in 1765 to the Baroque design of Antonio Bibiena who even designed the costumes and scenery for the first performance.

In 17th and 18th century Bologna, ten stage designers and theatre builders known as the ten Bibiena dominated theatre building in Europe and, popularising Baroque theatre with rows of boxes atop each other, take credit for the design of La Scala.

Street Life

Bologna is a city with a semi-village outlook. It has a democratic tradition and is known as a town where one can walk around safely in the evenings.

Around Ugo Bassi is the centre of the street life. In the student quarter, around Via Zamboni and the university, plenty of little pubs and **bars** exist. We had a fine time in October when the students were back and the bars full – particularly the *Irish pub*, which was packed with Guinness drinkers till happy hour, ended. Also on the Zamboni is the packed place-to-be-seen *Café Museo*, dancing in *Lord Lister's* and the trendy *Kinky* bar for those with money.

Other streets with plenty of bars are Via Mascarella with its late night *Jam Club* and Via Pratello. *Birriera Meddix* in Via Mascarella boasts a huge selection of beers and a 90-minute long 'happy hour' from 7.30pm nightly. *Corto Maltese* in Via del Borgo di San Pietro goes even further with a two hour 'happy hour' from 7pm and a discobar till 3am. Another owl's paradise is the Cuban *La Habana Vieja* in Via de Griffoni with its variety of tapas, Cuban musicians and Latin dancing.

Café Commercianti on Strada Maggiore is worth a visit before those late night sessions as there are plenty of aperitivi nibbles on offer until 9pm when it closes.

During the day, Piazza Maggiore is a fine place to sit, have a drink and watch life go by. Sunday brings a **Puppet Theatre** re-enacting the adventures of 'Fagiolino', 'Sganapino' and 'Pinocchio'. During the summer the municipality organises concerts in the square accompanied by showing silent movies with an orchestra playing especially composed film scores.

Thousands turn out in Piazza Maggiore on New Year's Eve to watch the firework display and the dancing. Only on this night does the huge bell of Arengo's Tower chime. The city's **Summer Dream Festival** brings the parks and piazzas alive with bands, concerts, theatre, mime and jazz.

For sport lovers in winter there's Serie A football at the Bologna **soccer ground** (tel 6145391) on Via Andrea Costa and premier league professional **rugby union** to watch at Bologna Rugby club's ground in Via dell'Arcoveggio (tel 352776 or website www.rugby.it.). The **horse racing** track is north of the city on Via di Corticella.

Cinema goers can see American films shown weekly at the *Adriano* in Via San Felice, *Tiffany's* on Piazza Porta Saragozza and *Cinema Lumiere* on Via Petralata for L8/10,000 (students L7,000).

Bologna Fiera on the outskirts of the city beside Via Michelino is a huge exhibition centre hosting industrial fairs and conferences. Some of the highlights include the **International Fair of Contemporary Art** (last week in Jan), Italian fashion and leather (early May), Leather fashion (mid November) and the **Motor**

and Motorcycle Show (mid December). For more details contact tel 282111 fax 282332. Access can be achieved by car or by the 226 autobus that shuttles between the airport and the central station.

BOLOGNA 2,000 – European City of Culture

The year 2,000 will see Bologna celebrating its status as one of the 10 European cities of culture. Visitors will benefit hugely by the city's emphasis on the cleaning and restoration of its plethora of historic buildings. Celebrated artists such as Bologna-born Umberto Eco have participated in the huge programme of exhibitions for the year long festival.

A highlight of the festival is the **Three Maestri and Morandi: Giacometti, Klee** and **Cezanne** exhibition at the **Morandi Museum** beginning in June, 2000 and displaying the portraits, drawings and sculptures from some of the most authoritative figures in 20th century art.

Another treat includes **The Shadow of Reason** exhibition at the **Modern Art Gallery** where the works of **Mondrian, Lucio Fontana** and **Francis Bacon** amongst others will be on show between April and October. In the historic theme, the Pinacoteca Nazionale will stage the **Bibiena** exhibition featuring the works of the great Bibiena family. The Bibiena's dominated the cultural scene of the royal courts, palaces and theatres of Europe during the 17th and 18th centuries. Examples of this local dynasty's architecture and scene-paintings abound in Emilia and the exhibition will begin in October 2,000.

Going back further in history to emphasise the city's key role in the history of European art, the Municipal Archaeological Museum will, between April and July, host the **Glow of the Middle Ages** exhibition. Exhibited will be paintings, frescoes, sculptures, stained glass, gold and ivory objects, and fabrics from the 13th century.

World-renowned architects will be in evidence at the Architecture Project in Palazzo Re Enzo, from the beginning of the year until summer of 2001. Theatre, music and dance will be celebrated with exhibitions and performances by leading figures in modern dance, jazz, chamber music and theatre and by artists from all over the globe.

Bologna's contribution to the European kitchen is trumpeted in the **Food Culture Festival** that will run through to Summer 1991 and provide a gastronomic delight for visitors.

BOLOGNA

With the **Land of Motors Festival** in the summer of 2000 at Palacongressi, the motor car is not forgotten. This is the region of Ferrari, Ducati, Bugatti and Lamborghini. What better for motor enthusiasts than an organised tour of the Ferrari, Ducati and Lamborghini museums linking up with major motor races in the region?

For further details contact Bologna 2,000's website at www.bologna2000.it.

Shopping

Bologna has some tremendous shops and the prices are not frightening. A normal shopping tour would take in Via's Ugo Bassi, Rizzoli, Farini, Santo Stefano, Massimo D'Azeglio and the Pavaglione.

South of Piazza Maggiore is the high fashion shoppers' paradise. Mercato di Mezzo Archiginnasio street just off Ugo Bassi contains high fashion shops and jewellers. Via D'Azzeglio is pedestrianised with many expensive shops. Alongside Via Farini and the Archiginnasio it is the city's premier spot for high fashion. Galleria Cavour has slightly cheaper shops (Gucci, Ferre, Armani, Versace and Trussardi) but, some say, just as stylish. Giorgio's, the boutique of chic designer, Mariella Burani is at 29 Via San Stefano, near the church complex. Forlini shoe shops, using leather from the local area, are very expensive but popular.

The city has several **markets**. Every Friday and every Saturday morning, Montagnola market takes place in Piazza VIII Agosto and offers a range of quality and cheaper prices with old **lacework, antiques** and second hand clothes. Another popular antiques market takes place every second weekend in the month at Piazza Santo Stefano. On the same days a **handicrafts market** takes place under the Two Towers.

Piazza Aldrovandi hosts a daily **food market**. Other covered food markets are held at the corner of Via San Gervasio and Via Belvedere and at the corner of Via Drapperie and Via degli Orefici.

The elegant Casa Fondata, Mayani's chocolate firm was established in the city in 1796 and makes some of Italy's best chocolates. Its cafe is in Piazza Galvani and is worth a treat for those with a sweet tooth.

In Via Caprarie's restored 13th century houses, Paulo Atti's shop has been selling the original tortellini of Bologna since 1880. We went in and looked at the wonderful display of fresh tortellini and tortelloni stuffed with ricotta cheese and spinach, which could be bought in boxes at L4,900 for 100 grams.

Next door at number one, the grand old shop of **Tamburini** has been selling tortellini, succulent mortadella, and Tamburini's own brand of Parma ham since 1932. It smelled so good that Muriel had to buy some. The shop (tel 051-234726) has a self-service bistro for meals and drinks open between noon and 3pm.

Via Pesceria Veccia, contains a vast array of fishmongers and market stalls displaying their fruit and vegetables. Nearby are old butchers, greengrocers, cheese stores and plenty of shops where one can buy tortellini and mortadella.

In Via Altabelli close to San Petronius we strolled down the narrow street and came to **Faccioli's wine bar**. The bar, in the Faccioli's hands for three generations, used to be under Asinelli's tower but moved with its old furnishings to this street. It is a lovely old bar with a friendly patron serving from his stock of 200 Faccioli wines made to the patron's order. Add a delicious plate of mortadella cubes served with bread and it's a delightful, popular, if fattening, place to eat and seats up to 30 people.

Shops open from 9am to 12.30pm and 3.30pm to 7.30pm. Supermarkets close on Monday mornings and other stores on Thursday afternoons. **Banks** open from 8am to 1.20pm and from 2.30pm till 4.30pm (closed weekends). Otherwise, the foreign exchange office at the main railway station opens from 8am until 7.45pm. The central **post office** is at 14, Via de'Toschi. Post office opening hours are 8.15am to 7.30pm (closed Sat p.m.). **Museums** are generally open from 9am till 1pm.

EATING OUT

Bolognese **tortellini** are the small stuffed pasta shells boiled in a meat broth or stock. There are many stories of tortellini's origin. One tale has it that the gods, Mars, Bacchus, and Venus had met at an inn in Castelfranco to arrange aid for Modena, which was being besieged by Bolognese troops. The inn-keeper saw Venus naked and was so in awe of her divine navel that he recreated the image as tortellini. At **Biagi's** restaurant one can see the reputed smallest tortellini in the world being made.

Those who wish to try the world famous **Bolognese sauce** need do no more than request a Bolognese ragu. The ingredients of the Bolognese are a little different to that offered in the rest of the world. The true recipe for Bolognese sauce includes beef, carrots, celery, onions, tomatoes, dry white wine and milk.

Cesari (closed Sun) in Via de'Carbonesi is a top-notch restaurant in the city with prices (L35/55,000) to match. **Torre de'Galluzi** in the mediaeval tower on Corte de Galluzi and **Drogheria della Rosa** (closed Sun in August) in Via Cartoleria compete for being the best for quality food. **Rodrigo's** (closed Sun) in Via della Zeccha is renown for its traditional recipes and was once frequented by Enzo Ferrari.

The cheapest places to eat here are the self-service cafes such as the **Bassi Otto Co-op** at 8, Via Ugo Bassi (L18,000 for a fixed meal) and **Lazzarini's** in Via Clavature

BOLOGNA

(L12/25,000). Others can be found in the student quarter, such as *Hostaria da Matusel* (closed Sun and Sat p.m.) in Via Bertoloni (L18,000). *Panabrasita* (closed Thurs.) in Via Pietralata is also cheap at L15/25,000.

Slightly above this range, with a variety of budget and more expensive meals (L20/40,000), are: *Birreria Lamma* (closed Sun) in Via de'Giudei with its large stock of beers, *Osteria dei Poeti* (closed Mon) in Via dei Poeti where musicians play from 8pm, *Trattoria Boni* (Fri/Sat noon) at 8 Via Saragozza, specialising in pappardelle with mushrooms and *Il Portico's* pizzeria (closed Wed) in Via Augusto Righi. *Cantina Bentivoglio* (closed Mon) in Via Mascarella is known for its simple authentic dishes such as sausage and bean stew and large mixed salads helped down by plenty of jazz music and wine.

The quirky *Al 15* on Via Mirasole serves Bolognese dishes and the *Papagallo* (closed Sun) in Piazza d. Mercandazia is known for its pasta dishes.

Otherwise a full meal with wine will cost L50,000 and a couple of plates, L30,000. Cheapest meals are pizzas or visits to takeaways such as the Greek *Gyrosteria* in Via Gioto.

Osteria, pubs and **wine bars** open between 8pm and 1am. The city has many historic wine bars, to the extent that the guides offer special tours of these bars. Restaurants are generally open from noon till 3pm and from 8pm until 11pm. Osteria often stay open till after midnight.

ACCOMMODATION
Hotels (area code 051)

Hotel prices are set for commercial travellers visiting the many industrial exhibitions which, taking place throughout the year, leave prices high in the city.

****The best stay in Bologna centre is reputed to be in the historic four stars ****Grand Hotel Belgian* (051 225445) at 8, Via Independenzia. A piece of a Roman street paves part of its ground floor and *Guercino* and *Carracci* frescoes adorn the museum vaults. The hotel has seen plenty of history being the favourite choice of the great and the good, and the bad – Vittorio Emmanuele, Marconi, Luis Armstrong, Clark Gable and Tsar Nicholas. Rooms cost £120/200 a night for a double.

Others in this range include the very modern *Jolly* (tel 248921 fax 249764) at 2, Piazza XX Settembre and the *Corona D'Oro* (tel 236456 fax 262679)in Via Oberdan with its beautiful painted ceilings. Bologna's *Sheraton* (tel 6415104 fax 6414090) is by the airport and is a snip at close on £200 a night. Cheapest in this range is the ****Amadeus* (tel 403040 fax 405933) at 39 Via Marco Emilio Lepido and charging £60/100.

***hotels include the relatively cheap *Holiday* (tel 235326 fax 234591) in Via Bertiera (£25/60) and *Palace* (tel 237442 fax 220689) at 92 Via Montegrappa (£30/55), the quiet *Il Guercino* (tel/fax 369893) close to the station on Via Luigi Serra (£70/100), the equally expensive *Commercianti* (tel 233052 fax 224733) in Via de Pignattari at £55/85 and *Hotel Orologio* (tel 231253 fax 260552) in Via IV Novembre at £55/100.

B O L O G N A

hotels include: *Hotel Dell'Accademia* (tel 232318 fax 554035) in the student quarter on Via delle Belle Arti for £25/45, **Centrale (tel 225114 fax 223899) on Via Zecca for £30/45. Otherwise the cheapest in the range is the *Tuscolano* (tel 324024 fax 327960) on Via Tuscolano at £25/40.

The *Marconi* (tel 262832) in Via Marconi is actually a pension and good value at £30. *Albergo Panorama* (tel 221802 fax 266360) on Via Linaghi with its inner courtyard is priced £17/25. Generally the 1 star hotels will charge £30 a night. They include: *Apollo* (tel 223955 fax 238760) at 5 Via Drapperie, *Giardinetto* (tel 342793 fax 342816) and *Lucky* (tel 304664 fax 346716) both on Via Massarenti, *Perla* (tel 302997) and *San Vitale* (tel 225966 fax 239396) both on Via San Vitale and, on the outskirts in Via Felsina, the 18th century *Villa Azzura* (tel 535460 fax 531346) with its quiet garden.

Bologna's **camp site** (tel 325016 fax 325318) costing £7 per adult is at 12/4 Via Romida. The two **youth hostels** are located in Via Viadagola (tel 501810 and 519202) and priced £6/7 per person.

Agriturismo with accommodation close to Bologna

South of Bologna
Sasso Marconi: *Le Conchiglie* (tel 840131), 76/1 Via Lagune, **Lagune** *Prati di San Lorenzo* (tel 841175) 5/3 Via Gamberi, San Lorenzo. **Paderno:** *Cavaione* (tel 589006 fax 589060), 4 Via Cavaione **Ozzano Emilia:** *Forlani Andrea* (tel/fax 798726) 81 Via Galvani

North of Bologna
Budrio: *Belle Lu* (tel 807034) 1 Via Banzi, Bagnarola **Castenaso:** *Il Loghetto* (tel 6052218 fax 6052254) 3/4 Via Zenzalino Sud, **Sacerno di Calderara di Reno:** *Fattoria San Martino* (tel/fax 6469000) 17 Via di Mezzo Ponente (£17/25)

i **Bologna Tourist Information Office** (tel 239660) is at 6 Piazza Maggiore and there is another office at the airport.

Travelling Around

Distances from Bologna of the main cities are: Ravenna 66km, Ferrara 34km and on Via Emilia, Rimini 113km, Modena 39km, Reggio Nell'Emilia 62km, Parma 91km and Piacenza 135km. Bologna is 154km from Venice, 106km from Florence and 379km from Rome.

Train Times (faster direct services)

Bologna Centrale to Modena 21mins, Ferrara 26mins, Forli 34mins, Reggio Emilia 37mins, Parma 50mins, Rimini 1hr, Piacenza 1hr 20mins, Milan Centrale 2hrs, Florence 1hr, Venice 2hrs, Rome 3 to 4hrs.

Trains around Bologna Province

Local trains run out of Bologna Centrale at the north end of Via Indipendenza to all over the province, covering the towns listed (journey times in brackets).

East from Bologna Centrale – Varighana, Castel S.Pietro, Imola (25mins), Riolo Terme (30mins)

North east from Bologna Centrale and Bologna Corticella - Castelmaggiore, San Giorgio in Piano, San Pietro in Casale, Galleria (30mins) and north east from Bologna Centrale - San Giovanni in Persiceto, Crevalcore (30mins).

West from Bologna Centrale - Anzole dell'Emilia, Sammoggia (15mins).

South from Bologna Centrale and Bologna Ruffilo – Pianoro, Monzuno, Grizzana, Castiglione (40mins).

South from Bologna Centrale and Bologna Borgo Panigale – Casalecchio (10mins), Pontecchio Marconi (15mins), Sasso Marconi, Marzabotto (35mins), Vergato (45mins), Porretta Terme (1hr)

Travelling by Road

Cars can be hired at Bologna airport or at the *Avis* office (tel 6341632) in Via Marco, Polo and **bicycles** from 4a Piazza Medaglie d'Oro (tel 6302015) at L15,000 per day. **Taxis** (tel 372727 or 534141) cost L1,400/km with a minimum fare of L4,500. The central **bus and coach** station is in the north of the city at Piazza Venti Settembre. **Bus passes** cost L10,000 for eight tickets. Monthly passes cost L55,000.

B O L O G N A

Bologna city

AROUND BOLOGNA
THE BOLOGNA APENNINES

Four main valleys lead south into the Bologna Apennines and across to Tuscany. The main route is the Setta, which is the route of the A1 autostrada after it leaves the Reno valley at Sasso Marconi. The Reno splits to the east and runs parallel to the Samoggia. To the west of the Setta valley is the Savena and then the Idice.

SOUTH ALONG THE RENO
Casalecchio di Reno

Six km from Bologna's centre, Casalecchio is better known as an exit point for the A1 autostrada than the spacious, green parkland of **Parco Talon Sampieri**. The park, referred to by Stendhal as Italy's Bois du Boloigne, has tree-lined avenues, undulating meadows, woodland, gorges and lakes. With huge summer rock concerts and a theatre at the Palasport centre, it's a good place to take the children.

Casalecchio was a haunt of Bologna's well-to-do as revealed by its many villas, the pride of which is **Il Toiano** built in 1559. Designed by Tibaldi, the house's garden had its many statues added in the 18th century.

Sasso Marconi

We drove off south to Sasso Marconi at the foot of the Apennines. We could have taken the Al from Bologna but our map was atrocious and we ended up taking an hour to escape the city and took the hill road to Sasso. It was dusk and as we passed the little village of Padorno we found ourselves on a tiny road going up into the hills. Dried by the hot summer, the sparse shrubs on rugged hills produced a Badlands type scene – quite lovely hiking country. We were assured of an awesome sunset view as we climbed the winding road at dusk. This time it was not to be. Mist and low cloud obscured the vista. But as we came to a stretch where the road fell away sharply on either side, we knew we were in some dramatic countryside.

The mist hunger over Sasso Marconi as we descended to cross the River Reno and reach the small village of Sasso Marconi and *Le Conchiglie's* **agriturismo** restaurant and guest house. On a sunny day, the adjacent mountain top hill offers a splendid view in which, we were told, we could spot 140 towns, Florence, Rimini, Modena, the Alps, the Adriatic and the Mediterranean.

Below we would have seen the **Roman aqueduct** at the foot of Mount Mariano. Built in the time of Augustus Caesar, it was reactivated in 1870 and still carries water to Bologna.

We ate some of the local arista de maiale, a delicious roast pork cooked in pepper. The meal was simple but deliciously country fresh. The L45,000 tariff included wine and five courses and was good value. It's worth considering a stop at an agriturismo near Bologna if one wants to see the city sights and at the same time take advantage of the Apennine countryside.

Le Conchiglie has rooms in its pleasantly set, no frill farmhouses at L50,000 per person and two person apartments for L170,000.

Sasso Marconi Agriturismo has quite basic rooms in the farmhouses. They have no telephones – so, no room service here – but they are very clean. The rooms offer lovely views of the surrounding mountains. The facilities include outdoor table tennis. The agriturismo has 260 Italian Friesian cows on the clean, modern farm.

Guglielmo Marconi

The son of an Irish heiress to the Jameson Whiskey fortune and a noble landowner, Guglielmo Marconi (1864-1937) is known as the inventor of radio. Born in Capugnano, he spent much of his childhood at the Villa Griffone in Pontecchio 8km south of Sasso Marconi. It was from Villa Griffone that the genius sent his first successful radio signal directed at the Celestini Hill. He sent off the carpenter Vornelli with an antenna to hold up on the other side of the hill and his brother with a rifle to record reception.

Villa Griffone is visitable and now contains a museum with equipment used by Marconi and a mausoleum in which the body of the great scientist is entombed.

Near to Pontecchio is the beautiful **de'Rossi castle**. Built in 1482 it gave host to the rich and famous including two popes and the poet Torquato Tasso.

Further up river and 24km from Bologna is **Marzabotto** home to the historic Etruscan township of **Misa**. Misa's life began in the 6th century B.C and soon the town gained an octagonal perimeter wall covering 3,500 metres. Archaeologists have discovered traces of a sophisticated drainage system and high quality buildings decorated with terracotta. With remains of temples, an acropolis and necropolis, it is definitely worth a visit. The main artefacts discovered in the town are displayed at the Pompeo Aria Archaeological Museum.

Marzabotto was a scene of opposition to the Nazis and at the end of the war 1,830 men, women and children were massacred and the village destroyed.

West of Marzabotto in the hills are mediaeval villages and the 15th century Torre dell Lame. Above the town splendid mountain scenery and mineral springs at **Fonte Cerelia** have attracted a tourist trade. Also close by is the attractive stone built Romanesque Rocca di Roffeno. The Rocca was a fortified religious complex but nevertheless boasts a lovely apse and old bell tower.

To the south east is **Grizzana Morandi,** the town recently adding the name of the great Bologna impressionist Morandi who adored the area's landscapes. The children might be interested in the town's **Mountain Sweets Festival** on August 15th. Close by is Montovolo mountain rising to 3,000ft above sea level.

Across the Setta valley to the east on the slopes of Monte Venere (3,000ft) is **Molino del Piero Golf Club** (tel/fax 051 6770506) which is on the Loiano road near the Rioveggio A1 exit. In Via Molino del Piero, the 9 hole hilly golf course has holes varying by 300ft in height in a scenic setting above the Savena valley.

Riola is near the head of the Reno valley, an area bathed in dense woodland. The town is known for its Roccheta Mattei close to the Riola bridge. This eccentric, almost **Art Nouveau** castle with its strange battlements was completed in 1871 to the Arab/Moor design of historian Cesare Mattei. The Santa Maria Assunta church beautifully set on the hill was built in 1978 to the design of the Finnish Alvar Aalto. It is a brilliant example of modern architecture complimenting both the past and the countryside.

Further on is **Borgo della Scola**, a well preserved mediaeval village of ancient houses, statues and towers and the church of San Lorenzo with its eight sided chapel. From Riola, a small tributary of the Reno flows from Mount Calvi (4,000ft). The last stop before Tuscany is the mediaeval village of **Castel di Casio,** 10km from Riola with its 100ft high tower that splits in two half way up. Near to the village is Lago di Suviana, a reservoir surrounded by pine forest and replete with chub, **trout** and carp. It has a **camp site**.

Roughly 5km from Castiglione dei Pepoli on road 62 to Camugnano is the 800metre long artificial reservoir, Lake Brasimone which is popular for **fishing** and **water sports**.

Porretta Terme

The Reno valley reaches up to the health spa resort of Porretta Terme, 11km south of Riola on highway 64. In a valley surrounded by dramatic mountainsides, beech, chestnut, fir and pine tree woods, the town centre has narrow cobbled lanes overshadowed by the mountains.

Modena

The Modenese Appennines

Snow expanses, kilometers and kilometers of ski slopes, cross-country skiing trails that meander through secular woods and sunny valleys.

Friendly people ready to meet the requirements of the tourist, inns in which to taste crescentine and have a glass of good Lambrusco wine: these are the Modenese Appennines.

www.studioarletti.it

Provincia di Modena
Assessorato al Turismo

E-mail: turismo@provincia.modena.it

The beach at Punta Marina Terme on the Adriatic Riviera

Dell'Uso Valley, Rimini

Mediaeval pageantry

Mediaeval pageant, Gropparello

Verucchio, Rimini

Pietra di Bismantova, Reggio

A mud volcano in Nirano

The Apennine foothills, Modena

Ferrara Cathedral

Via delle Volte, Ferrara

Castello Estense, Ferrara

Vialle Bertuzzi, Po Delta

San Francesco Basilica, Bologna

In the Modena kitchen tigelle, tortellini,
tortelloni, tagliatelle and ricotta

Making chestnut flour

Palazzo Ducale Di Colorno

Lago Santo, Bologna

Piazza Maggiore, Bologna

The Anatomical Theatre, Bologna

The Twin Towers, Bologna

Arcades in Bologna

Farnese Theatre, Parma

Verdi's birthplace near Busseto

Food from the Modena farms

Pavarotti in concert

Modena Cathedral

Pomposa Abbey

Making Ferrara bread

Ferrara Palio

Trepponti Bridge, Comacchio

Brisighella

In San Vitale Basilica, Ravenna

Riolo Terme spa

The Ferrari Gallery, Maranello

On the Po in Reggio

The events of Bologna 2000

The Bologna 2000 program envisages approximately 600 events including: The International Dance, Music and Theater Festival, the exhibition of the most important works of European Twentieth Century artists such as Bacon, Fontana, Munch, Giacometti, Cézanne and Klee. Peter Greenaway shall liven up the city with his light and music shows whereas the summer of the year 2000 shall be animated by "Per Te", a music festival with musicians coming from five continents.

The menus for Bologna 2000

The Bologna 2000 scientific-cultural project on food seeks to enhance the typical products of the region (parmesan cheese, balsamic vinegar, raw ham, mortadella and typical wines) and to create new dishes and menus dedicated to the event. Tours and itineraries to the production areas of the regional oenogastronomic traditions have also been organized. To enhance the typical products, a committee shall select the best dishes and menus of Bologna 2000 which shall then be proposed by the restaurants connected to the events. The best Consortia producing typical wines of the Bologna hills such as the Pignoletto, Sauvignon, Barbera and Merlot shall be selected by a commission and by sommeliers who shall determine which CAO wines shall represent Bologna 2000.

The land of motors circuit

The "land of motors" circuit proposes the legendary path covered by the important racing and luxury automobiles and motorcycles in the area around Bologna, such as the Lamborghini and the Ducati in the Bologna area, Ferrari and Maserati in the Modena area and the many motor manufacturers in the Romagna area.

The jubilee

The year 2000 also coincides with the Jubilee and the city together with the restoration of many historical buildings to be dedicated to new cultural spaces is carrying out important restorations to churches and basilicas including the Cattedrale di San Pietro, Basilica di San Petronio, Santa Maria della Vita and the San Luca porticoes

B O L O G N A
Città Europea della Cultura

Bologna 2000 European City of Culture

Bologna's appointment as a European City of Culture in the year 2000 is not simply an important acknowledgement by the European Union. Indeed, it constitutes an important opportunity for the city to relaunch its image in the global tourism market. The first positive data was recorded in the improvement of the reception structures to tackle an increase of approximately 300,000 night stays and one million visitors foreseen for the year 2000. Furthermore, intense promotional activities have been carried out abroad to support Bologna's position in the booming and growing international cultural tourism market and increase its fame internationally.

City of towers and porticoes, of squares which are full of life: the bolognese, the students, citizens of the world

Bologna is a unique city and certainly one of the most beautiful in Italy. Its historical center is one of the best conserved in Europe and it is one of the largest in Italy. However, its most characteristic trait is the porticoes extending for over 42 kilometers. The portico leading to the Santuario della Madonna di San Luca comprising 666 arches is the longest in the world. Bologna is also famous for its mediaeval towers. The most famous are: the Torre degli Asinelli and the Torre Garisenda with its characteristic inclination (3.22 meters) which has been immortalized in Dante's Divine Comedy.

The places of Bologna 2000

The program of urban renewal envisages important renewals which shall be completed in the year 2000. They include: the former Sala Borsa which shall house Italy's largest Multimedia Library, the former Tabacco Factory area which shall house the new Center for Visual Arts, Communication and Performances, Palazzo Sanguinetti shall house the Music Museum, the former Convent of S. Cristina shall become the "Risorgimento" Museum and the National Women's Library. The Salara Space to enhance creativity in young people has been operational since the summer of 1998.

Comacchio
and the Coast

Ferrara
terra e acqua

Provincia di Ferrara

The healing powers of Porretta's spring waters are legendary. About 2,000 years ago a bull, too sick to continue pulling his farmer's plough, is said to have been let loose by a peasant. The bull wandered off and stopped to drink at the 'Puzzola' well. Its health was restored and it returned to pull the plough. Ever since the bull has been the symbol of Porretta.

Etruscans, Romans, Lorenzo the Magnificent, Luigi Bonaparte and even Machiavelli in his play Mandragola, stopped off at the spa to take advantage of its sulphurous and sodiobromidiodic waters. Today they are registered by the government's health department as among the most curative in Italy and used to deal with respiratory, digestive, dermatological and vascular problems, and even as a cure for some hearing and gynaecological problems. Beauty treatment is also on offer.

Porretta Spa (tel 0534 22093, fax 24260) is situated at 29, Via Ranuzzi and hotel accommodation such as at the Castanea is often linked with treatment at the major centres, the 18th century Bovi Leone and the Donzelle built in 1814.

In the town, the old narrow streets such as Via Falcone are a pleasure to walk around. Also of interest is the 17th century church of Santa Maria Maddalena. The council also has a good sports pavilion for playing tennis, basketball, skating and an Olympic swimming pool. For those who are so inclined, the town also hosts the semi-finals of the annual Miss Italy contest.

The area of Porretta has a distinguishable cuisine based on the mountainside. Proximity to Tuscany has created a delightful combining of Tuscan and Emilia Romagna cuisine. Most famous is the **Porretta truffle**, its harvest being the occasion for a special local festival in November. There is a wide variety of edible mushrooms including morette, bloetus, red fairy clubs, shoestring fungus and the ovular mushroom.

From the chestnut forests come chestnut flour, chestnut polenta, fritters and cagnaccio. Fried crescentine pancakes are served with local bacon and salami and the local sausage meats.

Halfway between Bologna and Florence, Porretta is an excellent staging post for seeing north and middle Italy and also a fine base camp for touring the fascinating Apennine locality. Close to Lakes Pratignano, Scaffaiolo and Suviana, Porretta offers plenty of walks among the mountains, rivers, waterfalls, fishing, boating, and winter skiing. The forests are host to plentiful flora, including wild mushroom, wild cherry, raspberry and the Porretta truffle, which is among the most rated in Italy. The rivers and lakes offer **trout**, crayfish, barbel and chub fishing. Feasting on all this are plenty of fauna, hares, foxes, marmots, pheasant, and partridge, woodpeckers, owls and golden eagles.

BOLOGNA

About 11km south of Porretta is another old tourist resort, Granaglione known for its August Somersaulting competition.

The beautiful mediaeval hamlet of **Castelluccio**, located 6km west from Porretta at over 2,500ft above sea level, offers splendid views of rugged Apennine terrain. Take a bus from Porretta to here and the walk back offers two hours of splendid trekking. Alternatively the trek up to the peak of Monte Piella at 4,000ft requires three hours for the return journey.

A few kilometres further west is the former Bolognese fortress outpost of **Lizzano in Belvedere** 2,000ft above sea level where the chestnut and beech forests host groundhogs, roe and fallow deer and the once almost extinct moufflon sheep. 1500ft higher up Mount Pizzo is the Rotonda, a pre-Romanesque round church and bell tower dedicated to San Mamante and believed to date back to the 8th century.

Skiing

Linked to Mount Pizzo by cableway, Lizzano is a winter tourist resort popular with visitors to the ski slopes. Most renown of these is on Corno alla Scale that peaks at over 6,000ft. Its 36km of ski runs and cross country ski routes for all levels are covered in snow till the end of April and also boast Olympic ski champion, Alberto Tomba's, presence.

SOUTH ALONG THE SAMOGGIA

Just west of Casalecchio and 10km from Bologna on the Vignola road is the town of **Zola Predosa**. It is notable for the 17th century Palazzo Albergati commissioned by the Marquis of the same name. His intention was to create the finest mansion in the area to host such worthies as the English James III, the Queen of Poland and Frederic IV of Denmark. The imposing but harmonious Renaissance exterior looks out on a large park decorated with marble statues. The interior, in contrast, is a blaze of Baroque with frescoes and a huge open gallery rising over 120ft. The next Marquis converted the main drawing room into a theatre, performing the plays of Voltaire and those of the vain Marquis himself.

Further west one crosses the river Samoggia to reach the agricultural town of **Bazzano,** over which looms the mediaeval castle dating back to when Matilda di Canossa occupied it. The side facing the river and the southern tower were built in the year 1000 and formed parts of the fortress presented to Matilda's father Boniface in 1038. The rest was later destroyed then rebuilt as his home by

Giovanni II Bentivoglio in 1473.

The tower is renowned for being where Italian writer Ugo Foscolo was imprisoned after certain political and amorous misdemeanours conducted in the false name of Lorenzo Alighieri. Otherwise the town is the centre for the thriving vineyard owners whose grapes produce Trebbiano, Barbera, Sauvignon and White Pinot.

Close to Bazzano and Ponte Ronca just off SS569 is **Bologna Golf Club** (tel 051 969100 fax 6720017) is on Via Sabattini in Monte San Pietro. The 18 hole course is par 72.

A few kilometres upstream from Bazzano on a rock outcrop is Matilda di Canossa's fortress hamlet of **Monteveglio** which can be reached via a winding road from the main town. Parts of the castle remain intact as is the Municipal Residence. Walking further one can reach the fine Abbazia di Santa Maria Assunta built in 1092 and still giving its name to a local wine, 'the White Wine of the Abbey.'

The abbey was built on the site of an early Christian temple enclosed in the crypt and the apse and a former Romanesque cloister incorporated into the north part of the building. The abbey's park includes the castle and the five peaks of Cucherla, Veglio, Morello, Gennaro and Alfredo as can be seen from its north-east facing 14th century mullioned windows. The park's woodlands, stream-crossed pastures and ravines are recommended for **trekking**.

Just off the road south on the Modena border west is the former fortified mediaeval hamlet of **Castello di Serravalle** where the 16th century tower, the drawbridge and 13th century house of the fortress remain. The hamlet also has the impressive Palazzo dei Ranuzzi, which was built in 1523. One former noble, Boccadiferro was said to have married many women then killed them. Their ghosts are believed to roam the castle seeking revenge.

The last town in the Samoggia valley is **Savigno,** 37km from Bologna and famous for a Risorgimento revolt led by the town doctor, Pasquale Muratori in 1843. The revolt was suppressed, many were killed and six revolutionaries were executed by the Papal government in Bologna's Prato di Sant'Antonio. Otherwise Savigno holds a **palio horse race** round the town on the 4th Sunday in may and a **cherry festival** on 24th June. The nearby hamlet of Vignola dei Conti is worth visiting for its lovely old mountain houses.

B O L O G N A

SOUTH ALONG THE SAVENA

The Savena river flows north into the Idice just beside the autostrada exit at Bologna San Lazzaro. The most notable town is **Pianoro,** 16km from Bologna. 1km before Pianoro Vecchia on the road from Rastignano is the 15th century Torre dei

Lupari which has interesting turrets, a fine loggia, a fountain and gargoyles. Pianoro Vecchia was reduced to rubble in the last war and the new town is 3km away.

From Pianoro one can view **Monte Formiche**, the mountain of the ants. 15km away from Pianoro, the mountain has the pre-Romanesque church of Santa Maria di Zena at its peak, the centre of a fascinating phenomenon every September 8th. On this day dedicated to the Virgin Mary, hundreds of thousands of flying ants swarm into the area to reproduce. After mating, the exhausted male ants fly off to die on the walls of the church. The dead males are then collected, blessed and distributed to the congregation for use in cures of rheumatism, toothaches and headaches.

The road to **Loiano**, 19km further up the valley is reputed to be one of the prettiest in the region and attracted Goethe who passed by in 1796. His "*Journey to Italy*" mentions the *albergo della Corona* in the town. The town is mainly known for being the home of Bologna University's grand **Astronomical Observatory** built in 1936. The Augustinian church of San Giacomo e Santa Maria was built in the 1300s though the bell tower is an 18th century addition.

The last stop before Tuscany is 8km south of Loiano in the town of **Monghidoro** once known as Scaricalasino, meaning 'unload the donkey'. Travellers into Tuscany had to unload their donkeys to pass through the Papal customs post. Easter Mondays and the town hosts an unusual fair, the **Festival of the Old Hag**. This mountainous area has many Renaissance buildings notably complimenting the surrounding countryside.

THE UPPER IDICE AND THE CHALK BADLANDS

Heading east from Bologna to San Lazzaro another road leads south towards Monterenzio in the Idice valley east of the Savena. A turn right after a few kilometres at Castel dei Botti brings one into the **Parco dei Gessi**, the chalk park where the rolling chalk hills have been ravaged by the elements and riddled with caves, ravines, waterfalls and gorges. Like the Badlands from a western movie, they nevertheless offer a wonderfully serene stroll away from the Bologna traffic.

Upwards of 200 caves remain, the most famous of which are the **Grotta del Farneto** and Spipola at La Croara. Weapons, tools and moulds for melting bronze have been found at Farneto indicating that these caves were inhabited 4,000 years ago during the Neolithic transition from the Stone to the Bronze Age. The main grotto is 145metres long and capped by a large Neolithic vault. The **Spipola caves** have a tremendous 5670metre long network of galleries – the longest chalk cave system in the world.

ACCOMMODATION AND EATING OUT

Apart from the agriturismo listed below, the area has several with dining facilities. The mountains in this region are noted for **truffles** and **mushrooms**, particularly the edible Boletus, meadow mushrooms, morette and royal agaric that find their way to the dining table particularly around Lizzano.

Food only Agriturismo include:

Lizzano in Belvedere: *Agritur*, 56 Via Serra, Sassochio (L30,000)
Marzabotto: *La Quercia*, **22 Via Quercia (L25,000)** Castello di Serravalle: *Fattoria Quercia*, 909 Via Mulino, Fagnano (L35,000) *Le Ariette*, 2781, Via Rio Marzatore, Acqua Salata (L30,000)
Monteveglio: *Al Pazz*, 57 Via Montebudello (L25/35,000)
Pianoro: *Tossani Marcello Pian delle Vigne*, 20 Via del Sasso (L30,000)
Pignanoli Ferrini Morandina, 3 Via del Sasso
Sasso Marconi: *Il Monte*, 59 Via Castello, Lagune (L35,000)
Monghidoro: *I Fondi* 1 Via Fondi (L30,000)
Benassi Clara 12 Via Vergiano, Vergiano (L30,000)

Agriturismo with accommodation

Lizzano: *Ca' di Fos* (tel/fax 0534 37029) 731 Via Ronchidoso, Ca' di Fos, **Gaggio Montano** (£25/night full board) *Ca' Gabrielli* (tel 0534 54049) 156 Via Ca' Gabrielli, La Ca' (camping only - £2.50/person)

Sasso Marconi: *Le Conchiglie* (tel 051 840131), 76/1 Via Lagune, Lagune (£17/bed)

Prati di San Lorenzo (tel 051 841175) 5/3 Via Gamberi, San Lorenzo (£17/bed)
Monte San Pietro: *Tenutu Bonzara* (tel 051 6768324) 37a Via San Chierlo (£200/£250 per week)
Paderno: *Cavaione* (tel 051 589006 fax 589060), 4 Via Cavaione (£30/bed)
Castel d'Aiano: *La Fenice* (tel/fax 051 919272) 29 Via S. Lucia, Rocca di Roffeno (£35/bed)

Monteveglio: *Corte D'Aibo* (tel 051 832583 fax 830937) 15 Via Marzatore (£20/bed a breakfast)
La Cavaliera (tel 051 832595 fax 833126) 11 Via Canossa (£25/£35/bed)
Porretta: *Calenz* (tel/fax 0534 43144), 108c Via Il Piano, Bargi, Camugnano (£20/bed)
Monghidoro: *I Fondi* (tel 051 6553600) 1 Via Fondi
Benassi Clara (tel 051 6544087) 12 Via Vergiano, Vergiano
Pianoro: *Il Rulleto* (tel 051 6516289) 3 Via Gorgognano (£25/bed+breakfast)

Hotels/Camp Sites

Sasso Marconi (area code 051)

Sasso has three ***hotels, *La Meridiana* (tel 841098 fax 6750273) at £30/65 and *Tre Galletti* (tel/fax 841128) and *Oasi* (tel 841608 fax 6751827) both at £50.

**La Bettola (tel 841376 fax 842174) in the village charges £40/45 and *Triana e Tyche (tel 6751616 fax 6751702) charges £30/45. Cheaper stays are offered in Mongardino near Pontecchio Marconi at *Del Loghetto (tel 6755192)*, Mon Jardin* (tel 6755190) and *Pilicchi* (tel 6755390) all at around £20/25.

Savigno has two 2 star hotels, *La Villa* (tel 051 6708027) near Samoggia at £25/30 and *Stella D'Oro* (tel 6708044) at £25/35. For golfers who want to stay in **Monte San Pietro** there are the ***Palmieri** (tel 051 6760371 fax 6760253) at £40/60, **Marchi** (tel 051 6760109 fax 6760920) at £30/40 and *Locanda Irene* (tel/fax 051 675 9228) at £25/30. **Castel D'Aiano** has the ***Merlino** (914652) at £15/35 and **Nuovo** (tel 914238) for £15/30.

Two **Camp Sites** can be found in **Marzabotto**, *Piccolo Paradiso* (tel/fax 051 842680) near Sirano and *Ca' Le Scope* (tel 932328) near Gardelatta. Charges are around £3 per adult with the Piccolo slightly cheaper.

Porretta Terme (area code 0534)

****Castanea** (tel 22051 fax 24260, *Santoli* (tel 23206 fax 22744) and *Sassocardo* (tel 23074 fax 24260) all cost around £45/70.

***Hotel Terme di Porretta** (tel 22394 fax 22094) 1 Via delle Terme is connected to the spa centres and costs L80,000 for full board in the off season. Standard in this range are the *Aurora* (tel/fax 23751) and *Bertusi* (tel/fax 22072) at £45 while the *Helvetia* (tel 22214 fax 22279) and *Italla* (tel 22039 fax 22279) offer doubles for £30/45.

The ***Cini** (tel 22161 fax 23902), the *Campana* (tel 22063) and *Dina* (tel 22161 fax 23902) all charge £17/35 while *Riomaggiore* (tel23049) and *Toscana* (tel 29352) charge £25.

i **Porretta's Tourist Information Office** (tel 22021) is at 11 Piazza della Liberta.

The **train station** is in Piazzale Protche. **taxis** (tel 22105), **car hire** (tel 31015) **post office** (Via Stazione)

Lizzano in Belvedere (area code 0534)

Lizzano has plenty of ***hotels including: *Miravalle* (tel 51044 fax 51818) with its solarium, *Monte Pizzo* (tel 51055 fax 51650) and *Villa Fedora* (tel 51122) all for £25/40. *Nappini* (tel 51011 fax 51070) is slightly cheaper at £20/30.

***Farnetti** (tel 51051) and ***Franca** (tel 51036) charge £30 and ***Belvedere** (tel 51144) charges £20/40. Prices for *hotels are around £20/30 with *Gasperini* (tel 51577) offering doubles for £15/20 and *Anna* (tel 51116) rooms for £17.

i **Lizzano's Tourist Information Office** is in the town hall (tel/fax 51052). The nearest **train station** is Porretta Terme. Lizzano's **post office** is at 47 Via III Novembre.

Pianoro (area code 051)

Top of the range in Pianoro is the *****Park Hotel** (tel 6516504 fax 6516402) at £60/110 and its ***subsidiary charging £50/100. The ***Bellevue** (tel 775762 fax 777026) for £20/40 and ***Da Mario** (tel 774865 fax 777225) charging £35. The only en suite *hotel is *Dollaro e Mezzo* (tel 777002) in *Musiano* charging £20/25. Other *hotels include: *Centrale* (tel 777025) at £10/15 and *Mediterraneo* (tel/fax 777130), *Nazionale* (tel 777083) and *Luce* (tel 777136) all charging £17/23.

Monghidoro has a **camp site**, *La Martina* (tel 6551466) at Parco La Martina charging around £3 per adult.

BOLOGNA

THE LOWLANDS

South of Via Emilia towards Imola is an undulating landscape, a junior nursery for the Apennines. North of Via Emilia and the A1 autostrada, Bologna province consists of tranquil stretches of the former Po flood plain now a prosperous rural area.

TOWARDS IMOLA

From Bologna, Via Emilia heads in a southeasterly direction towards Imola and on to Rimini. It is tracked by the A1 autostrada and is a more interesting route if one has the time. About 23km along the old Roman road we arrived at the picturesque health spa town of **Castel San Pietro Terme**. Close to the border with Romagna, the town had dell'Emilia added to its name to stress its strong Emilian allegiance.

The town was founded at the end of the 12th century and again in the 13th but by the 14th century the spa's importance was recognised. The town was important enough for the seat of Bologna University to be moved here both in 1306 and 1338 when the city had problems with the Popes.

A clock tower built in 1119 forms the entrance to the town and leads to Santa Maria Maggiore. This church was built in the same period but the bell tower is 15th century. The town is also known for its lamb dishes and a special honey. It also stages an inviting **Pork Chop Festival** on the second Sunday in September.

Fegatella is the name of the spa's oldest spring. Its curative powers were discovered in 1337 when the cattle stock was saved from an epidemic. The waters were long known for curing liver disorders. The spa also uses local mud and claims to be one of the few spas not using regenerated mud. It also specialises in dealing with obesity and acne. **Castel San Pietro Spa** (051 941247 fax 944423) at 1113 Viale Terme has modern equipment, a health, beauty and fitness centre, a swimming pool, sports centres, night clubs, cinemas and its own hotel.

Close by are many historic towns some dating back to Roman times. To the west, **Varignana** has a church with a crypt built in the 800s. **Frassineto Vecchio** has a castle built in the 900s. **Castel Guelfo** was a fortified hamlet and is still almost surrounded by the bulging 15th century walls with their huge corner bastions erected at the behest of the Malvezzi family. Opponents of the Bentivoglio, they turned the town into a mini city-state and we could still see the city gates that were locked after dark every night till the end of the 18th century.

At Castel Guelfo's heart is a lovely 18th century triangular square surrounded by porticoes. The porticoes have lozenge shaped columns designed to prevent thieves and assassins from hiding behind them. The town is also noteworthy for its

15th and 16th century buildings, particularly Palazzo Marchionale and Palazzo del Podesta.

To the south, just off Via Emilia, the imposing Rocca Sforzesca built in the 1200s and restructured in the 1500s overshadows the town of **Dozza**. Once owned by the Sforzas, the castle has interesting prisoners' graffiti in the dungeons and a collection of torture instruments. Add this to the trap door just in front of the chapel's altar and one gets a rather chilling view of the former owners. The castle also has a display of antique furniture and the regional wine store is in the vaults.

The houses of Dozza may be old but their facades sport colossal contemporary murals, some of them the outstanding works of artists such as Matta, Saetti and Zigaina. The murals are the products of the town's **Painted Wall, Fresco Competition** that attracts artists from around the world. The biennial festival is held each September when the year is an odd number.

The area also offers pleasant walks. Just 4km away from Castel San Pietro are the woods, streams and canals of **Casalecchio dei Conti** and 15 kilometres away are the ancient scenic woods of **Monte Caldero** that peaks rising to 2,000ft

IMOLA – MORE THAN A GRAND PRIX TOWN

Once a year **Imola**'s **Dino Ferrari Racetrack** hosts **a World Formula One Grand Prix**, attracting the international racing community. Ironically Imola's racing history actually began in the 1940s with two wheelers – motor bikes. Just 34km on the A14 autostrada from Bologna, 75km from the Ferrari town of Maranello and a two-hour drive to San Marino, it makes for part of an excellent itinerary for racing enthusiasts. The track stages other car races and still hosts international motorbike competitions.

One of the earliest of the warring Sforzas, Museo Attendolo Sforza, went from Imola to found the great dynasty of Milan dukes. Later in the 1300s Giangaleazzo Sforza built the castle in its present form. The most famous occupant was however Caterina Sforza who ruled the area between Imola and Forli from the late 1400s, until ousted in 1502 by the infamous 'Il Valentino', Cesare Borgia.

Caterina Sforza was one of the great Renaissance figures of Emilia. Faced with a rebellion in which her husband Girolamo Riario was killed and his body thrown from a window, the seven month pregnant Caterina took charge ordering the cannon to be directed at the rebels who succumbed.

Borgia only held the fortress for two years but secured the services of none other than the renowned genius, **Leonardo da Vinci**, to carry out further modifications to the structure. The castle had been badly damaged when captured from the Sforza and Leonardo's military mind was put to effect to modify the castle.

While in Imola, da Vinci also drew a map of the town now kept as part of the royal collection of Windsor.

The fortress (tel 0542 23472), which is open to the public, has been excellently and atmospherically restored and contains displays of antique weapons and ceramics.

Along Via Emilia, Imola's main square is the attractive **Piazza Matteotti**, which is flanked by elegant loggia and 14 arches of the Renaissance Palazzo Sersanti. Opposite is the Palazzo Comunale in Gothic/Romanesque style with evidence of an 18th century restoration. The paintings of the city's patron saint, San Cassiano and of Pietro Grisologo in the two niches beside the balcony are also 18th century. Inside the town hall has many rooms decorated with frescoes.

A few metres away from Matteotti is Piazzetta dell'Orologio, the clock square where the locals gather in the bars and on seats in the sunshine. Just on the side down Via Appia is the 13th century Gothic palace, Palazzo Pighini. Close by is another building from the same period, the Chiesa and Convento di Santo Domenico, which contains a work by Carracci, the Martyrdom of St Ursula. The town theatre alongside it was once a 14th century church but now has a 19th century design.

In a former Franciscan convent, the town library also houses the Archaeology, Natural History and Risorgimento museums. Pride of place is the collection of 400,000 books, the nucleus of which was created by the Franciscan monks. Two interesting 13th century books on show are a gold leafed Latin Book of Psalms and a Hebrew bible.

Next door in the former Dominican convent is the art gallery, La Pinacoteca, with a collection of Carracci, Reni and Bastianino paintings and the more contemporary de Pisis, Guttuso and Cantatore. (Opening times, 9am-12am, 2.30pm-6.30pm)

Imola is part of the ceramic eastern plain specialising in **majolica** jars. Over 400 are on display alongside vases and tiles at Farmacia dell'Ospedale, a building on Via Emilia dating back to 1736.

Just outside the town, 4km to the west on Via Emilia, is another key part of its history, **Il Piratello**, a sanctuary to the Madonna.

Piratello comes from piradel or 'little pear' after a tree that grew beside a pillar with a painting of the Madonna in the 15th century. Pilgrim, Stefano Mangelli stopped beneath the tree on the way to Loreto. Seeing a candle illuminate the

B O L O G N A

Madonna, he heard a voice telling him to build a shrine built on the spot. After a siege of Imola, Caterina Sforza ordered the construction of the shrine.

Later Cesare Borgia vowed that if he took Imola without blood he would build a chapel at the shrine. Despite the partial destruction of the castle indicating a violent struggle, Il Valentino built the chapel bringing Leonardo da Vinci along to decorate the chapel with a picture. The classical Renaissance shrine includes interesting frescoes by Guardassoni.

A pleasant place for relaxing in the town is **Il Parco delle Acque Minerale**, the mineral water park, so-called because of a spring of sulphurous water. Holm Oaks, plane trees and maidenhair offer shade. Otherwise outside the town are Tozzoni Park and the nature reserve, **Frattona Wood**. The wood is of interest especially because of the presence of the sands or Sabbie di Imola, relics of Imola's prehistoric shoreline.

EATING OUT

For eating out, Imola is well known as home to many gourmet chefs. Many of their best have gone to the USA and Europe but still it's worth asking for the local specialities of **strozzapreti** and **garganelli** with a ragu sauce. Nearby Ponticelli holds a macaroni festival on the first Sunday in Lent. The **Grand Hotel Donatello** has a **discotheque**.

Close to Imola town there are two dining **agriturismo** – **Monte Frascineto** at 2 Via Chiesa Pediano in Tre Monti (£12 a meal) and **Locanda Solarola** at 5 Via Santa Croce in Castel Guelfo. Ozzana dell'Emilia has three **agriturismo with accommodation**, **Dulcamara** (tel/fax 051 796643) at 78 Via Tolara di Sopra in Settefonti (£10/night), **El Poggio** (tel 051 6515358) at 8 Via Montearmato (£25/double) and **Forlani Andrea** (tel/fax 051 798726) at 81 Via Galvani (£12/30/bed).

ACCOMMODATION

Imola (area code 0542) has three ****hotels for race goers, namely, **Grand Hotel Donatello** (tel 680800 fax 689514) at 25 Via Rossini charging £75/120, **Molino Rosso** (tel 63111 fax 631163) at 49 Via Statale Selice charging £60/110 and **Olimpia** (tel 28460 fax 26500) at 69 Via Pisacane charging £50/100.

Of the ***hotels, **Il Castello** (tel 657018) at 55 Via Bergullo, **Moderna** (tel/fax 23122) at 22 Via XX Settembre and **Zio** (tel 35274 fax 35627) at 14 Via Nardozzi charge around £40. **La Perla** (tel/fax 600023) at 15, Via Malsicura charges £60/90.

****Motel Villagio** (tel 641889 fax 640006) on Via Riccione may have only two stars but expect to pay £65. ****Del Turismo** (tel/fax 22771) at 45 Via C.Pisacane charge £25 and ****Rivazza** (tel 26052) at 39 Via del Colli charge £17/35.

Cheapest of the *hotels is **La Collina** (tel 626200 fax 42627) on Via Mercatone at £25. **Rio Gardi** (tel 22426) at 15 Via Busa in Piratello is an **agriturismo** with eight rooms.

Castel San Pietro Terme (area code 051) has one ****hotel, **Castello** (tel 940138 fax 944573) at 1010 Viale

Terme and charging £60/100.

*****Park Hotel** (tel 941101 fax 944374) at 1010 Via Terme charge around £40 while *****Nuova Italia** (tel 941932 fax 941398) with its **discotheque** at 73 Via Cavour and *****Hotel Parigi** (tel/fax 943585) at 860 Via Terme charge £40/60.

Hotels include: **Corona (tel 941462) at 48 Via dei Mille charging £20/40, **Due Portoni** (tel 941190) at 133 Via Mazzini charging £30, **La Torretta** (tel 941340) at 1559 Via Terme (£25), and **Il Gallo** (tel 941114 fax 944520) at 34 Via Repubblica (£30/40). The ***Maraz** (tel 941236) in Piazza Vittorio Veneto

charges £20 for a room with shared bath.

A stop in **Castel Guelfo** at ***Da Tartaglia** (tel 0542 53321) costs £20/25 a night.

Dozza (area code 0542) has ******Hotel Gloria** (tel 673438 fax 673439) charging £45/100 and ******Monte del Re** (tel 678400 fax 678444) charging £60/100. Cheaper stays are offered at the *****Cane** (tel 678120 fax 678522) and ****Da Marino** (tel/fax 678112) for around £30.

i For **Imola Tourist Information Office** telephone 0542 602308

UP THE SANTERNO VALLEY

Imola is on the Santerno River and travelling up the valley on the Via Montanara (SS610) offers some pleasant towns and scenery. Roughly 12km from Imola is **Borgo Tossignano** and the road left there brings one to the old town of Tossignano settled since the Villanovan era.

Apart from its 'Cisterna Pubblica' the town is best known for its annual Mardi Gras polenta festival that has been celebrated in the ruins of the castle since 1611. Further along the valley road is **Fontanelice** most of which was swept away, castle and all, in the 1748 landslide. On Easter Monday one can stop here for another festival, the Sagra della Pie Fritta, and try the Pie Fritta, a sweet, fried local tortilla. Above the town on Monte Volpe is the Grotto di Re Tiberio, a cave that gave birth to a legend reminiscent of that concerning the death of King Theodoric of Ravenna.

King Tiberio is said to have brought his court to hide in the grotto after he was warned that he would meet his death via a bolt of lightning. He ventured out for a stroll

on his horse when he saw the sun shining in a clear blue sky, only to be struck by a stray thunderbolt.

The final stop 24km from Imola at the head of the valley is at **Castel del Rio**, a former territory of Matilda di Canossa and later a fiefdom of the Alidosi family. Their castle, Palazzo degli Alidosi, built in 1504 is a fine Renaissance example of a fortified residence and now the municipal town hall. The castle houses the Museo della Guerra displaying items from the last war. Another reminder of Alidosi rule is the 42metre-high hump-backed bridge across the Santerno built in 1449 and called Ponte degli Alidosi.

Locals call themselves Alidosiani but they are better known for the local chestnut, the marrone di Castel del Rio or Castel del Rio brown, which is a mark of quality. Come the chestnut harvest and they celebrate with a **gastronomic festival** on the second Sunday each October. June brings two other interesting events, the historic pageant of the **Burning of the Witch** and the **Jostling Contest** of the Mediaeval Quarters.

BOLOGNA

Accommodation and Eating Out
(area code 0542)

Castel del Rio has an **agriturismo with accommodation**, Ca' del Rio Zafferino (tel 96022) at 24 Via Rio Zafferino, Giugnola (£10/night).

Castel del Rio's ***Gallo** (tel 95924 fax 95380) and ***Villangela** (tel 95684 fax 95380) charge £30/40 while

Corona (tel 95917) and **Il Galletto** (tel 95331 fax 95380) are slightly cheaper. **Fontanelice** has the ***Centrale** (tel 92710) and **La Pergola** (tel 92562 fax 92254) both charging around £30 and **Ca' Monti** (tel 97666) **agriturismo** at 4 Via Monte Morosino with rooms for £15. **Borgo Tossignano** has **Richi** (tel/fax 91033) charging £25/30.

Castel del Rio has a **camp site** at Le Selve (tel 95806).

THE NORTHERN PLAINS

North of Bologna the province is a stretch of rich reclaimed marshland for which the Reno River provides the northern border. The main roads radiate out from Bologna City and provide different tourist routes meandering past beautiful villas and tranquil farms on the eastern, northern and western plains.

About 11km from Bologna's Porta San Vitale on Via San Vitale (SS253) one arrives at **Castenaso** a former Roman castrum named after the Consul Publio Scipione known as Nasica because of his large nose. Hence, Castenaso – the town of Big Nose. The Consul made his name in a great victory against the Gauls, which is recorded in the village coat of arms. Nearby is the Baroque Santuario della Madonna del Pilar where the composer **Rossini** was married in 1822 to soprano Isabella Colbran. Rossini and Sra Colbran lived near Castenaso for ten years during which he wrote *Semiramide* and *The William Tell Overture*.

A ten-minute detour from SS253 and a 5km-drive north from Castenaso is **Budrio**. One locally made instrument, which may be on display, is the *ocarine* a terracotta wind instrument sometimes described as a flute and sometimes as a mouth organ. The ocarine, made in a range of tones and shaped like sweet potatoes, were invented in 1853 by Budrio born Guiseppe Donati who became internationally recognised.

The pride of Budrio is however outside the town walls, 4km away on the road to Granarolo in the hamlet of **Bagnarola**. The Bentivoglio built the four-towered Palazzo Odorico here in the 16th century. In the early 18th century Torreggiani designed the gardens and villa known as Floriano Complex and they were soon dubbed, the '**Bologna Versailles**'.

The Malvezzi tried to outdo Floriano and nearby built the Casino L'Aurelia

Complex as their summer home replete with gardens, swings, fishponds and three chapels. Their guests included many royals and in 1727, the Stuart, James III. The 18th century Villa Ranuzzi Copsi only added to the Versailles-like grandeur.

North east of Budrio a turn right just after Vedrana brings one to the feudal 15th century village of **Selva Malvezzi**, another former fiefdom of the Bologna's Malvezzi family. Of interest here is the marvellous facade, clock and bell of Palazzo del Governatore and Palazzo Padronale's double ramp staircase offering differential access for man and beast. The village also contains the Neoclassical church of S.Croce designed by Venturoli.

Continuing 17km along the road north east from Budrio one comes across the town of **Molinella** famous for its tagliatelle cakes first baked in the 1700s. Here the River Idice is populated by many water mills, which were used to grind flour in this once oft-flooded area. The town's skyline is dominated by its leaning tower and the Torre Stefano built in 1402.

Guiseppe Massarenti (1867-1959) is the most celebrated figure in the town. One of the first socialist mayors in Italy and one of the first founders of the agricultural consumer co-operatives, he was persecuted by the fascists. Mussolini's men even sent him to a mental asylum, from where he was only released at the end of the war.

Molinella is also close to the Ferrara marshlands or 'wetlands' of Campotto's La Valle.

Also leaving Bologna via Via Zamboni north past Granarolo and east of Ca' de' Fabbri is the village of **Minerbio** dominated by Rocca Castello degli Isolani. 150 exiled families from Lombardy founded Minerbio in 1231. But in 1303, the Cypriot Isolani family built this fortress and became the feudal lords in 1403. Apart from when the Isolani were expelled by the Bentivoglio, they have lived in Minerbio ever since. In 1530 they were considered worthy enough to entertain Emperor Charles V here as he travelled to his coronation in Bologna.

The three splendidly frescoed rooms of Marte (Mars), Astronomia and Ercole (Hercules) were the work of Amico Aspertini in 1527. The castle has an interesting octagonal dovecote with cells to allow for 5,000 nests.

Facing the castle is Palazzo Isolani with Bolognese school frescoes and sculptures from the same era. Also in the town centre is the church of San Giovanni Battista built in the 1300s but extensively redesigned by Donati in the 1700s.

Just 3km east of Minerbio is the mediaeval hamlet of **San Martino in Soverzano**, which is dominated by the wonderful 15th century Castello del Manzoli. The Manzoli dynasty took over the castle after the family of Ariosto, the Renaissance poet, had built it. In 1883 it was extensively restored and boasts fine crenellated battlements. Entry requires contacting the current owners.

The northern plain consists of the area close to the A13 autostrada from Bologna towards Ferrara. From Bologna one can take the provincial road towards Galleria or the A13 exit at Bologna Interporto which soon brings one to **Castel Maggiore** beside the Navile Canal. The Navile Canal has furnished this rich reclaimed agricultural area since the 12th century. Close to Bologna, it was settled by many rich Bolognese families as evident by the many splendid 17th to 19th century villas dotted around the plain.

Next to the A13 autostrada and 4km east of San Giorgio lies **Bentivoglio**, a town that grew rich from its access to the Navile. Indeed until the Bentivoglio arrived, the town was known as Ponte Poledrano after its bridge across the canal. The importance of the waterways to the economy, military fighting on the plain and the town's closeness to Ferrara gave the town a strategic importance.

The castle was erected in the late 1400s by Giovanni II Bentivoglio to strengthen the town as a military outpost. But the castle has other associations. It was the rendezvous for Alfonso D'Este I and his future bride, the notorious Lucrezia Borgia. An elegant castle, as wars subsided, it became more of a delizia. A courtyard description describes it as a *domus jucunditatis* or happy house.

Continuing up north from San Giorgio one arrives after 7km at **San Pietro in Casale** where in 1443 Annibale Bentivoglio defeated the north Italian troops of the powerful Visconti. The church of San Pietro e Paulo in the town's attractive main piazza has an 11th century bell tower and an interior boasting 16th century frescoes by the Ferrara school. The 16th century Villa Padoa is now the seat of the town council.

Heading west from Bologna on SS568 and taking the turn off to Cento, one arrives after 14km at **Sala Bolognese** with the simple Lombard-Romanesque style church Pieve di San Biaggio. The ram's head of Aries carved into the marble table on the main altar is thought to be evidence that the pieve was built in 1066 on the ruins of a Roman pagan temple. Also of interest is the 13th century gallery in the largest of the three apses.

Castello D'Argile is 9km further north. Its name means, 'castle of clay' and one can visit what is left of the rocca. Just 5km north of Castello D'Argile is **Pieve di Cento**, adjacent to its twin, Cento that lies just across the boundary with Ferrara province. The attractive mediaeval town is known as 'Little Bologna' owing to the number of ancient wooden beamed porticoes, the best of which can be seen at the 1272 **Casa degli Anziani** on Via Garibaldi. Much of the encircling walls, battlements, and the 15th and 16th century gates, are still intact, inviting visitors into a treat of mediaeval, Renaissance and Baroque houses, palaces and churches.

Central to the town's history is the Torre della Rocca castle built in 1387 and designed by the same de Vincenzo who drew up the plans for San Petronio in

Bologna's Piazza Maggiore. The castle was the scene of many battles as Bologna fought with Ferrara for control of the town.

The town takes its name from the Collegiate church of Santa Maria Maggiore in Piazza Andrea Costa, which was rebuilt, in Baroque style in the early 1700s. The interior contains works by Guercino and the apse has Guido Reni's *Palla dell'Assunta*. But the most notable feature is the impressive 13th century cypress wood crucifix beneath which Popes Julius II, Clement VIII and Pius IX knelt to pray. More of Reni and Guercino's works can be found in the 18th century Palazzo Mastellari's Pinacoteca Comunale public art gallery alongside works from 20th century artists.

Another route following the SS568 leads to Crevalcore (26km) via **San Giovanni in Persiceto** (16km). Villanovan relics found near the town indicate that it has been settled for thousands of years. The concentric circles of streets at San Giovanni's centre testify to its mediaeval past as does the 12th century wooden portico on the Palazzaccio next to the town hall. Giovanni II Bentivoglio had the town hall built in 1498, along with Castello o Villa la Giovanni near Decima with its five towers and marvellous Guercino frescoes covering the walls of six rooms.

The Collegiate church of San Giovanni Battista has work by Albani and Guercino and bas-reliefs by Pio whose work is also in the 15th century church of Crocifisso. Emperor Charles V visited the town in 1532 but the town is more known for its struggle for democracy, trade unions, co-ops and struggles against fascism.

San Giovanni in Persiceto's main festival is an historical pageant held in June, when floats carry scenes from stories about the legendary Bertoldo and related in *Bertoldo e Bertolino* by San Giovanni-born Giulio Cesare Croce. Performances may sometimes appear in the beautiful hall of the town's public theatre.

The town of **Anzola** is south of San Giovanni in Persiceto and can be reached by taking Via Emilia from Bologna (13km). At its heart was the 13th century Torre di Re Enzo where King Enzo was also imprisoned for a time after being captured at Fossalta in 1249 by the Bologna Comunes. The tower is all that is left of the castle. **Enzo** was watched over by Count Michele degli Orsi, the lord of Anzola. They became friends and the count tried to smuggle his ward out of a castle in a pannier. Enzo was subsequently moved to a palace in central Bologna's Piazza Maggiore.

Just 6km west of San Giovanni on the road to Nonantola is **Sant'Agata Bolognese**, so-called because it was on the Modena border and control was contested by the Modenese. Today it is best known as host to a **Lamborghini factory**. Nevertheless, the town's Torre tower is a national monument. It also has the old Porta di Sotto town gate with parts of its old drawbridge. Sant'Agata has pretty Renaissance churches like Sant'Andrea and the oratory of Spirito Santo which has fine frescoes. The splendid Sala Consigliare is also worth a visit.

ACCOMMODATION AND EATING OUT
(area code 051)

Budrio has ***Sport** (tel 803515 fax 803580) at £40/60 and *Del Teatro* (tel 800208) charging £40 while *San Francesco* (tel/fax 801490) charges £25/40. **Belle Lu** (tel 807034 fax 801034) at 1 Via Banzi in Bagnarola is an **agriturismo** with **accommodation**. *Fondo Fornasella* at 4 Via Dritto in Pieve is a dining **agriturismo** as is *Libertas Immobiliare* at 30 Via Rabuina.

Bentivoglio has ***Hotel Bentivoglio** (tel 6641111 fax 6640997) at 18 Via Marconi charging £40/65. Minerbio has ***Nanni** (tel 878276 fax 876094) £50/65 and ***Prim Hotel** (tel 6604108 fax 6606210) charging £45/80. Molinella has ***Mini Place Hotel** (tel 881180 fax 880877) charging £40/80 and *Stadio* (tel 881144) charging £20/30. Pieve di Cento has ****Nuovo Gran Hotel Bologna** (tel 6861070 fax 974835) with a **discotheque** and charging £120 and *Locanda le Quattro Piume* (tel 6861500 fax 974191) at 15, Via XXV Aprile at £30/60.

The tomb of Giovanni Legnano, Bologna

BOLOGNA

The Council of Ministries of Culture of the European Union has awarded Bologna's cultural vitality by nominating it European City of Culture for the year 2000, together with Avignon, Bergen, Krakow, Helsinki, Prague, Reykiavik and Santiago de Compostela. For this reason, and thanks not only to the town's public institutions but also to the many citizens' associations who are the main characters of the town's cultural life, we will celebrate the new millennium by opening new spaces for culture and with a programme of unprecedented intensity and height: 585 projects, more than 1800 events - exibitions, shows, festivals, multimedia initiatives - will bring the Italian culture into Europe, and the European culture into Italy.

TOURIST INFORMATION OFFICE (I.A.T.)
P.zza Maggiore 6
Tel. 051 239660 - Fax 051 231454
E-mail: touristoffice@comune.bologna.it

BOLOGNA 2000 INFOLINE
For information about Bologna 2000 events. **166 00 2000**
Internet: **www.bologna2000.it**

PAVAROTTI'S **Modena**

Leaving Bologna for Modena we managed to end up on the old Via Emilia which being a direct but relatively narrow road is slow moving. I had forgotten that on the roads the green road signs alone indicated directions via the autostrada and the blue signs referred to lesser roads. In error we took a blue sign and ended up on the Via Emilia instead of the A1 autostrada which would have saved 25 minutes from our hour long journey westwards.

Travelling westwards, the Apennine mountains came into view in the south, while to the north were the flat fields stretching out over the plain to the Po. It was a classic picture of the part Via Emilia plays in dividing up the provinces of Emilia. Eventually we arrived in Modena city, administrative capital to the province of Pavarotti, Umberto Eco and Enzo Ferrari.

The streets are relatively wide in this prosperous, industrous city, home to **Maserati** and **Ferrari** car plants. Like most of Emilia-Romagna, Modena's grand structures tend to be devoid of marble, using clay brick, river stone, or sandstone. Laws in the town strictly control the colour schemes of buildings. The streets painted in ochre, yellows, browns and light greens conveyed welcoming warmth.

We arrived at the Hotel Roma in the centre by driving straight down the Via Emilia, so straight that we drove straight through a No Entry sign finding ourselves directly behind a Carabinieri police car. We drove on with not a beep or a whistle from the police and we soon reached the hotel. Only later did we discover that, in Modena centre at least, tourists are allowed to pass through the No Entry signs so that they can see the sites and reach their hotels conveniently.

MODENA'S HISTORY

Modena's early history can be traced back through the Palaeolithic Age to the Roman era, begun by the driving out of the Celts and the creation of a castrum on Via Emilia. The castrum was the location for a battle in 44 B.C when the troops under Brutus laid siege to the town held by **Mark Anthony**.

Modena's name is thought to derive either from the Celtic or Etruscan word for a small mound. However, being on the flood plain, the city was at times hit by devastating floods. These floods, post-Roman invasions, and earthquakes have left no architectural trace of the early city.

Plenty of digs and finds have unearthed artefacts from these eras. Pre-Roman artefacts are on display in the Museo Civico, and the plentiful Roman finds are displayed in Museo Lapidario Estense.

As in most of Italy, the post-Roman era saw a major decline in population and civil life. Only after 400 years did production and population revive sufficiently to allow the return of great works. The array of Romanesque buildings around the province, and the jewel of **Modena Cathedral**, are testament to the strength of this new age.

Matilda di Canossa played a part (1075-1115) in this revival. Modena subsequently passed through Comune rule until the nobles began another significant era for the city.

In 1289, the warring Modena nobility sought stability by offering power to Obizzo D'Este, Duke of Ferrara. The tyranny of his rule led to a republican uprising in 1306 when he was chased from the city. It was not an auspicious start but the Este duke returned and he and his heirs ruled for the next 500 years. In 1598 the Estense were expelled from Ferrara and set up base in Modena.

The Estense had a big presence, erecting palaces and churches, particularly after they had left Ferrara, and made Modena the capital of their dukedom. They chose Modena because it had links to Ferrara. The great moat around the palace was connected to a canal flowing into the River Po, and down to their beloved Ferrarese domains. Also important in this era were the Pio family, nobles residing in Sassuolo and Carpi. Marco Pio increased his power by marrying a Farnese princess from Milan. So, to consolidate their rule in their new capital, the Estense immediately killed Marco Pio. His family was well linked to the Estense and the act was a demonstration of their ruthless determination.

AROUND MODENA CITY
Piazza Grande

With the town hall and the cathedral, the historic centre of the town is **Piazza Grande**, a wide square used as the city's market place up until the inter war period. Today the fruit and vegetable market is in a covered hall in Via Albinelli and the Monday market that used to be in Piazza Grande has moved to Parco Novi Sad.

One corner of the piazza is a large marble stone known as the **ringadora** or haranguing stone. Originally used as a rostrum for proclamations and as a Hyde Park-like speakers' corner, the ringadora was then used for debtors. To avoid being declared bankrupts, they had to have their hair cut off and walk naked three times around the piazza on three Saturdays. They would then have to beat on the stone, which was covered with turpentine, three times with their bare backsides to complete their humiliation.

When failed traders were not mooning it, the stone had a more macabre role as the place on which the drowned were dumped while they awaited identification.

The piazza is packed on January 31st, the **feast day** of patron saint, **San Geminiano** and on Giovedi Grasso, the Thursday before Shrove Tuesday. On the latter day thousands pack the square to hear an actor dressed up as **Sandrone**, a legendary Modena peasant, address them from the town hall balcony in Modenese dialect.

The last Sunday in May brings thousands of children to a huge show as part of the modern festival, **The City is Mine**, dedicated to the child. The square is also a centre for concerts, shows and theatre during the summer. However, this may be at an end as the authorities are considering erecting a cafe concerto here.

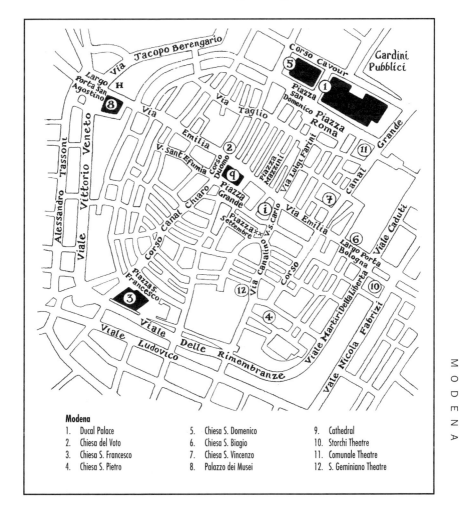

Modena

1. Ducal Palace	5. Chiesa S. Domenico	9. Cathedral
2. Chiesa del Voto	6. Chiesa S. Biagio	10. Storchi Theatre
3. Chiesa S. Francesco	7. Chiesa S. Vincenzo	11. Comunale Theatre
4. Chiesa S. Pietro	8. Palazzo dei Musei	12. S. Geminiano Theatre

The Cathedral

Modena's cathedral is the city's most famous monument. Begun on June 6th, 1099, it is a masterpiece of the architect Lanfranco and includes bas relief sculptures by Wiligelmo. The structure has worn well over the centuries and remains a classical Romanesque building. The dramatic southern side facing out over Piazza Grande is probably more impressive than the façade. However many of the original pieces are preserved in museums.

During the Mediaeval period each town was self-governed, hence it was very important to build a powerful cathedral to demonstrate one's wealth and might. Modena often fought against the town of Bologna and the intense rivalry was reflected in the size of the municipal structures. A general assembly of the people of the city decided to fund the building of the cathedral, which is why it was both a religious and civic building. Its effect was also to shift the centre of the city.

The marble for the exterior came from ancient Roman buildings and the lions at the base of the columns of the Porta dei Principe Principi (main entrance) are considered too realistic to have been mediaeval, and therefore were probably taken from a Roman villa.

The bas reliefs by the German artist, Wiligelmo stand beside and around the main door. In the Middle Ages a popular means of relating biblical stories and religious tales and messages to the illiterate population was to decorate the church facades with sculptures portraying the various legends.

The other entrances were added later and the bas reliefs shifted to above the doors. As in Verona a white whale bone hangs on a chain above the main door. A 17th century book states it was found on the square during a 16th century excavation, but more probably it was bought.

Entering we moved out from bright sunlight into semi-darkness. The very simple interior was a sharp contrast to the heavily embellished exterior. The huge rose window above the main window was only inserted in the 14th century so we could imagine how much darker the Romanesque duomo was intended to be.

Interesting features at the rear on the apse wall are the engraved measurements indicating the cathedral's standard size for a yard, a pole, a roof-tile and a brick.

Also to the rear is an archivault with a bas-relief of the legend of King Arthur and Genevieve is seen locked in a tower. Our guide insisted that King Arthur came from Brittany and not England. Whatever his origins, nobody knows how King Arthur made his way into the 12th century art of this Italian cathedral.

One of the most peculiar reliefs is the so-called Metopes statue high up on the wall showing two people one stood and the other upside down- the antipodes, a

MODENA

hermaphrodite, and a half-man half bird figure eating a fish. The hermaphrodite is sometimes said to represent the Putta of Modena, a legendary unmarried woman who was said to have died giving birth to her 40th baby.

The cathedral, like the Ghirlandina tower to its rear, leans. The lean resulted in the insertion of a Gothic arch that stands between the two buildings ensuring that they do not meet. The incline is put down to the land beneath being still ridden with water and upset by many past archaeological excavations.

The Ghirlandina Tower

Just behind and looming over the cathedral is the historic landmark, the 11th century Ghirlandina Tower, Italy's third biggest leaning tower after Pisa and Bologna. The construction began during the same period of the cathedral, the main work being done during the 12th century. The tower is 82 metres high and not only symbolic, but a key defence centre for the town where important archives were kept.

Its base was begun at the same time as the cathedral. The octagonal and pyramidical upper parts were Gothic additions by Campione, and were called *da Campione* or *Campiones*, completed in 1319. At its base are two round indentations that were for measuring cheese wheels. Modena's popular ricotta cheeses would be brought here to see whether they would cost three or five coins.

The Stolen Bucket

In 1325 Modena's troops defeated Bologna's army at Zappolino, and carried off a wooden bucket belonging to the Bologna soldiers, as a victory trophy. The bucket was then for centuries kept under guard in the Ghirlandina Tower. Alessandro Tassoni, who wrote a mock heroic poem about the bucket in 1622, is commemorated with a statue in the square.

Ten years ago a group of Bolognese students kidnapped the bucket and demanded a ransom from the Comune of Modena for its return. The Comune agreed to the students' demands and they received their booty – some hams and cheese. The bucket was returned but now it is kept in the more secure town hall. A replica remains on display in the tower

M
O
D
E
N
A

The Town Hall

Also in the square, the **Palazzo Comunale** town hall is thought to have been built earlier than the cathedral, but they are from approximately the same era. The town hall facade was completely restructured in the 17th century as a Renaissance building with arcades. The **Torre dell'Orologio** clock tower in the middle remains as a 15th century work.

On the end of the arcade in the corner close to Via Castellaro is the statue known as **The Bonissima**, a popular local figure whose origin is unknown but under which four marble columns carry indications as to the official weights and measures standards of 1268 when it was erected.

The first floor has a gallery where we saw the Stolen Bucket, surrounded by finely painted wooden 16th and 18th century panels in the Sala del Fuoco (Fire Room) named after its huge fireplace. In the Mediaeval Ages merchants would arrive bringing wood to burn, taking hot embers out to the piazza to keep themselves warm on a winter's day. Paintings by the artists of the time portrayed the city as having leaning towers even then.

The emblem of the town is shown as a blue cross on a white background similar to that of Parma. The old town council meetings were held in the **Sala del Vecchio Consiglio** (Old Council Hall) which has black and white 17th century frescoes illustrating the legends of San Geminiano and the art of government. The Sala degli Arazzi (Tapestry Room) contains a magnificent 300-year-old locally made tapestry.

On Via Canalino, the curvature of the ancient street has led people to suggest that the corner was the site of the old Roman amphitheatre. This area was the site of the town walls but they were demolished long ago. The area outside the walls now has a large park area. The old town had been built with an extensive system of canals, many of the streets that replaced or ran along them bear their names. Hence, Canalino meaning *little canal,* Canalchiaro, *clear canal*, Canal Grande, *big canal* and so on.

Of note is **La Chiesa del Voto**, construction of which begun on the day after the townspeople stopped carrying out their dead struck down by the Great Plague. The plague killed off 40 percent of the city's people and led to the covering over of the canal system.

Corso Canal Grande follows the path of what was once the city's main canal and was well worth a stroll. Many of the splendid old buildings are still owned by noble families. The street also contains what is said to be the nicest hotel in town, the frescoed **Hotel Canal Grande**, owned by **Alejandro De Tomaso**, the famous car builder.

Via Emilia's large arcades are 19th and 20th century, and taller than those of

MODENA

Renaissance style. Modena has no particular mediaeval area, save around Via San Geminiano and Via Largo San Giacomo, and the many ancient monasteries dotted around the city. Off Piazza San Giacomo are several suitably dark and narrow streets with arcades of mediaeval origin. Here the arcades vary in size because not all complied with the request to reduce their arcades in size so as to facilitate the widening of the canal.

Just along Via Caselle, close to Corso Canal Grande, we were told of a legendary spot where a walnut tree once grew. During the Middle Ages, the local witches (considered in Modena to include all red-haired women) would gather here. Women's bare hands should collect the walnuts for the nocino liqueur on June 24th , the night of San Giovanni when witches come out, guaranteeing a bewitching effect on the drinkers. After Witches Night the nuts are soaked in alcohol and allowed to mature, producing a sweet potent drink.

The arching twist of the Via Mondatora has led local historians to suggest that the site is that of the city's former Roman amphitheatre. Down the street is the 100 year-old food market, open from very early in the morning till 1.30pm, a good stop off for cheap and high quality food.

Wherever else we went in the city, we seemed to be surrounded by Renaissance and Baroque buildings. Modena went into decline in the post Romanesque period and only began to revive with Estense rule. The late 15th century **San Pietro Abbey** and other monasteries cling to the old canal street. San Pietro's on Via San Pietro is a fine early Renaissance example with its beautiful cloister and facade of circles, rectangles, triangles and vertical and horizontal lines. Terracotta was used both in the decorations and the building work. In summer the abbey's ancient organ is used to stage concerts for the public.

The Ducal Palace

A short walk from Piazza Grande brought us to the Piazza Ducale and the large 12th century **Ducal Palace**. The site was chosen because it was at the centre of the canal system and the surrounding moat fed into the canals. It became the official residence of the Estense dukes. Most of the building is in the Baroque style, popular in 1635 when it was altered at the behest of Este duke, Francesco I. The east wing is a later Neoclassical addition.

MODENA

The simple style reflected Modena taste and the high cost of transporting marble. That the palace rises only three stories is because the diplomatic dukes took respectful pains to ensure that it was no taller than the town hall. The clock in the central tower was installed in 1756 and is still working. The elegant inner courtyard and staircase are home to the Military Academy and a library containing many precious books and paintings. Visits are allowed on Sundays mornings.

At Largo Porta San Agostino the 18th century **Palazzo dei Musei** (Open 9am-2pm, closed Mondays) contains the **Galleria Estense** collection of paintings and artworks collected by the Este Dukes. Sadly, the Estense were in the habit of profligate spending and many of their best paintings were sold off to raise funds. They then raided their other cities to maintain the collection and these, including works of Tintoretto, Carracci, Guercino and Guido Reni, are on display on the 2nd floor.

The ground floor holds the **Museo Lapidario Estense** with artefacts from the Palaeolithic to Mediaeval Ages. Other sections of the building include displays of items from the letters of Lucrezia Borgia to 15th century illustrated Bibles and material from the Risorgimento.

We drove off to see the old city wall on the Marte De Libertad **Martiri della Libertà** road. Covered in ivy and just four feet long, that is all that is left of the mediaeval city wall – one of Italy's smaller monuments.

We noted in the central park, popular for promenading, how the statues of Garibaldi and his men were hidden behind trees. We were told that the people were rather ashamed of the quality of the statues, but rather than destroy the work of art, they surrounded it with foliage!

On the Trail of Pavarotti

We arrived at the Pavarotti restaurant once owned by the great opera singer. That the maestro hails from Modena has been a great modern spur to the city, which hosts an annual festival known as, "Pavarotti and Friends". The star's fans flock to the city hoping to catch sight of him.

His father used to work in a small bakery that has a white tent on Via Emilia just outside the city centre on the road to Bologna. Inside hangs a picture of the young Pavarotti, who sang in the cathedral choir, making the bread.

His former villa, now belonging to his ex-wife, can be reached by travelling along Via Giardini towards Sassuolo. Arriving at the small village of Saliceta San Giuliano, one can spot the villa surrounded by poplar trees in a huge garden. The villa was being built close to **Restaurant Europa 92**, off the Nuovo Estense road to Montale. Restaurant Europa 92 (closed Mon) at 8 Stradello Nava used to belong to Pavarotti and is still the location for the **Pavarotti International Horse Show**, begun by the star due to his love of horses.

Eating is a popular activity in Modena with its special cuisine using Parmesan and Balsamic vinegar. The central area has plenty of restaurants and bars to choose from.

On Via Farini one can find an old salami shop, **Giuseppe Giusti's**, one of the oldest in the world. Giusti's famous shop began in 1605 in the Jewish ghetto and ever since has made salami in-house.

Between the cathedral and the Ducal Palace is a network of pedestrian streets with plenty of eating houses. Of these, **Da Enzo** (closed Mon) at 17, Via Coltellini is one of the cheapers, serving meals at L35,000. Another in this range is **Al Boschetto** (closed Wed) at 202, Via Due Canali. Also on Via Coltellini, **Da Danilo** (closed Fri) offers meals at L40,000, and **Aurora** (closed Mon) serves up meals at L45/70,000. **Borso D'Este** at 5 Piazza Roma (closed Sun) is said to be among the best and most expensive restaurants (meals L80,000).

Albina is an eating house built especially for merchants who attended the market place. The atmosphere is almost sixties style with meals available for L20,000. **L'Incontro** (closed Sun) at 32, Largo San Giacomo in the south of the city is reputed (at L45,000) to be one of the better restaurants in the city.

Ermes Trattoria on Via Ganaceto is only open till lunchtime but it is very popular. If you eat there you have to order a primo, a secondo, a side-dish and a coffee, but if you want to order less you will be probably invited to order a whole meal or invited to leave: these are Ermes' rules. This is one of the most reputable places for hand-made pasta: cookery-writers generally prefer to go to Ermes rather than Fini! You don't really need a reservation. Ermes is a historical restaurant: it was meant, as Aldina, for those coming to work in town. Ermes prepares all very traditional food you generally don't find in restaurants. All this for 25.000 lire.

Venezia 2 at 44 Via Galluci (closes 8.30pm) in the south east of the centre is a popular pasticceria with a friendly atmosphere, imaginative menus and plenty of pasta, "like we make at home".

At **nights** we went for a drink at Modena's young and trendy **Embassy Bar** at the corner of Via Bellinzona and Via Vignolese. It's a bright, loud but friendly place for a night out with lots of salami, quails eggs, prawns, parmesan, artichokes, olives and other snacks coming free with the drinks. Meals are available at lunchtime and the little terrace is popular in the summer.

Piazza Grande is the July and August venue for a season of **plays**, **concerts** and **operetta** in the open air in front of an auditorium seating 2,000 people. Between October and May, **opera, classical music and ballet** are performed at the 1,200 seater **Teatro Comunale** on Corso

M
O
D
E
N
A

Canalgrande. **Plays** are staged at **Teatro Storchi** nearby in Largo Garibaldi. During summer the monastery cloisters are used for various types of **concerts**.

Cinemas include *Filmstudio 7B* that puts on new art films. The *Embassy* shows good commercial films in the original language, while in the summer *Supercinema Estivo* puts on commercial films outdoors. There are few **night clubs** in the centre but many are outside coming to life in the students' term time.

The Communist Annual Festival, **Festa de l'Unità**, now more of a carnival, takes place in September and attracts thousands to its restaurants, concerts and stalls in Ponte Alto. Another place to visit is the **Antique Market** that takes place every fourth weekend of the month in the area of Novi Sad Park.

ACCOMMODATION
(area code 059)

Modena is host to many industrial fairs and exhibitions so hotel space can be at a premium. Booking in advance is advisable.

Hotels

****At £45/90 per night, the cheapest of the four star hotels is *Central Park* (tel 522225 fax 225141) at 10, Viale Vittorio Veneto. *Canalgrande* (tel 217160 fax 221674) at 4 Corso Canalgrande, *Grand'Hotel Raffaello* (tel 357035 fax 354522) at 5 Strada per Cognento and *Hotel Real Fini* (tel 238091) at 441 Via Emilia Est have rooms costing £70/200).

The ***Europa* (tel 217721 fax 222228), *Milano* *** (tel 223011 fax 225136) and *Principe* (tel 218670 fax 237693) are just behind the Ducal palace by the Public Gardens on Corso Vittorio Emanuele. Cheapest in this range at £30/50 is the *Estense* (tel 219057 fax 211755) at 11 Via Berengario just west of the palace.

**Cheapest of the two star hotels is *San Geminiano* (tel 210303) at 41 Via Moreali for £15/35. Others include *Astor* (tel 365037 fax 371250), *Castello* (tel 361033 fax 366024) at 321 Via Pica and *La Torre* (tel 222615 fax 216316) at 5 Via Cervetta.

Bonci (tel 223634) at 59 Via Ramazzini and *Del Pozzo* (tel 360350) at 72a Via del Pozzo offer rooms for £14/25 while *Leoncino* (tel 334190) at 407 Via Emilia Ovest and *Sole* (tel 214245) at 45 Via Malatesta offer rooms with shared bath for £20.

For the cheapest option, **guest rooms** are available at £10 a night in homes. Contact Tourist Information for more details.

Camp Sites
International Camping Modena (tel 206660) is sited at 111 Via Cave di Ramo and open through the summer. Charges are £5/6 per adult.

i **Modena Tourist Information Centre** is at 17 Piazza Grande (tel 206660 fax 206659).

Web: www.comune.modena.it e-mail: iatmo@comune.modena.it

The **main post office** is in the centre on Via Emilia. It closes on Saturday afternoons and Sundays but Via Rainusso's post office opens all day Saturday.

Travelling Around

Biking is very popular in Modena city because of restrictions on entering the centre of the city. The council because of city congestion encourages cycling and bicycles can be hired at Parco Novi Sad or at Policlinico hospital for L1000 for the first hour and L500/hour thereafter. It's a pleasant way to see the town and avoid parking problems. Our guide Elena warned, "It's great but watch your way. There is hardly a street in the city where cars are totally prohibited and bus drivers are rather daredevils."

Special permission to drive in the city centre is available from the Polizia Municipale but tourists heading for their hotel do not require it. Maps of **bus routes** are available at the tourist information office in the town hall. Buses are frequent if relatively expensive compared to other cities.

Distances from Modena of the main cities are; Ravenna 105km, Ferrara 73km, Rimini 152km, Bologna 39km, Reggio Nell'Emilia 33km, Parma 52km and Piacenza 94km.

Train Times (faster direct services)

Modena to Bologna 21mins, Reggio Emilia 14mins, Parma 27mins, Piacenza 57mins, Rimini 1hr 40mins, Florence 1hr 40mins, Milan Centrale 1hr 40mins, Rome 4hrs.

Trains around Modena Province

Trains run frequently from Modena station to Carpi (11mins) and trains run south west to Sassuolo and south east to Spilamberto and Vignola. Mirandola, San Felice sul Panaro and Camposanto are on a line which runs from Bologna to Verona.

SOUTH OF MODENA
ALONG THE UPPER SECCHIA VALLEY
Cognento Parmesan Dairy

Around 7km south west of Modena city centre and south off Via Emilia at the turn off for the Modena Nord autostrada exit, we drove 2km through the corn fields. On the flat plain in Cogniento, Hombre dairy farm and parmesan plant is situated in Via Corletto Sud. Modena is one of the four provinces registered to make Parmesan or parmigiano reggiano. The large farm owned by the Panini family is worth a visit. For seeing more traditional small scale production one needs to contact a tourist information bureau.

Sr Panini's Parmesan is creamy, soft and very tasty. Every parmesan producer has a shop and, at L25,000 a kilo it was cheaper to buy from Panini than in the delicatessens and supermarkets.

As we walked around a sleek red Maserati was cruising around the site. Sr Panini is also the proud owner of forty or so sports and racing cars which he has turned into a **vintage car exhibition** on the site. A large building houses the pick of Sr Panini's cars, including a Maserati which won three grand prix, and another in which the British ace, **Sterling Moss**, won a grand prix.

Oldest in the collection is a 1909 Roland Poullain, with a huge great klaxon that scared the life out of me. Twenty motorbikes and a dozen or so tractors make up his fine collection all of which can be seen for free. The trip rounded off with a visit to the bar beside the veteran vehicles. (For visits tel. 059 510660)

Sassuolo

Just 18km south of Modena and the A1 autostrada on the SS486 is the town of **Sassuolo**. Evidence of early settlements around Sassuolo come from Roman coins and weapons found near Salvarola. In the 16th century healthy oils were found in the ground by the Secchia River and Sassuolo became famous throughout Europe for these oils.

Sassuolo is one of the world's great ceramic centres and unsurpassed in its production of floor and wall tiles. Vast stocks of tiles sit around in warehouses waiting to be exported around the globe. The ceramic factories produce a great deal of dust into the air but if you are a ceramics enthusiast or a lover of art and history, it will not put you off. Some of Italy's greatest actors visit the town for its renowned theatre, as we would find out when we bumped into them at the popular Salvarola Terme hotel.

First we visited the pretty and historic town centre arriving in the dark in **Piazza Garibaldi**, known in the town as, 'the little square'. Off the piazza is Via Ducale that was built to connect the palace to the Ducal Palace in Modena city.

Surrounded on all sides by Renaissance arcades and buildings, the piazza leads directly to the Ducal Palace. It is a very becoming quiet town centre with plenty of parking space. It was also one of Italy's first squares to be designed with a drainage system. One can still see where the water would flow through from the Secchia river to be used by women for washing and by the horses for drinking.

Once a beautiful statue of Napoleon stood at its heart but Napoleon didn't like it. His troops brought up a cannon and blasted it to bits. Apart from that, Sassuolo only credits the 'little general' with having robbed their best art works for the private collections of France.

MODENA

Ducal Palace

Via Menotti brought us to Piazzale della Rosa, the lovely cobbled square in front of the Ducal Palace. The 17th century facade of the palace looks out over the piazza which, being at the end of a narrow cul-de-sac, was extremely tranquil.

Sassuolo's ceramics industry began in 1741. Previously the area's rural beauty attracted the noble families to erect summer residences here. The Estense held the palace. Then in the late 15th century, the Pio family arrived after the Estense had forced them out of the castle in Carpi.

The central part of the palace was a fortress and, at the rear, parts of the 11th century foundations remain. The structure of the castle is mainly attributable to the rule of the Pio. From the first floor one can see that the palace was built on top of the 1350 ramparts of the old fortress. The grounds to the rear of the castle were a vast ducal park and hunting ground, split by a small road flanked by poplar trees along its length. Near the line of poplars is a pond and old fountains used for water displays.

The derelict but charming palace swimming pool, the Peschiera, has the Estense eagles at the core. It was a bathing pool and the young dukes would paddle around in boats. Around the edge were little sheltered areas where they could sit shaded from the sun.

In 1599 when the Estense were forced out of Ferrara, they moved to Modena and murdered the last Pio lord, Marco III Pio di Savoia. They then took over Sassuolo castle as their summer palace or delizia. The majority of what are magnificent frescoes were commissioned for the Estense during the 1640s.

Few of the region's noble summer residences have been able to preserve their frescoes intact but in Sassuolo, all the rooms are decorated from floor to ceiling with frescoes by French and Italian painters. The palace is one of the best examples of Baroque decoration in Italy with plenty of Grotesque figures in the apartment of the Duchess. Trompe l'oeil is used to increase the impression of height and form to the ceilings.

Around the walls are incredible stucco creations of animals and other creatures. The main work was carried out by Brescian artist, Ottavio Viviani, who created the architectural perspectives of the various rooms. French artist, Jean Boulanger, decorated the frescoes.

M O D E N A

Entering the palace one is faced with statues, terracotta coloured columns and a large courtyard still used by the military. A grand staircase took us up two flights of stairs to the first floor. Don't miss what's beneath you because each room has differently designed marble flooring.

The floor is split between the rooms of the Duchess' Apartment and those of the Duke's Apartment and antechamber. Linking them is the Bacchus Gallery with its story of the triumph of the god of 'wine and sexual prosperity'.

Once a dining room, the Jupiter Room has plenty of cupids looking on the banqueting Jupiter and Juno. The Duchess had her own banqueting hall and ballroom, they contain magnificent frescoes of the muses among the two putti playing with two Estense eagles.

The frescoes in **the Duke's Apartment** are the prize of the palace. We passed through the Room of Fortune where Boulanger painted, *"The blind fool Fortune who lets happiness or bad luck fall from the tree of life"*, depicting allegories of luck and ill fortune. Of special note is the Hall of Love with frescoes of the legendary lovers and their foolish episodes, Orlando Furioso, Samson, Mark Anthony, Hercules and Solomon.

The hall of the Estense Duke has original stucco frames some with gold leaf decorating frescoes of distinguished episodes of the Estense family. At the Room of Aurora we came to a succession of rooms which formed the Duke's private apartment. Next came the Room of Aurora then the Duke's bedroom, the Room of Dawn where Francesco II died in 1694.

The bodyguards of Francesco I slept next door in the Camerino of the Moor. Here the staircase leads to the secret passage by which the Estense could enter the ducal gallery of their chapel.

As for the paintings and furniture, what the Estense had not sold off to raise funds was removed when "Napoleon arrived and stole everything". Paintings and sketches by Orsi, Cavedoni, Guercino and Ludovico Carracci hang in the Paris Louvre. Some of them were temporarily returned and on display in the palace.

Outside the front of the palace on the left was **the ducal chapel**, San Francesco church. It was moved from the opposite side of the square so that the ducal family could arrive via the secret connection form the palace. Rebuilt in 1650, it had a healthy display of gold leaf and monochrome paintings. On the right the chapel has a relic of Christ from Jerusalem, which is hidden behind a special painted panel only opened for special occasions such as feasts and special prayers.

The panel was lifted for us revealing a fresco with putti surrounding the cross. The great organ is 17th century and still used for services. The centre of the cross in the chapel was said to have a piece of Christ's crucifix in it.

The street in front of the palace housed the courtesans. Today this street houses the library. The **town hall** in Via Fenuzzi was a 17th century prison used especially to imprison wealthy Ghibelline opponents of the Pope, later Ciro Menotti, local leaders of the Risorgimento and then the left opponents of Mussolini. The prison was finally closed in 1965.

Some of the cells have kept their original doors and have been neatly restored as offices. We could still see some of the prisoners' graffiti with '1848' and love hearts etched into the thick walls. Worth a visit, even if just to see how the staff are coping. Behind on the right are some very old houses used to house the poor.

Terme della Salvarola

The health properties of local Nirano clay has given rise to the health and beauty centre of Terme della Salvarola (covered in more detail in the introduction). The first records of a spa at Salvarola come from the 13th century and from Matilda of Canossa's use of the spa. Today the clay for the mud packs is brought from elsewhere and saturated for two years to emulate the Nirano mud.

When we arrived in La Salvarola, Umberto Orsini, the famous Italian theatrical actor was sat having breakfast. The singers Caterina Caselli and Pierangelo Bertoli have stayed at Terme hotel. Many other famous artists, singers and writers come here to visit the Sassuolo theatre.

The large centre lies on a hill in Salvarola, 2km from Sassuolo and the best sign posted site we ever visited. Here magnesium sulphate and sodium bromides are used in the health treatment particularly for respiratory health, rheumatism and the intestines. Other preparations are used for bathing and mud packs for the body.

Actress Dominic and Sam, a singer and dancer from London were at the new beauty and fitness spa for four days.

"We went into the pool with the warm water cascading onto us. That was fantastic. We did the beauty therapy. It was fantastic and it took a layer of skin off . It's been such a marvellous time. We've really been pampered.

It was wild. We didn't know what to expect in Sassuolo. We came here to meet some friends. Other friends asked why Sassuolo but it's a really lovely place. The palace knocked us out. The baby whose eyes followed you on the fresco – that was freaky."

Salvarola Terme's hotel really is a smart four star hotel and a cut above a three star. Besides the Terme, its grounds also house extensive gardens, a small shopping centre, a fairground, a restaurant, a pizzeria, two bars and a chapel.

Around Sassuolo

For those who wish to trek, one can walk or mountain bike 5km through the forest up to the castle of Montegibbio which overlooks Salvarola. The castle sits above a beautifully serene valley that almost appears cut off from modern civilisation.

Garibaldi Square hosts many festivals including the 500 years-old **October Fair** featuring music concerts, traditional food stalls and antique fairs. Every Thursday night in the summer sees music performances.

Roteglia's shop in Piazza Garibaldi has been open since 1848 and remains as it was, still producing lovely nocino. The Renaissance square surrounded by arcades opens onto the shopping area, Via Menotti. Along Via C.Battisti street on the corner of Via Menotti is Bellei's nice pasticceria.

Modena Golf & Country Club (tel 059 553482, fax 553696) lies 5km north of Sassuolo in Formigine at 4, Via Castelnuovo Rangone. The 18-hole course was the scene of Italy's 50th **International Open Championship**.

EATING OUT

La Paggeria restaurant (closed Sun) at 19 Piazzale della Rosa is in attractive rooms formerly used as the arsenal for the palace. Heraldic symbols surround the walls and add to a sense of style and occasion. It has excellent food, a broad selection of wines and friendly, cultured staff making for a relatively inexpensive (L40,000) but quality dine out. Another stylish place is Enoteca '*La Cantina*' at 1, Via Monzambano.

The restaurant at **Terme La Salvarola** offers meals at L30,000 and also has a pizza restaurant guaranteeing a cheap meal. Cheaper eating places are in the town. *Ancora* at 216 Via Circonvallazione specialises in fish and pizzas.

Charlie Pub at 34 Via Mantova (closed Wed) opens for breakfasts at 7am, has a happy hour for cheap drinks from 7pm till 8pm and only shuts at 1.30pm.

ACCOMMODATION

At 109, Via Salvarola Terme, **Salvarola Terme****** (tel 0536 871788 fax 872160) is Sassuolo's class hotel with rooms at £55/65, a friendly bar and excellent service. Otherwise there is **Hotel Michelangelo*****(tel 0536 998511 fax 815410) at 85 Via Circonvallazione Nord Est where rooms cost £30/60. Guest rooms are available for £17 a night with Malavasi Beniamino (tel 801594) at 1 Via Stazione.

The Mud Volcanoes of Salse di Nirano

About 7km from Sassuolo on the Maranello road we turned right at Spezzano. After 3km we stopped at a hollowed out valley just beyond Nirano village. We had found the amazing mini mud volcanoes of Salse di Nirano steaming away. It's clay provided the material for ancient buildings, the ceramics industry and the mud packs of Sassuolo beauty centres. Nirano provides a bizarre monument to Sassuolo's historic role.

On our first visit eight mud volcanoes formed of grey cones rising up to twelve feet high were intermittently expelling gas and bubbling away. The mud lava oozed down the sometimes steep slopes which when dry would be safe to climb. Elsewhere, dormant formations were spread over an area of several hundreds yards.

The flora is also of interest producing a grey desert notably more akin to a coastal area. Salt water prevents many of the areas normal plants from growing here and many species found on the site are only find otherwise on the coast.

Central Italy is well know for being an unstable geological area. The underlying rocks, still being forced up from east to west, from time to time create devastating earthquakes. There are no volcanoes in the north but Nirano is the mini-equivalent.

Subterranean activity produces steam which rises, bringing up the clay and salt water below. The escaping gases and steam produce the effervescent crater and dump the wet clay on the edges. Dried by the sun, the cone builds until the rising gases are insufficient to carry their load any higher. The clay is then deposited in the chimney plugging the crater, which eventually collapses as the gases find a new vent to escape from and form new cones elsewhere.

We climbed to the top of the volcanoes finding them completely safe if requiring heavy shoes. With nobody else around we sat and listened to the bubbling brew and wondered, "where was everybody?". Nowadays it is a protected area and taking away the mud is forbidden.

In the past the site was popular as the mud was believed to have healing properties and, even today is considered so excellent for the skin that it is exactly replicated for use in beauty treatments. The water is also used for spa bathing and to produce steam for those with respiratory problems.

Nirano town has a few restaurants but we climbed the hill above enjoying the panorama and the *calanchi* – vast grey furrows cut into the hillsides - and took our snack sat by the roadside.

MODENA

Maranello – Ferrari Town

Modena province can rightly call itself the home of the sports car. It's a must for car enthusiasts. Not only the home of Ferrari, the area also produces **Maseratis**, **De Tomaso**, and **Bugatti's** for the world's jet setters. With Panini's display at Cognento, and Imola and Monza nearby, what better treat for a sports car enthusiast than to visit this area?

Maranello lies on the SP3 which branches off SS486 after Casinalbo village. Just 16km south of Modena, the town is a 10km drive eastward from Sassuolo. Maranello's link with the Formula One racing circuit is further emphasised with it being the home of one of its most renowned drivers, **Michael Schumacher**.

We were lucky to see the towns on a grand prix racing day. Bars and shops were festooned with red flags from Imola to Modena. In Maranello a big screen was erected in the town centre for everyone to see the race. Schumacher won again bringing great celebrations.

Ferrari's status in the century's racing world is unchallenged. The pride of the region and Italy has won more than 40 world championships and over 100 Formula One races. The team can be seen racing at the grand prix circuits of **Imola** and **Monza**. Alternatively, a cheaper way to see the doyen of speed in action is to go to the training track in Maranello and Fiorano and watch from the outside, on the road to Sassuolo.

Founded more than seventy years ago by **Enzo Ferrari**, the firm has a quality name over its sports and luxury cars. Maranello is the centre of Ferrari's operations and the 1,700 workers pride themselves on the quality of the sports cars produced here over the decades. At one time they even had a big push to rename the town Maranello Ferrari. In turn, when Enzo's young son died of muscular dystrophy, the magnate funded a mechanics school and many other works in the town.

On the edge of town we visited the **Ferrari Galleria** at 43, Via Dino Ferrari and saw a marvellous collection of Ferrari sports, and sleek saloon, cars. One of the cars was a Nigel Mansell Formula One racer from 1990. Medals, trophies and memorabilia of Enzo Ferrari, down to his clothes, spectacles and signed cheques, are on display. More than 16,000 visitors arrive annually from all corners of the globe to this shrine to Enzo and his creation. Each year new cars and information are added to the gallery.

M O D E N A

Display boards are in English (one of the few places in the region) and film clips show Enzo and his drivers at work. Enzo died in Modena in 1988.

Entry is L15,000 and groups can arrange visits to the Ferrari factory by appointment. (opening hours: 9.30am-12.30pm, 3pm-6pm, closed Mondays)

Accommodation (area code 0536) in Maranello is limited but there is the ***Hotel Domus** (tel 941071 fax 942343) at 38, Piazza della Libertad at £35/55, the £35/40 **Europa** (tel 940440 fax 941612) at 11, Via Mediterraneo and **Fondazione Manni** (tel 943406) at 60 Via Nazionale for £35/45. Guest rooms are available for £6 a night in **Artuso Rosina** (tel 945294) at 41 Via Lazio.

Ristorante William is at 1, Via Flavio Gioia and the pizzeria **Domus Desideria** is in Piazza Liberta. For an **agriturismo**, try **Il Luoghetto** at 1, Via Gaiano.

The quickest way to travel south from Sassuolo and up the Secchia valley is to cross the Secchia into Reggio province, and turn left onto SS486 to **Montefiorino**, 35km away. Sat on the hillside in Val Dragone, the 13th century castle, which once belonged to the Montecuccoli, is now the town hall. Inside is a museum celebrating the wartime '**Republic of Montefiorino**'.

In these parts many older residents can recall the sites where fighting occurred and still point out bullet ridden shrines. The partisan's republic held out in 1944 from 18th June to 30th July controlling large tracts of hillside in Modena and Reggio Emilia. The castle played a part in the republic and, completely intact, it adds atmosphere to the museum.

Over the valley on Monte S. Giulia a terrible massacre took place in March 1944 partly inspiring the creation of the republic. The Hermann Goering Division of the German Army slaughtered 136 of the residents of Monchio, Susano and Costrignano hamlets in a single day. 136 trees in Monchio Park commemorate the dead. Nearby is **Monte S.Giulia Park** also dedicated to the Resistance. The Romanesque church at the top of the hill was destroyed by a German bombardment but most of it has been reconstructed.

TO THE UPPER PANARO VALLEY AND THE APENNINES

We drove 10km down the SS12 from the east side of Modena city and turned right just after Colombaro passing through Castelnuovo Rangone, a town famous for its pork industry producing salami, prosciutto, mortadella, and zampone. Indeed, the symbol of the town is a statue of a bronze pig that we saw opposite the church in the town square.

The town processes 80 percent of Italian cured pork production. The road south from the town has the largest meat processing plant in Europe with the capacity of slaughtering 4,000 animals a day. The town has the world record for making the biggest zampone, 400 kilograms. They say that when approaching the town you can *really* smell the zampone.

MODENA

Due to the town mayor's affection for the former Beatle, the town commemorates **John Lennon's** death every year. Town council newsletters often contain a drawing by John Lennon, and the lyrics of Imagine are on a sign in **John Lennon Park**, which also contains a statue showing Lennon walking, Abbey Road-like. Although the statue was only unveiled last year, someone stole his glasses and a firework caused damage.

Once again we were off through the lush Modena countryside. This time we drove 1km eastwards on SP16 before turning left at Settecani village to take the SP17 south for 4km to Castelvetro. **Castelvetro** is in real **Lambrusco country**, where the hills are bedecked with vineyards and orchards. The hilly territory also provides for many castles that controlled the valleys and trade routes to Tuscany. The castle here was built in 1200 and is thought to be the oldest in the province. From Roman times the area was important, as illustrated by discoveries of Roman ceramics.

Lambrusco is a very light, sparkling red wine typical to the region that sits well with the locality's heavy cuisine. We were here to eat in a farm restaurant and we found the **Le Casette agriturismo** (tel 059 799086) at 63 Via Ghiarone. The friendly family run kitchen produced a huge and excellent meal from home grown produce for L30,000.

We were eating gnocco fritto, traditional food from the Modena kitchen. We started off with an antipasti and a salami sausage, followed by tortelloni, a lovely plate of pork cooked in Balsamic vinegar and flour, then plenty of freshly picked and boiled vegetables.

We finished off our dessert with a juicy red and yellow coloured sponge with lemon peel, chocolate and orange, known as 'English Soup' – Zuppa Inglese – an English mixture rather than a broth. It was thrown together by someone preparing a meal for his or her English guests and therefore took its duplicitous name.

We passed by a superb clay brick castle Levizzano in **Infadeo**, with its clock tower rising above the town of Castelvetro. We arrived at Castelvetro castle where one can see Lambrusco being made and taste the local wines. It's an Enoteca open on Saturdays and on Sundays when tasting is organised and advice given as to which to buy. Entry is free from 3pm to 6pm at the weekend and at public holidays.

Castelvetro hosts its annual **Absurd Festival** of street parties and strange happenings and a more traditional festival in the third week in September to celebrate the grape harvest.

Vignola

We drove 7km further eastwards on SP17 to Vignola on the Panaro river. Sleepy hamlets sit among the cherry orchards and vineyards in the countryside to the south. Vignola is famous for its vast cherry orchards. The Vignola cherries are canned and used for cocktails and chocolate all over the world.

Each June as the cherry harvest is gathered, the townspeople organise great feasts with large horse drawn carriages decorated completely with cherry flowers. On the first Sunday, locals bring out a vast cherry pie, the biggest in the world. It's as long as a street but the bonus is that visitors get a free piece.

The Modenese believe that Vignola's Castle is the most beautiful in the region. We drove up through the busy little town and through the mediaeval area of tiny close packed streets to the castle on Via Garibaldi. With its ramparts, battlements, drawbridges and huge walls and towers, it is a fantasy castle, a good place to bring the children.

Other hints of the Middle Ages are still present, for example the Gothic arches. The brickwork was added in the 15th century and the castle today is more Renaissance in character. Two

VIGNOLA CASTLE

drawbridges remain to cross to get inside to the original keep. There were three keeps, reflecting the three stages of expansion of the castle.

In the Middle Ages, the castle with windows to keep watch on the Panaro river, was purely a fortress defending Modena from Bologna. Vignola is on the river Panaro flowing from Monte Cimone and, in the lowlands, forming the border with Bologna. In 1247, the pro-Guelph King Enzo led his Bologna army against Ghibelline Modena and had the castle burnt down. The Renaissance brought an end to most of the fighting between the two city states and the castle became a palace.

The Grassoni dynasty lived here in the 12th and 13th century. They were followed by the Contrari, allies of the Estense. The Contrari are responsible for much of the castle decor. They ran out of heirs in 1575 and the castle was bought by the Boncampagni who owned the castle till 1965 when replaced by the Cassa di Risparmio company.

MODENA

The restored late 15th century frescoes are quite tremendous and swamp the castle walls and ceilings. Frescoes adorn some of the outer walls looking out onto the courtyard, and a tower, indicating that the external walls were probably covered in frescoes. The Este double eagle symbols are everywhere reflecting the Contrari's subordination to the Estense.

We came across some graffiti made by an angry prisoner in the tower who declared that he had been misunderstood. One tower in the castle is known as the Women's Tower. It is where women were imprisoned for betraying their husbands.

Filippo, a Spanish sailor went to **Spilamberto** *on the Panaro near Vignola in the 17th century to sell millinery. He had an affair with a married woman and when discovered was thrown into prison where he died. He scratched his story onto the walls of his cell protesting his innocence. His graffiti remains in Spilamberto castle as, it is said, does his spirit. On a stormy night, they say that one can hear Filippo crying out.*

The staircase we took upwards to the tower was the servants' staircase and aptly difficult. It's unsafe for children. Some of the rooms had been extended and though the castle is a fine example and wonderful for taking children into a fantasy world, some of the heavy restoration has detracted from its attractiveness.

Of note are also the frescoes in the Ducal Chapel and Uguccione Contrari's study. One could easily imagine from the surfeit of brightly coloured frescoes the gaiety of life that must have existed in the Contrari's castle. It's almost kitsch. On the third storey we found the soldiers' quarters. No frescoes here, just a floor of roughly hewn brick. Their billet looks down on the keep. The fourth floor offers excellent views of the women's tower and a sight of the prison cell where Ugo Foscolo, the poet was kept in the late 18th century.

A moat surrounded the castle. In front of the mediaeval castle is a small empty square. It's certainly lively and with the castle moat and courtyard, a venue for concerts, jazz festivals, cinema, conferences, exhibitions and parties.

The piazza is quite beautiful retaining its 17th century flavour. Opposite the castle entrance is the strange Barozzi palace which is now a municipal building. *Pasticceria Gollini* cake shop on the corner of Via Garibaldi, is worth a visit. Gollini make **Torta Barozzi**, their own legendary chocolate cake with its registered trade mark. With this, the cunning Mr Gollini retained the secret recipe, starting the legend. Lots of cookery writers have tried to discover the ingredients, some even trying underhand methods to extract the truth. It is said that an American woman admitted that she tried to get Gollini's heir drunk in order that he would tell her

Accommodation and Eating Out

Vignola has the ***Eden** (tel 059 772847 fax 771477) at 49 Via C.Battisti for £20/35 and **Castelvetro** has the **Sant'Eusebio** (tel 059 702782) at 44 Via Spilamberto for £30.

Agriturismo without accommodation but serving food include **San Polo** at 5, Via San Polo and **Le Casette** at 63a Via Ghiarone, both in Castelvetro district. In Vignola there is **La Casetta** at 624 Via Frignanese.

i **Vignola Tourist Information Centre** (tel 059 764365 fax 764311) is at Via Selmi 5.

TO THE APENNINE MOUNTAINS
The Panaro Valley

The main roads to the south are the Secchia and the Panaro valley roads. Panaro Valley road offers a slow scenic route to Florence. South of Vignola, the SP4 valley road twists through increasingly rugged countryside. Every now and then a rocca pops up on the hill tops. It is trekking territory with the occasional rock face that might tempt climbers.

The area is particularly popular for nature studies and a 45km ramblers' track leads along the river from Modena past Vignola and Rocca Malatina to Monte Cimone. Other tracks lead off it and the superb four day route can be taken by foot, horse or mountain bike. Along the way are relatively cheap guest houses right up to Scaffaiolo lake.

We wound our way up through the hill roads to **Guiglia** and its old pieve sat on the Passo Brasa road on the east side of the Panaro. Guiglia is on the edge of the natural park of Sassi di Rocca Malatina. It was a grey misty September day reminding us that the sun doesn't always shine in Italy. However, it was still a warm 21°C.

In the lowest part of the Apennine range, 700 metres above sea level, **Guiglia Rocca** and its sandstone chalets with their sloping roofs appear almost Alpine.

We drove south to **Sassi di Rocca Malatina** with its spectacular views. It is Modena's second natural park. At the park's heart, Rocca Malatina rises a sheer 1,000 feet from its base reaching 2,000 feet above sea level. The sandstone rock outcrops jut out and dominate the valley and, though it is too soft a rock for rock climbing, this protected site has become the home for families of peregrine falcons that soar, then swoop down on their prey below.

Walking is possible on one of them and requires paying L3,000 to the park office. There is a hut for birdwatchers (L3,000 a day) and April/May brings enthusiasts to watch the sparrow hawk and five species of falcon during their breeding season.

Around the rocca is a beautiful natural park of woodland, gurgling streams, pastures and isolated farmhouses. Stags, lizards, marmosets and wild boar forage in the forest. Sheep and goats graze in the valley studded by oak trees and cherry orchards and the streams attract water snakes, heron, river crabs and kingfisher.

We visited the macro-biotic restaurant of **Casa Val di Sasso** (tel 059 795841), an agriturismo well set on the hillside in Via Castellino. We ate in the restaurant and for the first time on our trip were offered no alcohol, no milk products and no meats. Instead salad, vegetables cooked in natural oil, fruits and soya and corn products with apple vinegar were put together in a tasty meal washed down with non alcoholic beer and a barley coffee. A complete meal here is L40,000.

Accommodation is available (L40,000 a night for a double, L30,000 with your own sleeping bag, L85,000 full board) and the stay is worthwhile as the views are quite spectacular. The spot is excellent for taking walks, which can take six hours, around the hills and the valley. **Horse riding** and **mountain biking** facilities are available. All together it is an excellent place for a country stay that still leaves the towns and castles within 90 minutes. **Samone** has a restaurant one hour's walk away that offers a break from macro-biotic food.

Above is the interestingly named **Castellino delle Formiche**, the castle of the moles, with its 14th century Gothic portal. Close to Guiglia, Rocca Dequili is a 15th century castle recently restored. Nearby is **D'll Faro's** restaurant and bar that looks out over the valley and directly onto Rocca Malatina. Beside the restaurant sunflowers had been hung out to dry as we sat outside and watched the falcon hovering. Beneath the Rocca we could see the caves once inhabited by the valley people.

Pieve di Trebbio only opens on Sunday. The hamlet is reached by taking the road south from Guiglia and turning left into the valley after Monte Orsello. We parked in the courtyard to see the Romanesque church first mentioned in 996 in the documents of Nonantola Abbey. In the 13th century this pieve was very prestigious, the head of 19 chapels. Thereafter it declined. The semi-capitals, splayed windows and arches are original as are the presbytery fence, the crypt and the baptismal font.

Close by is the park's natural museum that gives a portrayal of the flora and fauna in the area. **Grotta di Ca Certea** has stalactites in the limestone area.

Towards the Bologna border is the village of **Zocca**. Surrounded by beautiful trekking country and ruined castles, it hosts a national conference on **Edible Snail Rearing** (tel 059 987018) in May. In the same month the village holds its **Festa del Maurino** which might tempt tourists more since the Via Mauro Tesi main street is packed with restaurant stalls giving away local foods.

The two **discotheques** in the town are on Via Dello Sport and Via Rosola and there is the *Bibap* discobar on Via M.Tesi.

Accommodation and Eating Out
(area code 059)

Zocca has ***hotel *Joli'* (tel/fax 987052) at 20, Via Pineta, *****Lenzi** (tel 987039 fax 986510) at 14 Via Cavour and *****Panoramic** (tel 987010 fax 987156) at 690 Via Maurio Tesi all at around £30/40. ****Bellavista** (te 987002) at 31 Via Bellavista and ****Belvedere** (tel 987020) at 37 Via XXV Aprile are similarly priced.

Close to Zocca are two **agriturismo** without accommodation; **Tizzano** at 1197 Via Lamizze and *Ca'Monduzzi* at 1130d Via Vignolese. Zocca also has a summer camp site, *Montequestiolo* (tel 987764) on Via Montequestiolo.

Guiglia has the *****Tre Lune** (tel/fax 792262) at 854 Via Michelangelo, ****Belvedere** (tel 792451) at 18 Via Roma and ****La Lanterna** (tel 792444) in Piazza Cantelli, all for £30/40. *Ca' di Marchino* (tel 795582) at 4 Via Buzzeda in Monteorsello is an **agriturismo with accommodation**.

i **Zocca Tourist Information Centre** (tel/fax 059 987073) is at 1096 Via Tesi.

Fanano

Further along the valley road from the pieve we passed waterfalls at La Ciocala Cicala and went along the Panaro on the Via Romea's road which took pilgrims to the Vatican. Romea was the name used for these pilgrims, which is why many roads south in the region take this name. Many pilgrims would stop off at Nonantola's monastery and then come down the Panaro valley.

The valley now splayed out with steep rock faces and woodland rising on each side. We were approaching the 1,000 years old village of Fanano (50 km from Modena), once an important stopover for pilgrims resting before having to climb into the mountains to reach Tuscany. Their task was hard but beyond offered beautiful sightseeing with the valley dissected by streams and waterfalls.

Trout fishing is popular here but the government operates a strict, no kill, catch and return policy. This town marks the beginning of the **Frignano park**, Modena's main natural park that stretches right across the mountains. The area we were in became known as Ospitale valley and the river, the Ospitale. Hospitals here began as travellers' rest houses. They would receive 'hospitality' but, after travelling a long way some needed medical treatment. Where there were no monasteries or ospitali to treat the sick, often private ospitali would do so. Hence the link with the English word, 'hospital'.

M O D E N A

Entering Fanano, the gateway to the mountains, the adaptation to the harsh countryside was apparent in the steeply inclined rooftops, wooden balconies, exterior staircases and the use of sandstone and stone rather than clay brick for the buildings. Streets twisted wherever they could be carved on the hillside.

We were struck by the appearance of polished sandstone sculptures around the piazzas and streets. Even the church has two large sculptures of hands outside its entrance. These sculptures are the pride of the village giving Fanano notoriety. The village streets have almost been turned into an art exhibition.

The church is off the main square. As it preceded the creation of the piazza there was little room available on the slopes around the church. Romanesque in origin, its facade underwent a Renaissance restoration. Inside it contains the classical Romanesque features in its poor light, and three aisles. But with Tuscany being just over the mountains, the architecture has greater similar with Tuscan churches. The arches, ceiling decoration and cupola are more Gothic and Renaissance additions.

Gesso, a more simple way of working in scagliola, producing simple colours out of the clay, is used here for imitation marble decoration.

Around the town we saw many *marcolfa*, strange distorted faces of men and women that appear on pictures and sculptures in the Apennines. Their appearance is not related directly to Grotesque but more to mountain church folklore.

We went into a bar in the piazza. The area is an important producer of mushrooms and truffles. It was **mushroom picking** season and the men were debating who had picked the biggest mushroom and the largest stockpile.

Today the town is developing as an Italian tourist resort for summer trekking and winter skiing on Monte Cimone. Outside the town are ski lifts and buses to take skiers up if they wish to leave their cars for the short ride. Nevertheless, the town remains unspoilt and hardly touristic in feel or appearance.

Other sports catered for here are **ice skating, canoeing, hang gliding, paragliding, mountain biking** and **orienteering. Rock climbing** is pursued on the rocky opholitic outcrop at Sassi di Varana near the town of Seramazzoni (tel 0536 952310), 18km south of Maranello. Otherwise climbing is difficult here because of the soft, sandstone rock and dense woodland. It is more suitable for **trekking**.

Fanano has plenty of restaurants and, in Via Aba, the *Discoteca Re Artu. Ricky's Pub* is in Via Roma.

Monte Cimone

We were on the road through the green mountainside to **Sestola Ski resort** on the edge of Monte Cimone, the Apennines tallest mountain. Sestola, 3km from Fanano, is the main ski station in the Apennines. Above was the Sestola castle. Below were splendid views.

We stopped off at the former Estense **Sestola Castle**. Set on the mountainous border with Tuscany, it was one of the most important rocca for controlling the trade route. The castle looms over the town. The Estense nominated the governors of the area and each had their own heraldic symbol as shown in the Council Room of the town hall. Sestola looks a little touristy with many souvenir shops in the square but the ancient sandstone chalets add a charm.

The main entry of the castle has a 13th century Arabic arch wide enough to take a cart and horse. Here the sandstone walls are plastered with the governor's symbols and the Estense symbol hangs over the fireplace. The main building in the castle dates back to the early 17th century as a home for the governors. Some of the 17th century decor survives.

The castle is a museum of mountain life and also has a fascinating museum of musical machines. Here the enthusiastic museum caretaker showed us round, winding up or turning on some of the instruments like the huge gramophone in the gramophone room. This room was formerly the torture room where water was dripped onto the heads of the prisoners to secure confessions before death.

The former private room of the castle governor is the piano and organ museum replete with century old wind up pianolo organs and dancing monkeys. The mountain life museum offers an insight into the Cimone world. Here the marcolfa are called *mama*. Farm instruments, wine vats and photos are on show.

Sestola town is a busy tourist resort mainly for winter sports. Accommodation and **restaurants** are plentiful while the town also has *Belvedere* **cinema** on Via Delle Ville. The two **discotheques** are on Via Stotale Ovest and Piazza Passerini which also is the site of the *Gosling Pub*.

Monte Cimone's peak rises to 7,100ft. On a clear day, even below its peak one can view the Adriatic, the Mediterranean and the Alps. This is fortunate because a military research centre making it out of bounds occupies the very top. On this day clouds were licking the mountain tops.

M O D E N A

The winter snow slopes of Cimone would attract world champion skier, Alberto Tomba as a young man. For many years he trained here until becoming champion of the world in the 1988 games held in Canada.

The recently retired, charismatic **Alberto Tomba** *and his fans still arrive in Passo de Lupo for the occasional reunion. From being a young boy, he regularly trained on the slopes on Monte Cimone winning three Olympic golds and 50 World Cup races. After the world cup he trained elsewhere but he remained a local hero.*

We drove up to the central station at **Passo del Lupo** (Wolf Pass) with facilities including cashpoints, restaurants, a hotel, discotheques, shops and the ski centre. Beneath Sestola one can ski in winter from Pian del Falco down to Sestola. Skiing has been a popular pastime here for over a century.

A chair lift brings visitors from Sestola up to Passo de Lupo. Ski lifts take skiers up the remaining 1,500 metres. About 25 ski lifts go up to the different ski stations serving 31 slopes stretching 51 km. The twisting and turning Black slopes are for the best skiers, Red for medium and Blue for low level skiers.

Cimone has a dozen or so routes for cross country skiing. Most of the skiers are from Emilia, especially at the weekends. Many Bolognese have second homes in the area. However it takes three hours from the Adriatic coast of Romagna to get to Monte Cimone. Polish, Turkish and French groups have been attracted from abroad because prices are cheaper, the transfer from Bologna airport is a mere 90 minutes and the Apennines offer a change from the Alps.

In general a week's trip will cost L1 million. Staying at the hotels costs the same or cheaper but the ski lift costs L130,000, 30 percent cheaper than a similar area in the Alps. Staying in the Dolomites is much more expensive and Modena has plenty of special ski-week cheap offers. In November the slopes are grass covered and the haunt of marmots. December and January are the best times to ski and plenty of snow machines are around which can cover half the slopes if the snow melts.

Skiers are serviced by 50 FISI ski instructors, fully equipped first aid posts, ski and boot hire. Smaller ski resorts include **Doccia**, 4km from Fiumalbo, **Piandelagotti** in the Dragone valley close to Frassinoro, **La Piane** near Lama Mocogno on the slopes of Monte Cantiere and, with its discos, cinemas and restaurants, **Santa Anna** on Monte Albano.

For **ski details** telephone Cimone Winter Resort Consortium (tel 0536 62350 fax 60021).

We visited the pretty site of **Nymph Lake**, a natural lake that would fill up another 1.5metres after the winter rains. The nymphs were lily-like wild flowers that would carpet the water. Today, the cleaning of the lake has led to their elimination.

It is said that a farmer was eaten by a monster from this lake but, the lake being only four metres deep, this legend has few modern believers. Its surrounds have a lot of fine tracks for ramblers. Close by are **riding stables** and the excellent, wonderfully set **Osteria La Cervarola** (tel 62356) in Cervarola, part of an agriturismo behind which Alpine cows and goats were munching in the fields.

Inside we ate rice with mushroom and pork followed by tortelloni in an unusual tomato cheese sauce. We drank dry red Lambrusco that went down wonderfully with the pasta. Then came a taste of truly Modenese Apennine cuisine, the tasty crescentina. Crescentina, tigella and borlenghi are typical of this area. We were invited to the kitchen to watch the crescentina being made with a special metal dish.

Normally, flour, water, salt, a little sugar and yeast for fermentation were kneeded together and placed in special terracotta dishes stacked one on top of the other then positioned close to the fire to allow the flour to ferment. After baking, the little flat round breads like round mini-pitta breads were ready for us to slit open and eat. Known more commonly today as tigella, the crescentina is often eaten with ricotta cheese.

Thereafter followed a tasty dish of rabbit, then a ricotta cheesecake for dessert all washed down with liqueurs of gineprino (juniper) and mirtillino (blackcurrants). La Cervarola offers full board for L80.000 a night.

A road along the west side of the Tagliole valley below leads up to **Largo Santo**, the biggest lake in the Apennine peaks. At 5,000ft on Monte Giovo, it lies in a glacial hollow. Popular with the Modenese in summer, it also offers a scenic walk through a pretty wood of beech trees and bilberry bushes to nearby Largo Bacco and other lakes. The mountains surround the beautiful landscape. **Monte Giovo** can be reached by foot. However one walk on Giovo involves negotiating Grotta Rosa, a sheer rock face, for several metres. A steel cable is provided for safety.

Interesting **local festivals** include:

First Weekend in *May*: Trofeo **Sestola** OK, international children's **soccer** tournament (tel 039 53662324)

First Sunday After 3rd *July*: **Montecreto**'s Paglio degli Asini, **donkey parade** and race.

July/August: **Pavullo nel Frignano**'s Protaganista a Casa Baldasarre avant garde **artists' shows and performances** (tel 039 53620675)

Third Weekend in *July*: **Pavullo nel Frignano**'s Pinone **Rock Festival** for new bands (tel 039 53623032)

August: **Montefiorino**'s Festa della Birra, **beer festival** (tel 039 536965606)

M O D E N A

August 15th: **Palago**'s (Montefiorino) Festa dei Matti **loony festival** (tel 039 536961519)

End *August/September*: Frassinoro's Concorso Internazionale di Violino, **international violin competition** (tel 039 536969141)

September: **Pavullo nel Frignano**'s Emilia Celtica' **Celtic and Emilian rock and folk festival** (tel 039 53623032)

BACK DOWN THE PANARO

Travelling along the sides of the hilltops, the mountain range is revealed as a plateau sharply eroded by the elements which have deeply incised into the soft rock creating deep valleys and ravines. From the top of the hill we could see Sestola's church sat like a large grey cat looking down on the valley.

Down in the depths of the valley ten minutes from Sestola, in a narrow country lane we found **San Giacomo,** a deserted, small Romanesque church. Its facade is classically Romanesque with motives, two small windows and different capitals.

Not all the sculptures on the soft sandstone have survived. The bas reliefs of grapes and wine drinking appear almost as a Bacchanalian celebration. Indeed it is said that a devil and witches occupy this church built in the 11th century. The church is only used once a year for a festival. Left to itself it is a little jewel.

Back on the top of the hill we looked down on the picturesque valley with its patch work of fields, copses, orchards, and spatterings of houses and church steeples. We were in the **Scoltenna** valley, which feeds into the Panaro valley. Above us was the 15th century castle of the Montecuccoli. Below we were heading for **Olina's Bridge**, an attractive donkey or u-shaped bridge across the river 15 minutes away from Pavullo nel Frignano on SS12.

Cobbled stones still pave the road of this steeply arched mediaeval bridge known as the 'Witches' Bridge'. However it is believed that it may be a Roman bridge. Beneath the waters flowed across the shale river bed. Around us woodland rose up the steep sides of the valley, swamping the occasional farm house. The bridge in stone rises to a considerable height in order to effect the wide crossing. A serene spot. The majolica crypt of the Madonna on top of the bridge is a replica. The original was stolen.

Fulenas Bridge is another 'witches' bridge where witches are said to meet in the night. Devil's Bridge carries a tale of a non-believer in the devil who was thrown down from the bridge. The bridge unites two rocks and appears like a cavern – a home for the devil.

'Witches' Bridge

ACCOMMODATION
(area code 0536)

Fanano has ***Park Hotel** (tel 69898 fax 69740) in Via Campo del Lungo, ***Parco Eden** (tel 68903 fax 68399) in Viale Rimembranze and ***Firenze (tel 68822 fax 68688) in Via Roma, all for £35/40. **Hotel Pineta** (tel/fax 69494) in Via Salvo D'Acquisto has some rooms for £12/17 and *Bologna (tel 68929) in Via C.Foli rooms for £20.

Agiturismo II Feliceto (tel 68409 fax 68696) at 454 Via Ca Zucchi in Ospitale has good accommodation. Accommodation is also available at *La Cervarola* (tel 62356) on Via Cervarola in Cervarola.

The *Capanna Tassone* (tel 68364) **mountain shelter** near Ospitale can be booked for £8/9 per night

Sestola has a range of cheap and expensive accommodation and a local **swimming** pool. The ****San Marco** (tel 62330 fax 62305) is in Via dele Rose and prices are £40/70. It's an old building but has modern facilities. ***Tirolo** (tel 62523) is on the same street. The collection of hotels on Corso Umberto include ***Nuovo Parco** (tel 62322) and its **satellite, ***San Rocco** (tel 62382), **Cimone** (tel 62531 fax 60842), **Piccolo** (tel 62525) and **Panoramic** (tel/fax 62321), all at £25/40. **Sport Hotel** (tel 62502) on Via delle Ville offers some rooms for £17.

Stays at the three hotels in the piazza at *Passo del Lupo* (tel 62338) cost £25/40.

Sestola has a **camp site** open throughout the year. *Camping Sestola* (tel 62324) is at 18 Via Palazzuola and costs £4/5 per adult. The *Ninfa* (tel 62324) **mountain shelter** near the Nymph lake can be booked for £8/14 per night

Other **mountain shelters** at altitudes of around 4,500ft are; *Rami Secchi* (tel 73909) near Fiumalbo, *Prati Fiorentini* (tel 967193) near Frassinoro and, around Pievepelago , *Vittoria*, *Marchetti*, *Giovo* and *Le Tagliole* all available by phoning 71304.

Villavasanto by Largo Santo has a variety of accommodation. Good value can be had at L80,000 for full board.

Frassinoro has a **youth hostel** (tel 965609) at 7 Via Perdelle costing £4/person/night.

i **Fanano** Tourist Information Centre is in the main square (tel. 0536 68825)

i **Sestola** Tourist Information Centre (tel 62762).

Travelling: Fanano and Sestola can be reached from Modena city in 75 minutes by car or a 90 minute bus ride.

MODENA

THE PLAINS NORTH OF MODENA
ALONG THE LOWER PANARO
Nonantola Abbey

We headed 11km north east of Modena on SS255 to Nonantola. The town was famous in the Mediaeval era for its abbey that was a key stop over for pilgrims travelling to Rome. The origins of the town go back to at least 186 B.C when it was a Roman settlement of the same name. In the 9th century the Longobard king, Astolfo, gave the area to his brother, the abbot, Anselmo who began the building of the abbey.

Like Modena, the Carpi, Sagra, Ganaceto and Pieve Trebbio, it is an example of the Romanesque buildings of the period which flourished, it is said, particularly because of the influence of Matilda of Canossa. The Tuscan queen longed to increase the status of the church in her domain and thus undermine the authority of the many notoriously sinful noble families.

The town grew up around the abbey on the Modena to Bologna road now called Via Nonantola. The abbey has a huge four storey building. Inside the almost warehouse like building are many important parchments relating to rulers such as Matilda of Canossa. This part of the building was restored and re-opened with an Internet facility in the spring of 1999.

In 1116 the great earthquake that hit the region devastated the abbey and much had to be reconstructed. Height was also added later for impression. The facade of the cathedral is a reconstruction but its design is Romanesque and divided into three parts representing the classic three aisle division of the period's churches.

The interior was quite dark as we stepped onto its 13th century floor paved in pink and white Verona marble. The ceiling was raised in the Gothic era and windows added but the very simple design is still deprived of light. In the 15th century the interior was reworked adding the cross vault and the rose window. The cathedral roof was reworked in the sixties to recreate its Romanesque impression.

The four columns with Roman capitals contain the sarcophagus and relics of Saint Sylvester moved here from Rome. Relics of other saints are kept in the altar. The origin of the 64 different Roman style capitals on the columns is debated as to whether they were sculptured by monks or taken from old Roman buildings.

In fact the capitals are called 'Nonantola capitals' because they are unique and their style cannot be said to be Ionic, Corinthian or Doric. The two capitals in front of the altar are said to be original. The cross is also said to contain a piece of Christ's cross.

Behind the cathedral in the monastery we entered the fresco covered friars' refectory. The frescoes are from 1080 and adorned with blue lapis. Greek style frescoes above use signs from the Orient, and reflect the wealth of the monastery at the time. Only important people and the rich attended the cathedral while the peasantry attended other churches. The lower floor is now an art gallery used for exhibitions.

The refectory also contains displays of locally discovered Gallic and Etruscan artefacts such as tools, flour grinders and even old skulls dating back as far as 1500 B.C. A large wall once circled the abbey. Later a church and hospital were added just outside the walls. The 14th century hospital is now the restaurant *Santa Maria Fiore* on Via Nonantola opposite the abbey. *Carlo Magno's* restaurant is opposite the abbey on the smaller piazza.

The town has two **palio** horse races. Palio dell'Abate takes place on the penultimate Sunday in July from Palazzo Partecipanza while Palio delle Due Torre takes place on the following Sunday from Parco della Pace.

Bomporto

We drove across the Po plain to the small town of Bomporto on the banks of the Panaro. The town is 13km from Modena and can be reached by taking SP2 along the left bank of the Panaro. It was a warm day late in October and we passed through the vineyards which had turned an earthy burgundy colour or like 'cooked blood' as Muriel would have it. We were heading to Campo Santo following the line of the Panaro. We arrived at a big estate in the centre of which was Villa Cavazza, a large recently restored manor.

The manor housed a temporary exhibition of life on the canal network dating back to the Estense period. Our guide, Christina, explained that a network of canals connected Modena and Venice, the first being the Naviglio Canal constructed in the 11th century. Bomporto, meaning 'good haven' was a key part of this network whereby the Panaro river was used to connect Modena with the Po, which took boats and barges down to Venice and the Adriatic.

As late as the 14th century Modena used both rivers and roads as the motorways of transport. Until locks were introduced, oxen and horses would tow the barges up river. The Italian, Leonardo Da Vinci is given credit for inventing the lock system first introduced by the Dukes of Milan, before spreading to the rest of Europe.

This area was a centre of Lambrusco wine. Pork and other agricultural products were traded for clothes with Venice. The area's prosperity is evident from the numerous grand old villas such as Villa Cavazza that speckle the countryside.

M
O
D
E
N
A

Walled with a large square courtyard with houses for the former servants, **Villa Cavazza** is a typical 18th century manor. The open attractive building was semi-derelict five years ago. Now the courtyard has a display of old barges, yachts and canoes used on the canals to transport agricultural produce, clay and sand. Beautiful hanging lamps surround the yard and on one of the two large clock towers is a slogan for the manor's employees, "If one wastes time, one will regret it."

The main villa houses other items used on the boats and barges. Even old stones used in catapults in times of battle, in particular against the Bolognese's attempts to sieze control of the canal system. A photographic and pictorial display with to scale models gives a vivid display of the semi-aquatic life on the canals.

Those who want to explore further can obtain maps of the canals where the towpaths have been turned into cycling lanes. Free of other traffic we found the towpaths serenely peaceful and safe. One of the most attractive routes is that between Bomporto and Finale Emilia to the north east which offers beautiful views of the countryside and the many old villas of mediaeval, Gothic and Renaissance style painted in the colours of the countryside, terracotta, oranges, sky blues and greens.

Lambrusco

This area produces the slightly drier Sorbara Lambrusco, said by some Modenese to be one of the three genuine Lambrusco, characterised in autumn when the vineyards turn to that rich burgundy colour. We had spotted Sobara 15km north of Modena city. Castelvetro in the south produces a slightly sweeter Lambrusco and the drier Santa Croce near Carpi produces the third.

We discovered that the province has a small production of white Lambrusco from the best grapes, which came as a surprise as everyone we had spoken to in the region laughed with incredulity when we told them that white Lambrusco was available in shops in England. They found this very amusing. White Lambrusco did not exist. It was "invented" for exportation. They thought that a white wine would have been more familiar to the uncultured foreigner, So they developed a new method with a slow fermentation and a little chemical assistance.

M O D E N A

Finale Emilia

We headed north east for 31km on SP2 tracking the Panaro and soon we arrived at the pretty little town of Finale Emilia. Actually, despite its population of just 15,000 people, Finale is officially designated as a city. In Italy today, towns must have at least 30,000 to 40,000 inhabitants to be called a city. But Francesco III designated Finale as a city back in 1729 because of its strategic importance. Dominating the town is the 15th century **Castello Estense**. The castle being on the Panaro, a fortress existed here from the 11th century onwards.

The oldest building is the **Torre dell'Orologio** clock tower at the east end of Corso Trento e Trieste. It was built in 1213 when the Estense first ruled over the town. Corso Trento e Trieste, which now passes through the town and past the castle, was once the Panaro river. Finale Emilia secured its name from being the final point of the Emilia state before the state of Bologna. As demonstrated by its magnificent ramparts, moats, towers and battlements, the **castle** was a military garrison rather than a palace. Though later, in more peaceful times the castle was transformed into a summer residence of the Estense. Frescoes are evident on the outside of the west tower.

The interior of the castle can be visited by appointment with the local comune in the town hall (tel 059 788111). However having been used as a local prison for many years and then to house the homeless people who fled the countryside after the war, despite 15 years of restoration there is still much work to do inside. Behind the castle were the old gardens and homes of the courtiers now turned into a delightful little square.

Also behind the castle which used to look back into the town centre are the old cobbled streets and the Piazza Guiseppe Verdi where one can find the town hall and three pleasant inexpensive cafes flowing onto the pavement. Nearby is the small red brick cathedral with its Baroque facade completed in 1807. The bell tower and apse date back to 1587 and the frescoed interior is quite charming.

At the front of the castle across Corso Trento e Trieste around Via A.Costa are the wondrous narrow mediaeval streets of a tiny old Jewish ghetto placed, as was Estense policy, as close to their castle as possible.

Also opposite the front of the castle beside the road are the old buildings that retain the structure from the time when the road was the Panaro river. Lines of painted porticoes delineate the old river's edge. The buildings and the porticoes were specially strengthened as a defence against floods. Some of the larger buildings jut out on the first floor for facilitating boats that would moor beneath the buildings to drop off cargo. Here we sat in an old bar with men seemingly as old passing the day away in conservation and contemplation. History pervaded the town.

As we passed a little bar at the side of the road, old men were speaking with a Ferrara accent testament to the origins of a section of the local community. Further on we walked beneath a statue of the Virgin Mary with the inscription," *When you pass under here say an Ave Maria.*"

MODENA

Opposite the castle is parking space and an open picnic area. The lemon-coloured, Liberty style **Teatro Sociale** just behind was built in 1907 and has re-opened for performances.

As we drove through the countryside towards San Felice we passed through an area of long reclaimed marshland now being re-flooded to stock fish. We discussed how so few of the houses in the region jar on the eye. Instead, modest, painted terracotta, blue, straw yellow and grass green, they tend to blend into each other and into the countryside. Our guides told us that there is quite strict municipal control of building colours, design and scale, mainly in the historic centre. All houses in Italy over 80 years old are protected by the government.

ACCOMMODATION AND EATING OUT

Nonantola (area code 059) has a collection of places to eat out including *Santa Maria Fuori le Mura* at 61 Via Vittorio Veneto (closed Sun) with meals at L45,000 and, outside the centre, *Osteria di Rubbiara* at 2 Via Risaia (closed Tue,Fri,Sun evenng) at L30/40,000 and *Trattoria del Campazzo* at 22 Via Farini (closed Mon, Tues evening).

Nonantola's only **hotel** is the **Abbazia* (tel 549754) at 101 Vittorio Veneto and costing £25/30. The town also has a **youth hostel** (tel 896511 fax 896590) at 29 Via Montegrappa costing £7/person/night.

i **Nonantola Tourist Information Centre**, 6 Piazza Abbazia (tel 896555).

Finale Emilia (area code 0535) has two **hotels**, ***Zuccherificio** (tel 97172 fax 97250) at 9 Via Ceresa costing £35 and ***Hotel L'Impero** (tel 98266) at 15 Strada Panaria Bassa costing £25. Guest rooms at £15 a night are available at 65 Via Pre Modena (tel 780210). *Ospitale Rurale* (tel 789977) at 30 Via Panaria in Ca' Bianca is an **agriturismo** with accommodation. The area also has an agriturismo without accommodation in *AL50* at 15 Via Finale S.Bianca (closed Mon, Fri).

On Via Imperiale, we passed a fishing areas and came, at 491, to *La Losca* **agriturismo** (tel 0535 37551) with its fish farms and leaping goldfish drawing the seagulls well inland. We ate **padinini sedanini** with a smoked ham and tortellini truffles boiled in a broth, followed by veal cutlets and chipolatas. Locally grown pumpkin followed. For the sweet, Torta Barozzi, coffee cake, arrived.

Bomporto has two **agriturismo**: *Garuti* at 16 Via Carlo Testa and *Marandello* at 3 Via Per Solara.

i **Finale Emilia Tourist Information Centre**, 1b Via Cesare Battisti (tel 788333 fax 788130)

MODENA

THE SECCHIA PLAINS
Campogalliano

One morning we headed off to Campogalliano, a 20 minute drive north east of Modena in the middle of a natural park. Just off the A22 autostrada at the Campogalliano exit, the museum is easy to reach. The area is one of a number of beautiful villas next to the Secchia river. With three large-scale factories, Campogalliano is Italy's capital for balancing scales. Even with the new factory of the legendary Bugatti car company, it doesn't appear like an engineering centre. The tiny town has a piazza where we found the **Museo della Bilancia,** the balancing museum by the Conad supermarket where we could park.

It's a popular venue for schools groups and families. Every October, the town has a scales festival. Campogalliano has been manufacturing scales for 120 years.

The museum with Braille explanations, a lift and disability access, contains a wide range of scales, from the most ancient and primitive of, to the most advanced, technologically. The tour begins with items that can be weighed representing those that can't.

I sat on a chair which, taking account of varying gravity, measured my weight on Earth, on the Moon and on Jupiter. I preferred my weight on the Moon. Software on computers explained the principles of scales.

Scales on display hail from the 13th century to the present. There are 19th century scales to weigh gold, 16th and 17th century scales in wood, metal and bone from around the world. 700 balancing machines are displayed here and few in England know of this museum, which includes 15th century wooden market scales for weighing fish.

The first floor contains some amazing machines, ranging from the last century to the most modern from this century. There are scales made to weigh the young Prince of Savoy, balances from 1831 used to weigh rain, barrels of wine and Parmesan cheese, and a lovely 19th century armchair for weighing people. The most modern machine didn't use the balancing principle at all. Instead it sent an electric circuit around a metal object, analysed its structure and calculated its weight.

A five minute drive from Campogalliano and we were in the fascinating **Secchia Flood Retention Basin Park**, a balancing act worthy of the city of scales. To prevent flooding the authorities dug huge ponds on the river's edge. Now when the river floods over its banks, the water flows into the ponds preventing danger to the cultivated areas and towns and when the river is dry in the summer the water from the ponds seeps back into the river.

The result was the creation of a picturesque nature park with woodland, plenty of bird life for the **birdwatchers** and yet spaces for a children's playground, sunbathers, water sports and fishing. Only 15 minutes from Modena, the park is a popular area for the Modenese and probably best avoided on Sundays by those who prefer peace and quiet.

We were off to the little village of **Ganaceto,** 5km north of Modena on SS413. Few historic churches in the region's lowlands have lasted through the centuries without substantial alterations. Ganaceto's early 12th century **Church of St Giorgio** still displays its Romanesque structure and decoration intact.

It was a Sunday morning and the old padre was greeting gaily dressed church goers young and old. The field that is the town square had been turned into a car park. The church bells stopped ringing and the priest entered his ancient charge. We remained outside watching the stream of unrepentant late arrivals dawdle through the side door. Inside the priest was sat in the confession box, his head in his hands and looking the worse for wear while his packed congregation burst out a hymn.

Built slightly later than Modena's cathedral, St Giorgio's was also a work of the Wiligelmo school. The principal elements of similarity are the little arches close to the apses, the slender decorative columns and the engraved motifs on the exterior.

The slit windows providing for a dimly lit interior are original. However the large rose window in the facade was, as in Modena cathedral, a 15th century Gothic introduction to bring some brightness to ceremonial proceedings when the roof was lifted. The church was carefully restored in 1980.

On to Carpi

Carpi is 15km north of Modena and a 10km drive on SS413 from Ganaceto. The fastest route from Modena city is to take the A22 autostrada towards the Brenner Pass and leave at the Carpi exit. On arrival in the small town of Carpi we weren't aware that we were about to witness one of the architectural wonders of northern Italy, the **Piazza dei Martiri**. This square is not only magnificent in its immensity (it is the third largest in Italy), but its perspective, the symbiosity of its structures and the marvellous Portico Lungo arcade.

Piazza dei Martiri inspired Austrian art historian, Hans Semper to describe the town as a 'princely Renaissance city'.

It is another example of how small noble dukedoms built grandly to impress their rivals. The square was the 16th centre product of rule by the Pio family. Carpi's history dates back further to 751 A.D when the Longobard king, Astolfo ordered the construction of the church of Santa Maria nearby in the adjacent

MODENA

Piazza Re Astolfo. The church was rebuilt in the Romanesque period. We began our tour of the town here to trace the town's historical development.

Truciolo, a form of art used in making bags, hats, and now employed in knitwear, (the main industry in the town) is important to the area, Pleasant tree lined boulevards run through the spacious modern town. The historic centre has been pedestrianised so we parked our car and walked. Very quickly we arrived in Piazza Re Astolfo, the small square once called **Piazza della Citadella** and the mediaeval centre of the town. We were here to view the Church of Santa Maria, another 12th century church.

The church of Santa Maria is nowadays only open for weddings which, in Italy, frequently take place on a Sunday. As it was a Sunday, a horse drawn cart bringing a cheerful marriage party to the front entrance delayed our entry. When we returned later it seemed as if the whole square had been covered with a blanket of fusulli, rice and confetti.

Consecrated in 1184 by Pope Lucius III, the church became known as the '**Sagra**' meaning consecrated. Peruzzi added a Renaissance facade for the Pio family in 1514. Much of the Romanesque decor has survived. The 9th century crypt built using the base of a 2nd century Roman villa is being restored following its recent discovery.

The apses and porticoes are what remains of the Wiligelmo work on the exterior. Little arches and a great arch decorate the apses and the bell tower at the side by Viale Carducci. A smaller church than in Ganaceto, this pieve which once reached out into the centre of the square, was reduced to one third of its original length when the Pio ordered the changes. A new cathedral was being built nearby and Santa Guilia pieve, 10km away, also provided for the area. So despite the relative importance of the town, the Sagra was not considered important enough to expand.

One window provides light into the church. Two circles high on either side of the facade represent the Renaissance attempts to provide balance to the appearance of the church. The Romanesque bell tower with its slit windows and tiny arches is said to be a leaning 50 metres high. Like Modena's Ghirlandina tower it is positioned close to the apses of the cathedral. On the other side of the church to the tower is the **Bishop's Palace** designed again by Peruzzi in the 16th century, its features displaying Renaissance geometry.

After the wedding we were able to enter the church that still carried the sweet scents of the fresh flowers used to decorate the ceremony. The interior walls and ceilings have some marvellous 13th century frescoes and those in the ducal chapel are 15th century. The church contains the sarcophagus of Carpi's first duke, Manfredo Pio. Praised in Dante's *Divine Comedy*, he was entombed here in 1350.

MODENA

A special feature almost unique to the Sagra is the way in which the beams have been painted with brightly coloured patterns. Romanesque beams carried no decoration and the design is 16th century.

The caretaker slammed the door, angry at the wedding litter of rice and confetti. She'd had enough for one day and it was time to move on.

Carpi and the Pio

In the 11th century Carpi fell into the hands of Matilda of Canossa before being held by the Estense till 1288 and, until 1327, the Mantova Bonaccolsi family. Real control under the Mantovans rested with the rival local clans of the Brocchi and Tosabecchi. The struggle was however resolved in 1327. The Brocchi's married into the Pio family who then held the fiefdom until their duke, Alberto III was driven out by the Spanish troops of Emperor Charles V. The emperor promptly handed the territory back to the Estense.

Across the way the huge warehouse-like but attractive 19th century building was once a factory for **truciolo** workings. Today it is a school. Alongside it**, Castel Vecchio** is an imposing 15th century structure built for the Pio family. Gothic porches and arches bring a hint of the previous eras into the Renaissance building. This is the oldest part of the Pio castle – **Rocca Vecchia**.

On our right was the 15th century **Palazzolo** and by its side, is the 16th century **Rocca Nuova**. To reach Piazza dei Martiri we took a passage through the Rocca coming across another wedding. A huge crowd laughed and shouted outside. This was a town hall wedding and, as the couple ventured out, not only rice and confetti, but raw penne, fusulli, spaghetti, and even the boxes were launched at the newly weds.

Between the two squares is a beautiful and classic Renaissance courtyard built to unite the squares. Built in terracotta brick, it is surrounded on four sides by a symmetry of marble columns, arches and windows. Maintaining their strict line, each side has seven arches, seven lower windows and above them seven more.

The **Piazza dei Matiri's** grandiosity is due to the demands of the Pio dynasty during their two hundred year rule and then to the Estense. When we came out into the square we were met by a cacophony of noise. The cathedral's bells peeled away while a large brass band dressed in bright uniforms oompahpah'd their way around the crowds. Hundreds of people, young and old were sat and stood around with their bicycles debating, laughing and swapping news. We would come back to the square one hour later to find it deserted and left to its own elegance. It was time for Sunday lunch, a typical scene in an Italian square.

What is not typical is the square's proportions. It is 276 metres long and 75

metres wide. 52 arches decorated with fired brickwork run along the **Portico Lungo** on one side of the square. The achievement of the Portico Lungo was that the arcades previously existed of separate buildings as can be seen by the heights of the blocks. Centuries ago they were linked and now form the 120 metre line of arcades.

Opposite stands the Palazzo or Castello Pio with its vast sprawl combining towers, turrets, fortifications and chapels etched on through the centuries.

At the top of the square is the huge cathedral of **Santa Maria Assunta**. At the opposite end the nine arches of the **Portico del Grano** former corn market seal the piazza. Nevertheless the square's size refuses to allow any single feature to dominate allowing a synthesis of the buildings.

Santa Maria Assunta was begun in the 16th century but building stopped and the facade was only finished in the 17th century. Consequently a Baroque facade, characterised by its many columns, statues, spirals and windows and the little domes on either side, fronts the Renaissance interior. Carpi is characterised by the use of scagliola in its decorative sculptures from the 17th century and the interior of the cathedral demonstrates a fine use of the skill to create imitation marble decorations.

Churches were built beginning with the rear. The tower behind the cathedral is the oldest part though even in this case it wasn't completed till the following century. It is simple, octagonal and noticeably discordant with the rest of the building attacking the symmetry. The Baroque facade of the cathedral should have been as big as the dome but the church ran out of money.

The pink building opposite the long arcade was the castle of **Palazzo Pio** but today it is the town hall. Next to it is the theatre built in 1860. The clock tower of the clay brick castle is a 17th century addition to the castle that was built in 1440. A canal that ran in front of the palace acting as a form of moat occupied part of the square. The main entrance had a drawbridge.

The square tower on the palace's right was built in 1327 and is one of the oldest parts of the castle. It was later used by Alberto Pio III to house his bird collection and is still known as the bird tower.

An entrance beside the castle leads to the **Deportees Museum** that occupies a 15th century wing of the castle including its vault. Grey sandstone brick gives a cool sobriety to the interior commemorating those politicians, revolutionaries, soldiers and Jewish families who were deported to the German concentration camps in World War II. It is the only museum in Italy to those who entered the concentration camps.

M O D E N A

A sketch of a deportee drawn by Picasso in 1960 for the museum and a poem written by Bertold Brecht adorn the walls. Graffiti scrawled by prisoners on the walls of huts in the concentration camps also appears on the walls. That of a non-Jewish inmate arrested for helping Jewish families to escape reads,

"If you had seen how I have seen what things they make the Jewish people suffer, you would have helped more Jews."

Displays of spoons, clothes, and other artefacts from former inmates, together with pictures of starved skeletal bodies dead and alive are displayed. In the Names Room, the walls are covered with the 14,000 names of those deported from Italy. From time to time a relative comes to find the names of their parents.

A silent museum, it's a moving experience. Schools and groups are welcome.

Fossoli Prisoner of War Camp

Fossoli is 6km from Carpi on the road to Modena and set on a gently undulating, suitably bleak plain. After heavy rain it may not be possible to get there because of the mud but we arrived on a sunny day. We parked just in front of the derelict outhouses of the former concentration camp. Hung on the camp gates were a bunch of red roses.

10,000 Allied soldiers, 5,000 political prisoners and 5,000 members of Jewish families were sent here. Benigni's last film *La Vita e Bella* gives a good portrayal of what life was like in Fossoli. After the war, the camp was turned into a home for refugees and an orphans' home, before it was left empty as a monument.

The first eight semi-derelict brick huts were a simple reminder of the horrors of the Holocaust. They held Jewish families who would then be separated and sent north. The camp's hospital, kitchens and huts have been left untouched. The barbed wire fences, machine gun turrets, barking orders and rifle fire are left to the imagination.

Fossoli was a transit concentration camp opened by the Italians in August, 1942 to house allied prisoners. The Italian army in the south sued for peace in July, 1943, signing the **Salerno Pact**, but Mussolini and the German army fought on in the north. On September 8th, 1943 the German troops arrived to take over and use the camp to intern Italian political prisoners and Jewish families before they were sent through the Brescello Pass to the north European concentration camps. The last train to **Auschwitz** left Carpi in August 1944. Then the camp held people who would be sent to work in Germany.

M O D E N A

The Partisans

The Committee of Liberation was set up involving the Communists, Republicans and other parties to organise the resistance that battled for two years. The Emilia-Romagna Apennines were the front line and thousands of the region's men and women joined in the struggle.

In early 1999, Modena police believed that they had found the gun used by partisans to kill Mussolini and his mistress Clara Petacci. A Modenese partisan is thought to have brought the gun back to his village of Montefiorino and buried the weapon in a church cemetery.

The former leader of the Italian volunteer army was killed in Fossoli along with 66 other prisoners.

The first camp for the English was to the east of the current fields. Turn right out of the camp and right again and one comes to the tomb of former government minister, Leopold Gasparoto machined gunned down in the fields at the age of 41.

Behind and just down the road from the old camp is the municipal shooting range behind which the camp's prisoners were executed by firing squad. Stand beside the entrance and the loud reports of rifle fire add to one's imagination of the scene for the 67 dying prisoners. One prisoner was pardoned by the comandante so that his skills as a mechanic could be utilised.

The first 20 prisoners were shot in the fields. Of the following 20, two escaped and the rest were killed by the shooting range. They were shot from behind while kneeling on the ground. Carlo Bianchi alone was shot in his chest, which has led historians to believe that he was trying to escape or making a last gesture of defiance against the Nazis.

Four cypress trees and floral tributes now surround the tomb where the men are honoured. Carpi train station carries an inscription, detailing the dreadful passage of prisoners through the station to the concentration camps in Germany and Austria. Still today, there are Carpi pensioners who remember aiding British and Allied prisoners to escape and ask the local comune for news of their escapees.

For those interested in the history of the Second World War, Land, Memory and Peace is an organisation arranging tours of the Modena region.

The municipality holds an **annual concert** to commemorate the Fossoli internees in Piazza dei Martyri during July.

San Felice

To the east is the town of San Felice with a well-restored and quite splendid castle. It's now the town hall and has a small museum. Built in 1340 and remodelled 100 years later, **Rocca Estense** is noted for its inner courtyard and staircase. In front in the central square are 15th century buildings including the church to San Felice with its 17th century Neoclassical façade.

Accommodation and Eating Out (area code 059)

Machiavelli wrote of the "gallant meals and glorious beds" he was afforded in Carpi. That was 500 years ago. Today **Carpi** has four hotels, the ***Touring** (tel 686111 fax 686229) at 1 Viale Dallai and ***Duomo** (tel/fax 686745) at 25 Via C.Battisti both costing £55/65, **Da Giorgio** (tel 685365) at 1 Via G.Rocca for £30 and **Lina** (tel 686752) at 40 S.S.Motta for £20/30.

Campogalliano has the upmarket ****Hotel Mercure** (tel 851505 fax 851377) at 160 Via del Passatore for £60/90 and ***La Gentile** (tel 525938 fax 526547) at 21 Viale Martiri della Liberta for £30/40. The hotel has an excellent **restaurant** serving meals at L40/50,000 with a main dish for L27,000. The staff are friendly and the food traditional. Italian soccer star, **Del Piero**, is known to visit the restaurant as is **Pavarotti** who, when dieting in Milan, would occasionally break his fast with a meal here.

MODENA

Modena

Modena

The Cathedral of Modena

heritage of humanity

1099 -1999

1999 marks the ninth centennial of the foundation of the Cathedral of Modena,

recognised by UNESCO as part of the universal heritage of mankind, along with the Ghirlandina tower and Piazza Grande.

Provincia di Modena
Assessorato al Turismo

E-mail: turismo@provincia.modena.it

Reggio Emilia THEATRE AND PAGEANTRY

We arrived in Reggio Nell'Emilia after a thirteen-minute train ride from Modena. At L7,200, the trip cost more than the much longer trip to Bologna. This emphasised the point that knowing a little Italian would have been useful to find one's way around – cheaply. The journey to the province's administrative and commercial centre took just 13 minutes and the sites in the city can easily be seen by foot or by bicycle.

REGGIO CITY

With a population of 130,000, Reggio Nell'Emilia is the principal town of Reggio Emilia province sandwiched between Modena and Parma. The town's origins are believed to date from Etruscan times.

The area attracted Etruscans then Celts to settle. The Ligurians from the Apennines then took over the area until driven out by the Romans who established the city as a military encampment around 187 B.C. This is shown by the bronze plaque on the Via Emilia which marks the spot which the Romans decided would be the geometric centre of the castra stativa, which preceded the city.

Roman Consul **Marco Emilio Lepido**, whose name was immortalised in the Via Emilia which splits the town in two, ordered the construction of the town as part of his plan to build a line of communication and defence between the Adriatic and the Mediterranean. Nothing is left to see of the Roman city save in the museums.

In 900 A.D Emperor Charlemagne, gave permission for the first city wall to be built. He put the Bishop in charge of the city which was defined by the wall and covered just the streets between the Piazza's Prampolini and San Prospero. In the 13th century, the expanding city required a new wall. In the 15th century an even longer wall was built defining the fortified city as a hexagon. Each corner had strong ramparts, of which the section at **Porto Costello** is the surviving remnant of the walls. Once outside the gates, travellers on the Via Emilia, pedestrian or not, had to pay a road tax which was collected until the end of the 18th century. Now one only pays when reaching the autostrada.

We came across the **Giardini Pubblici**, public gardens built in the late 19th century. The centre of the gardens was once the site of a mediaeval citadel, a town fortress built in 1339 by the ruling Gonzaga family. The Gonzagas, after a war with Milan, seized control of the city and built the fort to protect themselves against its unappreciative citizens. Eventually they in turn were thrown out by the Estense dukes in Ferrara who took over the city in 1401 and ruled for 400 years. Estense rule was only once broken when the Vatican gained control of the city for a brief period and also seized Bologna and Ferrara.

REGGIO EMILIA

In Corso Garibaldi we were on the city's only wide and winding road, winding because, until 1280, a river was flowing there. The river was canalised and placed outside the city for defensive purposes, leaving its old route as pebbles and sand. On this street we visited one of the few Baroque churches in the city, the **Basilica Beata Vergine della Ghiara**, its name Ghiara being the Reggio dialect for pebbles and sand.

The site of the basilica is said to be that of a miracle in 1596 when a 17 year old boy who was deaf and dumb stopped one night to pray in front of a painting of the Holy Virgin and child. Marchino was cured of his disabilities and the bishop of Reggio declared it a miracle. One year later the first stone was laid for the church dedicated to the veneration of the Madonna. Financed by the city's craft guilds and the Comunes, it was completed 22 years later.

Ghiara basilica belongs to the municipality but its guardians are the Florentine Fathers Who Serve Mary. Today it is a popular destination for pilgrims who arrive from all over Italy.

The architect of the church was Cesare Balbo of Ferrara. Its facade displays the simplicity of the early Baroque style and contrasts quite dramatically with the magnificence within.

Inside the Ghiara basilica, the perils facing churches in this part of Italy was evident as craftsmen were up aloft repairing the dome damaged by a ten-second earthquake in 1996. The church is in the style of a Greek cross with each arm of equal length, and is distinctive inasmuch as all other churches in the city have the Latin shape. Of great height, it is a marvel of colour; reds and gold, browns and blues coming from every side in gloriously bold paintings and frescoes. It was easy to understand why our guide, one of the monks, said the basilica took 40 years to decorate. Yet many of the paintings were stolen by an Estense duke and now are exhibited in a gallery in Modena.

The main altar is close to the entrance and on its right is the altar of the Madonna with a magnificent fresco of the Madonna made in 1569 by **Lelio Orsi**, a Novellara artist, inspired by Michelangelo. The supplicant Madonna looks on the child whose right hand gives the benediction to the people of the city. Emilia's most famous painter, Guercino from Ferrara, created the Palla by the altar.

The ceiling is stucco and gold plated with putti's everywhere in the Baroque style. The frescoes on the ceiling above the church organ were the work of 17th century painter Luca Ferrara who borrowed from the style of the Venetian school, anticipating the paintings of Tiepolo by 100 years.

If the fathers have time, they will show you to a place beside the organ to see the 'eternal clock' made in 1646 by a Ghiara friar. Three discs are moved by a pendulum and show the time, the date, the horoscope, and the seasons. Each day was given a saint, even in leap years, and, in all, 21 different aspects of the calendar are detailed.

The clock was fixed to show details till 2002 A.D but, the friars, forced to flee by Napoleon in 1797, returned in 1926 to find that the clock had gained its own millennium bug and stopped working. The friars could get the clock going by their own endeavours but for only six hours at a time. Except during exhibitions, they prefer to leave it dormant. The basilica's friars also created the 450 year old church bells which, now restored, chime away

In Via San Pietro Martire where it meets Via Fioredibelli, the lemon coloured 16th century home of architect **Antonio Casotti**, who built the city hall's tower, still displays his initials on the corner of the house. The cobbled stones and narrow passages testify to the mediaeval origin of this street and the other streets surrounding the main square, the Piazza Prampolini.

Being a Monday many of the museums, palaces, shops and restaurants were closed. Nevertheless Monday has its advantages as the town centres are even quieter and we strolled around in the sunshine in relative tranquillity.

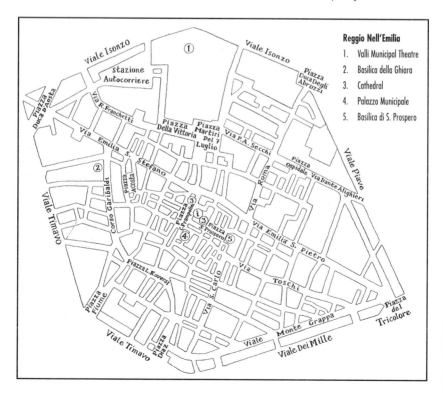

Reggio Nell'Emilia

1. Valli Municipal Theatre
2. Basilica della Ghiara
3. Cathedral
4. Palazzo Municipale
5. Basilica di S. Prospero

Piazza Prampolini

The main square was named after Camino Prampolini, a socialist who fought against an infamous grain tax, campaigning in the columns of La Justicia newspaper for the citizens to join in demonstrations against the Duke. Out of this movement came the first co-operatives so common in Emilia today.

With the cathedral, city hall and the Romanesque Baptistery, the mediaeval square, known locally as the 'Piazza Grande', is the busy centre of the town hosting a thriving market on Tuesdays and Fridays, concerts and protest demonstrations.

We sat facing the **Palazzo Monte di Pieta**. Built in 1188, the palace was the seat of the town hall from the end of the 13th century till 1400. In 1280 an overpass was constructed to the Palazzo Capitano demonstrating the close link between the Capitano and the elected representatives of the Comune.

The red brick building with its bell tower was replaced in 1401 when the new city hall was constructed. In 1494, part of the palace was used by the Monte di Pieta (pawnbrokers) conferring on the building its unflattering name.

The City Hall

Opposite the Palazzo Monte di Pieta across the square is the City Hall whose facade was completed in 1417. The three arches of coupled pillars were added some 60 years later. Apart from functioning as an administrative centre, the ancient building is also a monument to the city's glorious struggles for freedom.

A plaque at the entrance records the 1946 votes in the referendum for post war democracy when 50,000 city citizens voted for Italy to become a republic and just 12,000 for the monarchy. A tricolour hangs outside the hall and beneath it is the slogan, *"This is where the Republic of Italy was born for ever."*

The Hall of the "Tricolore"

We visited the grand **Tricolour Hall** where a prototype of the green, white and red Italian Republican flag hangs. The French flag was the model for the republic and the three strips originally horizontal rather than vertical. In the middle is a basket with the heralds of the four cities that met in the town hall to declare a republic in 1797.

Architect, Ludovico Bolognini, designed the Neoclassical hall as an archive for the Estense Duke in 1774. It was here, just 23 years later on 7th January, 1797, that the Cispadane (Po Plain) Republic was born, uniting Reggio with Modena, Bologna and Ferrara under the Tricolore flag.

Inspired by the French Revolution the people rose up against the Estense dukedom holding great marches in the square to demand the duke's departure and call for Napoleon to take over the city. The duke fled to Austria and the **Republica Reggiana** was born alongside the Cispadane republic.

Reggio's republic lasted but a few months before the Estense, using Austrian troops, forced their way back following several defeats of Napoleon's armies. A battle was ensued by bloody reprisals. The bells tolled announcing executions in the square and many people were imprisoned. In 1805 Napoleon again passed through the city but this time left the Estense's in control. The last duke died in 1831.

Nowadays, each Friday 40 city councillors meet with their mayor to administer government of the city. The archive's galleries are used to seat the public. On view is the town's green, white and red mediaeval standard which displays the city coat of arms, the Madonna della Ghiara and the saints Prospero, Grisante and Daria.

The standard also includes a gold medal awarded to the city for military valour in the struggle against Nazism. Reggio Emilia was a particularly strong partisan recruitment area for the liberation war in the Apennines. The names and portraits of those who gave their lives are shown at the city hall entrance.

Viewing of the hall is by appointment (tel 0522 456662)

Santa Maria Cathedral

Piazza Prampolini is dominated by Santa Maria Cathedral whose origin dates back to around 857 A.D. Many centuries ago the bishop ruled over the town and the cathedral's two great circular windows facing onto the square look like they were prepared for cannon.

The brick building has a Romanesque facade that was ordered to be coated over in marble in the early 1600s. However, the work directed by sculptor Clemente was not completed, some say because of Clemente falling out with the bishop. The mediaeval bell tower is octagonal and the facade is topped by a gold-plated 16th century statue of the Madonna with child.

Originally the facade was covered in frescoes depicting religious stories to the illiterate, but these were removed early this century and are now kept in the cathedral's library. Having undergone many restorations, only the crypt in the interior remains from the Romanesque period. The chapels inside are mainly 16th century and the widespread use of finely sculpted marble illustrates the wealth of the city.

To the rear of the cathedral is the lime-green, Baroque style sanctuary inside which are silver caskets containing the relics of other saints. Entry requires permission from the priests.

REGGIO EMILIA

The Roman Baptistery

Being a Monday afternoon our entry into the city's Baptistery next to the cathedral was barred. Constructed in the 12th century with its edifice redesigned in the 15th century the Baptistery's mediaeval structure and some of the decoration overlain by works in the 15th century are apparent. One feature of note is the painted lunette on the exterior that was used until the 15th century.

Il Palazzo del Capitano del Populo

Well, actually it's now the **Hotel Posta** and stands on the edge of the main square. The name Hotel Posta comes from the 16th century when the building became a stage for changing horses. The riders would arrive beneath the porticoes and take on another horse. Prior to that the Palazzo del Capitano del Populo played an important role in the city's history.

The red brick Palazzo was constructed with its Ghibelline swallow-tail battlements in 1280, after the local people had decided to demolish two houses to make way for the People's Captain.

Reggio had been ruled by Matilda of Canossa. After her death, the free city state of Reggio was born in 1115 A.D. This was followed by internecine warfare, until the election of the People's Captain by the craftsmen's guilds and the people in 1278. As ruler of the city, the people's captain was head of the militia and this brought some political stability.

People's Captains had to be over 30 years old, from outside the city and were forbidden from owning property in the city or bringing their children with them. They were elected at least every six months by consul representatives of the guilds. Until 1326, they were the rulers supreme in the city. The takeover by the Gonzaga ended the role of People's Captain and the palace became a seat of the Dukes' Regent.

Each captain would have his coat of arms painted on the walls of the building. The result, on the exterior walls and in the **Great Hall** on the second floor, is a wonderful array of mediaeval coats of arms. In the Great Hall, the olive painted walls are decorated with an Oriental fresco of peacocks dating back to 1300. The Captains were well supplied with views from the balconies and windows of the hall, which looked out onto the square and a mile down the Via Emilia. The hall is now used for conferences and functions.

In the centuries that followed, the Palazzo was converted from a palace into a mint, then the Red Hat Inn and finally into the elegant and luxurious, four-star Hotel Posta.

Piazza del Monte

The Piazza del Monte gives a fine view of the Via Emilia twisting its way out of the city south eastwards towards Modena (Via Emilia San Stefano), and north eastwards to Parma. We headed on foot on the Via Emilia San Pietro in the Parma direction through the busy pedestrian shopping area.

Opposite Hotel Posta on Via Emilia, the three storeys of 17th century **Palazzo Bussetti** were once the seat of Reggio's university. The Estense dukes were happy to relieve Reggio of its treasures. One of their members 're-located' the university from Reggio to Modena. To this day the university has not returned to Reggio.

The Bronze Plaque

We came to the intersection with Via Roma 100 yards on, where the bronze plaque sits in the middle of the road marking the centre of the old Roman city. We had to take our lives in our hands to get close to the plaque. With bicycles, taxis, minibuses and lorries, Reggio has the busiest pedestrian area that I'd ever witnessed, and that was on a Monday when the shops were shut!

The plaque was discovered beneath the spot on which it sits. Nearby, grains of seed were found which eventually allowed archaeologists to surmise that the Consul's accommodation would have been close by, concluding that this was indeed the original centre of the camp.

The plaque's position suggests that the east-west Via Emilia was the decuman maximo and the north-south Via Roma was the carde maximo, the central axes of the encampment. All other streets would then be traced out in a radiating octagonal layout as was the norm

San Prospero's Basilica

The Basilica di San Prospero overlooks San Prospero square, known as the 'Lion's Square' for the large red lions which have sat at the base of the basilica's six columns since the 16th century. **San Prospero** was the bishop of Reggio during the 5th century. A legendary miracle maker and the city's patron saint, he ruled the city, protecting it from invasion. A statue at the top of the facade represents his personage.

The clay brick church was consecrated in 997 but was rebuilt in the 16th century. Most of the facade was reworked in the 18th century. Its fine sculpture contrasts sharply with the ruggedness of the grey octagonal bell tower built of stone from the city's old river bed. The tower was never completed.

REGGIO EMILIA

The apse has an interesting cycle of frescoes depicting the Final Judgement painted in 1589 by Camillo Procaccini from the Bologna school. The painter visited the Sistine Chapel in Rome. Both he and Zacetti (who worked with Michelangelo and also painted part of the apse) were heavily influenced by Michelangelo's works. The wooden choir stalls dating back to 1546 are also of interest, with marvellous carvings inlaid portraying country life, landscapes and urban perspectives.

The Valli Municipal Theatre

Reggio has a great theatrical tradition. Despite the small size of the city it has four main theatres. The most popular is the Municipal Theatre on Piazza Martiri del 7 Luglio. Teatro Municipale Valli is named after Reggio-born Romolo Valli, who was a popular comic actor. The theatre was originally designed as an opera house and operas and ballet are performed here.

The Municipal Theatre's facade is in Neoclassical style with the lower part supported by 12 columns forming a portico. Of interest are the 20 statues looking out at the visitor from the top of the building. From left to right on the facade the statues represent Tragedy, Vice, Glory, Drama, Virtue, Truth, Instruction, Pleasure, Fable, Jest, Dance, Caprice, Comedy and Sound. On the left side, three other statues represent Silence, Curiosity and Remorse and on the right, Painting, Modesty and Remorse. I was exhausted just thinking about them.

As we entered the theatre, little was left devoid of fanciful decoration with 1850s period monochrome paintings and Venetian stucco everywhere.

The interior is a bright and quite glorious blaze of scarlet, greys and gold. A series of 106 boxes and four tiers of galleries arch around the stage to seat 1,100 visitors. A magnificent 3.75 metre high, 3 metre wide chandelier hangs from the dome at the centre of the ceiling. Note the now disused camerine rooms behind each box where the high paying nobles could eat and party during and between performances. The central and largest box was reserved for the Duke of Estense.

It was here three decades ago that **Pavarotti** won his first public operatic contest singing La Boheme. Performances at the Municipal Theatre are generally sold out by the start of the season. Out of season the theatre is in state of permanent restoration. Guided tours, which include the mirror room, dance rehearsals and exhibitions of ancient theatrical equipment, can be had by appointment (tel 0522 458811).

Ariosto's theatre, **Teatro Ludovico Ariosto**, is named after the locally born poet, Ludovico Ariosto. Born in 1474 in the Gonzaga's Citadel, he became particularly known for his great epic poem, Orlando Furioso. An 1851 reconstruction of the building has not harmed the splendour. Its design is Neoclassical but the interior decoration of the theatre's dome is a 1927 Art Nouveau work of Anselmo Govi who was inspired by Ariosto's greatest poem.

Guided tours are by appointment (tel 0522 458811).

Palazzo Magnani

When the wealthy Luigi Magnani died in 1927 leaving no heirs, the Municipal Theatre fell into the hands of Reggio's provincial government. Palazzo Magnani was his home and is now a gallery sumptuously decorated with monochrome frescoes common to the last century.

The building was first referred to in 1608 but since then has undergone a great deal of restoration and transformation. The first floor decorations are 18th century and the ceiling of the dining room is in the gay Grotesque style. Magnani's collection of important paintings is displayed at the **Villa Magnani** just across the Parma border in the village of Mamiano. Open air concerts take place in the courtyard during the summer. There is also an amusement area and a bar.

Street Life

Beside the cathedral in the main piazza is an arcade known as the **Broletto**, a local name for the priest's orchard that existed behind the cathedral. In the arcade we found a butcher, *Salla Maria*, selling beautiful hams and salamis. Via Emilia San Pietro contains many banks and boutiques, including the fashionable **Maximara** clothes store. It is a popular area for promenading in the summer and spring evenings.

From Piazza Martiri 7th Luglio, we walked on down Vicolo Trivelli. With its plentiful **boutiques** and street decorations, it is known as Reggio's *Carnaby Street*. Via Antonino Franzoni has a lovely display of 100 year-old engravings of what was sold in the street's shops. Shops close at 12.30pm on Thursdays and few are open on Sundays or Monday afternoons.

Corso Garibaldi has a thriving annual Ghiara trade fair; a **handicraft market** with stalls displaying ironwork, furniture, wood carvings, wool clothing and other goods. It takes place from 3rd September to 8th September.

Reggio is famous for its children's education and kindergartens for children aged 3 to 6 years old. The Diana kindergarten in the city is reputed to be one of the world's finest.

ACCOMMODATION AND EATING OUT
(area code 0522)

Papardella, tagliatelle and gnocchi are worth a try in Reggio's many eating establishments. Reggio is home to **Balsamic vinegar** and **Parmigiano-Reggiano** which, taken together, are quite superb. The area around **Piazza Prampolini** is littered with restaurants and the square itself offers a nice place to sit and dine al fresco.

For a cheap meal, try the self-service *Free-Flow Job's* at 2 Piazza Gioberti near the centre, just off Via Emilia San Pietro.

A **free booklet** is available detailing some of Reggio Emilia's **Parmigiano-Reggiano recipes** in English, by writing to Consorzio del Formaggio Parmigiano-Reggiano, Casella Postale 1056, 42100 Reggio Emilia, Italy. Details of Reggio recipes for

Balsamic vinegar can be had by contacting the Balsamic Vinegar Consortium c/o Camera di Commercio di Reggio Emilia, 1 Piazza della Vittoria, 42100 Reggio Emilia (tel 796225 fax 433750 e-mail reappennino@reappennino.it.).

The ****_Hotel Posta_ (tel 432944 fax 453737) opposite the town hall on the edge of Piazza Prampolini is the most sought after location with international visitors. As a hotel, its tradition dates back centuries, and it is by far the oldest in the city. The owners have done all in their power to ensure that the whole building, from the reception area to the 43 air-conditioned bedrooms, is revealed in all its true period elegance. Rooms are £90 per night with breakfast. Although it has no restaurant, there are plenty nearby.

****_Astoria Mercure_ (tel 435245 fax 453365) is at 2 Via Nobili and, like ****_Delle Notarie_ (tel 453500 fax 452602) at 5 Via Palazzolo, charges £80.

Cheapest of the ***hotels are _San Marco_ (tel 435364 fax 452742) at 1 Piazzale Marconi and _Airone_ (tel 92411 fax 515119) at 20 Via Aeronautica, charging £50. At the upper end are _Cristallo_ (tel 511811 fax 513073) on Viale Regina Margherita and _Nova Hotel_ (tel 531053 fax 531077) on Via Tirelli, charging £60.

The **_Ariosto_ (tel 437320 fax 452514) on Via San Rocco, **_Brasil_ (tel 455336 fax 455379) at 37 Via Roma, **_La Rosta_ (tel 283683 fax 322866) at 19 Via Passo Buole and **_Cairoli_ (tel 453596 fax 453148) at 2 Piazza XXV Aprile, all charge around £35.

Cheapest of the *hotels are _Haiti_ (tel 300884 fax 382409) at 172 Via F.Cervi and _Sirena_ (tel 516882 fax 922625) at 2 Viale Ramazzini, charging £25. _Stazione_ (tel 431270) at 1, Via Turri, also charges £25 but only has rooms with shared bath.

The _Tricolore_ **youth hostel** (tel 454795) just off Via Emilia San Pietro at 8 Via dell'Abbadessa charges £5.

_i_ Reggio's **Tourist Information Office** (tel 451152 fax 436739) is at 5 Piazza Prampolini.

Travelling Around

Distances from Reggio Nell'Emilia of the main cities are; Ravenna 138km, Ferrara 106km, Rimini 185km, Bologna 72km, Parma 19km, Modena 33km and Piacenza 61km. The **train station** (tel 452444) is in Piazzale Marconi and the **bus station** is on Via Trento Trieste. **Taxis** (tel 453345) run from Piazza Martiri 7 Luglio.

Train Times (faster direct services)

Reggio to Modena 14mins, Bologna 37mins, Parma 23mins, Piacenza 43mins, Milan Centrale 1hr 25mins, Florence 2hrs, Rimini 2hrs, Rome 4hrs 30mins.

Trains around Reggio Province

Trains run east from Reggio city to Rubiera (10mins), west to S.Ilario d'Enza (15mins), south west to Scandiano and south west through Bibbiano, S.Polo d'Enza to Ciano d'Enza.

A private line runs north from Reggio City to Biagnolo in Piano, Novellara, Guastalla, and Luzzara.

Another line runs west through Luzzara, Guastalla and Brescello to Parma.

THE PLAINS OF REGGIO'S BASSA
Gualtieri

We arrived at the tiny town of Gualtieri, close to the River Po. Hidden on the plain, we were about to find one of the region's most attractive and neatest historic towns. As we passed through the cobbled streets and rows of centuries old houses to the beautiful Renaissance central square all was at peace. We were in a rush but I threw a coin over my shoulder swearing I would one day be back to spend more time savouring the serene and time-free atmosphere of the town.

Benedictine monks long ago reclaimed these lands from the Po marshes. The nucleus of the village is believed to have been a church, the **Chiesa di San Andrea** which is in the 11th century Piazza Felice Cavallotti. Up to the 13th century the area surrounding the village was under the state of Parma, after which followed the period of the free comunes. Its modern history began in 1479 when the area came under the control of the Este Dukedom based in Ferrara.

Gualtieri, with an important position on the Po, became an outpost for the Estense who faced the Parma rulers to the east and the Mantovans to the north. The Mantovans had the Gonzaga family as allies in Guastalla, a town just a few kilometres away. To fortify there position the Estense's handed 'Castel Gualtieri' to their vassals, the Bentivoglio family who in 1594 set about reclaiming land and building a fortified palace.

Palazzo Bentivoglio was completed in 1600 and, with its piazza and surrounding terraces and arcades also created under Bentivoglio instruction, forms a classic example of Renaissance architecture. The grandeur of this palace set in countryside can only be imagined as today's palace was only the front of the old fort.

What remains formed part of a large square fort that stretched out to its rear, encompassing a large courtyard. In 1750 the other wings were dismantled and their bricks used to construct a flood barrier. Viewing the turreted, fortified wings of the palace one can derive some appreciation that the Palace was much more than

REGGIO EMILIA

a summer pleasure house for the Bentivoglio. The Bentivoglio ruled for 100 years until they ran out of male heirs and the dynasty became extinct. Thereafter, the palace fell into the hands of the Estense.

Piazza Bentivoglio

The palace was designed to look out on the beautiful **Piazza Bentivoglio**, a 50-metre square with a circular ornamental garden. Surrounded on three sides with typical Emilian Renaissance buildings containing arcades, the piazza was constructed both to support the palace courtiers but also to impress the Bentivoglio's rivals. Not only is it a very winning Renaissance balance of symmetry, squares, arches and circles but the square is virtually empty, as if the whole town has disappeared for a long siesta.

The buildings around the square have been painted lemon yellow on the ground floor and peach on the second, contrasting with the terracotta clay bricks of the palace. Their roofs have been covered with the rare combination of clay and white coloured tiles. This pretty pebble-dash effect is coming back into fashion amongst the region's well-to-do. Each roof is then decorated with a series of obelisks interspersed by chimneys.

Directly opposite the palace entrance is the town's clock tower. Standing in the middle of the terraces its archway forms the entry into the square. At 44 metres high it offers excellent views of the countryside and the rest of the town. Note the first floor iron balcony for the municipal representatives to appear and look out over the square. Under the vault, about 12 ft above the ground, is an inscription pointing to a line marking the height where a great flood once reached.

Inside Palazzo Bentivoglio

We entered through the huge archway beneath the facade, up a grand stone staircase to the first floor and through the main doors. It soon became clear that even if the Bentivoglios kept the simple facade of the fortress, inside they spared little on their elaborate furnishings and decoration.

The palace has undergone a process of restoration over the last 30 years. After the Estense left, the building fell into disrepair. During the post war period it was used to accommodate homeless peasants migrating from the south and the mountains to find work on the northern plains. The refugees lit fires in the rooms in the winter months causing some damage to the frescoes.

In the Salone dei Giganti, or **Hall of Giants,** we could not but be impressed.

Hidden away in this sleepy little town the Bentivoglio had ordered the construction of this massive ballroom. At 31 metres long, 17 metres high and 14 metres high, it seemed as if the whole town would have had to be invited to fill it.

Reaching right to the ceiling, the original wall frescoes add height and posture to the hall. They comprise of three tiers of monochrome painted frames creating a series of 'windows', in which appear portrayals depicting Roman legends. The painters were Badalocchio of the Bologna school and Battistelli of the Guercino school, who was responsible for the monochrome paintings.

The **Tirelli Exhibition** is housed in the east wing of the palace. Born in Gualtieri, Tirelli was a tailor and clothes designer particularly famous for the exquisite costumes in period style he made for the theatre and film industry. Both his own costumes, some worn by **Romy Schneider**, and the best of others he collected are on show.

The Icarus room is so-called because of the large painting of Icarus' plight by Battistelli in the monochrome style. The room adjacent is dedicated to the local Naïf painter, **Antonio Ligabue**. When he died recently, the inspiration he had drawn from the palace resulted in the gallery becoming an exhibition of his work. Particularly interesting in his splendidly aggressive paintings is the collection of self portraits.

The room to the left of the entry hall formed a theatre in the 1700s. When we visited it was being restored and converted into an art gallery.

Outside the square the tranquil streets and houses around Corso Garibaldi are almost as they were in the Renaissance save that is for the clothes shops and restaurants. We came to **Cavallotti Square** once known as 'New Square'. The piazza is overlooked by Chiesa di San Andrea and is believed to be the former centre of the village.

We asked why the church walls were riddled with holes, as if someone had removed bricks to make a pattern. The palace guide said the holes were to strengthen the church against earthquakes. These holes are a common and unattractive feature in many of the region's historic buildings. But opinion was divided as to their function. The best guess was that the holes were created to support ancient wooden scaffolding, which would have been necessary to repair walls and windows. Like many skilled craftsmen the scaffold erectors probably left, not bothering to put the bricks back in place.

The fountain in the centre of the square was the only source of clean water for the villagers during the 18th century, when the area was riddled with cholera. The third weekend in June each year sees a special fountain festival in the town. "Does the fountain get turned on?" I asked. "What for? We drink Lambrusco!" came the reply.

Guastalla

Upon leaving Gualtieri it took the painted roundabout on the road to bring me back to the 20th century. Then again we travelled back in time as we drove across the Torrente Crostolo canal towards Gualtieri's long term rival, the town of **Guastalla**. Within ten minutes we had arrived by way of Via Garibaldi at the oldest part of the town. The town was littered with Renaissance porticoes and cobbled streets.

Flanked by the 15th century arcades of its houses, Via Garibaldi's cobbled street barely allows sufficient room for a car to get through. Nevertheless it is the location of many of the town's important sites including the historic **Maldotti Library** and the town's oldest and most celebrated inn, **Trattoria Fratellanza**. Further on at number 23 is Garibaldi House where the Risorgimento hero stayed during a night in August, 1858. Among Via Garibaldi's unobtrusive shops are ice cream parlours and restaurants.

Nearby is the tiny, cobbled and sloping square, once the old town centre. The **Piazza Mazzini** is not actually a square but a peculiar misshape, as if suffering like Emilia's towers from the wear of time. The piazza and porticoes around it are over 1,000 years old. Above the porticoes the houses sport balconies decorated in wrought ironwork and stone. The steep incline was considered a bonus for clearing flood water back in the direction of the River Po.

In the 13th century, Corso Garibaldi was the main barrier against the Po. Today, the river is still only 500 metres away.

Ferrante Gonzaga, who once ruled the town, had the bronze statue of him made in the 16th century. The statue has Gonzaga overwhelming his opponent. Work on the Concattedrale di San Pietro began in the same period but the **Palazzo Comunale** is more likely an early 15th century construction. Once the Palazzo Ducale, its fine Grotesque works completed in 1586 are being restored.

Trattoria Fratellanza

Trattoria Fratellanza (tel 0522 824690) dates back over 150 years and doesn't seem to have changed much. Wooden benches and chairs, the wizened faces of old men sat about in contemplation or debate, and various country bric-a-brac hanging on the walls added a rustic timeless air.

Garibaldi ate at the Fratellanza. As the kitchen casually went about preparing our meal while discussing the fine points of philosophy, it seemed as if they were consumed with all the questions the soldier politician had to grapple with.

We ate **tortelli**, a pasta dish packed with cheese and vegetables, boiled in water and then coated in a little butter, common to Reggio Emilia. Thereafter followed the local speciality, donkey. Each household would often own a donkey for doing heavy work. When the donkeys became too old to work, they were eaten (said our guide Alessandro) out of respect.

The donkey (azina) is boiled for six hours (stracotto is the term for well boiled meat) in water, with vegetables such as carrots and onions added to taste, providing a broth. Called **somarina,** it was served with polenta and quite delicious.

Desert followed. Another experience. A dry sponge cake, **bisulan,** was served. We waited while a white wine was poured into our glasses and then dunked our cake into the wine before eating it. Including a mushroom tagliatelle starter, the meal would have cost around L28,000 and would happily have fed two people.

The **Biblioteca Maldotti** is a massive old library donated to the town in the 15th century. It holds over 100,000 volumes including examples dating back to pre-15th century. Around 1,500 books produced in the 16th century attract researchers from all over the world. With the musty smell of old paper, portraits, and pieces of ancient local sculptor, it is a visit of interest to any culture vulture. It was interesting to note that the early books were all in Latin. Only in the 15th century did Italian appear as a language worthy of these books.

From Garibaldi Square we continued along Via Giuseppe Verdi, off which were neat little lanes with terracotta painted houses. We came to an orange and lemon coloured building, the facade of Guastalla's **theatre**.

The theatre was built in the late 18th century and still contains its original panels. The building has been restored but with its four U-shaped galleries and a glorious mix of gold and reds, it is a classic example of the attachment to the arts of even the smallest towns in Emilia. It is one of the few theatres in the region with the U-shape design more common to the 17th century.

The ceiling was renovated in the 19th century. A crystal chandelier hangs down from a glorious representation of the muse on the ceiling. During a recent restoration the theatre took on a more democratic look. The special boxes for royalty and the town officialdom were removed.

Dedicated to **Ruggero Ruggeri**, whose mother came from the town, the theatre stages performances of drama, ballet, opera and music concerts.

Art enthusiasts can also visit Villa Superiore in the town of Luzzara, 12km north east of Guastalla on the banks of the Po. Luzzara was the birthplace of Cesare Zavattini (1902-89) and seen as the home of Italy's Naïf school of artists. The villa houses the **Museo Nazionale del Naïf** in a deconsecrated monastery (Open 9am-noon, 3pm-6pm)

We went off to **Lido di Po**, a small recreation area surrounded by poplar trees on the river bank. The lido's buildings are charmingly old-fashioned, yet provide facilities for young and old. **Horse riding** stables, a cafe, a grey clay beach, a picnic area, a children's play area, a small football pitch and **volleyball** court, **rowing, canoeing, walks** on the river bank, **fishing**, a youth hostel and restaurant mean that almost everyone is catered for.

Anglers would be enticed by the photos of successful catches of sturgeon and 70 kilo catfish with their captors grimacing beneath the weight. Swimming is not recommended in this section of the river at the moment but the water is being purified to the extent that the sturgeon has returned to the Po.

Novellara

We took the 16km road south east to the town of **Novellara**, once the centre of another tiny city state. Just as in Guastalla, the ruling dynasty left behind many treasures of art and architecture. In this case the most influential rulers were the Gonzaga family who dominated the plains' town for 400 years.

The Gonzaga lived in a house just past the crossing on the right of Via San Bernadino. Originally inhabited by the Sessi clan, it was occupied by the Gonzaga until Guido Gonzaga reconstructed the Rocca. The simple exterior of the Rocca hides many treasures of a dynasty that courted Popes, emperors, kings and queens until they were ousted by the Modena Estense in 1728.

The Gonzagas amassed such riches that an inventory of paintings owned by the family in the early 18th century listed 1006 pieces, including works by Michelangelo, Raphael, Titian, Leonardo da Vinci, Tintoretto and Carracci. At their height in the 1500s the Gonzaga issued their own currency. The house of the old mint can still be seen on the corner of Via E. De Amicis and Via della Liberta opposite their first family home. Some of the coins are on display in the castle museum.

The Bentivoglio and the rulers of Correggio originally built the Rocca as a moated castle for purely defensive purposes protecting the family from occasional assault. It was modified and added to over the centuries until relative peace allowed the Gonzaga to turn it into a delizia. Today it is home to the town council, several museums, and boasts a fine theatre, **La Casa della Commedia**, created in 1567. The tranquil inner courtyards housed the many courtiers and the dungeon for less welcome visitors is still evident below the Torre della Computisteria tower.

The jewel of the castle is however the extensive work by the Renaissance artist, **Leoli Orsi** (1511-1587). Novellara-born, Leoli's father was Captain of The Gate at the castle. By the age of 19 Leoli was being described as a maestro and was taken on as the Gonzaga court artist. His earliest work in Novellara is believed to be the painting on the exterior of the clock tower in Piazza del Duomo.

In 1546 Orsi was forced to flee the tiny state, having been implicated in a murder case. Claiming innocence, he survived for six years outside Novellara, only returning when such evidence emerged proving that he could not have been involved in the murder. By 1563 he was given the job of redesigning the town. The design of the historical part of Novellara one sees today was Orsi's work. He designed some of the houses in the centre, San Stefano church in Piazza Maggiore, the Jesuit convent, and the rocca's second floor and loggia. He decorated the theatre, the splendid Salone Gonzaga hall and the piano nobile.

The Salone Gonzaga is now the meeting place for the local comune. Most of his work is on show, some in the museum. The theatre is a later design by Antoni Tegani, completed in 1868. Probably the best of Orsi's work was the cycle of frescoes adorning the Gonzaga's Casino di Sopra delizia on the road to Reggio. The frescoes now hang in the rocca museum.

Novellara's centre owes its origin to the Mediaeval period. The Renaissance sector of the town includes Chiesa di Servi (1654) on Via V.Veneto, the Jesuit convent (1571) on Viale Roma and the Beata Vergine della Fossetta sanctuary (1654) at the junction of Via C.Cavour and Contrada del Portico Lungo.

We stayed over night at the 16th century Nuova Agricola Riviera (tel 668189 fax 668104) guest house in the Novellara countryside. It's a good place to stay in the marshlands where spring brings sandpipers, snipes, teals and sheldrakes to join the herons, little egrets and buzzards that compete for air space.

We ate duck in a massive dining hall with a welcome bar. It's a large old villa with whitewashed houses at the centre of a large farm. The farmer and owner provide basic accommodation and, for those interested, have an artificial **fishing** lake and **pheasant hunting** grounds.

Boretto

Travelling back to Guastalla then parallel to the river on the way to Brescello, we came across **Boretto**. From the quayside, a twice weekly passenger ferry takes people on the two hour trip to Venice – a fascinating way of carrying on one's onward journey in peace.

Brescello

Heading east a mist had settled on the plain. It would clear with the hot sun. By October, the fog lingers all day. Soon we arrived in the sleepy town of **Brescello** – sometimes called the home of **Don Camillo**. For it was in Brescello's tranquil square that the scenes of the great Italian comedy series were filmed.

Don Camillo was a character created by Italian novelist, Giovannino Guareschi. In his novels Guareschi used Don Camillo, a church priest, and Communist mayor, **Peppone**, to comically portray the post war conflict between the church and the political left. The popularity of his novels such as *The Little World of Don Camillo* spread throughout Italy and Europe.

In turn, the novels were turned into films that were once again a huge success in Italy. Brescello was chosen as the main setting because of the peculiarity of its main square. Traditionally in Italian town squares, the town hall is on the opposite side of the square to the church. But Brescello's Piazza Matteotti has its town hall on the left hand side of the square when facing the church. French director, Julien Duvivier, wanted this unusual juxtaposition to portray the relationship between the Communist politicians and the clerics as not being totally at war but wary of one another, throwing sidelong glances.

It's an Italian story, never at war but never at peace. Always at odds but always prepared to co-exist. Today filming has long since ceased and the main income from Don Camillo comes via tourism – evidenced by the Peppone and Don Camillo cafes, puppets, mugs and various other effects.

Don Camillo's Church

The church dedicated to the birth of the Virgin Mary dates back to the 17th century. Inside the richly decorated church are beautiful frescoes. The facade of the church was changed at the behest of the filmmakers.

"The crucifix in the church was often used in the films. On one occasion, the crucifix had to be filmed being carried to the river. A dog was supposed to follow it. In the end the crew had to tie some meat to the cross which is why in the film you can see the dog following but jumping up and down."

Opposite the church are several restaurants. Otherwise the large square seems pleasantly unaffected with its barbers, pasticerria, greengrocers, clothes shop and ice cream parlour.

A short walk from the square in Viale Soliani is the **Peppone & Don Camillo Museum** celebrating the five 1950s films, their actors and technical staff. There is an interesting display of old motorbikes and a sidecar used in the filming plus a replica of an American tank used in a particularly humorous episode. The museum (tel 0522 96215, fax 684422) is open between 10am and noon and 2.30pm and 6pm every day.

Correggio

Antonio Allegri was born in the town of Correggio in 1489. As his celebrated paintings and frescoes became known he acquired the nickname of Correggio, becoming the town's most celebrated son. A monument to him stands in the square outside the Basilica of San Quintino, and the Civic Museum displays copies of his work.

Antonio Correggio

After a childhood in Correggio, Antonio moved to Parma, carving out a career as one of Italy's great Renaissance artists. A contemporary of Michelangelo and Raphael, he developed the illusionist devices of Mantegna, north Italy's first great Renaissance artist. Correggio trained in Mantova but was also influenced by the Venetian school, Leonardo da Vinci and Michelangelo.

He mastered chiaro scuro (light and shade) and the creation of three dimensional figures. Many figures stand out so firmly that they appear to be in relief. This great technical skill is seen as the reason why he was considered more of a technician than artist. As a result he is accused of eclecticism, lacking in emotional aspect. Most treasured are his paintings of mythological scenes. He died in 1534.

The town is 14km south east of Novellara on the frontier with Modena. Matilda di Canossa, the da Correggio earls and the Modena dukes all held the town over the years. At the centre of the town is Corso Mazzini, still cobbled and containing a double lane of granite laid out for the carriages that would pass along it. Also in the centre is the red brick Renaissance **Palazzo dei Principi** built in the early 1500s. The palace has an elegant marble gateway. Inside is the Civic Museum. Next door is the fine Neoclassical Teatro Comunale 'Asioli' built in 1898.

ACCOMMODATION AND EATING OUT
(area code 0522)

Gualtieri Stays at ***Antonio Ligabue** (tel 828120 fax 829294) in Piazza IV Novembre cost around £35. **Guastalla** has the ***Old River** (tel 838401 fax 824676) on Viale Po and ***Carolina** (tel 830405 fax 830520) on Via Pegolotti, charging £35/40. ***Leon d'Oro** (tel 826950 fax 824060) on Via Verdi is a pleasant local hotel with restaurant. With bed and breakfast for two at £35 and a full meal for L25,000, it rates an inexpensive stay for carousing around the Padane, as the plain is called. For those looking for cheaper accommodation, the nearby Lido di Po on the riverside has a **youth hostel** (tel 824915) in Via Casa Pontieri charging £5/person.

The town has plenty of pizzeria and restaurants. **Bolina** on Via Sacco e Vanzetti is a self-service restaurant. Apart from **Trattoria Fratellanza**, diners might also be attracted to **Valle Quinta dining agriturismo** on Via Valle Quinta in San Girolamo.

Brescello has the ***La Tavernetta del Lupo** (tel 680509 fax 680848) on Piazza M.Pallini charging £35, ***La Capannina** (tel 680291) and ***Luppi** (tel 687173) both on Via Cisa Ligure and charging £25/30. The cheapest stay in town is *Alla Stazione* (tel 687157) at 11 Viale Venturini for £20. The main square has a few restaurants and an **ice cream parlour.**

Novellara has ***Alexander** (tel/fax 653570) at 1 Via Cartoccio and ***Nubilaria** (tel 661363 fax 652441) at 64 Via della Constituzione both charging £35/40. Cheap accommodation is provided in the countryside at the **agriturismo Nuova Agricola Riviera** (tel 668189 fax 668104) on Via Riviera in San Bernadino. Novellara's **bars**, **cafes and pasticceria** are concentrated around Piazza Unita d'Italia and Via Colombo has several restaurants.

Correggio has the upmarket ****Dei Medaglioni** (tel 632233 fax 693256) at 6 Corso Mazzini charging £80, ***Locanda della Vigne** (tel 697345 fax 697197) at 8 Via Ruota and ***President** (tel 633711 fax 633777) at 61 Via Don Minzoni, charging £55/65. ***Rose e Crown** (tel 690276 fax 690388) at 80 Via Fosdondo charges £45.

Losara, near Carpi on the Modena border, contains a small Asian community with a Sikh temple and, for travellers wanting to cook up their own curry, a shop selling Indian spices and vegetables.

i **Tourist Information** is available, in **Novellara** at 1 Piazza le Marconi (tel 655454), in **Brescello** from the town hall (tel 687526 fax 684422), in **Boretto**, from the town hall in Piazza San Marco (tel 964221) and in **Gualtieri** from Palazzo Bentivoglio (tel 828696).

Transport
The regular and efficient **train service** from Parma to Darra stops at Brescello, Boretto, Guastalla and Gualtieri and costs no more than L5,000.

SOUTH OF REGGIO
THE LAND OF MATILDA DI CANOSSA

Taking SS63 for 28km south to Casina and then turning north east for 13km brings one to **Canossa**, heart of the former territories of one of Emilia and Tuscany's great historical figures, Matilda di Canossa. Set in green, rolling hills close to the border with Parma, the town pays homage to this important feudal queen who ruled over large tracts of Emilia, Mantova and Tuscany during the 11th century.

The Humiliation of Canossa

Matilda is best known for hosting the grand meeting of Pope Gregory VII and the German Emperor of the Holy Roman Empire, Henry IV in 1077. The two leaders represented the main religious and political authorities in Europe. Pope Gregory had set about reforming a church, which had succumbed to heresy and debauchery as Europe emerged from the Dark Ages with new found wealth.

In its darkest hour the church had been forced to concede power to the German Frank armies. In 800 Pope Leo III had crowned Charles the Great, known as Charlemagne, as the first Emperor of the Holy Roman Empire. Pope Gregory VII however came to power in 1073, insisting that the church was above man and above the German troops. He declared that he had the power to dismiss Emperors as he pleased. Henry IV objected and the tussle between the two ended up in Henry IV being excommunicated.

This weakened Henry IV's position by freeing his subjects from paying homage to him. By 1077 the German was ready to compromise. Matilda brought Gregory and Henry to the castle and mediated between them. Asserting his victory, Pope Gregory kept the Emperor waiting barefoot in penitence outside the castle for three days while the snow fell. The subsequent agreement became internationally known as 'the humiliation of Canossa'. Only when Henry V came to power was a lasting agreement made whereby the Emperor retained ownership of the bishops' lands.

Matilda di Canossa

Countess Matilda, also known as Matilda of Tuscany and La Gran Contessa was one of the great figures behind the spread of the Romanesque church designs of Wiligelmo. Her reign occurred at a time when the church was in disarray, with many bishops and feudal lords flouting the elementary mores of Christianity. She allied herself to the campaign of Pope Gregory VII known as the 'Gregorian Reforms'. He re-emphasised the practice of the more pious Christian ways.

Matilda encouraged the creation of new ecclesiastical buildings to reassert the religious role of the priesthood. In all she was said to have ordered the construction of 100 churches. The design of the churches re-created the earlier Christian simplicities, emphasising the values on which the church had been founded. Church bas-reliefs carried friezes no longer declaring that man's toils were a punishment by God for the original sin. Instead the new climate required an emphasis on work as a means to salvation.

Matilda also ordered the construction of new roads, bridges and hospices for pilgrims passing through to Rome. Resting on the church she secured allegiance from vast areas of Emilia. At first she reigned with her mother, Beatrice of Frassinoro, from 1074 to 1076. From then she reigned alone till her death in 1115. Her pious mantle however didn't stop her from donning armour to lead her troops into battle. Nor did it stop her, at 43, from marrying a 17-year-old and scandalising the nobility.

Ironically, her great works programmes stimulated the city's middle class which, once strengthened, took power. The middle classes broke up her dominions after her death and issued in the rule of the Comunes.

Atto Adalberto built a castle for Matilda's family in 940 A.D on the top of a white sandstone rock. Today it is a majestic ruin overlooking a verdant countryside (closed on Mondays. Opening times are in April-September, 9am-12.30pm and 3pm-7pm and from October to March, 2.30pm-5pm. Entrance is free). Adalberto also built the church of San Apollinnio close to the castle.

The castle is host to historic pageants and festivals commemorating Matilda's rule. **Quattro Castella**, with its modified 11th century Bianello castle, was a resting place for Matilda and holds the most important of the festivals. Annually they re-enact in full costume the reconciliation between Pope Gregory and the Emperor. Plenty of restaurants serve chestnut and mushroom-based foods, tortelli alla Matilda and Parmigiano-Reggiano in the local village. **Matilda di Canossa Golf Club** (tel 0522 371295 fax 371204) on Via del Casinazzo in San Bartolomeo has an 18 hole, par 72 course crossed by a stream.

Around Canossa

Canossa is in a beautiful part of the lower Apennines. It overlooks the Enza river that divides Parma from Reggio province. Tiny hamlets with tower-houses traditional to this part of the Apennines give a special character to this agricultural region.

Eastwards past Casalecchio on the road to Ciano d'Enza is the imposing castle of **Rossena** (940 A.D). Its impressive Rossonella tower perches on an outcrop of basalt. Little remains of the three wall defensive complex which once made this castle the most impregnable in Italy. It's open on Sundays between 4pm and 7pm.

Castelnovo ne'Monti lies 16km south of Casina on SS63 below a huge rock plateau, la Pietra di Bismantova, which rises out of the countryside. The town is a good base for trekkers with plenty of accommodation and reasonable prices.

THE REGGIO APENNINES AND PARCO DEL GIGANTE

Reggio's Apennine district is a vast protected area now called Parco del Gigante covering 23,400 hectares. The highest peak is Mount Cusna that rises to around 7,000ft. The main river valleys cutting through the mountains are those of the Enza on the Parma border, the Secchia which stretches towards Modena and the Dolo which forms the Modena border and joins the Secchia river at Cerredolo.

Here lush valleys sit beneath rugged and rolling hills covered by forests and pastures, and, in winter, snow. The snow-bound slopes provide for skiers and the area provides plenty of **trekking** country with lakes and waterfalls amongst moorland and forests of chestnut, beech, pine and fir trees. The natural inhabitants are wild boar, moose, deer, wild sheep, marmots, and overhead, fly eagles and hawks.

Leaving SS513 at Vetto the road south to **Ramiseto** ambles its way into the upper reaches of **the Enza valley**. This is a thick wooded area popular both in winter and summer with trekkers. Pratizzano has a cross country ski trail and, among the many lakes, Lake Calamona is said to be the most beautiful in Reggio. Southeast of Ramiseto are the villages of Miscoso and Cecciola where short, arch-shaped underpasses link the 15th century houses.

The upper reaches of the **Secchia Valley** can be arrived at by taking SS63 southwards from Castelnovo ne' Monti for 15km to **Busana**. At the foot of Mount Ventasso, Busana is famed for its **spring waters** from Fonti di S.Lucia and **thermal treatments** at **Cervarezza**, which is on SS63 6km to the north. The area is dotted with tiny hamlets such as Nismozza and Marmoreto with ancient stone houses and the old communal wash-houses.

The spring waters of Cervarezza are rich in chloride, sulphur and iodine. The Fonti di S.Lucia spring rises in a shaded wood above the village. The spring's waters are utilised at **Cervarezza Spa** (tel 0522-890143) which is only open from March to October.

The town of **Ligonchio** is another winding 16km upstream from Busana on the road left off SS63 just after Busana. The town lies beneath Mount Cusna. Sheer sandstone crags and deep glacial coombs are common. A popular trip is to Lavacchielo waterfall.

Continuing south on SS63 leads to **Collagna** that has a beautiful setting being encircled by Mounts Cavalbianco, La Nuda, Alpe di Succiso and Casarola. The town is a base for seeing the hills, as is **Cerreto dell'Alpi** a few kilometres southwards. Mounts La Nuda at 6,000ft, and Succiso (6,500ft) can both be climbed from Cerreto. Lake Pranda is on the slopes of Mount La Nuda and one recommended walk is through Passo d'Ospedalaccio to a vast **glacial amphitheatre** that is the source of the Secchia. Lake Cerreto has plenty of hotels and guest houses and an **indoor ice rink**. It also boasts a **ski resort**.

The main town in the upper **Dolo Valley** Apennine area is **Civago** that sits opposite Mount Prado (6,500ft). Civago can be reached by taking the valley road from Cerredolo or an 18km drive south over the hills from Villa Minozzo. The area has plenty of designated walks and tempting fields of blueberries, strawberries and raspberries around the Pass of Lama Lite (6,000ft).

Winter **ski resorts** include **Pratizzano** (tel 817300), **Ventasso Laghi** (tel 817300), **Cerreto Laghi** (tel 898150 fax 898310), **Ospitaletto** (tel 899138), **Alpe di Cusna** (tel 800156) and, with its discotheques, **Appenninia** (tel 807125).

ACCOMMODATION AND EATING OUT
(area code 0522)

Quattro Castella has *****Casa Matilde** (tel/fax 889008) with its historic Bianello room at 11 Via A.Negri at £85 and ****Maddalena** (tel 887021 fax 888133) at 5 Via Pasteur at £30. **Agriturismo with accommodation** include, in **Canossa**, **Antichi Poderi di Canossa e Riverzana** (tel/fax 877208) with its **swimming pool** at 21 Via Riverzana set in rolling hills and **Montefalcone** (tel 874174) at 8 Via Montefalcone in San Polo D'Enza, both with **horse riding**. **Dining agriturismo** in the locality include **Glicine** at 5 Via Martiri di Marzabotto in Roncolo and *Il Rifugio* at 5 Via Cernaieto in Trinita, Casina.

In **Castelnovo ne'Monti** most hotel stays cost £30/35 including, ****Bismantova** (tel 812218) at 151 Via Roma, *****Flamingo** (tel/fax 812292) at 83 Via Bagnoli and *****Miramonti** (tel 812300 fax 812578) at 7 Via Bagnoli. The ****Dante** (tel 812245) at 63a Via Roma charges £25. *Il Ginepro* (tel 611088 fax 812549) on Via Chiesa in Ginepro is an **agriturismo with accommodation** as is **Le Scuderie** (tel/fax 618118) at 77 Via San Donnino in Regigno near Carpineti.

Cervarezza has the ***Ilton** (tel 890175 fax 890506) on Via Statale at £30, ***Belvedere** (tel 890106) on Via della Molinella for £25 and ***Al Monte** (tel 890148) on Via P.Mentone and *Ventasso** (tel 890137) on Via della Resistenza for £20. Busana town also has the cheap *Bianchi** (tel 891164) on Via Liberta for £15. **Camping Le Fonti camp site** (tel 890126 fax 890390) is at 1 Via S. Lucia and charges £3/person.

Collagna /Lago Del Cerreto hotels cost around £30 including at ***del Bosco** (tel 898110 fax 898216) and ***Degli Sciatori** (tel/fax 898100) in Piazzale del Lago and ***Alpino** (tel 898150) in the Passo del Cerreto. *Stella Alpina** (tel 898109) in Via Provinciale offers a cheap stay for £20.

Ramiseto has several *hotels charging £15/20 including *Calamone** (tel 817139) near Ventasso Laguni, *Cicogna** (tel 817246) at 3 Via del Lago and *Jole** (tel 817110) at 87 Via Bombardi. Rooms with shared baths are available at *Del Lago** (tel 817114) at 6 Via Bombardi for £11, *La Montanara** (tel 892103) near Miscoso for £15 and *Al Ponte** (tel 614983) at 43 Via Ponte Enza for £15. **Camping Il Faggio camp site** (tel 817228) is near Ventasso Laghi and charges £3/person.

The Apennine areas have several **Alpine Refuges** for mountaineers at an altitude of around 5,000 feet. They are **Cesare Battisti** (tel 897497), **Segherie** (tel 807222), **Rio Pascolo** (tel 5115760, **Citta di Sarzana** (tel 892103), **Rio Re** (899619) and **Bargetana** (tel 627756). Each refuge is equipped with a kitchen and beds. Some are available only to experienced groups.

Ligonchio has ****Villa Montanarini** (tel 820001 fax 820338) on Via Mandelli which charges £60 for single rooms only. Elsewhere expect to pay £20/25 for an en suite double. Hotels include ***Del Lago** (tel 899118) on Via E.Bagnoli, *K2** (tel 891156) on Via Centrale, *Il Faro** (tel 899592) in Via al Frassine, and *Pineschi** (tel 899216) and *Tini** (tel 899138), both on Via Pradarena

i **Castelnovo ne'Monti Tourist Information Office** (tel/fax 810430) is at 12 Piazza Martiri della Liberta. Tourist information is also available for **Canossa** from Castello di Canossa (tel 877127), for **Cervarezza** from 3, Piazza Maggio (tel 890530) and for **Ramiseto**, from Centro Polivalente (tel 614555).

Visiting Centres for the **Parco del Gigante** can be contacted at Busana (tel 891587), Ligonchio (tel 899370), Cerreto Laghi (tel 898347) and Civago (tel 807276).

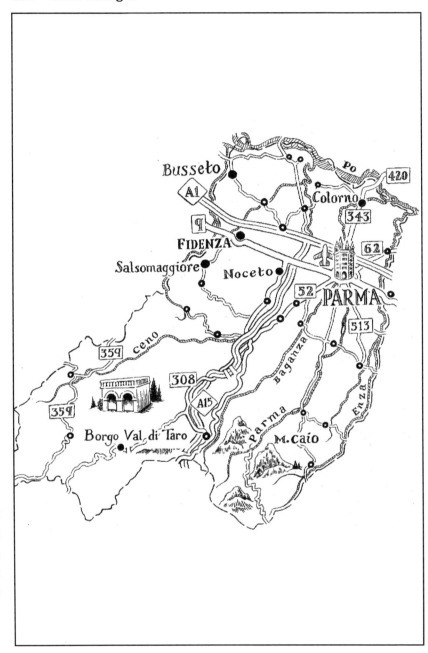

CULTURED **PARMA**
THE CITY

Parma, with 400,000 inhabitants, is the region's second largest city and lies on the Via Emilia between the plain and the Apennine hills. Parking in the city centre is difficult but we found spaces off Strada Farnese on the opposite side of the Parma river to the town hall. Crossing over the Parma River, it was summer time and the grand bridge of **Ponte di Mezzi** spanned a large river bed with a trickle of water passing through.

Beneath the Mezzi bridge is a piece of the old Roman bridge testifying to the age of the Roman city, said by Livy to have been founded with Modena in 183 B.C on Via Emilia. After the Romans came the Franks and the Holy Roman Empire, during which time the city flourished as an administrative centre. In 1106 its weakness led to the rule of the Comunes, followed by feudal strife that ended in Parma city with the seizure of the city in 1341 by the Visconti of Milan. The Terzi remained in control for 5 years before the Sforza families seized power as the leaders of the warring noble families.

The **Farnese** came to rule Rome by making important political marriages. When Farnese Pope, Paul III declared his son Pier Luigi Farnese ruler of Parma and Piacenza in 1545, a period of stability, construction and great works of art ensued. This was not before the Farnese had overcome the opposition of some of the ruling families. Pier Luigi was assassinated. By 1612 Farnese Duke Ranuccio I had gained the upper hand. He accused Barbara Sanseverino of treason. She and several nobles were executed in Parma's Piazza Garibaldi.

A point of note in Parma's history is the period following the death of Duke Ottavio, the heirless Farnese in 1731. Power passed to the **Bourbon**, Carlo, son of Spain's Phillip V and Elizabeth Farnese. But Carlo also assumed the throne to the Kingdom of Naples in 1734 and promptly stripped the ducal palaces of all their wealth. Bourbon rule lasted until the arrival of Napoleon's troops in 1802. They left, defeated in 1814 and the Congress of Vienna gave Parma to **Marie-Louise of Austria.**

From 1816 through to her death in 1847 Marie-Louise ruled in absolutist fashion. But her rule was very popular as she introduced many reforms and new public works, many of which have survived in the province. On her death, power passed back to a Bourbon, Duke Charles III who was stabbed to death in Parma in 1854. In 1860 Parma became part of the united Italy.

P A R M A

Mediaeval Parma

Only a few of Parma's mediaeval structures remain due to the grand plans of the Farnese, the Bourbons and Marie-Louise. Nevertheless, the historical centre of the city contains several jewels, making Parma one of the most visited of the region's cities.

Until the 12th century Parma maintained the dimensions of the Roman city. The Bishop's Palace, part of which remains on Via Cadalus, was first built in the 11th century, unusually outside the walls of the city. The palace was started in 1065 and the arch is original, lying close to the route of a Roman canal that linked the city, to the Po port of Brescello. Antipope Bishop Cadalus, who held power in the city, built it as a fortified stronghold. After the palace and church were built the walls were extended. It's the only area where one can feel the mediaeval city.

Walking to the edge of the city centre we came to the tranquil **Piazza del Duomo**, home to the magnificent Romanesque Baptistery and Parma Cathedral. **Parma Cathedral** was built between 1060 and 1073, but was severely damaged by an earthquake in 1117 and rebuilt and lengthened. The facade dates to 1178 but differs very much from the Romanesque styles used by the Wiligelmo school in Modena only because of its many transformations. The facade is an eclectic combination of styles.

The cathedral was to have two towers similar to the Fidenza church designed by **Benedetto Antelami**, the great Romanesque architect. He began this project but neither tower was built. The Gothic bell tower was added only in the late 13th century. We noticed that the tower was leaning but our guide informed us that the structure leans because it was built on a slope.

The Lombard porch was added in 1281. Interestingly, the Romanesque lions with animals caught beneath their paws at the front of the cathedral are said to represent Christ entrapping evil. In most other Romanesque churches the lions do not have animals beneath their feet, representing Christ having destroyed evil.

The patchwork nature of the sandstone façade, interspersed with marble which must have been left over from internal decoration, illustrates the age long interest in the cathedral. The three tiers of the facade were added in the 13th century. Much of the sandstone came from the city's vast Roman amphitheatre that would have seated 20,000 people.

The Cathedral contains beautiful interior decoration ranging from the Romanesque to the Baroque eras, with Mannerist frescoes on the ceilings and walls. Above the women's galleries are 17th century friezes representing the life of Christ. The stain glass window is not common to Italy and is quite modern.

The cathedral interior, like the facade, is stylistically eclectic. The Romanesque church was originally lower and the trussed ceiling was raised to create the vault and allow light to enter. The side altars were opened at the beginning of the 15th century and contain Gothic arches. The pulpit is a later Baroque introduction.

Correggio was considered one of Italy's greatest Renaissance artists. He is less well known on account of the fact that he never worked in Venice, Florence or any of the other major artistic centres. He worked in Parma, which at the time did not have a major court, the Duchy of Parma having not yet been founded. Had he lived longer he may well have been called to Rome because he was responsible for some of Italy's greatest decorations.

The artist decorated three domes in the city of Parma. The first two were in the Benedictine Monastery. The third fresco is in this cathedral where he represented in the cupola the ascension of the Virgin Mary. Today this fresco is considered to be the prototype for the Baroque style. His method was a new way of creating the appearance of space, and he is said to have inspired the great 17th century artists of Rome.

The fresco was painted between 1526 and 1530. The dome or cupola contains putti or cherubs dangling their legs as they carry the Virgin to heaven. From directly below, the worshipper would see the Virgin at the centre of the cupola But when we climbed the priests' steps closer to the fresco we could see that Correggio had created a cyclical movement or vortex, opening up the sky, destroying the architecture of the dome.

Correggio was ahead of his time and, with legs and arms in bountiful appearance, his masterpiece was decried as a frog's nest. Correggio took offence and, though he loved the city, he never returned. After Correggio's death, the bishop of the cathedral demanded a refund from his family for the money paid out to the artist.

The dispute continued for some years until Titian visited the city. Marvelling at the cupola, he remarked that if the dome were turned into a giant ball and filled with gold it would still have not been sufficiently paid for. The bishop relented.

P
A
R
M
A

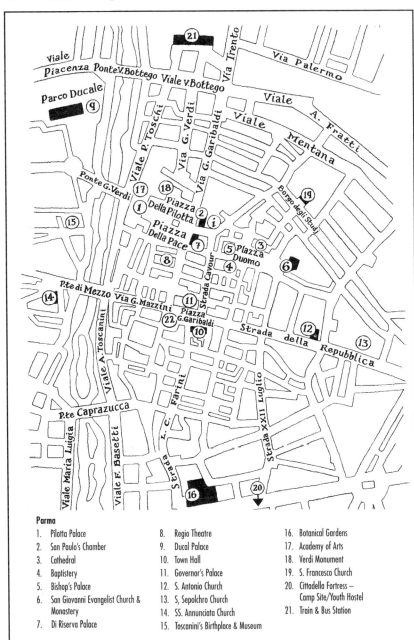

Parma

1.	Pilotta Palace
2.	San Paulo's Chamber
3.	Cathedral
4.	Baptistery
5.	Bishop's Palace
6.	San Giovanni Evangelist Church & Monastery
7.	Di Riserva Palace
8.	Regio Theatre
9.	Ducal Palace
10.	Town Hall
11.	Governor's Palace
12.	S. Antonio Church
13.	S, Sepolchro Church
14.	SS. Annunciata Church
15.	Toscanini's Birthplace & Museum
16.	Botanical Gardens
17.	Academy of Arts
18.	Verdi Monument
19.	S. Francesco Church
20.	Cittadella Fortress – Camp Site/Youth Hostel
21.	Train & Bus Station

We sat down for a rest in the pedestrian square in surprising peace, only disturbed by the occasional bicycle or shopper. The Piazza del Duomo, though not as lovely as many elsewhere in the region, is reputed to be one of Italy's finest for its harmony, blending together the buildings. With the correct evening light the Baptistery is quite beautiful.

To the left of the cathedral we could observe, in all its beauty, the octagonal, pale pink and white **Baptistery** with its exterior of Verona marble. The Baptistery, also by Antelami, was initiated in 1196 and is a masterpiece of Romanesque art. It contains height, rich decoration and also illustrates the beginning of the transition from the Romanesque to the Gothic style of architecture.

The portals are of French, if not Gothic influence. Some of the arches begin to be pointed rather than round. The Gothic height of the Baptistery represents reaching for god but also reflects the development of increased technological know-how to achieve greater height with buildings. For example, the pointed arches allowed for lighter structures.

Baptisteries

Baptisteries originally existed for those not allowed to enter the church. Only Christians could enter church and baptisms were performed annually at Easter or sometimes during Pentecost. Only a bishop could perform the baptism and only on adults. He would immerse the heathen three times beneath the water, representing the individual's symbolic death and rebirth as a Christian.

Once the Christian doctrine became more complex, other concepts such as limbo were created. The church needed 'limbo' as somewhere to put people such as prophets of the Old Testament, who were not Christian but could not be confined to either hell or heaven. Then, others who had become Christians feared that. should their children die young and unbaptised, they would enter hell. This ushered in the baptising of children.

Baptising began to take place in churches and baptisteries ceased to be constructed in the rest of Europe in the 8th century. Only in Italy and, in particular Emilia and Tuscany, did baptisteries continue to be built. Nevertheless, the Italian baptisteries became more symbolic than necessary. Their construction appeared in the large commercial cities such as Parma and Pisa.

The Baptistery is octagonal but not all sides are equal. This design is believed to have attempted to make the building appear more rotund. The eight sides

THE BAPTISTERY

represented the eighth day – the beginning of a new life. In addition the octagon is the geometrical pattern closest to the square and the circle, the square representing the earth and the circle representing the heavens.

The Baptistery is a very complex mixture of styles. The structure is part of the decoration. The columns are different and were probably recycled, as was much of the marble. Above the altar Christ stands in glory.

Beginning in the 12th century Romanesque period, women's galleries which may have been used previously, were now placed higher than any other decoration and themselves became purely decorative. Unlike in the cathedral, the tiny steps and gallery of the Baptistery were probably left unused.

Above the women's gallery is a typical Romanesque fresco of the cycle of labour of the months accompanied by their zodiac sign. The Roman calendar had ten months, with March as the first month as demonstrated in the cycle.

Nearby is **San Giovanni Evangelista**, a Renaissance church and abbey first founded in 980 A.D. The mediaeval structure was destroyed by fire in the 15th century and was to be rebuilt with a Baroque facade of white marble. The prayers commence at noon so we had to hurry. Close to the Cathedral, San Giovanni is very different. Occupied by the Benedictine order, it was the church of high society while the Cathedral was that of the people.

During the Renaissance period San Giovanni was one of five Benedictine churches in the city. Before the arrival of the Farnese, the absence of a rich court concentrated intellectual life around the Benedictine order. Money flowed in and when the church was rebuilt Correggio was probably invited in 1522 to design the cartoons for the frieze of *Hebrew and Pagan Sacrifice* around the nave. The terminal of the fresco decoration is that of the Correggio decorated dome, Correggio's second (the first is in St Paul's).

PARMA

The dome is much higher than what one sees, but it seems that he never considered the lighting conditions as is it was rather dark. Often people consider the cupola fresco to represent the ascension of Christ but, as we could see, Christ is not in fact ascending to the heavens, but falling from them. In addition, the men seated on heavenly clouds are apostles. It is unlikely that Correggio would have portrayed the apostles as having ascended to heaven before Christ. Rather, the other apostles are actually watching Jesus descending to gather John the Evangelist, last of the apostles, from earth.

It is suggested that the monks were trying to achieve a double interpretation. From their congregation Christ would appear to be ascending to heaven while only from the monks choir could John the Baptist be seen.

Here, Correggio painted his first dome with an open sky. Still a northern painter, his depiction of men are much more down to earth, unlike the gods of Michelangelo. Correggio's men are very much ordinary workmen and here they are sat in a simple osteria. He also decorated the area of the apse but the original fresco was destroyed in the late 16th century. Today the fresco is a copy made in 1586.

Outside San Giovanni's we went over to the Benedictine Pharmacy, Italy's first public dispensary. Opened in 1201 as part of the **Benedictine Monastery**, it must be the longest running shop in the world. Through and beyond the courtyard we came to three elegant cloisters open to the public, and still decorated with some 16th century frescoes (open 6.30am-noon, 3.30pm-8pm).

The pharmacy was part of the fourth largest monastery in Italy. Today the monastery is a national monument owned by the government. The dozen or so monks who inhabit the monastery run the shop selling jars of honey, fruit juices and other products from their monasteries outside the city. Benedictine monks were famous for their contribution to literature, laboriously copying books by hand. Above the pharmacy is a printing shop equipped with a modern printing press.

There is also a small Renaissance library with fascinating decoration, and open to the public on Saturdays. Again, we had be out by midday to make way for prayers.

Renaissance Parma

We were standing between Piazza del Pilotta and Piazza della Pace. Restoration work was continuing on the **Pilotta Palace**, built as the palace of the Farnese Dukes' servants and troops. When the Farnese family arrived in Parma they found a provincial city without grand palaces in the splendour they were already constructing in Rome. They set about creating palaces they considered worthy of their duchy.

First Ottavio Farnese ordered the building of the **Garden Palace** or Palazzo Ducale on the opposite side of the river across Ponte G.Verdi. It became the Farnese's pleasure palace and was decorated with figures celebrating love. The religious duke Ferdinand had the evocative figures plastered over at the turn of 18th century. Today the palace is the headquarters of the regional Carabinieri. In the middle of the Parco Ducale, it contains a 16th century core and 18th century additions carried out for Marie-Louise by Petitot.

P A R M A

The Carabinieri permit visitors to visit some of the frescoed rooms on the first floor. Particularly of note is the **Bird Room** or Sala degli Uccelli. It's not a prison but a hall decorated with splendid stucco in 1766 by Benigno Bossi. Bossi's stucco work portrays 224 different species of birds.

We went out into the spacious **Parco Ducale**, one of Italy's few surviving royal parks. It's a pleasant place for a break from the city. Begun in 1561 by Duke Ottavio, the park was given a French design by the 18th century Bourbons, before being altered to more of an English garden style by Marie-Louise. When the palace existed it was accompanied by garrisons and orchards. The Austrian Duchess opened the park to the public and the council took ownership in 1866.

The north side of the park contains a Neoclassical temple and the south, Palazzetto Eucherio Sanvitale. The latter is a Renaissance building dating from 1520 with four corner towers connected by loggia. The *Madonna and Child* fresco inside is thought to be an early work of Parmigianino.

With the Palazzo Ducale in place, the **Pilotta Palace** was built by Ranuccio I, in effect, as a corridor, including a wooden bridge across the river to connect the various ducal structures. To these structures were added wings for offices, secret archives, kitchens, warehouses, stables and barns. The Ducal Palace was then attached.

One main courtyard of Pilotta was reserved to play the Basque game of pelota. Hence the name of the palace.

It is a grand structure and housed between 4,000 and 5,000 people. Its ad hoc creation around three courtyards meant its appearance lacked the type of harmony of other palaces and one courtyard remains unfinished.

In the 17th century it was converted into a gallery, the **Galleria del Duca,** for the art collection of the Farnese's, who lost their palace in Rome. In 1743, the Bourbon duke, Carlo carted the collection off to his new Kingdom of Naples.

Today the palace contains the **Palatine Library**, the **Archaeological Museum**, the **National Gallery**, the **Farnese Theatre**, and the offices of art institutes. The *Virgin of Saint Jerome* by Correggio and, *La Scapigliata*, a small extraordinary drawing by Leonardo da Vinci are the **National Gallery**'s prize pieces. Other works on display include Parmigianino's beautiful *Turkish Girl*, and important paintings by Correggio, Tiepolo, Carracci, Guercino, Canaletto, Van Dyck and Bruegel (open 9am-2pm).

From Veleia in Piacenza, the **Archaeological Museum** contains the largest bronze inscription from the Roman world and fragments from ancient Egypt (open 9am-1.30pm, closed Mondays). The **Palatine Library** contains the largest collection of Hebrew manuscripts outside of Israel (for visits tel 0521 282217).

One of the greatest creations in the Pilotta was the **Farnese Theatre**, built in 1619 on the orders of Ranuccio I. The Theatre, holding 4,000 people, was also

PARMA

one of the greatest extravagances. It wasn't opened until 1628 and in the 104 years before it closed down only nine performances were given. Otherwise it was used for state weddings, galas and the like. Allied bombs destroyed the building in 1944 and today's theatre is a careful restoration (open 9am-2pm).

We crossed Strada Garibaldi into Via Melloni and turned left arriving at the fascinating **Camera di San Paulo**. Once part of the Benedictine monastery, it housed the apartment of the Abbess. In 1519, the feisty Abbess, Giovanna de Piacenza, had the vast umbrella vault with its 16 segments decorated in frescoes by Correggio. Putti in playful poses, animals and hunting scenes sit in a vast trompe l'oeil (open 2pm-5pm).

Back towards the Pilotta and down Strada Garibaldi we turned left into the Strada Carlo Pisacane and the **Teatro Regio Opera House** built by Duchess Marie-Louise in the 1820s. Dedicated to Verdi, it stakes a claim as one of the country's most influential opera houses. Like many other monuments, the building is painted in ochre – the colour of Marie-Louise. The colour was probably derived from the Hapsburg yellow.

On the corner of the strada is the **Palazzo della Riserva** which was formerly a guest house for the duchy before being turned into a gambling house by Petitot, Marie-Louise's great designer. Today it houses a small museum featuring the Duchy during the 18th and 19th centuries, and particularly Marie-Louise's reign.

Other places of note in the city include **Casa di Toscanini** at 13, Borgo Tanzi  off Strada Farnese near the park. The house was the birthplace of the great conductor, **Arturo Toscanini** and is now a museum dedicated to him (open 10am-1pm, 3pm-6pm, closed Sunday p.m. and Monday). Toscanini was an opponent of racism and fascism. When Mussolini introduced his race laws, the conductor insisted on performing with an all Jewish orchestra in Tel Aviv.

TOSCANINI

In the same area at the start of Strada Massimo D'Azeglio is the wondrous elliptical church of **Santissima Annunziata**. Built in 1566 with a facade of alternating concave and convex lines and ten radial chapels, it was one of the most innovative designs in the region. The interior contains a high ceiling, plenty of stucco work, frescoes and statues and a beautiful cloister.

A kilometre south of the centre, just past Viale Martiri della Liberazione, lies the spacious green area known as the **Cittadella**. At the centre is the Citadel (fortress) planned by Pier Luigi Farnese in 1546. Started in 1591, it contains pentagonal ramparts and five corner bastions. The moat has gone but the fine marble gateway remains.

PARMA

Hanging around for a train at Parma station, one might fill in the time by visiting the nearby **Collezione Borsari**, perfume museum in the Art Deco building at 30, Via Trento. Borsari manufacture the famous 'Violetta di Parma' (open 9am-1pm, 2pm-5pm, closed Saturdays). Their shop, *Borsari 1870* in Via Mazzini, sells Parma violet and other perfumes.

Stendhal's 'Charterhouse of Parma'

The Charterhouse of Parma can be found in the north of the city by going from Piazzale Vittorio Emmanuele II, along Via Emilia Este to Via Mantova on the road to Cisa. La Certuse de Parma contains a two-columned entrance into grounds that now only host the church of the Carthusian monks who had run the charterhouse since 1285. The original structure was demolished long before Stendhal.

The church was built in 1722 maintaining a slender pillared 15th century cloister and the 16th century sacristy and main cloister. It is worth a visit for its marvellous illusionist, trompe l'oeil by Alessandro Baratta and Natali.

Enthusiasts of the French classics will doubtless be intrigued as 'The Charterhouse of Parma' was the title of one of Stendhal's great novels. The novel is set in northern Italy around Parma, Milan and Lake Como. His hero Fabrizio del Drongo passes through Ferrara, spends some time in contemplation in the coolness and serenity of Bologna's San Petronio Basilica, and comments on the number of poor people who used to swarm Bologna's Piazza Maggiore. He is imprisoned in Parma.

Stendhal spent many years of his life in Italy but while his comments on Parma's Farnese Fortress ring true, with regards to Parma, his writings are sketchy. Many critics believe that his descriptions of life in Parma represent his composite experience of life in the cities of northern Italy. Nevertheless, those critics accept that Stendhal's evocation of court lives and intrigue hit the mark.

Stendhal is believed to have based his novel around the stories of Farnese Pope, Paul III's, rise to power. When the weight of the cities' historic architecture drags one back several centuries, scenes from his novel whisper life into the ancient bricks and mortar.

PARMA

Street Life

Piazza Garibaldi, located on the Via Emilia, is the centre of the city. The decuman or central axis was Via Emilia and the cardinal was the Strada Cavour. They met at the Roman forum, now the spot occupied by the square.

From here we passed along the street into the main shopping areas. We walked up the Strada Del Cavour that leads to Piazza Garibaldi. This is the part of the city where the young people stage their *passeggiata*. The people of Parma pride themselves on their fashion awareness and rival Rimini in this respect. On Saturday afternoon the street was filled with young people promenading, studying one another and meeting their friends.

The full range of Parma's gastronomic specialities are available in the centre from *Salumeria Piazza* at 11 Via Gramsci and *Specialita di Parma,* where garlands of **ham** decorate the windows at 9 Strada Farini. Parmense **bread** and fresh **pasta** are available from *Forno Rosetto* at 10 Strada XXII Luglio. **Parmigiano Reggiano** can be bought direct from the producers, *Tagliavini Ario* at 45 Via Fraore in San Pancrazio district. **Maps** and **cook books**, amongst other publication, are available at Parma's oldest bookshop, *Fiaccadori* on Via al Duomo. It was founded in 1829. Shops close on Thursday afternoons.

EATING OUT

Dining out in Parma can be expensive but a gastronomic delight. The centre boasts a wide range of dining establishments to choose from. Parmesan cuisine has been developed beyond its traditional dishes and some of the top-notch restaurants pride themselves on their innovation. These include the air conditioned *Angel D'Oro* (closed Sun) in Vicolo Scuttelari and *Greppia* (closed Mon/Tue) at 39 Strada Garibaldi where meals cost L100,000. For a similar price, the air conditioned *Parizzi* (closed Mon) at 71 Via Repubblica offers more classical fayre.

For L50/60,000 one can taste Parmesan cuisine at *Cortile* (closed Sun and noon Mon) at 3 Borgo Paglia, at the historic *Croce di Malta* (closed Sun) with its stuffed tortelli at 8 Borgo Palmia and *Da Marino's* (closed Sun) in Via Affo. *Parma Rotta* at 158 Via Langhirano (closed Mon) specialises in fish dishes for around the same price while a cheaper option for fish is the *Casablanca* (closed Wed) at 19 Via Marchesi east of the Ducal Park.

Meals for L50,000 are offered by the *Canon D'Or* (closed Wed) in Via N.Sauro, *Corrieri* (closed Sun) in Via Conservatorio, *Barricata* (closed Wed) in Borgo Marodolo and the nearby *Aldo* (closed Sun eve & Mon) in Piazzale Inzani. Traditional trattoria of note are the *Corrieri* (closed Sun) at 1 Via Conservatorio serving **bollito** and **straccoto**, made from horse meat and *Sorelle Picchi* at 29 Strada Farini serving **guinea fowl** and **lasagne**.

For a snack try the *Caffe Bistro* in Piazza Garibaldi and the *Caffe Armeno* in Via Carducci. Two pasticceria of note are the *S.Biagio* at 41 Strada Garibaldi with its cream puffs and, at 61, the *Torino* reputed to have the best coffee and cakes in the city and a **sweet spinach tortelli** to the recipe of Maria Luiga's chef. **Wines** galore are available with pasta dishes in *Enoteca Fontana* (closed Sun/Mon) at 24a Via Farini.

PARMA

ACCOMMODATION

(area code 0521)

****Grand Hotel Baglioni** (tel 292929 fax 292828) at 12c Viale Piacenza (£125) overlooking the Ducal Park and ****Palace Hotel Maria Luiga** (tel 281032 fax 231126) at 140 Viale Mentana (£130) are the most expensive and modern stays in town. The Art Nouveau ****Verdi** (tel 293539 fax 293559) at 18 Via Pasini and **Park Hotel Stendhal** (tel 208057 fax 285655) at 3 Via Bodoni are cheaper, charging £100. The Stendhal was once part of the Pilotta Palace, hence its spacious rooms. ****Villa Ducale** (tel 272727 fax 780756) at 35a Via del Popolo charges £80 but has no restaurant.

Most ***hotels charge £50/60. Among these are **Astoria Executive** (tel 272717 fax 272724) at 9 Via Trento, **Brenta** (tel 208093 fax 238783) at 12 Via G.B.Borghest and **Savoy** (tel 281101 fax 281103) at 3 Via XX Settembre, are near the station. **Torino** (tel 281046 fax 230725) at 7 Via A.Mazza near the Opera House, **Button** (tel 208093 fax 208094) at Borgo Salina and **Residence Liberty** (tel 227100 fax 283903) at Ple Salvo D'Acquisto, are in the centre.

The **Moderno** (tel 772647) at 4 Via A. Cecchi near the station and **Amorini** (tel/fax 983239) at 37 Via Gramsci, charge £35.

The two *hotels with en suite rooms, **Brozzi** (tel 272717 fax 272724) at 11 Via Trento near the station and **Lazzaro** (tel 208944) at 14 Via XX Marzo in the centre, charge £30. Near the station, **Leon D'Oro** (tel 773182) at 4 Viale A.Fratti charges £25 and on the edge of the city, **Ligabue** (tel 645101) at 285 Via Emilia Lepido charges £15.

The cheapest option is to take rooms in the small *Affitacamere* private **guest houses** (contact the tourist information office). The Cittadella **youth hostel** and **camp site** (both tel 961434) are at 5 Parco Cittadella.

i **Parma Tourist Information Office** (tel 218889 fax 234735) is on Via Mellone.

Travelling Around

Distances from Parma of the main cities are: Ravenna 157km, Ferrara 125km, Rimini 204km, Bologna 91km, Reggio Nell'Emilia 19km, Modena 52km and Piacenza 42km.

The **railway station** is on the north side of the city centre in Piazzale della Chiesa.

Train Times (faster direct services)

Parma to Modena 27mins, Reggio Emilia 23mins, Bologna 50mins, Piacenza 28mins, Milan Centrale 1hr 10mins, Florence 2hrs 10mins, Rimini 2hrs, Rome 4hrs 40mins

Trains around Parma Province

Trains travel out of Parma and Fidenza stations to the towns listed (journey times in brackets).

West from Parma – Castelguelfo, Fidenza (15mins)

North from Parma – Colorno (15mins)

South from Parma – Collechio (10mins), Fornovo (20mins), Berceto (32mins), Borgo Val di Taro (1hr)

North from Fidenza – Busseto (20mins), Villanova d'Ardua (25mins)

South from Fidenza – Salsomaggiore (10mins) Fornovo (20mins)

ACROSS THE NORTHERN PLAIN
The Palazzo Ducale of Colorno

We arrived in the small town of Colorno via Brescello in Reggio Emilia. En route the road running alongside the Po was being repaired, little more than a mud track along a raised bank beside the cornfields and woodland. The Po is known for its colourful landscape. However, this year it was dry.

Crossing the River Enza we entered Parma province and were first struck by the number of church steeples invading the skyline. We passed through **Mezzani** and the **Parma Morte Nature Reserve** beside the Po. Mezzani town hall does guided visits in the park when one can apparently come across the Ultricolaria, a rootless flesh-eating plant.

The outskirts of Colorno include modern houses and apartment blocks and it was as if we were returning to the 20th century – that is until we reached the town centre. We were there to see the **Palazzo Ducale** that towers over the main square. Nearby is the River Parma. Here it is merely a brook, particularly by the end of the dry summers.

A main road bisects the piazza so it is not as peaceful as others are. However, it has ample parking and the Cafe Posta for a rest after seeing the palace.

Until the 12th century Colorno was known as the Castello dei Parmensi. Thereafter it came under the rule of the Correggio's, then the Terzi. In 1458 the Sanseverino took control of the area and felt strong enough to convert the fortress into the palace that would become the toast of Parma's high society.

The last marchioness of the Sanseverino, Barbara, died in 1612 at the hands of the Duke of Parma, Ranuccio I Farnese, who accused her of plotting with other aristocrats to murder him. Confessions were forced out of them and they were all beheaded in Parma's main square. The murder of the Sanseverino placed the Colorno palace in the Farnese hands.

Some remains of the 14th century castle still exist in a corner of the palace grounds but the palace mainly dates back to the period of Farnese domination in the 17th century. Following the ousting of the Sanseverino the Farnese began converting the building into their biggest summer palace.

P
A
R
M
A

Added to the facade is the coat of arms of another significant resident of the palace, Napoleon's second wife, **Duchess Marie-Louise**. In love with the splendid palace, she would spend at least two months of each summer in residence. Her tenure is responsible for the restoration of several rooms.

Marie-Louise was one of the grand children of Maria-Theresa and daughter of Hapsburg Emperor Franz I and therefore survived Napoleon's exile after his defeat in 1815. The Hapsburgs had desired control of Parma to increase their influence in Italy. The Bourbons were in control of Parma but were sent to a small city in Tuscany. The Duchy of Parma, Piacenza and Guastalla then fell into Marie-Louise's hands.

Franz I sent his generals and diplomats to assist her in ruling Parma. She fell in love and had children to one of her court even prior to Napoleon's death. After Napoleon's death, the Duchess married the father of her new children and had rooms at the palace redecorated.

In 1847 the palace passed back to the Bourbon Duke of Parma but with the unity of Italy in 1859, the duke was killed. The other Bourbons fled to Spain and the people of Parma voted to be annexed to the kingdom of Savoy. With plenty of other summer residences, the king did not need the palace and sold it to the provincial government.

During the 17th century the facade of the palace was what is now the rear. This is easily recognisable when one climbs the grandiloquent steps to the first floor entry. The magnificent facade overlooked the Parco Ducale gardens and a forest once used as hunting grounds. On the right is the original palace orangery. Today it is used as a museum to display a collection of rural instruments used to make products such as Parmesan.

The Farnese inheritance line shrivelled and through one of their nieces, Parma passed into the hands of the Bourbons of Spain. In 1732, the Bourbon Carlo arrived as the new duke. Within two years Carlo departed having been crowned Carlo III of Naples, later to become Carlo III of Spain.

Carlo cleared the palace of furniture, statues, paintings, and whatever else he could carry off to his kingdom, even the Baroque windows and doors. Only one fresco remains from the period of Farnese occupation. On becoming the new duke, his brother **Filippo** found not only Colorno but also all his other palaces empty.

Filippo then had the palace entrance reversed to have the facade facing the square and redecorated the interior in the style in evidence today. He married **Louise Elizabeth**, daughter of the king of France and some of the best French artists were brought to the duchy. They, and later **Marie-Louise**, brought French style. The duchy had Italy's first boulevards and street lighting, and Parma city took on the title of *Little Versailles*. The wealth brought to the province was immense and, unlike most other buildings in Emilia Romagna, in this palace we could see marble everywhere.

Marie-Louise's link with Napoleon was demonstrated by the appearance of the Napoleonic eagle in the frescoes. The gallery on the west wing looking out on the garden contains a useful plan of the palace. The children's rooms were decorated with angels and Grotesque style fantasy creatures. Others were decorated with putti and masks.

The best preserved rooms are the two 18th century Chinese rooms with Chinese masks and, surprisingly, Japanese geisha girls, and a women's room for sewing. Next door is an ante-chamber with striking monochrome paintings. The monochrome style was particularly popular in Parma at the time of Marie-Louise, and features heavily all around the palace.

The Salla Dudiensa has an 18th century marble floor but the Grotesque fresco on the ceiling is from the period of Marie-Louise. As we passed through the palace we also noticed that every floor was different. Many rooms have ceilings of rococo plaster from the period of the Bourbon Filippo.

We then came to the main room, the Neoclassical Salla Grande, whose balcony looks over the park. In imitation of Versailles, the room was used for night parties that would empty to watch ballet or plays, or for dancing, in the once floodlit grounds. Petitot and the French sculptor, Boudard, designed this room, the most important in the palace.

The apartment occupied by the duchess contained refined tapestries. Only plaster decorations remain with rococo plaster. Filippo's wife, the Duchessa Louise Elizabeth, tried in every way to recreate her native Versailles. In evidence are paintings of lions, another symbol for the strength of the Bourbon dynasty and the Bourbon lily. She had several rooms for sleeping in, including the Camera Daletto. Now only two remain. The Daletto looks out onto the garden that was bathed in sunlight during the morning. The other room gets the sunshine in the afternoon so the duchess could choose which room she would sleep in according to the temperature and sunlight.

The paintings by Lacroix and the marble 18th century console by Petitot are the only movable items left on show from the original palace (open Mon-Fri 10am-1pm, 3pm-6pm, Sat till 6.45pm, Sun and public holidays, 11am-4pm. Admission fee. Guided tours only).

The palace's church is dedicated to **San Livorio** and was the ducal chapel. Prior to the building of the church, the Farnese had had a smaller chapel. They dedicated it to San Livorio. Following the French Revolution in 1789, the duke, Don Ferdinando the Bourbon, decided to open up the chapel to the people, and oriented the church so that its entry was on the road beside the palace. Napoleon's troops arrived in 1796 and the art-loving, pacific duke was left nominally in control.

In the pure classical style, the church is of interest. Its construction was begun in 1777. Completed in 1789, the facade was then turned around very quickly and the work completed by 1793. The decoration was carried out by masters of Parma's school of art, the sculptor Macceti, and the painter of the dome, Commuti.

The ironwork and silverwork is original. Of particular interest are the exquisite carvings on wooden choirs. Above them is a huge Ferrazi organ still used today for concerts. A masterpiece with 2,898 pipes, it was completed in 1794 and though cleaned, its tone is completely original.

Close by, right out of the church is a fascinating old service wing of the palace. Don Ferdinando had it transformed into a small apartment so that he could relax and study well away from the busy court. The first floor room is wonderful, decorated with frescoes, angels peering down from the corners and trompe l'oeil perspectives to add a sense of height and width to the small room.

To get to the **Observatory** on the second floor we had to climb fifty steps. It was marvellously decorated with the signs of the zodiac and two putti on each wall playing with astronomical instruments. Here, Ferdinando would track the stars with his telescope and philosophise on the turmoil then facing his country.

Polesine Parmense

From Colorno to Polesine Parmense involves a picturesque drive across the plain. Little villages dot up now and then until one reaches the River Stirone and the village of **Roccabianca**, named after its castle. The imposing 15th century structure is still relatively intact but the finest of its interior decorations were stripped and taken elsewhere.

Now we were well and truly in the country of **Parma Ham** and **culatello ham**. Up out of the corn fields rose the village, Polesine Parmense. That this was an area of severe flooding is testified by the origin of its name. Polesine is believed to derive from polecini (islands), carried down by flood water and their progress arrested by the river bank. The village is said to sit on such polecini.

We were mainly in the village to taste, the local speciality and Parma delicacy - culatello ham. We managed to do so at the stylish, upmarket **Al Cavallino Bianco** (tel/fax 0524 96136, a superb family-run restaurant in a villa set amongst hedgerows and fields on the outskirts of the village on Via Sbrisi.

P A R M A

Culatello

First, Massimo, one of the two brothers who run the restaurant, took us across the road to a small cottage where their culatello joints were hung as part of the ham's preparation. On the way across Massimo insisted that culatello was a cut above Parma Ham – for which the province is so famous. While Parma Ham production is a big industry, culatello is a carefully controlled enterprise of the small farmers. The consortium stamp of quality only appears on the hams of a dozen producers.

Culatello is produced on the northern plains of Parma but only in those areas close to the Po River. Culatello's preparation requires a very high level of humidity. Before the culatello is ready to cut, it will take one to two years of preparation. Production only takes place between November and February, the cold months when fog scours the plain. Salami made using different parts of the pig such as fiocetto, spalaconda (the shoulder) and pancietta (the stomach) are also made here but, in Massimo's opinion, culatello is king.

Hanging in damp, musty rooms were 2,000 joints. Whereas small pigs are used to produce prosciutto, culatello pigs must weigh over 2,000 kilos. At first the fresh ham will be hung on the airy first floor to sweat and dry for two or three months. Then it is sent into the damp cellar. The ham will be massaged, seasoned, then left in a ligature to hang.

Production is a delicate process. No cut will taste the same as the other. The very taste, perfume and texture of the culatello varies with the seasons and the micro-climate. Even the storage houses have to be specially chosen by location, orientation, winds and dampness. So, just across the Po, the Cremona pig farmers cannot produce culatello.

Lunch started with a sweet white local wine, Fontana. The starter was salami crespone and culatello. The next plate was served on a large white platter and we looked forward to receiving a cut from the large white slab – until we realised that it was lard.

Next came a Lambrusco sparkling red wine to accompany our tortelli, followed by a very tasty Parma speciality, rice with pigeon in a wine flavoured sauce, **Il tambilino di riso con piccioni**, which in turn required a glass of a dry red wine. Finally we relaxed our way through a beautiful sorbet with which we were advised to sip **ramondello**, a fruity oriental liquor. Altogether a fabulous meal. All delivered with panache and for a snip at L80,000. A great splurge for those in the mood for a treat.

P
A
R
M
A

ON THE VERDI TRAIL
Busseto

At Busseto's heart is the neatly laid out Piazza **Guiseppe Verdi**. Not surprisingly, a statue of the maestro stands in the centre of the square which includes a library, the town hall, the rocca, a church, and a couple of restaurants, a bar and pizzeria and the Teatro Verdi.

The Verdi Theatre

The peaceful square had ample parking space and we strolled up to the Renaissance style theatre. The theatre was built in commemoration of Verdi between 1856 and 1868. Verdi boycotted the theatre, never setting eyes on it. Some say that it was on account of his pique at a theatre carrying his name being so small and located in a tiny town. Instead he suggested the town worthies build a hospital for the aged.

Verdi had long been hostile to the local high society who disapproved of him living in sin with the famous opera singer Guiseppina Strepponi. They in turn, having paid for him to study in Milan, felt they had brought him success and felt slighted.

The attending room at the front of the theatre was used for chamber concerts. The orchestra would play from a small balcony and would be virtually out of sight of their audience. This was offset by the large three metre mirror placed opposite the musicians allowing the guests to see them playing. During the opera all the men were expected to wear a green (verdi) tie.

We passed through the smoking room and the foyer to the main theatre where Toscanini directed opera in 1913 and 1926. The theatre used to sit 400 people but improved safety now allows for only 300 seats. Each box is still owned by private families in the town. However the last public performance was in 1984. As

PARMA

we arrived the theatre were preparing for a performance of Verdi's opera, *Alzira*, but this was for a tour group. Opening hours are 9.30am-12.30pm and 2.30pm-5.30pm except during rehearsals. Tickets cost L5,000.

Verdi once owned the nearby Palazzo Orlandi which houses the **Museo dei Cimeli Verdiani**, displaying musical instruments, paintings and documents associated with the composer. Opening times in the summer months of April to September are 9.30am-12.30pm and 3pm –7pm.

VERDI

Villa Pallavicino

Parking at the junction of Via Provesi and Via Mascagni we had come to see the Villa Pallavicino. But we went back to look at the massive Gothic, Franciscan church of Santa Maria degli Angeli on Via Mascagni. This church was built in clay on the orders of Pallavicini Pallavicino and his brother between 1470 and 1474. The interior is grandly austere but on the outside is a fine terracotta frieze.

The Pallavicini were a small dynasty that ruled over the eastern area of the north Parma plain. Busseto was the Pallavicini capital and they had the Villa Pallavicino constructed in the early 16th century as a summer residence just outside the town's centre. In the 18th century it was enlarged and its style, is mainly Baroque, though the perspective and symmetry of the villa reveal its Renaissance origin.

We walked up a tree-lined avenue surrounded by a silence, only broken occasionally by a solitary bird twittering in the afternoon heat. We passed through a huge rococo entrance and the parched, ill kept but beautiful gardens. As we entered the semi-restored, semi-derelict villa one got a sense of the decline and ruination of the noble family that once tried to cling on to this small territory.

Surrounded by a moat, the villa is made up of five buildings set like a chess board, the central one being the early villa. Outside is a large, fascinating horseshoe-shaped stable block with a central bell tower. In the cemetery are two large bushes that are **bosso** (box) trees. Now virtually extinct locally, this local species gave its name to Busseto town.

Some rooms at the villa's heart are dedicated to Verdi and worth a visit. One room displays letters to and from Verdi, pictures, prints and furniture used by the composer and his relations and his death mask. The other interesting room is the room dedicated to the story of the Pallavicini. It contains 18th century frescoes and a fine stucco ceiling from the same period. The villa is open everyday between 9.30am and 12am and 3pm and 7pm.

Sant Agata and Villa Verdi

We were off on another Verdi trail. This time to Sant Agata just outside Busseto. This is a rural area with huge villas, farms with ancient machinery, set in woodland. Leave yourself some time to find Villa Verdi. We dubbed the composer's house 'unfindable' after wandering round the district for twenty minutes and passing the house twice.

Opening times are between April and September, 9am – 11.40am and 3pm - 6.45pm (closed Mon). Entry costs L8,000 but groups are charged L6,000 per head. All entering are given a guided tour in Italian lasting around 40 minutes.

As we first toured the large garden, our guide related how the young Guiseppe's ambition was not to be a composer but a farmer. As his wealth grew, the maestro bought up hundreds of acres of land and set to running his farm. The composer's manuscripts are sometimes covered with numbers, believed to have been records, detailing the volume of farm produce that he could see in his wagons passing the courtyard. Verdi also loved to walk on his massive estate, which included woodland, and would often hunt from early morning.

Verdi is reputed to have had a quick of temper but he was also known to have been extremely generous. He may have been shunned on account of **Strepponi** (his live-in mistress, a target for insults) by society in Busseto, but his love for the people still led him to build a hospital for the local villagers. In his will he bequeathed an annual donation to 100 poor people in the village. The payment would be made on 11th November, the traditional day for the villagers to pay their annual rent.

The democrat Verdi and his music were extremely popular with the Italian people. His name became synonymous with **Victoria Emmanuel Rege d'Italia** –V.E.R.D.I., Victor Emmanuel, King of Italy. Therefore, when the crowds shouted out, "Viva Verdi!", they were proclaiming their demand for the unification of Italy.

Already famous, Verdi arrived at the villa in 1851 at the age of 38. He had the house extended and set about designing the garden in the style fashionable to the era. Traditional Italian gardens were laid out in a symmetrical pattern with tiny clipped hedges and floral beds. But the 'English garden' came into fashion in Italy during the 19th century. Villa Verdi's garden contains one 200-year-old plain tree, the only tree on the property on Verdi's arrival. Plain trees were then introduced, surrounding the house, and seven chestnut trees were planted opposite the main entrance.

Verdi loved his garden spending a fortune on turning it into a classical 'English garden' of romantic winding pathways through woodland and shrubs. A tiny wooden bridge took us across a large artificial pond for which Verdi brought beautiful trees from California and carp. The pond had another function. When it froze over in the winter, its ice would be taken to the ice hole, packed, and stored underground for the summer.

By the edge of the lake is a grotto created while Verdi was writing **_Aida_**. In the piece, the heroine who has betrayed her lover meets him in a grotto, which becomes her tomb. The cool grotto, full of bats, is no longer open to visitors but is seen to be connected to the story.

Entering the house was like coming across a Marie-Celeste, as if Verdi had left and the house had been embalmed. Verdi adopted, Philomena, the daughter of a cousin. Philomena then married a son of Verdi's lawyer. Verdi bequeathed them the house on condition that it was preserved as it was.

Verdi's bedroom still contains the four poster in which Strepponi died in 1897 and many of the couple's paintings, furniture, nic-nacs, his piano, her opera costumes, trunks, and other artefacts.

Roncole Verdi

Verdi was born 5km south east of Busseto in the small town of Roncole Verdi. The church of San Michele displays the font in which the genius was baptised and the organ on which he practised as a boy. It's even possible to visit the building where Verdi was born (entry costs L3,000).

ACCOMMODATION AND EATING OUT

Colorno's restaurants include **Stendhal** (closed Tues) at Sacca and the cheaper **Al Vedel** (closed Tues and Mon eve) on Via Centrale in Vedole. **Adele** (closed Sat) and **Rustica** (closed Sun) are next door to each other on Via Belloni. Close by in Polesine Parmense is the upmarket **Al Cavallino Bianco** in Via Sbrisi and Colombo (closed Tues) in Santa Franca. **Café Posta** is opposite the Ducal Palace in Piazza Garibaldi.

For **hotels**, **Colorno** (area code 0521) has the ***Residence Il Borgo** (tel 312320 fax 312322) at £35 and ***Versailles** (tel 312099 fax 312322) at 3 Via Saragat for £45. Polesine has a small guest house at 12 Via Roma (tel 0524 96106).

Busseto has plenty of dining establishments, including **Teatro** at 39 Piazza Verdi by the Verdi theatre. **Hotel Sole** in Piazza Matteotti has a restaurant (closed Mon) serving Parmesan cuisine and **Ugo** (closed Mon/Tues) at 3 Via Mozart serves up Emilian cuisine. Local specialities include sturgeon, catfish and spongata, a cake filled with honey and dried fruit.

Hotels in **Busseto** (area code 0524) include ***Sole** (tel 93011 fax 930021) at Piazza Matteotti and ***I Due Foscari** (tel 930039 fax 91625) at 15 Piazza Rossi near to the theatre both charging around £45.***Aurora** (tel 97157) which charges £20 has no en suite rooms.

i **Tourist Information** centres can be found in **Busseto** at the town hall (tel/fax 0524 92487) at 1 Piazza Verdi and in **Colorno** at the Palazzo Ducale (tel/fax 0521 816939) on Piazza Garibaldi.

PARMA

TOWNS OF THE CENTRAL PLAIN
San Secondo Parmense

About 10km east of Soragna lies **San Secondo Parmense**, the former domain of the Rossi family and Pier Maria Rossi. The town has been associated with the Rossi since 1365 when Bishop Ugolino Rossi granted it to his nephew. Every year on the first Sunday in June, San Secondo commemorates the marriage of another Rossi, Pietro Maria III, to Camilla Gonzaga with a **horse race** around the area. It's a popular festival accompanied by a costumed parade and **re-enactments of battles.**

Pier Maria Rossi presided over the construction of San Secondo's castle in the 1450s. At 15 years old he had been married off to the daughter of Count Torelli of Montechiarugolo. He installed his wife in the castle, leaving her while he spent time in Milan where he met his mistress Bianca Pellegrini, for whom he built the Roccabianca and Torrechiara castles.

In the 1500s San Secondo castle was transformed into a delizia. Frescoes were painted on the vaults and fireplaces of Verona marble were installed. Some of these rooms can be seen (closed Mon, guided tours 11am, 3pm, 4pm, 5pm, 6pm, April to September). The Rossi still have an apartment in the castle that now houses the town council on the first floor.

Fidenza

The second town of the province is **Fidenza,** on the banks of the Stirone river, 23km west of Parma along the A1 autostrada or Via Emilia. With just 23,000 inhabitants, like all the provincial towns it is dwarfed by Parma city. Up until 1927 Fidenza was known as Borgo San Donnino. A courtier of Roman emperor Maximian, San Donnino converted to Christianity and fled. The emperor's soldiers pursued him and he was decapitated on the banks of the Stirone in 291 A.D. Subsequently, the town gained its Roman name of Julia Fidentia when the martyr's body was discovered during the 8th century.

PARMA

The town became a pilgrimage centre and a stop off point for merchants. The English bishop Sigeric, who later became Archbishop of Canterbury, passed through on his way to Rome in 990. Later, Archbishop **Thomas A Becket** would arrive in 1167 stopping at Cabriolo. Emperors, kings, Popes and bishops would all stop off in the town.

The most impressive building in the town is still the **cathedral** in the cobbled Piazza del Duomo dedicated to San Donnino. In Romanesque style with the standard three naves, the building was designed by Lanfranco and consecrated in

1106. The school of Benedetto Antelami was brought in to create the current facade flanked by two towers in the 12th century. The statues of prophets Daniel and Ezekiel are attributed to Benedetto himself.

Shortage of money left the upper gabled part of the facade unfinished. Instead, when money was available in the 16th century, the side chapels and the bell tower were added. Frescoes dating from the 13th century in the interior depict the Last Judgement and the life of San Donnino, while the relics of the saint are kept in a marble tomb in the crypt.

A statue of the apostle Simon still holds a scroll saying, "The apostle Simon says this is the road to Rome." Borgo San Donnino became a key point along the Via Francigena, the pilgrims' route to Rome. Travellers would pass through from all the corners of western Europe. From the Borgo they could then take the westerly route across Mount Bardone via the Cisa Pass or the eastern route via Forli. The town was so fought over by Parma and Piacenza that the fortifications were often destroyed. Archaeologists have identified city walls from at least seven different eras.

Rocca Sanvitale in Fontanellato

P A R M A

The Via Francigena in Parma

The Via Francigena were the pilgrim routes to Rome. Documents from as early as 400 A.D record the travels of devotional Christians to the holiest of places, in particular, Rome with its tombs of the apostles, and Jerusalem. Travellers would arrive from London, Bremen, Spain, and as far away as Iceland. There were several main routes through Emilia Romagna including south through Piacenza, through Parma, through Forli and a coastal road through Rimini.

To get to Rome the pilgrims had to make the taxing and dangerous journey through the Apennines. This problem dictated their routes as much as the wish to stop off at secondary shrines along the way. Many churches with the relics of saints in their crypts would be visited. Pilgrim routes also varied as the weather destroyed bridges, blocked passes, and difficulties arose out of the almost continuous wars between rival city states.

In 1538 Farnese Pope Paul III took the Via Francigena north through Parma to Provence to meet Charles V. He travelled through Parma with 22 cardinals, 800 horses and mules, 150 Swiss and German infantrymen and 80 Italian light cavalryman.

Most pilgrims would walk the journey with their burdon (mule) to carry their essentials, a stick for defence and a hollowed out pumpkin full of water. Only the rich would travel by horse. Places of shelter grew up along the route. Often the monasteries would look after the pilgrims. If they were no monasteries then 'hospitals' would be set up sometimes by the local church. These hospitals would also look after the sick. Later xenodochia were set up specifically to look after the sick.

The pilgrim traffic left its mark on the areas it crossed. Tariffs levied on pilgrims and merchants for travelling made the routes so lucrative that castles were built to administer the routes. Inns were built and the pilgrims from northern, western and eastern Europe brought new ideas.

In Parma, pilgrims would arrive at Fidenza then travel down the west bank (or east bank, if they wanted to visit Parma city) of the Taro. The routes would link up at Fornovo and then the Monte Bardone road through Cassio and Berceto crossed the Cisa pass. Napoleon began building a proper road on the route which became known as the Napoleonic Road (Now it is the SS62), though Duchess Marie-Louise largely completed it.

The cathedral is at the centre of the mediaeval area of the town with its concentric arch of streets. To the right of the cathedral towards Via Cavour is the mediaeval city's old gate, Porta San Donnino built in 1364. To the left is Via Frate Gherardo, which is interesting for the rows of old buildings, built from recycled materials. The Palazzo Comunale in Piazza Garibaldi has existed since 1191 but was destroyed by the French and Spanish armies in the 16th century. It was rebuilt and the facade is a 19th century addition in imitation Lombard-Gothic style. Its most famous visitor was Guiseppe Verdi, who in 1861 was elected as the borgo's MP in the first Italian parliament.

ACCOMMODATION AND EATING OUT

San Secondo Parmense has *****Hotel Sant Angelo** (tel 0521 8733780) charging £35. No dining establishments of note here but there is *Salumeria Attilio Cavalli* at 24 Via Roma which specialises in cured **shoulders of ham** and **Parmesan**.

In **Fidenza**, *I Gemelli* (closed Mon) at 14 Via Gialdi specialises in fish dishes, the **Astoria** hotel (closed Mon) on Via Gandolfi specialises in mushroom dishes and **Duomo** (closed Mon) on Via Micheli, in Parmesan dishes. **Parmesan** can be bought direct from the consortium at *Caseificio Commenda*, 3 Via Cabriolo.

For **hotels** Fidenza (area code 0524) has *****Ariston** (tel/fax 528452) and *****Astoria** (tel 524314 fax 527263) at 5 Via Gandolfi, charging £35/45 and the £30 a night ****Due Spade** (tel/fax 523389) and ****Ugolini** (tel/fax 522422). The cheapest hotels are in S.Faustino locality where ***Ponte** (tel 522115) charges £15 and ***Pinguino** (tel 522115) has no en suite rooms but charges only £10.

i **Fidenza Tourist Information** Centre is at 2 Piazza Duomo (tel 0524 84047)

The Pallavicino Hills

The area south of Via Emilia and boarded by the Stirone, Taro and Cento rivers is hill territory once the domain of the Pallavicini dynasty who were the dominant nobles of the territory for over 500 years until the 16th century. The Pallavicini left behind many fortresses among the beautiful pastures and woodlands of this part of south east Parma.

Salsomaggiore Terme

A trip along the plains can finish with a well-earned rest in the gentle hills of the spa town of **Salsomaggiore Terme**. Just 34km from Parma city and 9km south east of Fidenza, the spa overlooks the Stirone river. Here cold hypertonic

PARMA

waters are drawn up from 3,000ft beneath the ground. Their saline density is three times that of the Dead Sea. The town, once a salt mining area, became a spa centre from the time of the Duchy of Marie-Louise. Regularly patronised by the Russian Tsarina and the Queen of Savoy, the town became one of Italy's main **spa centres.**

The resort expanded particularly in the early 20th century, which explains why Salsomaggiore is one of the few towns in the Po valley with extensive Art Nouveau architecture. Most notable of the spas is the *Berzieri* complex (tel 0524-578201) on Via Roma. Completed in 1923, it has a splash of early Art Deco by the artist, **Galileo Chini**.

Galileo Chini also had a hand in the redesign of the **Grand Hotel des Thermes** including the portico-veranda overlooking the park, the Moorish hall and the 'Taverna Rossa'. Once a hotel, the building is now the headquarters of the tourist office promoting the spas.

Lorenzo Berzieri was the doctor who in the 1840s discovered that treatment with the waters was curative. Since Dr. Berzieri the town has amassed a number of spa resorts, including the *Baistrocchi Thermal Institute* (tel 0524-574411) on Viale Matteotti and the *Tommasini Spa Hotel* (tel 0524-575041) on Viale Corridone. Another spa just 5km away is at *Tabiano Bagni* (tel 0524-564111) on Viale delle Terme. Duchess Marie-Louise bought the sulphurous Tabiano springs in 1838, set up the Bagni, and visited *Spa Tabiano* regularly.

The centres all provide **beauty treatments** and have their own hotel accommodation. Sporting facilities are either located at most hotels or close by. Other visitors have included Verdi, Caruso and Pavarotti. During September and October the Toscanini Symphony Orchestra organises a **Mozart Festival**. Film buffs might wish to view the dramatic **Moresco Hall** in the town's Conference Building. Bertolucci used it when filming *The Last Emperor*. For those interested, the town also hosts the final of the *Miss Italy* beauty contest in late August. A pleasant aspect of the town is that the spacious Parco Mazzini starts near the centre behind the Berzieri complex.

Other local places to visit include the well preserved, 12th century Romanesque church in **San Nicomede** on the Fidenza road, and the 11th century castle and Piacentina tower, built by the Pallavicini in **Scipione**. **Salsomaggiore Golf Club** (tel/fax 0524 574128) at 105 Case Carancini has an 18-hole par 72 hilly course.

Pellegrino Parmense lies 17km from Salsomaggiore near the source of the Stirone River. Once in the hands of the Pallavicini, their former castle on the top of the hill dominates it. The castle was built in the 12th century and subsequently became the property of the Fogliani then the Meli Lupi.

P A R M A

ACCOMMODATION AND EATING OUT

The town has plenty of places to eat out and Via Matteotti has several grouped together. Of note is *Tartufo* (closed Wed and out of season) at 30 Viale Marconi which specialises in mushroom and truffle dishes. **Agriturismo with accommodation** in the locality include *Antica Torre* (tel/fax 575425) with its outdoor swimming pool at 197 Case Bussandri in Cangelasio and **Le Lame** (tel/fax 579195) at 40 Via Lame in San Vittore.

Salsomaggiore (area code 0524) has the province's only *****hotel, **Grand Hotel et de Milan** (tel 572241 fax 573884) with its swimming pool and gardens at 1 Via Dante (£130). The ******Cristallo** (tel 577241 fax 574022) at 1 Via Rossini (£55), ******Excelsior** (tel 575641 fax 573888) at 3 Via Berenini (£70) and ******Grand Hotel Porro** (tel 578221 fax 577878) at 10 Viale Porro (£80), all have indoor swimming pools.

***hotels are plentiful but may be closed in the winter. One exception is *Primarosa* (tel 575549 fax 573954) at 12 Viale Valentini (£50). **Hotel Valentini** (tel 578251 fax 577878), also at 10 Viale Porro (£60), has an indoor swimming pool. ***hotels at £30 a night include **Appennino** (tel 578377 fax 575666) at 13 Viale Milite Ignoto, **Cantuccio2** (tel 577643 fax 577644) at 1 Viale XXIV Maggio, **Doria** (tel 578364 fax 575174) at 27 Via Matteotti, **Pagoda** (tel 573015 fax 573928) at 9 Via Milano and, on Viale Cavour, **Giglio** (tel 572214) and **Capitol** (tel/fax 575380).

The ****Ambrosiano** (tel 773391) at 9 Via Valentini and **Diana** (tel 573539) at 3 Piazza Liberta have rooms for £20. The ***Marinella** (tel 578297 fax 577160) at 8 Via Castellazzo, ***Zanardi** (tel 573471) at 10 Viale Milite Ignoto and the ***Ancelle del Santuario** (tel 573512) and ***Torinese,** both on Via Matteotti, are also around £20. Cheapest of all, at £15, is ***Vittorio Veneto** (tel 577024) at 8 Via Marzaroli.

Arizona **camp site** (tel 565648) is in the district of Farolde/Bargone.

Being a spa centre, **Tabiano** also has plenty of accommodation and cheaper ****stays than in Salsomaggiore. Two **agriturismo with accommodation** can be found in Tabiano Castello. **Il Tondino** (tel/fax 62106), on Via Tabiano specialises in buffalo meat. **Rangona** (tel 62106) is nearby.

******Napoleon** (tel 565261 fax 565230) at 11 Viale Terme (£50) has an indoor swimming pool. ******Pandos** (tel 565276 fax 565287) on Via Fonti, ******Ducale** (tel 565132 fax 565150) on Viale Respighi and ******Farnese** (tel 565148 fax 565160) on Via Terme, are similarly priced.

Viale Fidenza is strung out with hotels. *****Boomerang** (tel 565228 fax 565348) at 43 Viale Fidenza (£45) has an outdoor swimming pool. There are several similarly priced ***hotels, including **Camillo** (tel 565332 fax 565680), **Pinuccia** (tel 565109 fax 565253), **Quisisana** (tel 565252 fax 565101), **Ridente** (tel 565390 fax 565590), **Sporting** (tel 565384 fax 565122), **Villa Maria Luisa** (tel 565801) and **Villa Rosa** (tel 565255 fax 565157).

P A R M A

The same street has the **Ada** (tel 565308 fax 565200), **Bienvenuti** (tel/fax 565220), **Carla** (tel/fax 565196), **Villa Doria** (tel 565527), **Villa del Sole** (tel 565300 fax 565742) and **Paradiso** (tel 565171 fax 565222), all with rooms at £25/30.

Also on Viale Fidenza is *Florida* (tel 565572 fax 565742) at £20. Similarly priced hotels include *Helvetia* (tel 565154 fax 565742) on Viale Fonti,

Laila (tel 565739 fax 565742) on Viale Terme, *Mirella* (tel 565600) on Viale Tabiano *and* *Villa Gioconda* (tel 565520 fax 565742) on Via Tabiano.

i **Salsomaggiore Tourist Information Centre** (tel 580211 fax 580219) is at 7 Viale Romagnosi. For Tabiano Information phone 565482.

TO THE PARMA APENNINES

South of Via Emilia, the landscape shifts from flat plains via undulating hills to the rugged mountains and afforested valleys of the Parma Apennines. The Apennines cover half the territory of Parma province and make for a tranquil area for trekkers. Outcrops of serpentine, sandstone and red jasper add dimension to the landscape once the home of the Ligurian tribes. The western area was under the control of the Roman authorities at Veleia Romea in Piacenza Province. Later the Landi dynasty would hold sway.

From east to west five rivers cut through the mountains, flowing north towards the Po basin. They form, from east to west, the valleys of the Ceno, Taro, Baganza, Parma and Enza. All were important transport routes and are lined with fortresses, palaces and ancient fortified villages.

Bardi Castle

ALONG THE TARO VALLEY

Flowing for 126km from the Tuscan border to the Po river near Sissa, the Taro covers the length of Parma. From the junction with the A1 autostrada, it is tracked by the A15 autostrada that passes through to La Spezia on the Mediterranean coast. The SS357 to Fornovo provides for a quieter, if longer trip. From Fornovo the SS308 travels up valley into the mountains.

South of the Via Emilia to Fornovo the area beside the river is designated as the **Regional Taro River Park** (for guides tel 0521 802688). Purple, white and riparian willows cling to the river banks. Hundreds of ducks and heron rest here during their autumn and spring migrations. Here, where the river rushes, poplar and alder trees provide a habitat for plenty of wild life including **wild boar**, foxes, weasels and skunks. The nutria, South American rodents, are new residents. They escaped from stock farms in the region and found that the Taro provided their best natural environment.

Picking up pilgrims on the road from Parma, the east bank road, now the SS62 Napoleonic Road was of greater importance and a key part of the Via Francigena to Tuscany. **Collecchio** was an important staging post for pilgrims after they had travelled from Fidenza or Parma city. Known in the Mediaeval era as Colliculum, the town is best known for the 11th century Romanesque church of San Prospero. Rebuilt in the 13th century and restored in the 20th, the church contains interesting animal headed capitals on the columns in the aisles. At the north entry to the town is the Baroque Villa Paveri Fontana, the work of Francesco Bibiena in the 17th century, with fine mythological frescoes.

Passing south down the SS62, a detour to the east brings one to **Talignano**'s Cistercian parish church dedicated to St Blaise. It was built in 1200 and has been restored. Of interest is the lunette over the main door, said to be a very rare example of Romanesque 'psychostasy'. The Last Judgement required weighing the soul of the dead and the scene depicts St. Michael weighing the souls of those who were tempted by the devil.

Castles along the way from Via Emilia on the west bank include, on the old road itself, **Castelguelfo**'s Torre d'Orlando, once a Pallavicino stronghold. The turreted fortress has undergone many alterations since it was built reputedly in the 1100s. A short distance south on SS357 is the 13th century **Noceto Castle** rebuilt by Pier Maria Rossi in the 15th century. The castle was altered in the 17th century so that residence could be divided between the Farnese and the San Vitale. Only its mighty keep, the internal wall and four corner towers remain.

On the SS62, 23km from Parma, on the SS357 from Castelguelfo and an exit point for the A15 autostrada, **Fornovo di Taro** is an important junction. In the past it was also important as the point where the Cento and Sporzana rivers joined the

P A R M A

Taro making the town a meeting place of routes into the hills. Travellers would rest here before or after making the wearisome trek across the Apennine ridge.

The town was the scene of a great battle in 1495. Charles VIII of France, while retreating after an unsuccessful attempt to take the Kingdom of Naples, was attacked by the Italian League army under Francesco Gonzaga. Of note today is the simple Romanesque church of **Santa Maria Assunta** founded in 854. When it was rebuilt in the 11th century, recycled Roman materials were used as can be seen. Evidence of the work of the Antelami school can be seen in the gabled facade and the wonderful scenes of *Hell and the Seven Capital Sins.*

THE UPPER TARO VALLEY

After Fornovo (500ft), the route divides. One road follows the Taro while the SS62 and the pilgrims would ascend the east side of the valley linking up with the Baganza valley to make the Cisa Pass. Ascending to **Cassio** to reach the Cisa Pass, the road takes the Scale di Piantonia, a series of sharp zig zags up Mount Prizera (2,500ft), writhing its way past serpentine crags to Cassio at almost 3,000ft. Cassio was once the home of a xenodochium, hospital for sick pilgrims. Today its narrow, paved streets still pass through houses assembled from roughly hewn grey sandstone.

The next stop on the SS62 is the mediaeval town **Berceto** that can be reached via a junction of the A15 autostrada. Berceto is dominated by the ruins of a 12th century castle. The castle was the birthplace of the great adulterer, Pier Maria Rossi in 1413. The town contains the small stone houses and cobbled streets traditional to the area. Many buildings are pre-17th century as is the many times restored Romanesque cathedral of St Moderanus.

East of Berceto is the mediaeval hamlet of **Corchia** which still has its arched underpasses in narrow, cobbled streets and typical mountain stable barns known as *toggc*. West of Berceto are the steep gorges carved by the Baganza River and Mount Cervellino which peaks at 5,000ft. To the south is **Guadine-Pradaccio Nature Reserve** with Mounts Marmagna and Sillara rising to almost 6,000ft and covered with beech woods. Interspersed are pockets of rare orchids, lilies and plenty of wild berries for picking (for guides tel 0521 235808). From Berceto, the **Cisa Pass** (3,400ft) is only another 8km away. The road then descends into Tuscany.

From Fornovo the SS523 road beside the Taro River arrives after 23km at **Borgo Val di Taro**. The town is also the last exit for the A15 autostrada before it rises to Berceto and the Cisa Pass. With 7,000 inhabitants, Borgo Val di Taro is the main town of the valley and an attractive holiday resort. Many fine 16th and 17th century buildings line the central streets beside the main road of Via Nazionale.

Important since Roman times when it was a castrum, most of the town's ancient buildings date from the Renaissance. The exception is the mediaeval tower at the northern boundary, once part of a fortress. Borgo Val di Taro is best visited for its gastronomic dishes, particularly the fungi porcini and Boletus mushrooms. The **mushroom fair of Sagra del Fungo Porcino di Borgataro** is held through September and October.

The hills to the north offer some fascinating visits like the village of Costella di San Pietro (where all the inhabitants carry the name *Costella)*, the joined twin towers of the 12th century church in **Tiedoli**, and **Lavacchielli** village with its monolithic doorways and portals.

Close by is **Testanello Valley** with spectacular rock formations, near vertical crags and waterfalls. In 1545 an earthquake, so violent that it split a house in two, swallowed up the vineyard of farmer Gian Antonio.

A few kilometres past Compiano and 14km from Borgo Val di Taro lies the summer holiday resort of **Bedonia**. Upstream above the valley are beautiful hills dominated by limestone crags on the edge of Mount Penna. They lead to the Bosso Pass and into Tuscany, just before which is the small town of **Tornolo**. Continuing on SS523 through Campi leads to the pass at **Cento Croci**, whose name means '100 crosses', believed to be a reference to the frequent murders carried out by brigands robbing passing travellers.

ALONG THE CENO VALLEY

The Ceno river flows into the Taro from the west at Fornovo. Its 50km long valley was a buffer zone between Parma and Piacenza and therefore well fortified. After 9km the road arrives at **Varano de'Melegari**. The town's huge square castle overlooks the valley. Built in 1208 on a sandstone crag and rebuilt in the 1400s by the Pallavicini, it remained in their possession until 1782. Nearby is the beautiful mediaeval hamlet of **Viazzano** with its houses in sandstone. For a different sort of holiday, the town, in conjunction with Alfa Romeo, offers the **Autodormo Riccardo Paletti**. It's a motor-racing track running courses organised by the International Centre for Safe Driving.

Another 9km along the Ceno valley is the village of **Serravalle** with its impressive castle also once controlled by the Pallavicini. Of interest here is the octagonal baptistery believed to be 8th century, and one of the few surviving in the villages.

The last stop in the Ceno is at **Bardi** whose huge castle sits imposingly on an outcrop of red jasper crags offering marvellous views of the surrounding hills and valleys. Legends say that Bardi received its name from being the final resting place of Barrio, the last of the 37 elephants Hannibal had brought to Italy. The town was

PARMA

once controlled by the Tuscans but by 1257 had passed into the hands of the Landi of Parma and Piacenza.

The main attraction here is the 13th century castle built by the Landi to consolidate their rule. The castle was continuously modified by the family over the following 400 years. It's a popular destination for tourists walking on its battlements and around the many towers and the massive keep, once the local prison. The **Princes Halls** off to the north and west of the main hall retain some of their 16th century Grotesque frescoes. From here there is access down to a lovely hanging garden known as the **Women's Garden**. (Open June 2pm-7pm, July, August 10am-7pm, other months Saturdays and public holidays 2pm-7pm, closed in winter. Admission fee)

Otherwise Bardi is an excellent spot for launching into the mountainside of tiny hamlets, Romanesque churches and ancient ruins dotted among the trees on the slopes of Mounts Crodolo (4,000ft) and Barigazzo (4,000ft).

ALONG THE BAGANZA RIVER

The Baganza river flows 50km down from Mount Borgognone, and has carved out a narrow valley before reaching the plain and joining the river Parma in Parma city. Travelling along the river requires taking road SS62 to Stradella then branching left to arrive first at **Sala Baganza**. Sala Baganza's Rocca became a summer palace of Duchess Marie-Louise and while quite sumptuous, retains few of its original features. It was built as a castle in 1477 for Gilberto III Sanvitale before being altered in the 1600s to become a summer residence of the Farnese.

The fortified manor contains many rooms for its servants and was extensively decorated. Frescoes have survived from the 16th century and the Salla dell'Apoteosi contains acclaimed 18th century rococo decoration. The importance for the Parma dukes of the rocca is emphasised by the **Assunta oratory** on the north side. It was installed in 1795 for Bourbon Duke Don Ferdinando. Close to the Rocca is **La Rocca Golf Club** (tel/fax 0521 834037) on Via Campi. The course, in acacia and oak groves is, a very technical 18-hole par 71.

Just 2km west of Sala Baganza stretching up to Collecchio are the age-old oak trees of the **Carrega Woodlands Regional Park**, the Parco Regionale dei Boschi di Carrega. The area was once the hunting ground of the Farnese and Bourbons. In the middle, surrounded by an English style lawn is the ducal villa, **Casino dei Boschi**. Built in Neoclassical style to the design of Petitot, it wasn't enough for Duchess Marie-Louise who added the arcaded wing for her servants and had the Villa dell Ferlaro built close by in 1828.

The lords and ladies almost hunted the park's roedeer to extinction. The 20th century saw the re-introduction of **wild boar** and **roedeer** and today the park contains plenty. Duchess Marie-Louise made a lasting contribution to the park. The Lebanese and Himalayan cedars, Canada spruce, American sequoia were planted and the Duchess first introduced the oriental thujas among the oaks (for guides tel 0521 836026).

Across the river from Sala Baganza is the small town of **Felino** famed for its salami. Otherwise of note in the town is the 9th century castle, altered in the 14th century and undergoing restoration (tel 0521 336020), and the 14th century Torreone tower.

Travelling south and up river, the road passes through the Apennine foothills for 17km to reach **Calestano.** Another gourmet town, the end of October and through November brings its annual fair celebrating the local speciality of Tartufo Nero di Fragno, or **Black Fragno Truffles**.

The road from Calestano to Berceto is quite beautiful with great crags cut into the mountainside. Past the mediaeval Pallavicini castle overlooking **Ravarano**, the huge grey incisors of **Soli del Diavolo** come into view. These awesome **Devil's Leaps** on Mount Cassio were cut out of sandstone and Palaeolithic rock and offer beautiful trekking.

ACCOMMODATION AND EATING OUT

Bardi (area code 0525) has an **agriturismo with accommodation** in the hillside at Castagneto di Gravago, *Castegneto* (tel 77141). The two hotels in the town are *****Sole** (tel 757100) and ****Bue Rosso** (tel 72260), with its restaurant in Piazza Martiri d'Ungheria, charging around £35.

Nearby the ski resort of **Bedonia** has *Carovane* (tel 825324) agriturismo with accommodation in the Bertoli district. Bedonia also has *****Belvedere U Rissu** (tel 826659) for £30 and single rooms at *****San Marco** (tel 824436) for £10. *San Marco's* restaurant (closed Tues) specialises in mushroom dishes. Double rooms with shared bath are available for £30 at ***Ponte** (tel 87118) in Ponte Ceno and ***Ferrari-Cecchino** (tel 824504) in Piane di Carniglia.

Monte Pelpi (tel 826626), a seasonal **camp site**, is at Largo Colombo.

Berceto (area code 0525) has *Ca' del Vento* (tel 0524 60165) **agriturismo with accommodation** near **Valbona**. The **hotels**, *****Fondovalle** (tel 68320 fax 68283) in **Ghiare**, *****Foresta di Bard** (tel 60248 fax 64477) at 64 Pra'Grande and *****Del Poggio** (tel/fax 60088) at 24 Via Nazionale, charge £30/35. *Foresta di Bard's* restaurant specialises in mushroom dishes. ****Gioli** (tel 64251) at 5 Ripasanta and ****Vittoria** (tel/fax 64306) at 5 Via G.Marconi charge £30.

PARMA

The **camp site, *I Panielli*** (tel 64521) in Berceto is also the main contact point for the **youth hostel**.

Sala Baganza (area code 0521) has ****Aemme*** (tel 836272 fax 836412) at 2 Via degli Antoni charging £45, ****Cecco*** (tel 833130 fax 833611) charging £30 and **Locanda Antico Borgo*** (tel 834788), for £20. ***Pifferi*** (closed Mon) on Via Zappati is a local restaurant with mushrooms as its speciality.

i **Tourist Information Centres** are at Bardi (tel 0525 43032 fax 71626), Bedonia town hall (tel 0525 824424 fax 824150) and Berceto, 4 Via Caprara (tel/fax 0525 64764).

ALONG THE PARMA VALLEY

Considering that the Parma river travels 100km from the Apennines into the Po, and was the cause for the creation of great bridges in Parma city, the sight of the Parma trickling through the city in summer is rather a disappointment. Only the winter rains and snow give body to this river. The peak of the valley contains several ski resorts, while the lower valley to Parma is mainly flood plain.

Torrechiara Castle – Pier Maria's Love Nest

Leaving Parma city the Langhirano road going south tracks the west bank of the river. About 17km out of the city the road arrives at the great impregnable fortress of **Torrechiara Castle**, a jewel of Parma province. Not quite a Taj Mahal, it nevertheless became a permanent expression of the lord Pier Maria Rossi's love for his mistress, Bianca Pelligrini, for whom it was constructed.

The large castle was built between 1448 and 1460, and defended by a triple wall with four corner towers on an outcrop overlooking the town of Torrechiara. The fantastic **Camera d'Oro** was the lovers' bedchamber. At the heart of the castle, it is adorned with frescoes attributed to Benedetto Bembo telling the story of Rossi and his lover. Some are rather kitsch, such as the linked hearts with the initials of Pier and Bianca joined by a ribbon declaring 'Nunc et Semper', 'Now and Forever'. Others depict quite explicit goings-on (tel 0521 852242).

The 16th century frescoes in the San Nicomede Oratory, the Salone degli Stemme and the Salone degli Acrobati were the work of Cesare Baglione. Pier Maria Rossi also had the more modest **Torrechiara Abbey** built in 1471, maybe to atone for his sins. The abbey sits on the other side of the valley and contains a 15th century fresco and in the north wing, a 17th

P A R M A

century terracotta image of the *Flagellation of Christ*. The Benedictine friars from San Giovanni Evangelista, in Parma use the abbey as their summer residence.

Across the Parma river from Torrechiara lies the spa town of **Lesignano de'Bagni**, whose thermal spa was re-established by Pier Maria Rossi in 1474. After Torrechiara the river road passes through increasingly mountainous countryside. On the east side of the valley, 7km from **Tizzano**, is the ski resort of **Schia** on Mount Ciao (tel 860152), containing 26 **ski** slopes and 7 ski-climb facilities.

At about 35km south of Torrechiara the road reaches **Corniglio**, with its frequently restored castle of mediaeval origin. Walter Madoi has frescoed the whole of **Sesta** village, 10km from Corniglio. The town is a stop off point for heading into the mountains and the beautiful **Lago Santo** glacial lake near Lagdei. The largest lake in the Emilia Apennines, it takes an hour on foot, or a chair-lift ride from Lagdei through the beech forests below Mount Marmagna (5,000ft). The area is a nature reserve and provides plenty of trekking routes.

ALONG THE ENZA VALLEY

The Enza River flows from the Apennines to the Po, forming the eastern border with Reggio Emilia province. South of the Via Emilia the valley rises through the rolling foothills of Canossa country. This is another land of knights of yore, containing castles and manors, Knights Valley and the Land of the 13 Courts. Feudal lords such as the di Canossas, Pallavicini, Sanvitale, Rossi, Terzi and Torelli sent out their armies to seize control of this route into Tuscany and Reggio Emilia.

The SS513 travels down the east side of the valley from Parma. After 10km a road to the left leads to the spa town of **Monticelli Terme**. Mud for beauty treatments was collected by allowing the waters to settle. Today Monticelli Spa contains modern facilities for respiratory disorders, irrigation, mud baths and beauty treatments. The spa (tel 0521 658521) is open from March to December and is linked to the Delle Terme and Delle Rossa hotels. Other facilities include thermal baths, hydromassage, a gymnasium and a hippodrome.

From Monticelli a road leads down for 6km to the Enza river and perched above it is the 12th century fortress of **Montechiarugolo**. As with Monticelli the previous fort was a victim of the feudal wars, being almost destroyed by the Parma army. The Farnese converted the castle into a fortified country manor in the 17th century.

Inside the moated castle has a large vaulted hall with 16th century frescoes,

P A R M A

heraldic shields and Grotesques thought to be the work of Cesare Baglione (open Sundays and public holidays March to November 10am-12.30pm, 3pm-6.30pm, tel 0521 686643).

Continuing down SS513 past Monticelli the road arrives at Traversetelo, 20km from Parma city. About 6km north west of Traversetelo is the village of **Mamiano**, location of the **Villa Magnani**. Since 1990 the building has been home to an important collection of over 100 paintings. The 19th century villa houses the private art collection of writer Luigi Magnani. On display are works by Titian, Rubens, Van Dyck, Filipo Lippi and Giorgio Morandi.

A few kilometres south west of Traversetelo and close to Torre is **Berzora** village that, for over 2,000 years, has played host to a group of continually erupting mud volcanoes or *barboi*. Travelling south and up into the hills on the west of the Enza, 45km from Parma city, the town of **Sasso** has the fascinating 11th century church of Santa Maria. Constructed to the orders of Matilda di Canossa from stone with a slated roof, the church stands on a rock outcrop. The interior contains a 12th century baptismal font carved from sandstone, while the terracotta columns decorate the nave.

The village of Selvanizza lies on SS513 and the Enza river. It's a starting point for entry into **Knights' Valley**, the source of the Enza. Dotted with rustic hamlets, the area's name came from the period of the Comune rule in the 12th century. The area remained a separate territory for the next 400 years. At the top of the valley is Rigosolo, once capital to the independent territory known as the **Land of the 13 Bishop's Courts**.

Selvanizza is also the junction for the road down the valley of the River Ceda, a tributary of the Enza. At the top of the valley set in beech and oak forests is the resort of **Monchio delle Corti**, which replaced Rigosolo as the capital of the 13 Courts in 1600 and acted as such until the fiefdom was abolished by Napoleon's armies in 1806. On the Tuscan border it contains many **trekking** routes on the slopes of Mount Sillara where, from 6,000ft, one can easily see the Tuscan coastline on the Mediterranean Sea.

P A R M A

ACCOMMODATION AND EATING OUT
(area code 0521)

Tizzano has two agriturismo with **accommodation**, *Ca' D'Ranier* (tel/fax 860304) in the hills of Groppizioso and *Casa Nuova* (tel/fax 868278) in Casanuona. The seasonal hotel ***Park Hotel Arena dei Pini** (tel 868630) at 1 Via Giolitti has a swimming pool and charges £25 as does *Miramonti* (tel 860134) in Schia. *Monte Fuso* (tel 866900) in Rusino offers double rooms with shared bath for £6

Corniglio has a few relatively inexpensive **hotels**. ***Le Mura** (tel/fax 880222) at 10 Piazza Rustici, *Ghirardini* (tel 889123) at 21 Via Provinciale, *Da Vignon* (tel 888113) in Le Ghiare and *Alpino* (tel 88257) charge around £25. **Stella Alpina** (tel 889175) in Bosco charges £17 for its rooms with shared bath.

Close to Corniglio there are two **Alpine refuges**, G.*Mariotti* (tel 889334) near Lago Santo and *Lagoni* (tel 889118) in Lagoni.

Monticelli Terme spa centre has ****Delle Rose** (tel 658521 fax 658527) **hotel** with its indoor **swimming pool** and charging £50 and ***Terme** and ***Quiete** (both tel 658521 fax 658527) charging £40. **Serenella** (tel 658226 fax 657026) and *Moderno* (tel 658230) charge £25. *Mariotti* (closed Mon), in Via Brigata Julia, is another **restaurant** specialising in mushroom dishes.

Monchio delle Corti has ***Scoiattolo** (tel 899134) **hotel** in Trefiumi and **Rita* (tel 899109) in Valditacca charging £25. **Ciambellino** (tel 896136) charges £20. The same price is charged by **Mariotti* (tel/fax 896127), **Tom* (tel 899185) in Pianadetto and *Berto* (tel 896126), none of which have en suite rooms. **Rifugio Prata Spilla** (tel/fax 890194) in Prato Spilla charges £10 for its en suite rooms.

i **Tourist Information Centres** are at Monticelli Terme (tel/fax 657519) in Viale alle Terme and Monchio delle Corti in the town hall (tel 896521 fax 896234).

Torrechiara Castle

P A R M A

CREMONA

Po

A1

PIACENZA

CHIARAVALLE della Columba

Castell'Arquato

Fiorenzuola d'Arda

Nure

Bobbio

Castel S. Giovanni

Borgonovo

Pianello

Tidone

Trebbia

Bétola

Veleia

M. Menegosa

Ferriere

M. Alfeo

10

412

461

586

45

354

Piacenza LAND OF THE CASTLES
PIACENZA CITY

It took us 3 hours from Ferrara to reach our destination of Piacenza, 188 km away, but it was worth it. We were again lucky finding a parking space close to the 16th century city walls beside the Po and Palazzo Farnese in Piazza Citadella. Piacenza is a deceptive city, the outskirts giving no hint of the historic and artistic treasures at its centre. The city was of pre-eminent importance during the Mediaeval era and, despite raiding despots, retains many of its treasures.

In 218 B.C, 6,000 Romans arrived in Piacenza and built it as a fortress town against the Gauls to the north. However their legions were not strong enough to defeat **Hannibal**. The African general and his elephant cavalry annihilated the Roman army in a battle close by on the river Trebbia. Nevertheless, on the vital Po river, Piacenza became the western outpost of Via Emilia which, stretching to Rimini on the Adriatic coast, was the supply route for the Empire's northern border.

Germanic, Hungarian and Goth invasions ransacked the city many times in the post-Roman era. Only in the 9th century under the Franks, did the city begin to recover. Of key importance was the city's position on the **Via Francigena**, the pilgrim route to Rome. That it became a major stopping off place is indicated by the number of churches along the pilgrim road through the city.

The city became a free comune in 1126 but by 1250 it had become engulfed by the many wars between the feuding nobility. Warlords such as the Pallavicini, the Scoto, Visconti and Sforza seized the city for varying periods until the Farnese dynasty, having secured the papacy in Rome, used the position to grab Piacenza as their fiefdom.

Reputed to have enormous appetites and problems with obesity, the Farnese married and prayed their way to power and the papacy. First, Farnese **Pope Julius II** gave Alessandro Farnese the bishopric of Parma. Alessandro took the papacy under the name Paul III and in 1545 handed both Piacenza and Parma to his son Pier Luigi. This began a dynastic rule that lasted through eight dukes and almost two centuries until in 1732 the dynasty was left heirless and replaced by Bourbon rule.

Certain members became important military leaders, wielding great power across Europe. Others gained grander reputations for their monstrous extravagances and follies, such as the Farnese Theatre. Nevertheless, architectural treasures left behind testify to the dynasty's importance in the growth of the city. If Parma is the city of Marie-Louise then Piacenza is the city of the Farnese.

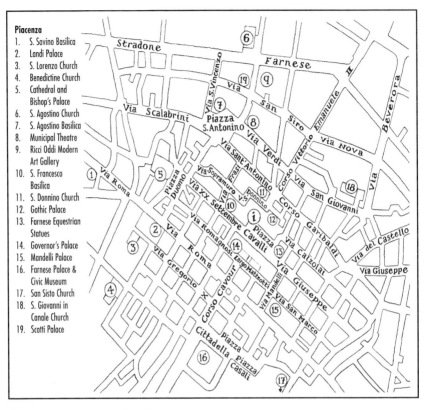

Piacenza
1. S. Savino Basilica
2. Landi Palace
3. S. Lorenzo Church
4. Benedictine Church
5. Cathedral and Bishop's Palace
6. S. Agostino Church
7. S. Agostino Basilica
8. Municipal Theatre
9. Ricci Oddi Modern Art Gallery
10. S. Francesco Basilica
11. S. Donnino Church
12. Gothic Palace
13. Farnese Equestrian Statues
14. Governor's Palace
15. Mandelli Palace
16. Farnese Palace & Civic Museum
17. San Sisto Church
18. S. Giovanni in Canale Church
19. Scotti Palace

The Farnese Palace

In Piazza Cittadella, the enormous **Palazzo Farnese** was originally a fortress owned by the Visconti. Traces of the original 14th century **Rocca Viscontea** can be seen on the towers to the left as one enters. Vignola designed the Palazzo Farnese in the 16th century under the instruction of Margherita, wife of the duke, Ottavio Farnese. Built as a fortress, but intentionally to look like a palace, the building has remained for 400 years only half finished. From the main road we could see how some of the window decorations were never completed.

As we passed through into the parade ground and courtyard, the wing of the three storey palace appearing on our right, looked like its outer wall had been peeled away. After centuries it was still awaiting completion. The old towers in front of us still looked out onto the river. To our right the building housing the tourist information office was being restored to house a collection of frescoes and paintings.

Inside the palace we found ourselves in the **duke's theatre** and a private ante-chamber of the palace, where the huge ornate fireguards are the only remaining pieces of furniture following the departure of the Bourbon duke, Carlo, for Naples. This section of the palace was worth visiting because it was awash with paintings depicting the story of the Farnese dynasty.

The alcove on the left was the duke's private room where only the most important people would have access to him. It was the most richly decorated, with stucco decor by Rissoni and paintings by Venetian, Sebastiano Ricci, celebrating the feats of Pope Paul III.

Pier Luigi's rule was unpopular with the Parma nobility. So much so that in 1547 he was killed in the Rocca Viscontea and his body thrown into the moat. His son, **Ottavio**, was in Parma and held on to the remainder of the duchy. Piacenza was lost for ten years but Ottavio subsequently married Margherita, the illegitimate daughter of Holy Roman Emperor Charles V, king of Spain, who restored Piacenza to his rule. But the couple quarrelled. Ottavio stayed in Parma while Margherita lived in Piacenza, supervising the construction of the palace. Later the Duchess went off to become governor of the Low Countries for her half brother King Philip II of Spain.

Ottavio's son, **Alexander**, re-established the authority of the regime, becoming commander of the Spanish troops in the Low Countries for his uncle, the Spanish king. Said to be the greatest European general of his era, he then became governor of the territory. His military feats are celebrated with monuments throughout the city.

The throne room still contains the original floor and everywhere is decorated with stucco and the lily, emblem of the Farnese family.

We passed through to the huge room 9, a 50 feet high first ante-chamber decorated in 14th and 15th century frescoes discovered recently in an old church. The paintings tell the story of Saint Catherine and are notable for the elegant dresses of Catherine and her entourage.

Room 11 displays 12th century sculptures from Piacenza and contains works of famous Romanesque sculptors. A unique piece on display in bronze is a 2,000 year old '**Etruscan liver**'. The Etruscans used the livers of animals to predict the future and the item on display may have been a teaching model or used for decoration. Each section of the liver is marked out to represent a particular god. Its examination would encourage soothsayers to predict good days and bad days.

Room 15 contains a collection of armour, some dating back to the 15th century, and over 300 weapons illustrating the evolution of swords, helmets, crossbows, and other battle artefacts. The first floor contains a vast collection of paintings and beautiful original frescoes on the ceilings, the best of which are probably in the duchess' ante-chamber. The room also contains a 1487 Botticelli

PIACENZA

painting of *Madonna Adoring the Child with the Infant St John,* confiscated by the Farnese from one of the families accused of conspiring against them. Room 22 contains plenty of stucco and tells again the story of Alexander Farnese.

The museum opens between 9.30 to 1pm and 3pm to 6pm. The free guided tour takes between 75 and 90 minutes. Entry to the museum costs L8,000 but an extra L2,000 to visit the **carriage museum**.

We walked from the rear of Palazzo Farnese in the direction of Piazza Cavalli, passing through narrow streets, including the Vicolo Angilberga, containing lovely old Renaissance buildings. It was a Sunday and the streets were quiet, save for the peel of church bells. It was a short walk to the Via San Sisto at the end of which stands **San Sisto Church**.

Founded by the Empress Angilberga in 874, San Sisto was the first mediaeval development to be based outside the walls of the old Roman city. Initially it was a powerful church given large tracts of land by the Empress. In the early 1550s it was rebuilt as a Benedictine monastery until suppressed by Napoleon. We couldn't visit the section of the monastery (once one of the most important in the north of Italy) because it is now owned by the army and used as barracks.

San Sisto, like San Sepolchro and Santa Maria di Campagna was designed by the renowned architect, **Alessio Tramello**, an associate of Bramante, northern Italy's greatest Renaissance architect. San Sisto is the most traditional of the three churches but nevertheless, its magnificent pointed brickwork vault is a remarkable example of Renaissance architecture.

The church is designed in the shape of a Latin cross, with three aisles containing naives on either side. The other churches exhibit a more revolutionary design and St Mary's contains a Greek cross. Renaissance architecture was based on using simple diametrical forms and the chapels on the left and right use the Greek cross for its ideal rectangular shape.

The most interesting area is around the altar. Above the high altar is **Raphael's** *Madonna Sistina*, but the painting is only a replica of one of the world's best known artworks. The original was painted for the church and hung there until sold by the monks who needed money to protect their land from the flooding Po. The King of Poland bought up the canvas in 1754 for 10,000 gold pieces and it now hangs in Dresden's museum.

Below the masterpiece are the splendid choirstalls, beautifully carved over 17 years by two local exponents of marketry, Spinello and Panbianchi, and installed in 1514.

On Via Roma, heading for the cathedral, we passed the 15th century **Palazzo Landi**, once home to the Landi, one of the great noble families of Piacenza. Confiscated by the Farnese after the murder of Duke Pier Luigi, it became the

PIACENZA

Farnese home and later housed Emperor Charles V. Now the Law Courts, it contains a magnificently ornate marble doorway and a courtyard decorated in terracotta. The facade was the work of two Lombard master masons, de Fondutis, who had worked with Bramante in Milan, and Battagio.

The Cathedral of Santa Maria Assunta

Constructed in the 111 years between 1122 and 1233, the Cathedral of Santa Maria Assunta in the Piazza Duomo is one of north Italy's finest examples of Romanesque architecture. The duomo took so long to build that it displays signs of the changes from the Romanesque to the Gothic style. Its massive, simple but elegant facade is said by some to have been the work of the Wiligelmo school, who designed many important churches on the plain including the cathedral in Modena.

That the base of the facade is comprised of pink and white Verona marble and the upper reaches, of decaying, local sandstone is due to the bishop running out of money.

The central entrance was reworked but the two side doors and the telamons on guard are original. The appearance of Wiligelmo's name on the elegant door on the left has led some to suggest that the great architect was himself involved.

We entered Piacenza's cathedral from the side entrance on Via Vescovado. Our guide correctly suggested that, seeing as construction began at the altar and moved to the facade, the cathedral was better approached from the rear to take in its treasures in their historical order.

From the outside we could see the leaning towers and walls, testament to the instability of the land beneath which suffered from the great earthquake of 1117. The earthquake destroyed the previous cathedral of Santa Giustina that stood on the same site. The Duomo has a steeple almost obscured by the tower that was introduced to allow for the high cupola, added in the Gothic period to the cathedral's ceiling.

PIACENZA

During three campaigns, funds for the cathedral were amassed from the clergy, the nobles, guilds, and common people. Most of the front and rear pillars carry plaques positioned 15 feet above the ground containing an inscription and picture illustrating which guild was responsible for financing it. The 'pillars' of the church included the guilds of the clogmakers, shoemakers, dyers and wheelmakers.

The choir stalls are 14th century late Gothic carvings. Starting with the painting of the death of Mary behind the altar, a series of paintings were gradually carried out over a 300 year period. Above the first painting is Mary's ascension and higher still, her crowning as queen of heaven.

Elements of the cathedral are said to show French influence on the design. As a trading centre, Piacenza was closely influenced by other cultures. As a result, some say that church is not truly Italian.

Down the steps in the dark Romanesque Greek cross-shaped crypt we were suddenly faced by 108 columns, each with a different capital – some ancient, some modern, one painted. Above us the organ pumped out its overture to the mass. **Santa Giustina** was martyred in the 3rd century. One of Piacenza's patron saints, her relics were brought to the duomo to rest in the crypt during the 11th century. As was tradition the relics, now upstairs, were kept in the crypt and the main altar is directly above where the saint's remains rested.

It is said that Piacenza was the most important city on the pilgrim route to Rome, with it being a point of convergence of routes from north and west Europe. The large crypt (which still has a door that looks out onto the pilgrim route through the city) was a major attraction for pilgrims.

Cathedral services held upstairs from the crypt in the main hall were long, in Latin, largely held solely for the clergy, and closed to pilgrims. Other services for the masses would be held outside. However, to pay homage to the saints who had been buried, these crypt held short services which were the meat or manna of those on the road to Rome.

Leaving via the main entrance upstairs we came out into **Piazza Duomo**. The piazza was shaped in the 16th century and is believed to have been planned as a square. Once again, due to a shortage of money, it remains just half a square. Close to Piazza Duomo is an open air **market** open on Wednesdays and Saturdays.

Turning left out of the duomo is Via Legnano, on which stands the fine Romanesque church of **San Savino**. The facade and entry portico are 17th/18th century but its interior is essentially Romanesque. San Savino church was first built in 903 before being rebuilt in 1000 by Benedictine bishop, Sigifredo. Saint Savino was Piacenza's second bishop. He died in 420 and his relics are held in the crypt.

Most worth seeing are the splendid 12th century **polychrome mosaics**. One depicting the eternity of time can be found in the presbytery, depicting the cardinal virtues of Prudence, Fortitude, Temperance and Justice.

Walking along Via Chiapponi we soon came to the church of **San Antonino**, with its huge 130ft high octagonal tower on Via Scalabrini. That the entry to the church is on the side was to allow access from the pilgrim road close by. San Vittore, first bishop of the city, had the church built in the middle of the 4th century. Germanic invasions destroyed the church and it was rebuilt in 1014.

A Romanesque church, it shows a dramatic 19th century Neo-Gothic development imposed on its ancient features. The authorities attempted to restore its mediaeval features but eventually gave up, leaving a remarkable concoction of

PIACENZA

architectural styles. Flying buttresses were erected over the centuries to prop up the exterior.

The octagonal tower was a Gothic addition. San Antonino is the patron saint of Piacenza. Beheaded near Travo in the Trebbia valley, his bones are kept in a glass case on view in the church. A series of frescoes celebrate his life, martyrdom and rise to heaven.

Nearby we took a look at the old municipal **Teatro Verdi**, a mini model of La Scala. The building was erected in 1804 and the facade completed in 1830.

Piazza Cavalli

The streets inside the area of the old Roman city are an attractive combination of mediaeval and Renaissance structures. The rectilinear streets define the area now slightly adjusted by developments over the centuries, including Via XX Settembre, Via Verdi, Corso Cavour and Via Scalabrini amongst others.

The city centre is not accessible for those who live outside of it by car so we had to make the short walk. We strolled down Via XX Settembre. The street, which formed part of the old Roman city, leads onto the grand **Piazza Cavalli**, the heart and hub of the city. This glorious square combines centuries of architecture, put together in such an ad hoc fashion that it is quite fascinating.

At its heart sits the lone splendid Gothic Palace, **Palazzo Gotico**. A descendant of a Scottish knight, Alberto Scoto, arrived in the city as part of the retinue of Charlemagne, and promoted the building of the palace. The base is an open structure with marble Gothic arches allowing for an arcade or covered market area. The floor above was built in 1281. Its Romanesque character is shown by the window decoration. Every window surround is different and beautifully decorated with terracotta. The façade has six windows above the five Gothic arches below, leading experts to suggest that, defying Gothic tendencies to mathematical balance which would have resulted in five windows, the palace is not truly Gothic.

A staircase leads to the first floor, which is simply a huge hall where meetings were held. The second floor contains rooms and swallow-tailed Ghibelline battlements, indicating the anti-Papist tendencies of the city rulers.

The ground floor was used by merchants and the middle floor by the people, leaving battlements above to government and military representatives. In addition a rose window similar to that in San Francesco Church was seen to represent the church. Hence, the building is said to be a symbolic representation of the unity between the merchants, government, military and clergy, all brought together on the middle floor in the meeting hall.

At the centre of the square are two bronze statues of Farnese dukes, **Alessandro** and **Ranuccio**, both on horseback. The statue of Ranuccio was the first to be erected in 1620. It pays tribute to Ranuccio who governed the dukedom while his father, Alessandro, was away fighting. Ranuccio is credited with developing the city's administration and executing 100 of his opponents, accused of conspiring against him.

Opposite the facade of the Gothic Palace stands the attractive, pink **Palazzo del Governatore**, built for the governor in 1787-1790 and now the Chamber of Commerce. One special features of the palace is the large sundial that hangs on the right side of its façade.

On the left is the **Church of San Francesco**, a classic Lombard Gothic building. The facade was altered to prevent the church from suppression when Napoleon arrived. Napoleon designated the building to be a hospital for, 'San Napoleon'. When Bonaparte left the church reassumed its former name. Built between 1278 and 1363 it was commissioned by Ghibelline Lord Ulbertino Landi and in 1848 was the scene for the proclamation of Piacenza's annexation to the kingdom of Piedmont. The radiating chapels indicate a Burgundy influence probably brought by the Cistercian monks. The frescoes and central portal are 15th/16th century.

Street Life

Piacenza city contains many splendid **palaces** built by the nobility between 1600 and 1900. Most are still in use and therefore closed to visitors. As in Ferrara the exteriors are interesting and occasionally one can take a peep into the decorous courtyards.

PIACENZA

Although Piazza Cavalli is the hub of the city with cafe and restaurants, many locals prefer to eat out in the countryside. Here, the new *Rocca Pescarola* is a popular restaurant and pizzeria.

A good place to buy **Piacentina** cured meats is *Scevi Carni* (closed Mon pm) at 17 Via Tansini, and the *Colmark* supermarket chain is a handy place for cheap groceries on Via Parmense and Vialle Dante. Sundays are definitely not a day for shopping here as we found almost every shop and office is shut.

Teatro Verdi on Via Verdi stages regular performances of classical music. There are a few **clubs** such as *Caprice* at 3 Via Tortona. Details of events can be found in the city's daily paper, *Liberta*. **Pubs** include bar *Bonnie Prince Charlie* (closed Tues) on Vicolo Perestrella and *American Bar* (closed Tues) at 75 Via Manfredi.

Cinemas include *Apollo* at 79 Via Garibaldi, *Roma* at 19 Via Capra, *Politeama* on Via San Siro and *President* on Via Manfredi, all of which show the occasional English language film – even if dubbed.

ACCOMMODATION AND EATING OUT
(area code 0523)

Il Pinzimonio (closed Tues) at 4 Via Cavaletto has a pizzeria and restaurant specialising in **mushroom** dishes and **fish**. *Ristorante Po* at 6 Via Nino Bixio is recommended for its traditional Piacentina dishes. Via Manfredi has some inexpensive dining establishments including trattoria, *Gasperini Danilo* (closed Sun) at 137, *Del Bivio Galleana* (closed Sat) at 130 and pizzeria and self-service places, *Catelli Marco* (closed Tues/Wed) at 78, *Corsaro Verde* (closed Wed) at 59 and *Mystic Pizza* (closed Mon) at 19. Via XX Settembre has a *McDonalds*. For a pricey splurge try the hotels *Best Western Park* and *Grande Albergo* Roma mentioned below.

An excellent alternative to a **hotel** stay in this cramped city, is to reside 15km out to the east in Roveleto di Cadeo at ****Le Ruote* (tel 500427 fax 509334 e-mail hotel.leruote@altrimedia.it) at 204 Via Emilia Parmense. The plush hotel provides good service, an excellent restaurant, fun nights in the bars and a discotheque.

Nearer to the city is *Motel-Ristorante K2* (tel 593220) at 133 Via Emilia Parmense. In the city ****Grande Albergo Roma* (tel 323201 fax 338534 website www.altrimedia.it/hotelroma) is at 14 Via Cittadella and the modern plush ****Best Western Park* (tel 712600 fax 453024, e-mail parkhotel@altrimedia.it) is at 7 Strada Valnure. ***Clarine* (tel 499074 fax 499115) is at 114a Via Emilia Pavese and ***Hotel Milano* (tel 336843 fax 385101) with no restaurant is at 47 Viale Risorgimento in the north of the city beside Piazzale Milano. *Moderno* (tel 329296) at 31 Via Tibini is one of the cheaper hotels.

i Piacenza City **Tourist Information Office** (tel 329324 fax 328843) is in Piazza Cavalli. Piacenza Province Office (tel/fax 305253 website www.piacenzaturismi.net) is at 62 Via Mazzini. **Tour guides** are available from the tour guide association at 21 Via Garibaldi (tel/fax 324591).

Travelling Around

Distances from Piacenza of the main cities are; Ravenna 200km, Ferrara 167km, Rimini 248m, Bologna 133km, Reggio Nell'Emilia 61km, Modena 94km and Parma 42km.

Train Times (faster direct services)

Piacenza **train station** is on Piazzale Marconi, a 15 minutes walk east of Piazza Cavalli.

Piacenza to Modena 57mins, Reggio Emilia 43mins, Parma 28mins, Bologna 1hr 20mins, Milan Centrale 39mins, Florence 2hrs 40mins, Rome 5hrs

PIACENZA

Trains around Piacenza Province

Trains go from Piacenza station to the following destinations (journey times in minutes).

East – Monticelli d'Ongina (20mins), Cremona (30mins) and – Pontenure, Cadeo, Fiorenzuola (14mins), Alseno

West – San Nicolo, Castel San Giovanni (25mins).

Taxis are available from Piazza Cavalli (tel 547511), the station (tel 323853) and Viale Dante (tel 754722).

PIACENZA'S HILLS AND PLAINS
UP THE TREBBIA VALLEY

Leaving the Palazzo Farnese, we travelled round the western side of the city along the Corso Borgeto beside the 16th century city walls. We were heading south on SS45 along the Trebbia valley to the historic town of Bobbio.

The road still contains old signs displaying the distance in Roman miles from Piacenza. Four Roman miles out one reaches the aptly named town of **Quarto**. Many Italian towns were named in this way and, at seven miles, one reaches **Septima**, near where the intriguing Etruscan liver in the Farnese palace was discovered.

Along the road on our right we passed Castello Vidiama, with its large rotund towers. Most of the 200 castles in Piacenza province are 14th or 15th century. Many are now in ruins but over 40 are in excellent condition. The land begins to undulate as we pass through the foothills of the Apennines. The increasing number of vineyards indicates that this is the beginning of the wine producing area.

This is the province's most important wine producing district. The best known wine typical to Piacenza is **Gutturnio**, a red wine which comes as a *frizzante* or still. **Barbera** is another common red wine produced locally.

Ortugo is a white wine only found in Piacenza. It is one of the few vines that survived a devastating outbreak of philoxera. White wine also comes as **Trebbianino**, a common Italian white wine or as the aromatic, normally sweet **Malvasia** in which to dunk one's cake.

Rivalta

Soon we were to pass **Rivalta** and its great castle. Here we find the river Trebbia, close to where Hannibal fought his first important battle in Italy. The African general and his elephants scored a total victory, routing the Roman legions. Hannibal left one of his wounded elephants at **Gossalengo**. The townspeople looked after it and eventually set it to work on the farms. To this day the elephant sits in the town coat of arms.

The tall turret and battlements of **Rivalta Castle** imposed themselves on the skyline as we approached. We explored the cobbled lane on which the gates to the castle's grounds look out. The old walls of the castle form one side. Beneath them are the walls of the village that grew up around the castle set on high ground above the river.

At the end of the lane is the 14th century church of Saint Martin, with its diaphragm arches quite unusual to the region. Inside are interesting frescoes and stucco decoration

The castle contains a beautiful Renaissance courtyard and a tremendous tower built in the late 15th century by **Solari**, the same Milanese architect later responsible for the towers on the Kremlin in Moscow. This castle is a favourite stay of **Princess Margaret** of England, and the guide took us into the simply furnished spacious bedroom that she occupies when on vacation here. Lying on the royal bed, I found it too soft and advised a replacement. In comparison the dining room was quite small though beautifully decorated with old frescoes.

This castle is a real treat. Heavily restored by the owners, the Landi family, it contains battlements, dungeons and turrets. There were 5 cells for prisoners in the dungeons. Our guide informed us that after sentencing by the lords, prisoners would be hung upside down here to secure a confession. Those who lived would be taken up to the tower, which contains a spiral staircase around a long drop or stairwell.

Halfway down the drop, sharp metal razors were once fastened across the gap. Those lucky enough to survive interrogation would be thrown down the drop and sliced to pieces. We weren't put off and climbed to the top of the tower that even at dusk, offers a panoramic view of the whole valley (tel 886258 fax 978300. Opens weekends and public holidays, 9am-noon, 3-6.30, March to Nov. Admission fee).

A short 1km walk away is the very popular *Avia* **discotheque and restaurant**. Located in the hills nearby is a beautiful 18th century mansion hosting the **Croara Country Club** (tel 0523 977105 fax 977100), notable for its 18-hole **golf course** which staged Italy's first Women's Open championship, and a **riding school**.

PIACENZA

To Bobbio

We headed off up the valley, the hills becoming higher and more rugged and the river faster flowing. This is a pleasant area for trekking, horse riding, cycling or mountain biking. Fishing is, however, not allowed on the river. We also passed **Travo,** site of an old castle with a church built into it. According to tradition this is where Saint Antonino, the patron saint of Piacenza, was martyred.

Several finds of pre-historic settlements were discovered in the hills behind **Travo Castle**, which contains a small collection of relics from these settlements.

Further along is the site where the Romans positioned the healing shrine of **Minerva Medica** that attracted citizens from hundreds of miles away. The church of Saint Mary stands on the site of the Roman Minerva temple.

The valley widened and just behind Bobbio one could easily make out the peak of Penice, 5000ft high. We passed through a tunnel and suddenly the valley sprawled out before us. We had reached **Bobbio**, a small country town on the banks of the Trebbia. The town gathered importance in the Middle Ages as it was on the main road to Genoa. Its narrow mediaeval streets twist up and down the hillside. The oldest houses are similar to those in Liguria, with low columns, porticoes, and traces of mediaeval decoration.

The main road is topped by a gate, the 12th century Porta Nova. The street contains some lovely shops and **pasticerria**. We stopped in one to buy **porcini**, the Apennine speciality of **dried mushroom** preserved in oil. We also tried the **black truffles** for which the village is famous.

We came to the main square, the tiny Piazza Duomo on a slope with narrow mediaeval streets leading off it. **Santa Maria Assunta** cathedral is essentially Romanesque. Its construction began in 1075. The cathedral's lower towers are original. The upper parts of the tower were added in the 17th century. On the right was the Bishop's Palace which is no longer used.

The entrance floor of the cathedral is higher than the inside. At first, the rains would flood in from the sloping piazza so in 1463, a wise Bishop had the facade built up as a little flood barrier. As was common during the Romanesque period, the ceiling was wooden and when the church was reworked with a brick roof it had to be lowered to facilitate its support. The interior contains interesting Grotesque frescoes and a mix of Romanesque and Neoclassical artwork. The cathedral cloister is often closed but offers a good view of the Romanesque mullioned windows.

PIACENZA

We walked a little way down from the cathedral and had an excellent view of the Trebbia river valley and Bobbio's, **Ponte Gobbo**, humpbacked bridge, said to have been constructed by the Romans. The 11 arches are remarkably different. Saint Colombano is thought to have added to it but the bridge only gradually achieved its full span, so what one sees today is an expanded 18th century version.

On the hillsides we could see small traces of footpaths. Many of these were walked by pilgrims on their way to Rome. Today they are excellent **trekking** routes. Up river from Bobbio the valley becomes quite charming, narrowing to a gorge with forested ravines.

Above the centre of the town sit Malaspina Castle and the grandiose **Abbey of San Colombano**. The 14th century castle is not open to visitors. We found a convenient parking space by the monastery. Saint Colombano, an Irish monk, founded the abbey in 614 A.D, and it became known throughout Europe as a centre for production and reproduction of literature. Another Abbot who arrived from the British Isles in the 7th century was the Scottish monk and bishop, Cumian. A tablet in his memory was donated by King Liutprand and is displayed in the adjacent museum.

The monastery also had its uses in overseeing the area for the Longobard and Frank kings. Much of the monastery was rebuilt in the 9th century by Abbot Agilulphus to house the 100 or so Benedictine friars who lived and worked here. As the whole abbey was rebuilt in the 15th century, the small apse and the bell tower are all that is left from the time.

The portico on the facade contains 14th century pillars and the gate at the entry is a fine example of 12th century ironwork. Inside, the church retains relics of the previous periods. Saints **Attalus** and **Bertulphus** were the second and third abbots of the monastery, and their tombs are covered by 9th century stone slabs and encircled by 15th century frescoes. The first chapel holds the 9th century baptismal font, while the crypt contains a marvellous 12th century mosaic floor, depicting the calendars of the month, and the Crusades as a Biblical battle scene from the Book of Maccabees.

Also of note in the main chapel is the fine inlaid and carved wooden choir made in 1488. The town museum, in the former refectory contains relics from pilgrims who visited the Holy Land and artefacts of village life (Open, Saturdays 4.30pm-6pm and Sundays, 11am-12am and 3pm-6pm. Groups of 10 or more must make a booking).

Since 1897 Bobbio has also been a spa town. The Marquis Malaspina had control of a sodiobromidioc spring at Piacansale for many years and handed it over to the Comune in 1927. San Martino spring was rich in both sulphur and sodium and opened in 1897, closed, and then re-opened in 1972 as **Bobbio Spa** (tel 0523 936250) at 20, Via San Martino (open May to October).

Swimming and **fishing** are common sights in the Trebbia and nearby summer resort, **Marsaglia,** has a **canoeing** school. East of Bobbio on Mount Penice lies the **winter sports** resort of **Passo Penice**. Bobbio is a 46km, one hour drive away from Piacenza. And, though a small town, Bobbio has as a **cinema**, *Le Grazie*, at 2 Contrada Ospedale.

P
I
A
C
E
N
Z
A

The Castles of Valtidone and Luretta

The Valtidone is the north west corner of Piacenza. Being hill country and on the border with the territories of Milan, it is speckled with castles. Travelling 30km west of Piacenza city on the A1 autostrada one arrives at the Castel San Giovanni exit. **Castel San Giovanni** *is also on Via Emilia and a good start for a castle tour. Just 6km south of the town are the quaint fortress in* **Borgonovo***, and the nearby castles of* **Castelnovo** *and* **Corano***.*

Sat on the banks of the Tidone river 6km further south is the resort town of **Pianello Val Tidone***, with its castle belonging to the Dalverme family. Another 5km southwards is the* **Rocca d'Olgisio***, where a fortress is thought to have existed since 500 A.D. The current castle was built in 1037 and has been recently restored. It sits charmingly on a rock spur overlooking the valley and contains no less than six boundary walls (for visits tel 0523 998075, open 10am-1pm, 2.30-7pm, Sundays and public holidays, April to Oct.).*

The French style country fortress of **La Bastardina** *is 10km east of Rocca d'Olgisio. Its mansion is still moated and the nine-hole* **golf** *course (tel 975106 fax 565274), and lake for* **fishing** *by boat offer a little more in terms of recreation. The castle was home to the Scotti and took its name from being a smaller version of La Bastarda fortress in Val d'Aosta. The interior contains Baroque designs and 17th century frescoes using Correggio's classic chiaroscuro methods to create the impressions of bas-reliefs (open April to October, 9am-12am, 3pm-6,30pm, tel/fax 975373. Admission fee).*

Close by and 1km from Gazzola is the elegant cloister and courtyard of the 14th century **Castello Agazzano***. Initially built in 1200 it was Scotti Castle, another haunt of the notoriously bloodthirsty Count Pier Maria Scotti. The interior contains many frescoes and period furniture (tel 886258, guided tours only. Admission fee). Travel 6km east and one arrives at the majestic castle of Rivalta in the Valtrebbia.*

PIACENZA

ALONG THE VALNURE

The Nure river flows northwards from Mount Maggiorasca (6,000ft) in the Apennines and arrives at the Po just east of Piacenza city. Due to its remoteness, the tranquillity of its highlands offer the best destination in the province. At its head the valley becomes the Passo del Tomarlo, the road for Tuscany and the Mediterranean.

Mounts Bue, Ragola and Nero offer some of the best **climbing routes** (including Ciapa Liscia and Groppo del Ali) in the region and students of nature will love the terrain, which contains clear evidence of glacial activity up to 8,000 years ago. The living reminders of that period are the dwarf pine (pinus mugo) trees a product of the rapid post Ice Age thaw. Lakes amid unusual geological and geomorphological formations give the territory a real fascination.

In the valley plain, 10km south east of Piacenza on Via Emilia is the town of **Pontenure**. About 3km south of this small town is **Paderna**, notable for the spacious 11th century fortress and manor, **Castello di Paderna**. Built in 1028 and surrounded by a moat, it has an early Christian chapel now used for organic farming (tel 511645. Open Saturdays 9.30am-noon. Admission fee).

The road south along the Nure river reaches **San Giorgio** after 7km. At its heart, the Palazzo Comunale dates back to the 11th century when it was a fortress. A 27km drive south into the foothills takes you to the resort town of **Bettola**, noted for the 15th century sanctuary and tall bell tower of Madonna della Quercia. Legend has it that while a shepherdess was sitting beneath an oak tree minding her flock, she saw the Madonna sitting on a branch, telling her to build a church. Until 1810 the sanctuary was in the care of the Franciscan Friars of the Tertiary Order, but it was rebuilt in the late 19th century. In 1913 Pope Pius X made Our Lady of the Oak (Madonna della Quercia) patron of the Valnure.

Just 4km away from Bettola, the tower in the village of **Pradello** is said to have been owned by the family of the adventurer, **Christopher Columbus**. A small museum celebrating his exploits can be found nearby. Beside the Nure, another 10km south, is the village of Farini, a road from which leads to **Mareto**, a village favoured for cross country skiing. The winter sports resort of **Selva** can be found 20km south of Farini, near the Tomarlo Pass in Liguria.

ACCOMMODATION AND EATING OUT
(area code 0523)

Along **Val Trebbia**, west of Rivalta in **Agazzano, Le Lische** (tel 976441 fax 976442) at 6 Via Lische is an **agriturismo with accommodation**. One special restaurant beside **Rivalta** castle is the *Locanda del Falco* (closed Tues) serving taglioni with mushrooms and roast shin of veal. Next door is a shop that retains its mediaeval appearance and sells meats and cheeses hung from the roof. **Rivergaro**, south of Rivalto, has a **dining agriturismo**, *La Sorgente,* at 55 Fraz. Cisiano in Cisiano and *River* **camp site** (tel 958996).

In **Bobbio**, An expensive but popular place to eat is *Enoteca* with its local speciality dishes using mushrooms or **truffles** and **snail soup**. *Ristorante Piacentino* (closed Mon) in Piazza San Francesco serves traditional local fare. *Tre Noci* (tel 931020) in Fontana, Coli, south of Bobbio, is an **agriturismo with accommodation** specialising in production of wines, liquors, nocino, gineprino and other beverages.

PIACENZA

Local **Camp sites** include **Ponte Gobbo** (tel 936927 fax 936068) in San Martino Terme, Bobbio, **Ponte Barberino** (tel/fax 937153) in Ponte Barberino, Coli and, south of Coli, **Marsaglia** (tel 934166) in Cortebrugnatella district (June/mid September).

In the **Valtidone** region around **Borgonovo Val Tidone**, **Il Cornilio** (tel 869293) in Castelnuovo Val Tidone is an **agriturismo with accommodation**. *Cantina Valtidone* at 58 Via Moretta in Borgonovo is a must for tasting and buying the **Piacentini** wines. *Vecchia Trattoria* in **Aggazino** is another recommended eating house and serves up **arrosti misti con anitra**, and vitello, **faraona**. An osteria of note in **Pianello Val Tidone** at 1 Vicolo al Tidone, is **L'Osteria del Re di Denari** serving rissotino alla Valtidonese.

Capitol **cinema** is at 20 Via S.Ziliano in Borgonovo while Sarmato near Castel San Giovanni has *Pierrot* **discotheque** (tel 887149).

In **Valnure**, south of Grazzano Visconti, Vigolzone has a **dining agriturismo, La Tosa** in Pizzamiglio, La Tosa. **La Favorita** in **Bicchignano** nearby, serves **tagliolini con sugo di Funghi**. **Cascinotta** camp site (tel 530113 fax 530260) is south of Pontenure in Rivolo village near San Giorgio Piacentino.

Bettola area has several **agriturismo with accommodation**: in Ponte dell'Olio, **La Conca D'Oro** (tel 712420 fax 453217) in La Valle Di Castione, **Il Castello di Folignano** (tel 876240) at 7 Via Castello in Folignano and **Torre Carmeli** (tel 877384) in Torre di Torrano, Torrano. **Le Rossane** camp site (tel/fax 910172) is south of Bettola in the Le Rosanne district of Farini.

i **Tourist Information Centres** are in Bobbio (tel/fax 803091) at 11a Piazzetta S.Chiara and in Grazzano Visconti (tel 870997) on Piazza del Biscione (open April-October).

PIACENZA

ON THE PO PLAIN

We drove out of Piacenza along the Via Emilia to the small town of **Roveleto di Cadeo**, containing some beautiful old houses. It also contains the popular Beato Vergine del Carmelo shrine on Via Emilia. Built in 1750, the shrine is thought to be the work of one of the Bibiena brothers from Bologna. The choir dates back to 1776 and the bell tower was added in 1850

We stayed at *La Ruote*, a large modern four-star hotel with a free discotheque. We drank and danced to rock music with the aged thirty-plus clientele until the early hours. The hotel cuisine was fabulous and the owners friendly and accommodating.

San Pietro in Ciero

The road west from **Villa Verdi** in Sant'Agata is studded with woodland, orchards, and vineyards. We came to a small village of tidy gardens and cherry orchards. This was red country – red cherries, red tomatoes, red clay, red tiles, red wine and red flags. After Naples, this area is Italy's most important cultivator of tomatoes (known locally as 'red gold') and pomodoro itself means 'golden apples'. Lorries abound carting off tomatoes and cherries to the canneries.

Set off the main road through the village down a long driveway, we came to **Castel San Pietro in Ciero**, a small but excellently restored 15th century castle in the village of the same name. The moat has been filled in but the drawbridge is still intact.

The Barattieri family received the fief in 1460 from the Visconti Duchess of Milan and only relinquished the property in 1994. The castle and its land were passed down to the eldest son, an unusual practice in Italy where property would normally be divided between all the sons.

During the Middle Ages, the castle was used as a military outpost, until the Barattieri took over. With increasing political stability the castle became a palace. Low down on the walls are round holes for canon. The former mediaeval castle had square corners, high towers and high walls. The method of defence would be from above, pouring down missiles and tar onto the assailants.

In 1453 Constantinople fell to gunpowder and canon. Military strategists realised the deficiency of the traditional fortifications. Round and lower towers were built for weaponry fired horizontally rather than from above. This castle was then lowered and round turrets were introduced over a 30 year period. However the tower, built in 1250, was kept and remains. A kiln for making bricks to rebuild the defences was recently discovered at the back of the castle.

The base of the castle is buried more than six metres beneath the ground. Passing into the keep through a six feet thick door, a side room had a mediaeval fridge where ice was stored deep underground in the winter and kept for the hot summers. Like most castles, this one was equipped with a chapel, a food store and a well (three in this case). At its heart was a typical Renaissance courtyard surrounded by ground floor arches each with two arches above.

The tower holds a grim dungeon where the feudal lords would imprison their captives after trials in the castle. We saw an impressive display of weaponry used in the castle including early 16th century long rifles, maces, and body armour before we went below ground to the cellars which contained huge vats for storing wine.

PIACENZA

During the war the German army used the castle as a military outpost, with gun nests in the towers, surrounded by tanks. One can see scrawls of German graffiti. Sr. Spaggiari finally bought the castle in 1994 and uses a corner of the building as his second home. The castle, which is still being restored, is open to visitors by appointment (tel 983711 fax 984722) or on Sundays and public holidays between 9.30am and 12am, and from 3 till 6pm. Smoking and photography are not permitted.

The town also has an old church and an excellent trattoria, the *Rizzi*, on Via Roma. They serve a first and second plate for as little as L17,000. Try their faraona (guinea fowl). It is delicious.

Another fine castle can be found just north of San Pietro in **Monticelli d'Ongina** on the Cremona road close to the Po. The huge square 15th century castle, with its cylindrical towers, dominates the town. Home to the Pallavicini who had it built in 1420, the castle is especially noted for its frescoes in the chapel by Renaissance artist, Benedetto Bembo (open June to September, Sundays 3pm-6.30pm).

Leaving Castel San Pietro in Ciero we took the SS462m road for 4km to the classical Renaissance town centre of **Cortemaggiore**. We were entering castle country in south east Piacenza. Hills rose up on each side of the road with castles gracing the highest of them. Cortemaggiore is a splendid town for those who love architecture. Laid out in grid lines with its beautiful square surrounded on three sides by arcades, it is considered one of the best examples of Renaissance architecture.

Once known as Curtis Maior, the town expanded under the Carolingans but thereafter declined until the 14th century. At this point the town was developed as the capital of a Pallavicini fiefdom. The Pallavicini lord had a classical plan drawn up for the design of the town and firmly implemented it. The Palazzo, now the town hall, stands in the middle of the main side of the square, with the church opposite. The mausoleum of the Pallavicini lies in the 15th century **College of Santa Maria della Grazie**, with frescoes by Filipo Mazzola. The main church is the Gothic Santa Annunziata built in the same period.

We headed off from Piacenza, 30km south eastwards to **Chiaravalle della Colomba** (tel 940132) by the A1 autostrada (just east of Fiorenzuola D'Arda) to see its formerly great abbey. The village is surrounded by cultivated fields, just north of Alseno on Via Emilia and close to the boundary with Parma.

Our progress into the village was arrested by a small mournful procession. It was All Saints Day, when people gather at cemeteries to remember their dead. Later we would be stuck for 30 minutes in a tiny village in the middle of the plain by a traffic jam created by vehicles leaving a crematorium. A day to avoid travelling.

The Cistercian monastery lies in the village. Most Italian monasteries followed

Saint Benedict. However the close of the 11th century saw the development of a reform movement at a place near Dijon called *Citeaux*, in Latin, *Cistercium*. Soon the Cistercian monks, led by the charismatic **Saint Bernard**, attracted huge numbers of recruits to their stern doctrine. Bernard, perhaps the most outstanding figure of 12th century Europe, became a powerful diplomat, visiting and resolving problems for the kings, queens, Popes and emperors of Europe.

Monasteries sprouted up and Bernard set up his abbey at Clairvaux. Chiaravalle was an Italianisation of Clairvaux, and Bernard visited what is now Chiaravalle at the request of the Duke of Piacenza. The local nobility founded an abbey here in 1135. According to tradition, a dove (colomba) flew down and, by dropping twigs, marked the plan of the monastery the friars were to build. Hence the name Chiaravalle della Colomba.

The Cistercians are known to have settled in many uninhabited areas. The area around what is now Chiaravalle was uninhabited marshland. They successfully began reclamation of this marshland. Gradually the monastery became rich and powerful, housing 100 monks.

The brick part at the base was the original mediaeval building. Another storey was added during the 17th century. However, the monastery was suppressed in the 18th century and the monks only returned in the 1930s, Very few remain in residence.

The very decorative church contains an interesting mixture of Italian and Burgundian influences. The Burgundy style arches reflect the French origins of the religious order. The crypt contains a fascinating mosaic of the zodiac signs as a calendar.

Outside is a beautiful cloister with the original and varying capitals still positioned on their columns. Note the corner columns with incredible stone knots around them. The abbey also contains a *parlour*. Cistercian monks were committed to total silence except in this one room, hence the name *parlour*.

The friars have a 19th century shop containing beautiful wood furnishings and selling their produce including royal jelly, the cure of Chiaravalle (an alcoholic drink), fruit wines and other beverages. Opposite the church is the old abbots' palace that was destroyed but is now being restored.

P I A C E N Z A

THE ARDA VALLEY

We left Chiaravalle della Colomba, taking the road south to **Alseno** on Via Emilia, then journeyed 10km south to **Castell'Arquato**, overlooking the Arda river. We approached a rugged rock outcrop and climbed through the winding narrow Via Dante and Via Sforza up the steep rocca of Castell'Arquato. We finally stopped in the cobbled Piazza Alta that sits like a grand elevated platform at the top of the hill.

This historic centre of the village includes the fifteenth centre fortress, **Rocca Viscontea**, which is intact and offers a clear view of the Arda valley. The Arda was an important route on the pilgrim road to Rome, as the fortress guaranteed control of this section of the valley and tolls from all who passed through.

The fortress, with its battlements, tall keep, and drawbridge, hangs on the side of a cliff face peering out over the valley. Built in 1343, it was clearly for military use. One could imagine the knights marching out with their foot soldiers. Later a more comfortable castle was built lower down the hill.

On another side of the square is the fascinating early 12th century Romanesque basilica of **Santa Maria**. It stands on the spot of the earlier church that was destroyed by an earthquake. Built of stone from the sedimentary rocks that formed the hillside, its walls and steps contain scores of prehistoric fossils. Three apses look out onto the square and overlooking it is the 14th century tower. The fine splayed portal has a picturesque 12th century lunette.

Fossils from the church and the surrounding rocks can be seen in the fortress. The **Museo Geologico** (open 9.30am-12.30pm, 2.30pm-5.30pm) on Via Dante contains more fossil specimens including that of a large whale calf found in the valley. The square contains a couple of dining establishments and the town is blessed with two **discotheques**, *Parco delle Driade* in Viale Rimembranze and *Stradivarius* in Via Sforza Caolzio.

About 6km eastwards through the vineyards and isolated farms of the Ongina Valley lies **Bacedasco Terme** (tel 0523 895410). It is Castell'Arquato's **spa**, equipped with baths, a playing area for children and surrounded by 200 hectares of ancient chestnut trees. Bacedasco itself is taken from the Longobard for 'Village of the Waters' – evidence of the long history of the spa site. **Castell'Arquato Golf Club** (tel 0523 895557 fax 895544) nearby contains a varied technical 18-hole par 73 course with fairways which can be quite steep.

Another village worth visiting is **Vigolo Marchese** in the hills to the north of Castell'Arquato. The 11th century church has a superb rotund baptistery next to it and is said to have been built in 1008. Inside is a baptismal font used in the time of the Roman Empire.

To the east, 1,000ft above the Stirone valley is the mediaeval village of **Vigoleno**. Encircled by walls built in 1395, the village contains many old towers. The Scotti fortress is an excellently preserved 12th century castle inside which is a Venetian style theatre of 18th century origin. Close to the castle is the Romanesque church of San Giorgio.

We stayed in Castell'Arquato at the **Conservatorio Villagi**, a labyrinth of a place accommodating up to 25 people. It's a former monastery built in 1750, though some of the walls date back to 1350. Set on the hill above the Arda Valley,

PIACENZA

it offers quite spectacular views of the surrounding countryside.

It's very well kept, with pleasant gardens where one can sit out and eat. Signora Baldini runs the premises and ensures fresh fruits from the garden are on the menu. A convent is next door and down in the basement wine cellar is an underground link with the nun's home that would be used by the monks.

Veleia Romea - The Roman Town

From Chiaravalle we headed south and west for 40 minutes to Castelliare. An autumn haze shimmered across the sun-drenched plain. Passing Santa Vittoria the Apennines came into view and we were about to get into the foothills. To the left an escarpment rose up, topped by a tower as we passed through Badagnano, a tiny village in the Chiavenna valley.

The road passed through between pretty rolling hills with little villages and church spires dotted around the landscape until we reached Veleia, 41km from Piacenza. Above the town by the church of San Antonino lay the excavated ruins of a Roman town, **Veleia Romea**.

We arrived well before closing times but the caretakers had decided to lock the gates early. We were left to stand on a bench outside the gate which fortunately allowed for a good view of the ruins and the lay out of the centre of the town.

In 1747, a farmer ploughing his field found a lump of metal. The farmer hacked at the object with the intention of finding buried treasure. Having retrieved the object, which was now in pieces, he then tried to sell what he had found. When he tried to sell the twisted pieces of metal they were recognised by a group of erudite priests who understood their value. They bought all the bits of metal and, fitting them together, discovered they had bought a classical inscription, now known as the **Tables of Trajan**.

The priests presented the tables to Duke Antonino as a gift. He then ordered the excavations. Fitted together, the tables are 15 feet by 6 feet sheets covered by dense writing, detailing records of mortgages to farmers. Trajan gave large sums of money to provide loans to farmers, encouraging them to invest. The interest was then used to house orphans. The tables along with the most important finds are now on display in the **Archaeological Museum** in **Parma**.

From the 1st century B.C Veleia was a Roman administrative centre for the Apennines area of Emilia and Romagna. Excavation began where the tables were found, uncovering the paved area in the centre of the city by the Forum. The marble tables and capitals are original but the columns have been reconstructed. These would have been surrounded by porticoes, shops and houses. The paving in the Forum is original and includes some of the inscriptions recording who paid for the paving. The drainage beneath is original as are half the steps.

PIACENZA

The basilica law courts were located nearer the entrance to the site that probably dates to the 1st century A.D. The many statues found there are now in the museum in Parma. Some of the foundations of the houses still clearly show typical Roman courtyards, as well as the bases of the public baths. More remains to be excavated – particularly the religious centre.

The area around Veleia is extremely subject to landslides and these are thought to account for the destruction of the Roman town (open 9am-one hour before sunset, Mon-Fri till 3pm, tel 807113). Guides for the Veleia visits are recommended and can be arranged by contacting the Tour Guide Association in Piacenza.

Gropparello Castle

Arriving at **Gropparello Castle** from Veleia required a 9km trip northward, along the scenic hill tops. The castle is based on an outcrop of hard serpentine rock that rises up out of the hillside, and provides a sheer drop on the other three sides of the fortress. Below is the Vezzeno, a small stream that flows through the valley before sliding over a gorge visible from the battlements. Part of the gorge is known as the Celtic altar, from where it is said that Celts conducted sacrifices.

The core of the castle is original to the 9th century when the castle was a garrison, housing troops to control the valley. Only much later did it become a noble residence. Many of the rooms have been altered and subjected to restoration over the centuries. A ghost is said to wander through the corridors at night.

Rosania married the lord of the castle. One day the castle was broken into while her lordship was away. Leading the assailants was the man she really loved and had wanted to marry. They had a wonderful night but Rosania was betrayed by one of the servants when her husband returned. She was put to death.

We stepped over the drawbridge into the keep. Its moat never contained water but was effective in making the tops of its walls even higher off the ground. As we entered, we had to go through a second gate surrounded by high walls, from which those breaking the first level of defence could be trapped and bombarded. Inside, people were stood around in mediaeval costumes enacting a play about events at the castle for a small audience of children and adults.

The great hall contains a marvellous view of the gorge and the coat of arms of the Scotti who occupied the castle for a period. Other rooms have 18th century furniture and frescoes. The castle contains comfortable well-decorated suites available to book, some of which include a small modern kitchen. **Mussolini** stayed at this castle and, since I had taken the opportunity to occupy Princess Margaret's bed at Rivalta, Muriel took to Mussolini's much firmer mattress. His past presence shouldn't put you off taking advantage of this special stay in a beautiful area.

The castle has a taverna and prepares meals for resident guests or for parties by prior appointment (tel 0523 855814 fax 885818). Castle opening times, 10am-12.30pm, 2.30-7pm Sundays and public holidays, March 19th-Nov 22nd. Admission fee.

The castle's spacious wooded grounds also have **Parco Deliciade**, including huts where special Sunday shows and mediaeval games are put on, and a playground area for children.

ACCOMMODATION AND EATING OUT
(area code 0523)

San Pietro in Ciero's *Trattoria Rizzi* (closed Tues evening/Weds) at 3 Via Roma serves good meals a la carte for around L37,000 with excellent tortelli and guinea fowl. To the west of **Fiorenzuola D'Arda** town is a **dining agriturismo**, *Poggio Caminata* at 105 Strada Bariana in Celleri village, Carpaneto Pino. Fiorenzuola has ***Hotel Smeraldo** (tel 984452 fax 983583) at 8 Via Gramsci, ***Albergo Domus** (tel 983800) and ***Albergo Concordia** (tel 982827 fax 981098) at 68 Via Matteotti, both found on website www.mathis.it. **Alseno** has ***Cortina** (tel/fax 948101) at 67 Via Centro.

Close to the Roman ruins, **Veleia Romea** has *Antica Locanda Veleia Romana* (tel 807109) which has 10 rooms and a large restaurant (closed Mon).

The upper reaches of **Val Arda** have two **agriturismo with accommodation** of note. Close to Vernasca in Cergallina village is *Cergallina* (tel/fax 898289), serving plates of **anatra al sugo** and **testina stufata**. Further up the valley is *Parco Monastero* (tel/fax 914257) at I Rabbini in Monastero, Morfasso serving pisarei e faso, polenta and anolini.

Castell'Arquato has plenty of eating establishments. The hotels **San Carlo** (tel 805138) at 39 Via Alighieri and **Leon D'Oro** (tel 803651) and **San Giorgio** (tel 805149) both in Piazza Europa have restaurants as does *Locanda le Rose* (tel 895548) in Case Ilariotti. *Conservatorio Villaggi* (tel 805245) up the hill at 27 Via Villagi is an excellent stay as is *Gropparello Castle* (tel 885814 fax 885818) at 84 Via Roma in **Gropparello**, £20 per night (full Board £40).

i **Tourist Information Centres** open April – September: Castell'Arquato (tel 870997) at 1 Viale Remondini, Cortemaggiore town hall (tel 836524).

P I A C E N Z A

Recommended Reading

Italy Today

Luigi Barzini *The Italians* (Penguin/MacMillan).

Charles Richards *The New Italians* (Penguin). On Italy in the 1990s

Tim Jepson *Wild Italy* (Sheldrake Press). A guide to Italy's flora and fauna

Umberto Eco *The Name of The Rose* (Minerva/Warner) A detective story set in Italy.

Italian Cuisine

Valentina Harris *Valentina's Regional Italian Cookery* (BBC Books)

Marcella Hazan *The Classic Italian Cookbook (MacMillan).* More regional recipes.

Italy's Past

Valerio Lintner *A Traveller's History of Italy* (Windrush Press/Interlink).

Dante Alighieri *The Divine Comedy* (Penguin). The great writer alludes to many places in Emilia.

Niccolo Macchiavelli *The Prince* (Penguin). An insight into the do's and don'ts for Italy's many princes and dukes during the Renaissance.

Ludovico Ariosto *Orlando Furioso* (Penguin). Classic tale from this Reggio poet

Denis Mack Smith *The Making of Italy 1796-1866* (MacMillan). On the Risorgimento and the Unification of Italy

Charles Dickens *Pictures From Italy* (Granville/Eco). The great novelist took in Emilia on his travels.

Giorgio Bassani *The Garden of Fitzi Contini* (Quartet). The book set in Ferrara's Jewish community in the era of Mussolini. It inspired the classic film of the same name.

Eric Newby *Love and War in the Apennines* (Picador/Penguin). World War II in the mountains of Emilia Romagna.

G.Guareschi *The Little World of Don Camillo.* Humorous tale of the day to day strife between a village priest and a Communist mayor in post-war Italy.

Italian Art

Frederick Hartt *History of Italian Renaissance Art* (Thames & Hudson)

Peter and Linda Murray *Art of the Renaissance* (Thames & Hudson)

Other titles in the MH*i* Publications Pleasure Seeking series

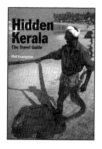

Hidden Kerala: the travel guide.

The acclaimed comprehensive guide to south India's paradise state. Phil Frampton and Steffanie Kalt travel from Kovalam Beach, through the cities of Kerala, and along the famous backwaters on a journey of discovery to the region's jungles, mountains and valleys.
Retail Price £9.95

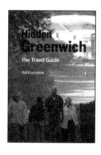

Hidden Greenwich: the travel guide

All and more of what the traveller needs to know about Britain's Millennium Borough. Phil Frampton and Muriel Savrot travel around Britain's most historic borough, a home to the kings and queens of England for almost a thousand years. The Millennium Dome, the National Maritime Museum, Greenwich Royal Park, the Thames Barrier, Eltham Palace, Queens House, the Royal Naval College, the Royal Arsenal, the ancient battlefield of Blackheath, the marshes of Thamesmead and forests of Shooters Hill, comprise just a few of the exciting sites in this beautiful part of London. Accompanied by details of hotels, restaurants and 'things to do', this guide will make you want to, and help you to, enjoy Greenwich time and time again.
Retail Price £10.95

Copies (post and packaging free for the U.K., £1.50 for Europe, £2.50 for the rest of the world) available from:
MHi Publications Ltd, PO Box 82, Manchester M32 8BX, U.K.
Fax 0161 881 5510 Website www.mhipub.co.uk